AMERICAN HISTORY
As Seen Through Currency

A Pictorial History of United States Currency as seen Throughout Important Historical Events

© Copyright 2003 - Dr. Edward and Joanne Dauer

•

All rights reserved
No material
may be used without
permission of the authors

•

ISBN 0-9728466-0-3

•

Cover layout and graphics by
Fred Wolfe - sfwgraphic@aol.com

•

Printed by Super Color
Hollywood, Florida

•

Bindery by Bind-Tech Binding Technology Inc.
Nashville, Tennessee

•

Published by Dr. Edward and Joanne Dauer
Ft. Lauderdale, Florida
Visit the new web site for this book
www.amhistoryuscurrency.com
For comments
e-mail: historycurrency@aol.com

•

A donation to the Dr. Maxwell and Reva Dauer
Scholarship Fund at the University of Miami
College of Engineering
will be made for each book sold

Come Travel w
as we Ride th

Foreword

As an educator, I am an advocate for learning about our nation's past. "American History as Seen Through Currency" guides the reader through the history of our nation as the epicenter for the world's trade and commerce. As experts in U.S. currency and historical documents, Edward and Joanne Dauer chronicle our nation's history using historical documents and legal tender U. S. currency notes from their personal collection.

Dr. Dauer is truly a renaissance man. A noted philatelist, his collection has been exhibited in our nation's top collection museum, the Smithsonian Institution. He and Mrs. Dauer are philanthropists, contributing generously to the University of Miami's academic scholarships, athletic programs and campus beautification endeavors, as well as other community efforts.

Dr. Dauer is one of the University's noted scholars and holds multiple degrees from his alma mater. In 1972, he was the first undergraduate at the University of Miami to study biomedical engineering and completed his senior undergraduate year and his first year of Medical School simultaneously. Most recently, he received his Masters Degree in Biomedical Engineering and is a Research Associate Professor in the College of Engineering. He serves as a trustee of the University. Mrs. Dauer is a former critical care nurse and hospital administrator who holds two degrees from Penn State University.

Aside from their intellectual pursuits, Edward and Joanne have amassed a significant collection of letters that chronicle the development of our nation's currency system. Through the use of photographs, reproductions of rare U.S. notes and original historical documents, dating from 1861 to 1929, they recall such great moments as the creation of the Federal Reserve System and the sinking of the Titanic. I invite you to journey back through time and learn more through this remarkable book.

Donna E. Shalala, Ph.D.
**President,
University of Miami**

American History as seen through Currency

TABLE OF CONTENTS

Chapter 1
HISTORY OF THE BUREAU OF ENGRAVING AND PRINTING — 17

Chapter 2
DEMAND NOTES — 23

Chapter 3
LEGAL TENDER NOTES — 49

Chapter 4
SILVER CERTIFICATES — 145

Chapter 5
TREASURY OR COIN NOTES — 211

Chapter 6
FEDERAL RESERVE BANK NOTES — 239

Chapter 7
FEDERAL RESERVE NOTES — 259

Chapter 8
GOLD CERTIFICATES — 289

Chapter 9
THE NATIONAL GOLD BANK NOTES OF CALIFORNIA — 349

Chapter 10
COLONIAL CURRENCY — 355

Chapter 11
NATIONAL CURRENCY — 363

January 3, 1961

Dr. Maxwell Dauer
Scientist, Educator, Philanthropist

UNIVERSITY OF MIAMI
SCHOOL OF MEDICINE
JACKSON MEMORIAL HOSPITAL
MIAMI 36, FLORIDA

DEPARTMENT OF RADIOLOGY

January 3, 1961

Lt. Col. M. Dauer
3410 Fielding Road
Baltimore 8, Maryland

Dear Colonel Dauer:

I have been advised by the Dean of the University of Miami School of Medicine that funds will be available to appoint you as Chief, Division of Radiophysics,* Department of Radiology at the academic rank of Associate Professor in radiology, beginning July 1, 1961. We have also received an oral comitment from Dr. Kermit Gates, Director of Jackson Memorial Hospital, that in the forthcoming hospital budget he would provide a sum of $3,000 for a Radiation Physicist.

Therefore, we are sure of an income of $8,000 per year until October 1, 1961, thereafter an assured income of at least $11,000.

If, for some reason, you would prefer to defer your plans until August 1st or September 1st, this would not cause any great conflict with my plans, although it would appear that the July 1st arrangement is mutually agreeable.

I shall look forward to receiving a letter from you giving me your reply to this offer.

With best wishes for the New Year.

Sincerely yours,

Raymond E. Parks, M. D.
Professor and Chairman

REP:las

*Radiation Physics

Assistant Medical Director, Washington, D.C., Manhattan Project (Atomic Bomb Project), Top Secret clearance

Radiological Officer, Atomic Energy Commission

Above: A section of the base of the crater formed by the explosion of the first atomic bomb at Los Alamos.

On July 1, 1946, the first underwater atomic bomb was exploded at Bikini Atoll in the Marshall Islands. Damaged and captured vessels from World War II were anchored in the lagoon in order to assess the damage an atomic blast would have on a fleet of ships.

Since there was so little left of the island after the blast, the two-piece bathing suit was named bikini, when it first appeared on July 5, 1946 at Paris, France, just 4 days after the blast.

Right: Cover sent by Dr. Dauer to his wife Reva. He was aboard the U.S.S. Haven. (Flagship)

January 3, 2003

Dr. Maxwell and Reva B. Dauer Clock Tower at the University of Miami library, Coral Gables, Florida

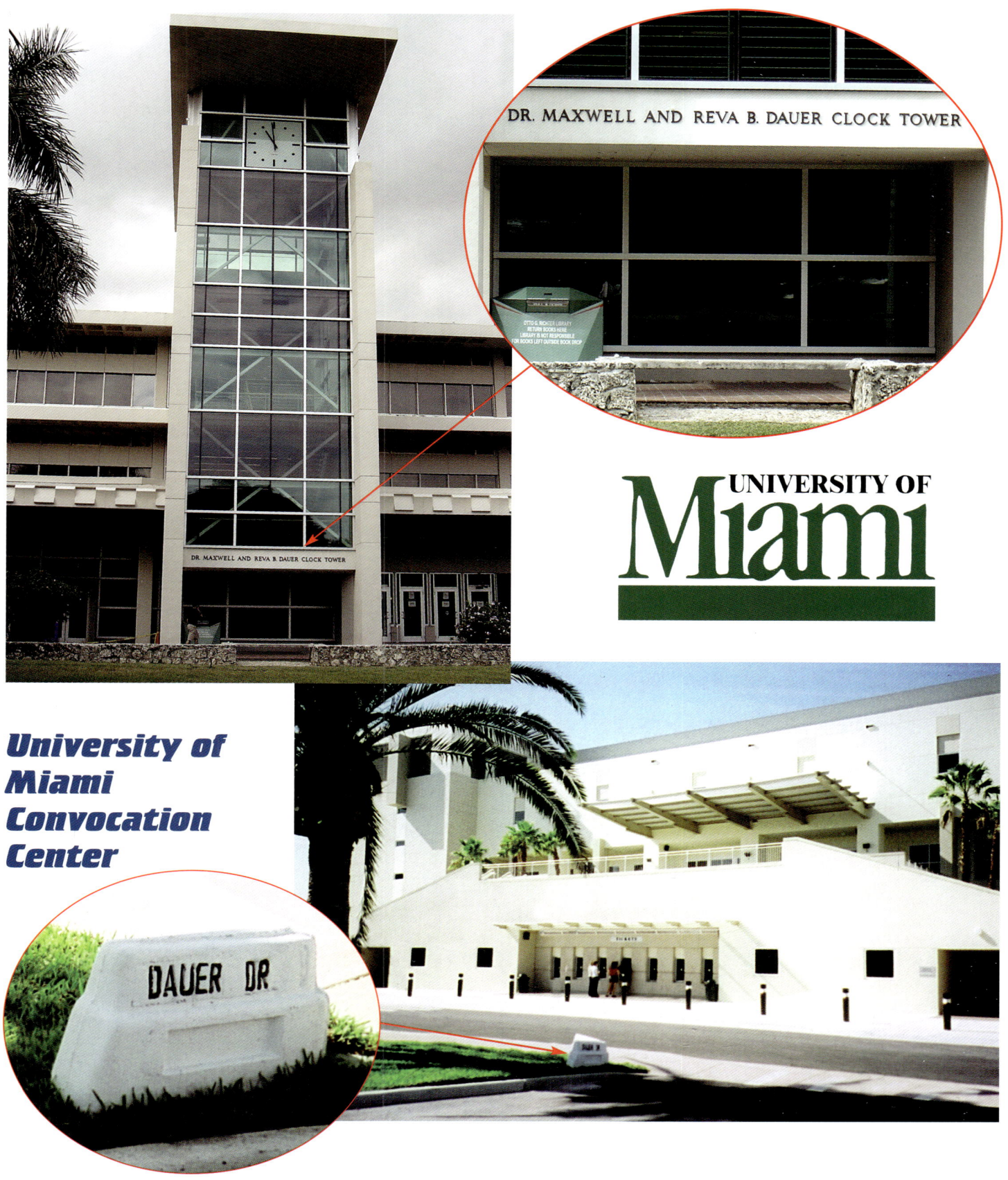

University of Miami Convocation Center

DEDICATION

Mary Elizabeth and Edwin Schlemmer

Reva and Dr. Maxwell Dauer

This book is dedicated to our parents: Mary Elizabeth and Edwin Richard Schlemmer and the late Reva B. and Dr. Maxwell Dauer who instilled in us the love and appreciation of living life to the fullest. It is through their kind encouragement throughout our lives, we have succeeded in our goals.

We also dedicate this book to our six children: Allison, Eric, Lauren, Marc, Ryan and Michael. You have all been a wonderful source of joy and excitement in our lives. We thank you for your constant expression of love and affection.

Large Size Currency

Large Size $5,000 Legal Tender Note Series 1878

Currency notes used by the United States from 1861 through the first half of 1929 were known as large size notes or "horse blankets." They were larger than the notes of today and the current small size notes were first printed in 1929 in an effort to save money by using less paper and ink. Large size notes are 7.42 x 3.12 inches in size. Small size notes are 6.14 x 2.61 inches, two-thirds the size of large size notes. One million dollars in current $100 bills would weigh approximately twenty-two pounds.

Date or Series

U.S. currency notes all bear at least one date or series. The series was originally the first date of production but not necessarily the date the note was printed, as it would change only if the design was modified or altered. It was common for the same series date to be used for many years with only changes in signature combinations or different types of Treasury seals.

The last series of large size notes was dated 1923. The first series of the current small size notes was dated 1928 although they were not released until July 10, 1929.

Reproduction

All notes in this book are reduced to less than 75% of their actual size. This is done to comply with Treasury Department regulations regarding color reproductions of U.S. currency.

Small Size $5,000 Federal Reserve Note Series 1934

Currency Paper

The paper used to print currency today is basically unchanged from the type used over a century ago. It is composed of 25% linen and 75% cotton. The blue and red fibers used to deter counterfeiters were made of silk prior to World War I. They are currently made of synthetic materials.

The Origin of the "$" Sign

Reviews of historical documents indicate the "$" most likely had its origin from the Spanish peso, pieces of eight, or piastres (P). The "S" gradually was written over the "P" in Mexico and eventually the "$" evolved.

The Color of Money

1878 - $10. Silver Certificate

1882 - $500. Gold Certificate

1861 - $5. Demand Note (Greenback)

The reverse of the first issue of U.S. currency, Demand Notes of 1861, was printed in green ink. This was to deter the reproduction of the notes by black and white photography. Green ink is also highly resistant to chemical and physical changes. Other colors were used on the reverse such as dark brown on the 1878-1880 Silver Certificates and a golden orange color on Gold Certificates. When small size notes were issued in 1929, green was used on the reverse of all notes because that color was available in large quantities. Green is also symbolic for the high credit rating and stable monetary policy of the Federal Government.

Condition of Currency Notes

Collectors prefer the highest grade and condition of currency notes. Uncirculated is the term used for a note that shows no trace of circulation and has never been used. It retains its original crispness. Most of the notes illustrated in this book have been acquired in the highest grade available. Some examples, especially notes like the $500 and $1,000 Legal Tender notes of 1869 ("rainbow" notes) are unique in collector hands and are only available in extremely fine or almost uncirculated condition. My common statement to a collector who only desires notes in uncirculated condition would be "It is unique and the only one around, so find another one!"

The Treasury Seal

The Treasury Seal is on all issues of U. S. currency except for the Demand Notes of 1861 and the first three issues of fractional currency. Many different varieties of the seal are shown in this book. It could be red, green, gold, yellow, brown, or blue, and have scalloped, spiked, or plain borders. The seal also varied in size.

The main design contains a shield with the scales of justice. The key pointing to the left represents official authority. Thirteen stars signify the original states and separate the scales from the key. The motto **"THESAUR AMER SEPTENT SIGIL"** translates into "The Seal of the Treasury of North America."

Small Red Scalloped Seal from the $10 Silver Certificate of 1886

Note: the key pointed left on above illustration

Series 1878 Silver Certificates were erroneously engraved and printed with the key pointing to the right. The mistake was corrected in the next issue (Series 1880).

Note: the key pointed right on above illustration

WHAT IS A FREE FRANK?

Free frank signed by George Washington in 1799 and addressed to Patrick Henry. The famous letter sent by Washington in this envelope was an appeal to Patrick Henry to support the Adams administration against its opponents who he warns will "Dissolve the Union" or bring civil war.

The Continental Congress established in 1775 the franking privilege. This law meant representatives, department heads, and other important leaders of the government including the President and Vice President would have the ability to send letters without fee or payment for postage, so that they could inform their constituents of official government actions. The origin of this privilege dates back to the English House of Commons in the 17th century.

The word "free" was stamped or written on the envelope and the sender's name was hand written on the envelope, usually but not always in the upper right hand corner. These documents that survive today provide a remarkable look back at the history of our country through the correspondence sent by many of our important leaders. The franking privilege still exists today but is only used for official government business and cannot be used for fund raising or other private correspondence.

Patrick Henry 1736-1799
Virginia House of Burgesses

Patrick Henry's personality was a curious antidote to the stern honor of Washington, the refined logic of Jefferson, and the well-tempered industry of Franklin. Young Henry was an idler and by many accounts a derelict; though everyone knew he was bright, he simply would not lift a finger except to his own pleasure. By the age of ten, his family knew that he would not be a farmer, and tried instead to train him toward academics. He would not apply himself to his studies either. At age twenty-one his father set him up in a business that he bankrupted shortly thereafter. Finally, the general public's disgust in Hanover and pressure from his young family (he had married at the age of eighteen) caused him to study for six weeks and take the bar exam, which he passed, and began work as a lawyer.

President Washington appointed him Secretary of State in 1795, but Henry refused the appointment. In 1799, President Adams appointed him envoy to France, but failing health required him to decline this office. He died on the sixth of June, 1799 at the age of sixty-two.

WHAT IS A FLIGHT COVER?

There are many examples of flown flight covers illustrated in this book. These were traditionally used on important or milestone airmail flights and were intended to commemorate an historic event.
They would commonly have a specially designed cancellation or a cachet printed on the envelope to describe the purpose of the flight. The value of a flight cover depends on the number of covers prepared for the flight as well as the historical significance of the flight. Rare and desirable first flight covers are illustrated below.

This cover was flown on the maiden voyage of the Hindenburg. It is postmarked May 11, 1936 and bears the official stamped cachet to commemorate the first flight.

This print shows the Hindenburg bursting into flames above Lakehurst Naval Air Station on May 6th, 1937 (The National Archives)

New York / Lakehurst, May 6th 1937, 7 pm:
The "Hindenburg" - a luxurious flying hotel, faster than any ship to date, is bringing its passengers to a landing in Lakehurst, N.Y.. With no prior warning, the pride of Hitler's Third Reich bursts into flames. In a matter of seconds, the largest airship ever built turns into a deadly inferno.

Surviving eye witnesses could never forget the horrible smell of burning flesh. Thirty-five people died in those flames. Was the "Hindenburg" disaster the result of sabotage, committed by opponents of the Nazi regime? Maybe the Zeppelin was struck by a bolt of lightning or was this just simply one of the most devastating accidents in aviation history of which the answer will never be found?

But new finds recently discovered by NASA state that neither the hydrogen in the hull nor a bomb was to blame, but a special fabric for the outer skin that, when ignited, burned like dry leaves.

FIRST FLIGHT COVER OF THE GRAF ZEPPELIN

This flight cover commemorated the first flight of the Graf Zeppelin from Lakehurst, New Jersey to Seville, Spain. It is postmarked May 30, 1930 and uses a special $1.30 commemorative airmail stamp to pay the airmail rate. The cancellation is a "wavy American flag."

The Graf Zeppelin ruled the uncluttered skies like no other monarch could. The sight of the silver ship gliding over head brought crowds of people streaming from their houses and into the streets. No other aircraft in history, with the possible exception of the Spirit of St. Louis, has been the focus of so much admiration by so many people.

In the period prior to and immediately after World War I, the Luftschiffbau Zeppelin operated excursion flights within Germany. In the mid to late 1930s, they added regularly scheduled passenger flights to both Rio de Janeiro in Brazil and Lakehurst, New Jersey in the United States. The "Graf Zeppelin" and "Hindenburg" were to be the forerunners of a transatlantic dirigible fleet.

What took months for a British military, heavy bomber to do, with many breakdowns and hardships, the Graf did in 12 days and 11 minutes in comfort and style with a full passenger load over much previously uncharted land. The trip was a complete success and the world, particularly the U.S., caught Zeppelin mania.

Examples of Modern Flight Covers

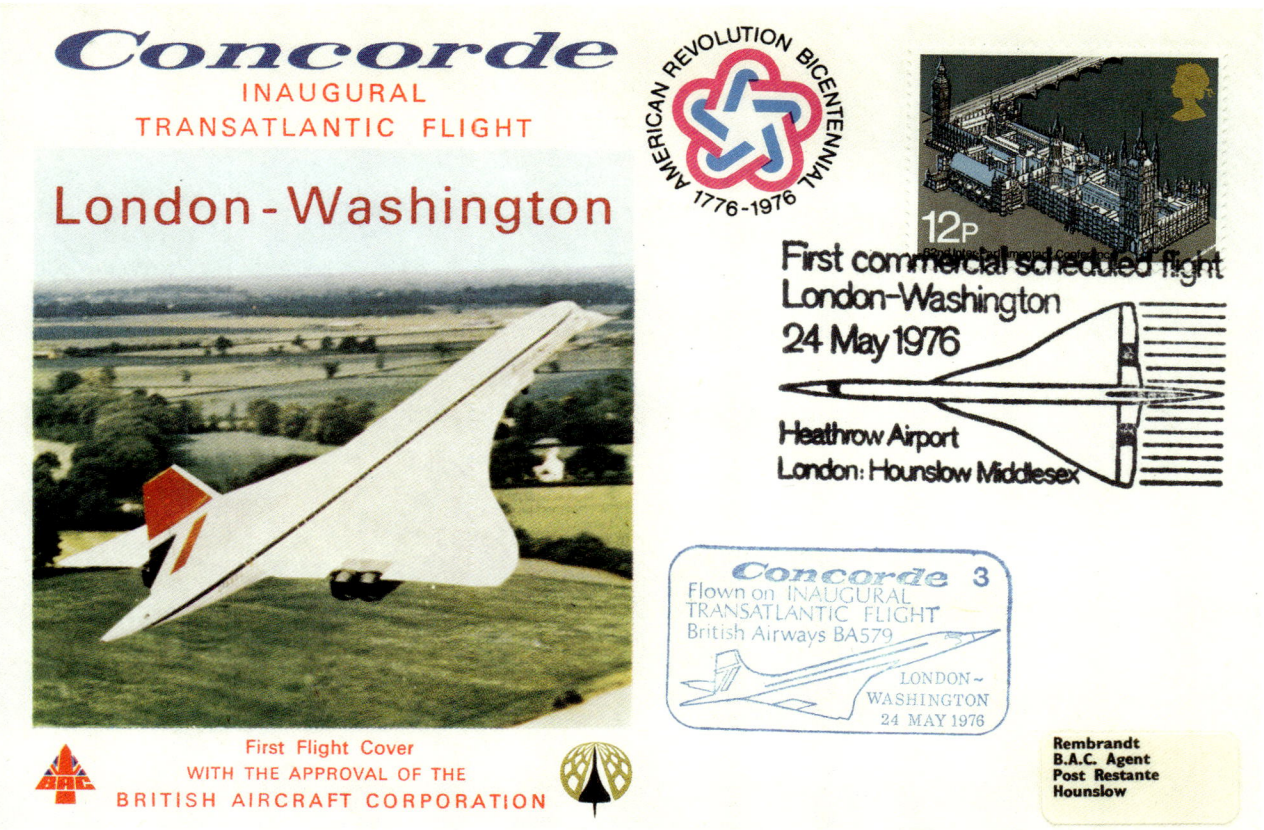

This cover was flown on the first scheduled commercial flight aboard the British Airways Concorde from London to Washington on May 24, 1976.
The Concorde flew 3,658 miles in 3 hours, 53 minutes at a speed of Mach 2.04 (twice the speed of sound) and an altitude of 57,400 ft.

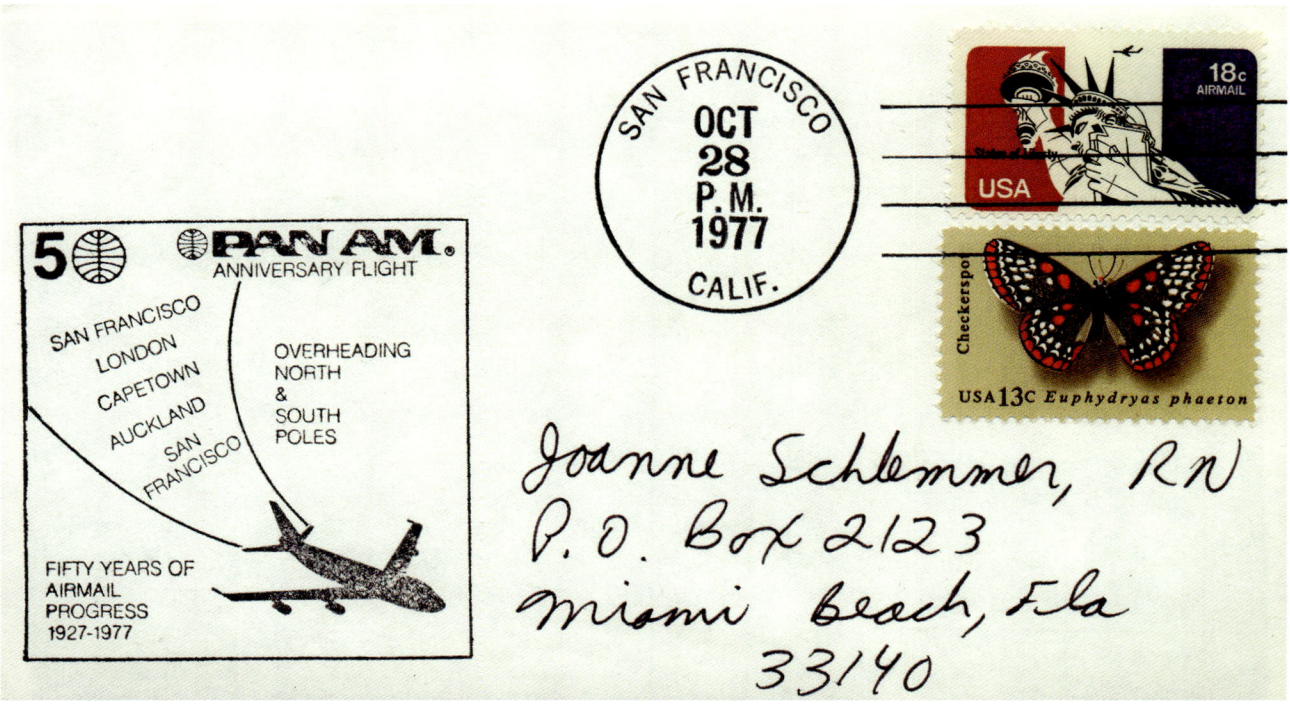

This cover was prepared and mailed by the author in 1977 to Joanne Schlemmer (Dauer). It was carried on a flight around the world by Pan Am Airways to commemorate the 50th anniversary of the company's first flight from Miami to Havana in 1927.

What is a brick?

Currency produced today is packed in bundles of 100 notes with a wrapper signifying the denomination. This is known as a "pack." Notes are shipped to the Federal Reserve Banks from the Bureau of Printing and Engraving in "bricks." A brick is forty packs of notes from the same denomination banded together and shrink-wrapped in plastic. The denomination, series, and serial number run is printed on one end. From the Federal Reserve Bank, bricks are broken up and individual packs are shipped to commercial banks for ultimate distribution and use by the public.

Unopened bricks of $1 and $2 Federal Reserve Notes. Packs of $2 notes are seen on top of the brick.

Why do I like collecting paper money?

I started collecting stamps at the age of four, intrigued by the beautiful engravings and colors. As I got older, I was similarly attracted to the intricate and detailed artwork on U. S. paper money. Currency designs and seal types were changed frequently prior to 1923. This wide variety of notes created hundreds of different types of banknotes—all of them illustrated in this book. This multitude of notes truly tells the history of United States in a fun and fascinating educational manner.
E.A.D.

Albert A. Grinnell 1865-1951

Albert A. Grinnell

Albert Grinnell was born in Shelby, New York and worked in his father's general store as a young boy. He first became interested in numismatics by searching through each day's change for unusual or rare coins.

He attended Rochester Business College and operated a coal and lumber yard in Oakfield, New York. He later built large grain elevators and warehouses for the storage of farm products. In 1910, he moved to Detroit and was affiliated with the Grinnell Brothers Music House until his retirement.

He is best known for acquiring over many years the finest and most complete collection of U. S. currency which was ultimately sold at a series of public auctions beginning in 1944. It is through his efforts that many of the unique and extremely rare notes survive today for future generations to enjoy. Even though he had an extensive collection of the finest specimens that existed, he was still not able to complete the type set collection. Several extremely rare notes illustrated in this book, such as the $100 1863 gold certificate, never became part of his collection. He was not able to locate or purchase them during his collecting career.

Chapter 1
The History of the Bureau of Engraving and Printing

All images are courtesy of the Department of the Treasury, Bureau of Engraving and Printing

First home of the Bureau, Washington, D.C. circa 1880

The United States coinage system was first established in 1792. Martha Washington's personal silverware was used to mint the first silver coinage of our country. In the early years only copper, silver, and gold coins widely circulated.

Various U.S. Treasury paper notes were printed from 1812 through 1857 and were used in commerce. It wasn't until 1861 that the first generally recognized United States currency notes were printed.

It was in a single room of the Treasury building on August 29, 1862, when the Bureau of Engraving and Printing was born. Six people, two men and four women, separated the notes and overprinted the Treasury seal by hand. This was done on one and two dollar U.S. notes that were printed by private bank note companies, the American Bank Note Company and the National Bank Note Company.

The first issue of United States paper money, the demand notes of 1861, and the legal tender notes of 1862 were printed privately by these companies. The actual printing of currency notes by Treasury employees began in 1863.

Martha Washington

The earliest picture in existence of the main Treasury currency printing press room was in the attic of the main Treasury building circa 1865. These were hand fed presses printing banknotes one sheet at a time.

The youngest employee ever hired by the Bureau was an eleven year old girl, Emma S. Brown, hired in 1865. Her brother, who was the main support of the family, was killed in action in 1864 during the Civil War. After Ms. Brown's Congressman heard of her family's misfortune, he arranged for her the appointment with the Bureau. After fifty nine years of continuous service, she retired in 1924. She worked in the trimming section and the Bureau's examining section.

Currency Plate Printing Pressroom - Attic of Main Treasury Building - circa 1865

In 1869, a new wing was added to the main Treasury building and construction of the present main Treasury building was completed. This was also the year that Congress recognized by legislation the Bureau of Engraving and Printing.

In 1880, an act of Congress authorized the construction of the Bureau of Engraving and Printing facility in their own separate building in Washington.

This red brick structure cost $300,000 to build. Expanding production needs gradually enlarged the building to its present size in 1914. It is now located south of the Holocaust Museum.

The Bureau added an annex building in 1938.

Destruction of Currency by Cutting - circa 1900-1920

View of Money-Shipping Entrance and Horse-drawn Carriages at Main Treasury Building - circa 1910

The annex of the Bureau of Engraving and Printing in the Department of the Treasury building as it is today - Built in 1938

M arcus Baldwin was an early engraver working for the Bureau, and one of the notes he engraved was the back of the $1,000 Federal Reserve Note of 1918. He is seen, upper left, at work in his office.

Marcus Baldwin, picture engraver, 1880

The eagle was engraved by Marcus Baldwin

Destruction of Currency by Cutting - circa 1900-1920

Worn out and mutilated currency was sent back to the Bureau for destruction.

This was accomplished by cutting the bundles of old currency into small pieces with currency cutting machines.

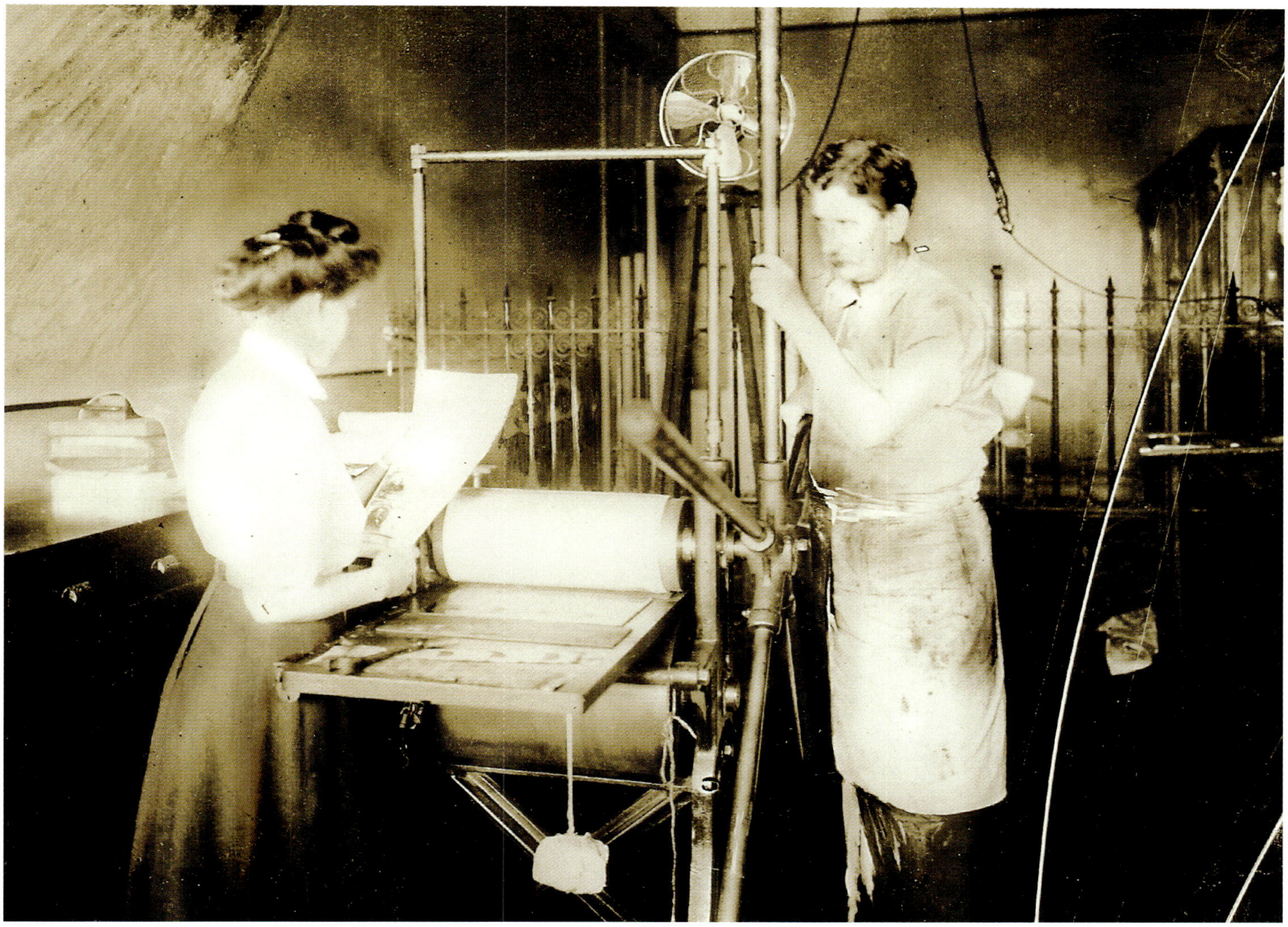

Spider press with plate printer and assistant, circa 1914

View of currency macerating room circa 1899

Money shipping carriages, carrying millions of dollars of banknotes from the Bureau to the main Treasury building (15th street sidewalk) - circa 1910

Francis E. Spinner
Treasurer of the United States

Francis E. Spinner

Francis Spinner, Treasurer of the United States from 1861 until 1875, was born in 1802 in the Mohawk Valley region of New York. He was unsuccessful as a merchant but rose to the rank of Major general of artillery in the state militia. He was elected to Congress in 1854 and later became a close and enthusiastic supporter and good friend of Lincoln.

His signature was the most difficult to duplicate or forge. He died in 1890 in Jacksonville, Florida at the age of 88 from cancer of the face.

Spinner's famous autograph signature of bold and decisive lettering appeared on all U.S. currency during his term as Treasurer.

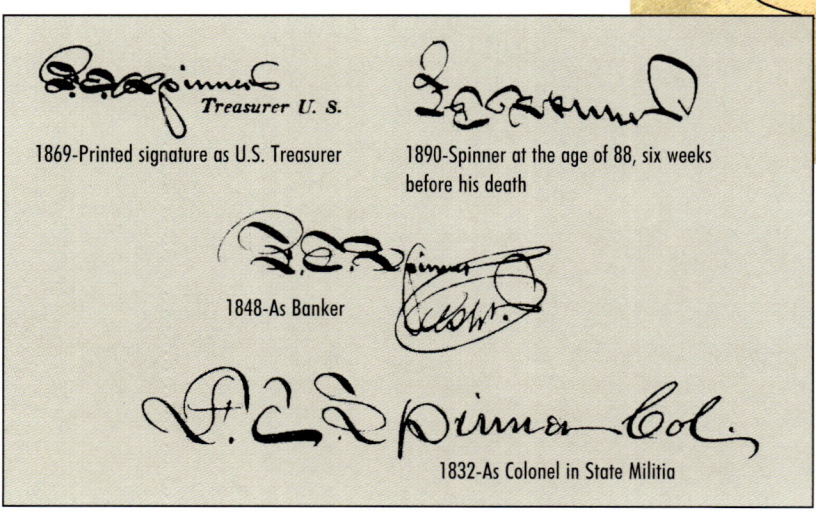

The Spinner signatures

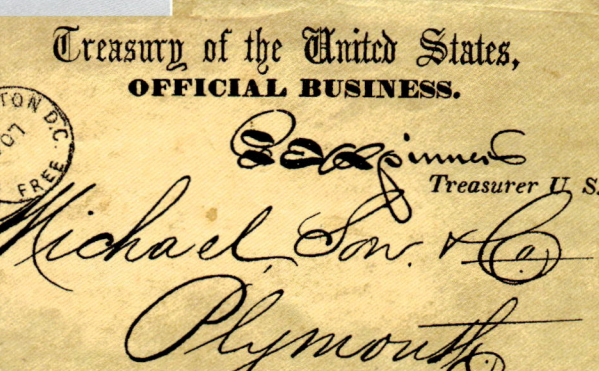

Francis Spinner's signature on a cover signed while he was Treasurer of the United States

Chapter II
Demand Notes
"GREENBACKS"

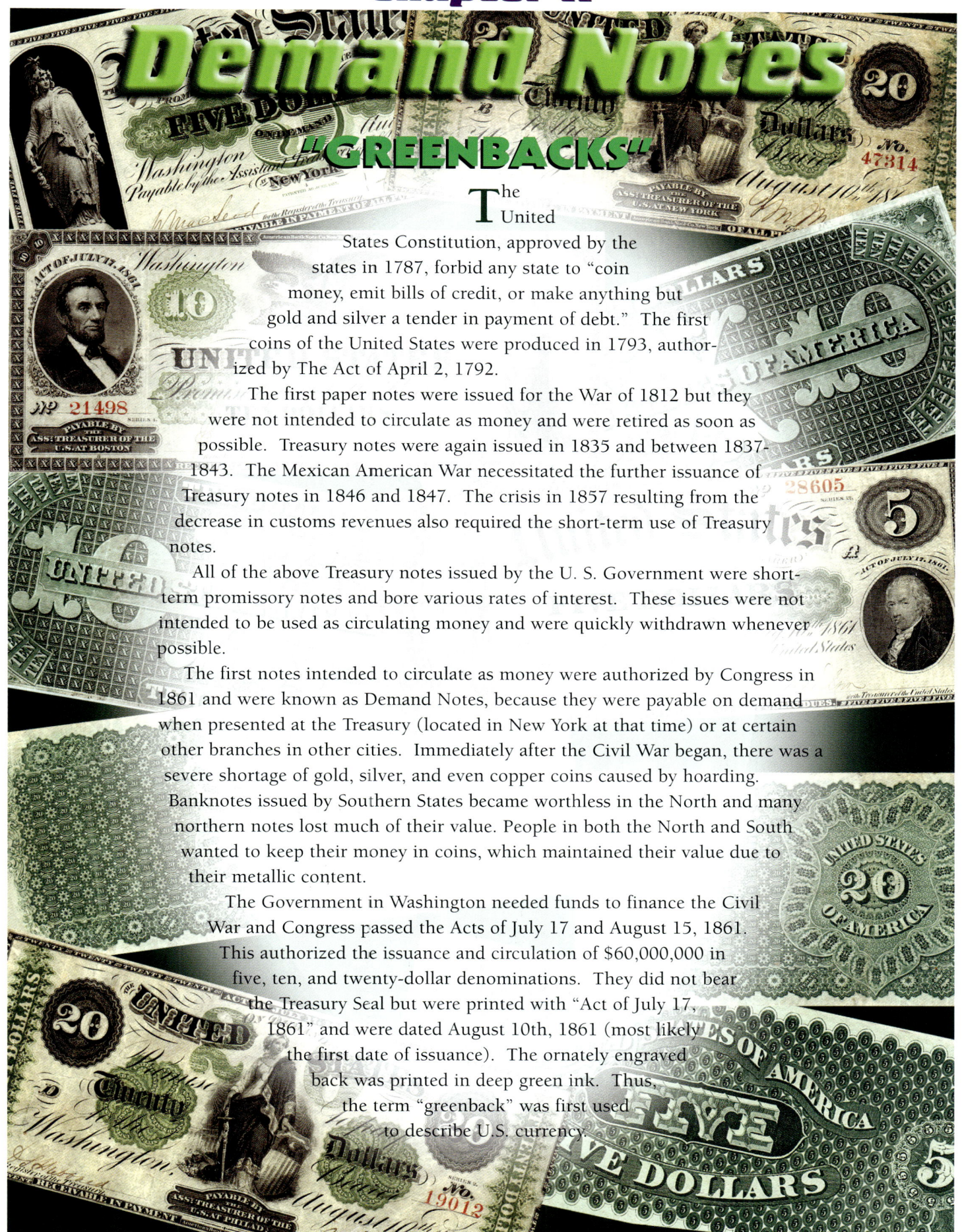

The United States Constitution, approved by the states in 1787, forbid any state to "coin money, emit bills of credit, or make anything but gold and silver a tender in payment of debt." The first coins of the United States were produced in 1793, authorized by The Act of April 2, 1792.

The first paper notes were issued for the War of 1812 but they were not intended to circulate as money and were retired as soon as possible. Treasury notes were again issued in 1835 and between 1837-1843. The Mexican American War necessitated the further issuance of Treasury notes in 1846 and 1847. The crisis in 1857 resulting from the decrease in customs revenues also required the short-term use of Treasury notes.

All of the above Treasury notes issued by the U. S. Government were short-term promissory notes and bore various rates of interest. These issues were not intended to be used as circulating money and were quickly withdrawn whenever possible.

The first notes intended to circulate as money were authorized by Congress in 1861 and were known as Demand Notes, because they were payable on demand when presented at the Treasury (located in New York at that time) or at certain other branches in other cities. Immediately after the Civil War began, there was a severe shortage of gold, silver, and even copper coins caused by hoarding. Banknotes issued by Southern States became worthless in the North and many northern notes lost much of their value. People in both the North and South wanted to keep their money in coins, which maintained their value due to their metallic content.

The Government in Washington needed funds to finance the Civil War and Congress passed the Acts of July 17 and August 15, 1861. This authorized the issuance and circulation of $60,000,000 in five, ten, and twenty-dollar denominations. They did not bear the Treasury Seal but were printed with "Act of July 17, 1861" and were dated August 10th, 1861 (most likely the first date of issuance). The ornately engraved back was printed in deep green ink. Thus, the term "greenback" was first used to describe U.S. currency.

FIVE DOLLAR DEMAND NOTES

Payable at New York
Obverse shows the Statue of Freedom, which is the crowning feature of the dome of the United States Capitol. The portrait is of Alexander Hamilton, the first Secretary of the Treasury from 1789 to 1795

These notes were nicknamed "greenbacks," a term that is still used today.

The U.S. Government had no facilities for printing currency notes in 1861 and these issues were printed by the American Bank Note Company. They were delivered to the Treasury Department where the signatures were applied by hand. These notes did not bear the seal of the United States Treasury.

Left: *The West Front of the Capitol*

Right: *View of the East Central Front of the Capitol*

Picture of Freedom

The Capitol Dome *Statue of Freedom on the Dome of the U.S. Capitol*

The Statue of Freedom was designed in 1857 by Thomas Crawford (1815-1857). Beginning in 1860, the statue was cast in five sections but work was halted in 1861, following the outbreak of the Civil War. It was finished in 1862 and was displayed on the grounds of the Capitol until it was installed on the dome in 1863.

Thomas Crawford also designed the Bronze doors of the House and Senate and the Pediment over the east entrance to the Senate wing of the Capitol.

The figure in the Center is America standing next to an eagle. Figures such as a woodsman, hunter, and Indians represent the early days of America. On the left are figures including those of a soldier, mechanic, and school children representing the diversity of human endeavor.

Senate Pediment
All photos from the Architect of the Capitol

What does "FOR THE" handwritten mean?

Payable at New York

"For the" handwritten

Spaces were left on Demand Notes for signatures of the "Register of the Treasury" and "Treasurer of the United States." Since there were millions of individual notes to sign, employees of the Treasury were required to hand sign each of them. As the actual Register and Treasurer never personally signed them, each employee had to add the words "for the" in front of the titles below the signature line. The plates were quickly changed to read "For the Register of the Treasury" and "For the Treasurer of the United States." Notes bearing the handwritten "for the" are extremely rare and valued today by collectors.

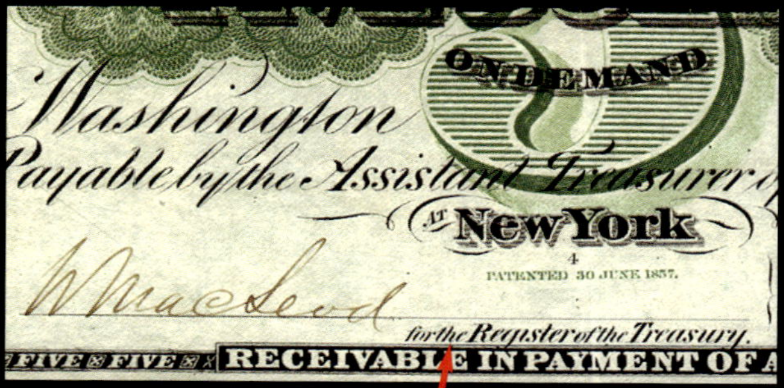

"For the Register of the Treasury"
Printed

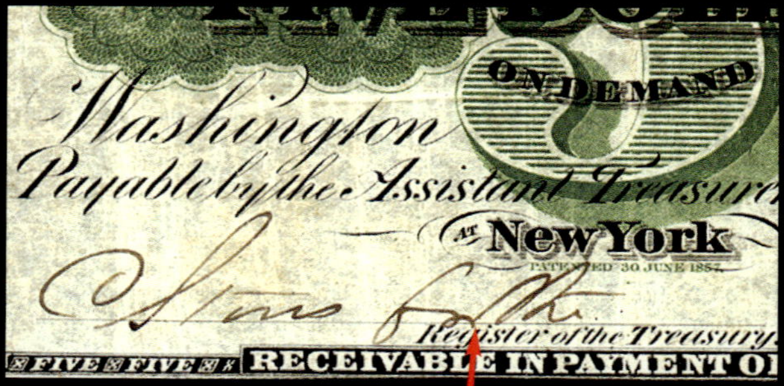

"For the Register of the Treasury"
Handwritten

"For the Treasurer of the United States"
Printed

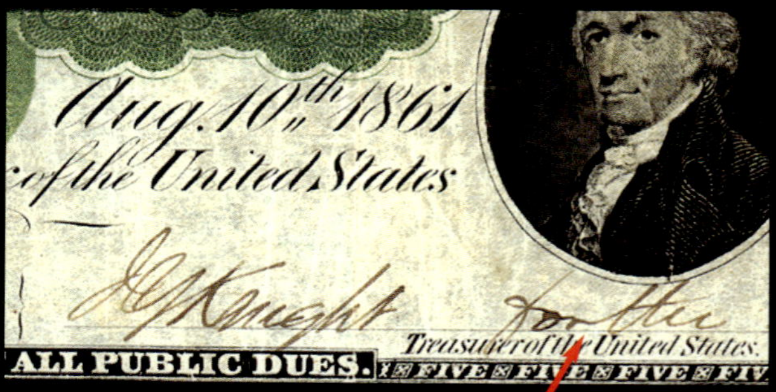

"For the Treasurer of the United States"
Handwritten

Payable at Philadelphia

Payable at Boston

"for the" handwritten payable at Boston
This note is unique

Payable at Cincinnati—only four other specimens are known

Notes payable at cities other than New York, Philadelphia and Boston are extremely rare.

Payable at St. Louis

Eight other examples are known to exist from St. Louis

The City of Cincinnati, Ohio as seen from atop Mt. Adams

The City of St. Louis, Missouri

TEN DOLLAR DEMAND NOTES

Payable at New York

"for the" handwritten
Only four other copies are known to exist

Payable at Philadelphia

Payable at Boston

"for the" handwritten
Payable at Boston—only one other copy exists

Payable at Cincinnati
Four other notes are known to exist

"for the" handwritten payable at Cincinnati
This is the only example known to exist

Payable at St. Louis—three other copies known

All ten dollar demand notes, printed in 1861, featured the portrait of Abraham Lincoln while he was still alive and President. The law was changed in 1866 allowing only deceased people to appear on currency.

TWENTY DOLLAR DEMAND NOTES

Payable at New York
Allegorical figure of Liberty holding a sword in her right hand. In her left hand is a shield featuring an eagle and stripes from the U.S. flag.

This is the only "for the" handwritten twenty dollar Demand Note that is known to exist. It is thus unique for type and design for those trying to complete a collection of Demand Notes. Even the Smithsonian and Federal Reserve Bank collections are missing this type. It was also absent from the Grinnell collection.

Payable at Philadelphia
This note is in extremely fine condition and is of the highest grade condition known to exist of all $20 Demand Notes. Grinnell owned this note when it was sold in 1944. It only appeared one other time at auction, in 1990.

Payable at Boston

Payable at Cincinnati
This is the only specimen known to exist and was once part of the Grinnell Collection.

FRACTIONAL CURRENCY

The beginning of the Civil War was a time for great distrust of paper currency. The Union was producing demand notes (greenbacks) and the Confederacy had their own currency. The currency printed by the losing side of this conflict was certain to become worthless.

Dimes, quarters, halves, and dollar coins were produced primarily from silver. The value of the silver in each of these coins approximated their face value. Since people were fearful of holding paper currency, silver coins were hoarded. This led to a shortage of coins that was initially solved by the practice of encasing postage stamps. Ultimately, the U.S. government had to produce fractional currency to provide a replacement for silver coins.

These notes were much smaller than dollar denominated bills and were printed on currency paper with the same engraving quality and technology as currency notes. They included the Treasury Seal but did not have serial numbers.

Congress passed the Act of July 17, 1862, which authorized the production and release of the first series of notes. There were four other issues of different designs, with the termination of fractional currency production finally occurring in 1876.

They represent an interesting reminder of our past history. Illustrated are examples of ten cent, twenty-five cent, and fifty cent notes. Also shown are complete packs of notes with the original Treasury strap—rare and desirable remnants of a difficult time in the United States.

Portrait of William Meredith, Secretary of the Treasury from 1849-1850

Reverse printed by the Columbian Bank Note Company

"This note is exchangeable for United States Notes by the Assistant Treasurers and designated depositories of the United States in sums not less than three dollars— Receivable in payment of all dues to the United States less than five dollars- except customs"

Five dollar pack of uncirculated ten cent notes

Portrait of Robert Walker, Secretary of the Treasury from 1845-1849

 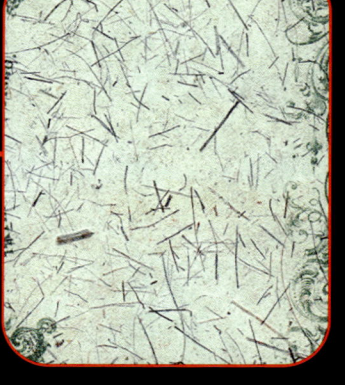

Note the extensive use of silk fibers used as a counterfeit deterrent

Ten dollar pack of uncirculated twenty-five cent notes

Portrait of William Crawford, Secretary of War and Secretary of the Treasury from 1815 to 1825

Reverse printed by Joseph R. Carpenter, Philadelphia

Original ten dollar pack of fifty cent notes in uncirculated condition

PONY EXPRESS

WANTED!!
Young, skinny wiry fellows.
Not over 18. Must be expert riders.
Willing to risk death daily.
Orphans preferred

Men Wanted!!
THE UNDERSIGNED WISHES TO hire ten or a dozen men, familiar with the management of horses, as hostlers or riders on the Overland Express Route via Salt Lake City. Wages $50 per month and board. I may be found at the St. George Hotel during Sunday, Monday and Tuesday.

William W. Finney

Above: Advertisement in a Sacramento newspaper
Right: An advertisement issued by William W. Finney for Pony Express riders

The year was 1861—The Civil War started with the attack on Fort Sumter, the first issue of U.S. currency Demand Notes or "greenbacks" were printed, and the Pony Express began its second and final year of operation.

The purpose of the Pony Express was to provide the fastest mail service between Sacramento, California, and St. Joseph, Missouri. It was started on April 3, 1860 with the hope of winning the million-dollar government mail contract for the Central Overland California and Pikes Peak Express Company. The trail was 1840 miles in length and the entire trip could be completed in ten days, half of the time normally required. It only passed through two states, Missouri and California. Nevada, Utah, Nebraska, Colorado, Kansas, and Wyoming were U.S. territories at the time.

The average age of the riders was twenty although the youngest was eleven and the oldest was forty-five. The pay was $100 per month. Horses traveled at an average speed of ten miles per hour and were changed every ten to fifteen miles. The riders were changed every 75 to 100 miles and there were approximately 165 relay stations. 400 horses were purchased for use on the route at a cost of $90,000. The owners invested $700,000 over eighteen months of operation, ultimately ceasing operations on October 24, 1861 with a loss of over $200,000.

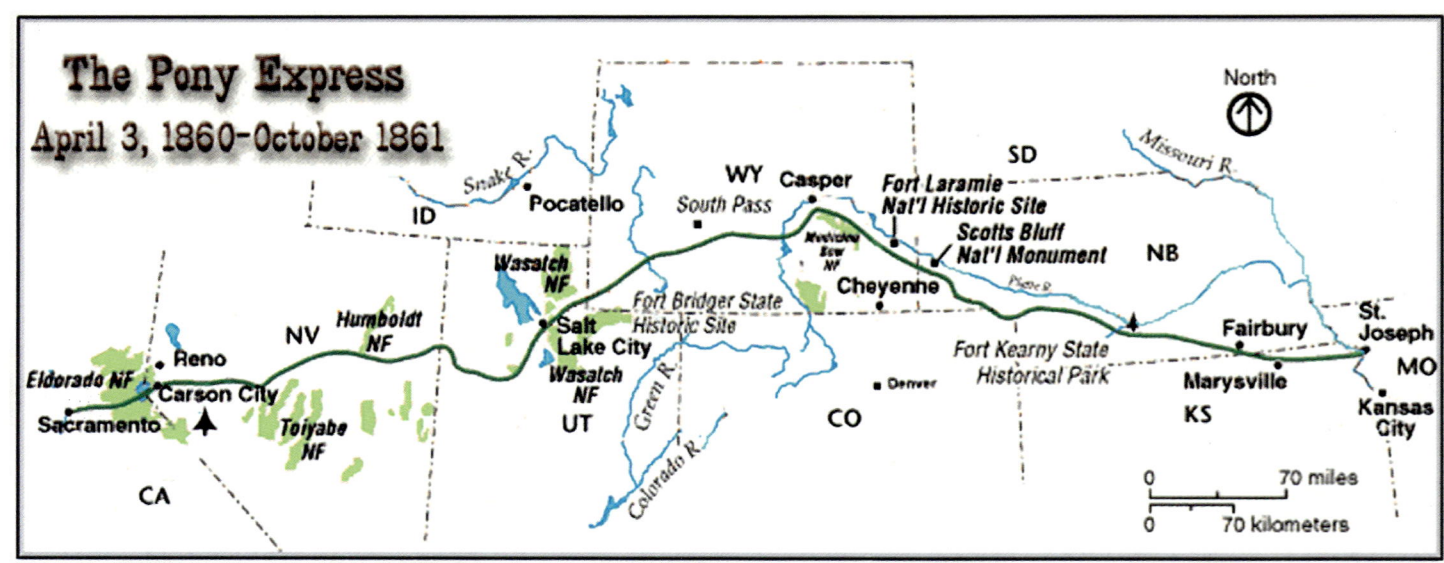

Map of the Pony Express routes from April 3, 1860 to October 1861

Founders of the Pony Express
"The Pony Must Go Spare neither Horses Money or Human Beings"

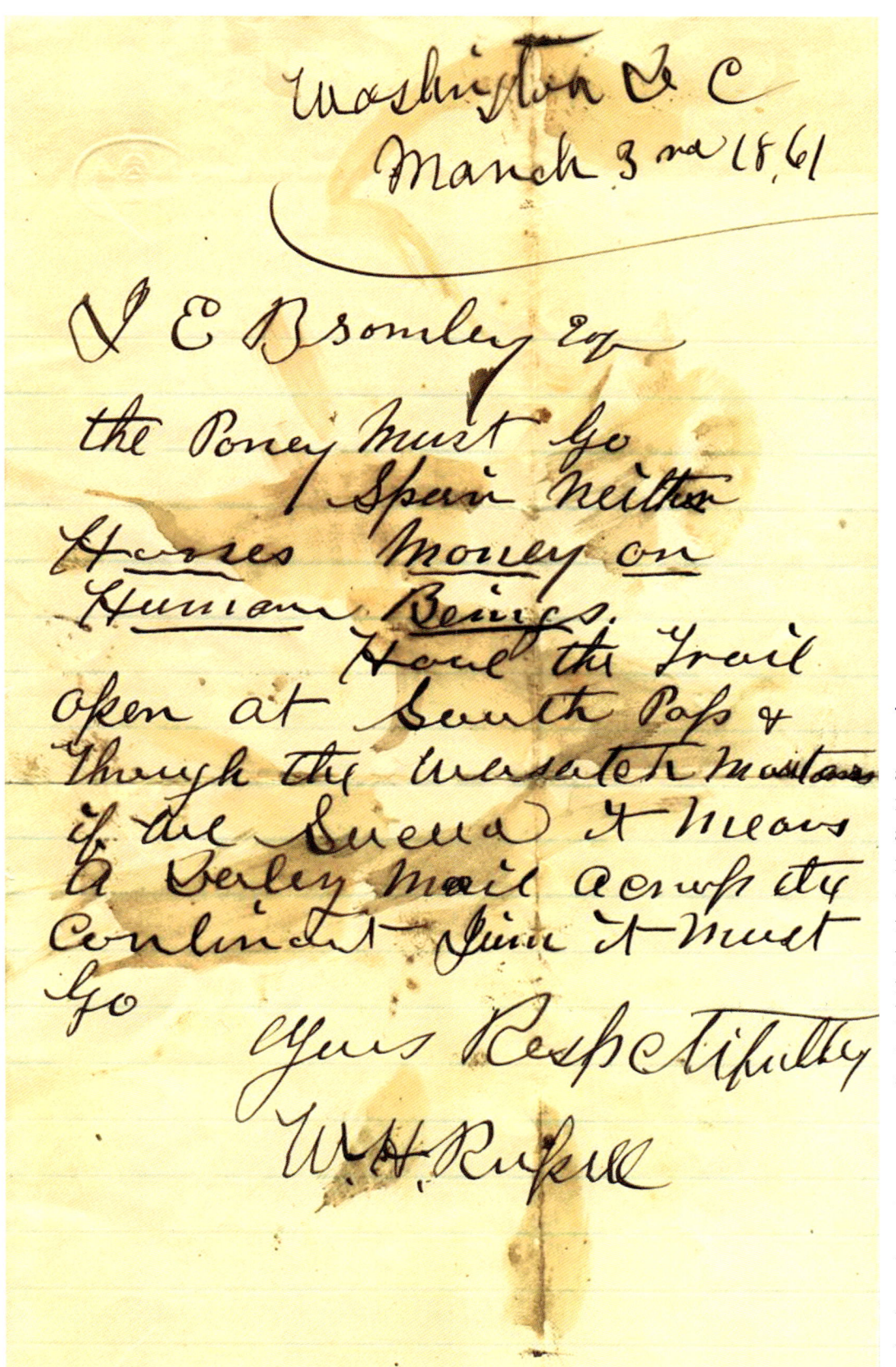

"the Pony Must Go Spare neither Horses Money or Human Beings. Have the trail open at South Pass & through the Wasatch Mountains if we succeed it means a daily mail across the Continent Jim it must go."

Yours Respectfully,

W.H. Russell

William H. Russell, Alexander Majors, and William Waddell formed the Pony Express as a subsidiary of their famous freight and stage company to prove that mail could be carried year round over the central route to California. They had hoped to obtain government subsidies to be able to operate at a profit.

Shown left is an important and historic letter dated March 3rd, 1861, the day before Lincoln's inauguration, and sent from Washington, D.C. by W. H. Russell to J.E. Bromley. It was written one month before ownership of the Pony Express passed on to Wells Fargo and Company in April, 1861. Russell resigned on April 26, 1861. This letter reveals the desperate attempts to secure a government contract.

Pony Express Stamps

The original charge to carry a letter was $5.00 per half ounce. The price gradually was lowered to $1.00 per half ounce. Regular U.S. postage stamps were used to pay the postage for delivery through the U.S. postal system at the destination city and hand franks or cancellations were applied at Pony Express offices to evidence payment of fees.

When Wells Fargo took over operation of the Pony Express, stamps were printed to pay the cost of sending a letter.

Original and unused block of six 25-cent stamps

Original and unused block of four $1 stamps

A rare used example of a $2 stamp with part of the Pony Express handstamp

Pony Express Abstract

TO	BILL NO.	FREE	DESCRIPTION	OUR CHARGES	PAID	COLLECT	DUE CAL
San Francisco	93	3	Letters		120.00		
Sacramento	11	2	"		20.00		
Virginia City	1		"		1.00		
Placerville	1		"		1.00		
Carson City	1		"		1.00		
Fort Laramie	1		"		1.00		
Fort Kearny	1		"		1.00		
	109	5			$145.00		
Saint Louis			C. W. Ford		27.00		
Wells Fargo & Co			New Envelopes Thro P.O.		107.00		
Leavenworth			J. W. Russell		2.00		
Saint Paul Minn			J. C. Terry		1.00		
Saint Joseph			Paul Coburn		8.00		
					$145.00		

PONY EXPRESS, ABSTRACT No. 17
From Saint Joseph, Mo., August 29th 1861 7 a.m.

This is an original page from the Pony Express Abstract book, page 17, dated August 29, 1861, from St. Joseph, Missouri. It details the letters that were carried on the westbound trip terminating in San Francisco.

A total of 109 letters were paid and five were free. The total fees collected were $145. Most of the letters were delivered in San Francisco but single letters were delivered to Carson City, Virginia City, Ft. Kearney, and Ft. Laramie.

The operating losses doomed the Pony Express and the completion of the transcontinental telegraph marked the final end of the Pony Express.

LETTER CARRIED BY THE PONY EXPRESS

This letter left San Francisco on October 5, 1861 and features the "running pony" hand stamp. It was postmarked October 19 in Atchison, Kansas and was ultimately delivered to New York City.

Above: Document from the Pony Express Museum reads "Legend has it Bronco Charlie Miller was just 11 years old when he first experienced the Pony Express."

Upper left: Hand stamp of "Running Pony" on cover illustrated above

Lower left: Detail of 1869 issue of 2 cents Pony Express stamp. This stamp was issued eight years after the Pony Express ceased operations and was part of the first issue of pictorial stamps issued by the United States.

PHILATELIC FOUNDATION CERTIFICATE

No. 48 569

APR 7 - 1975

THE PHILATELIC FOUNDATION
99 PARK AVENUE
NEW YORK, N.Y. 10016

EXPERT COMMITTEE

We have examined the enclosed USA 1861, 10¢, deep green, Scott 143L3.

submitted by

of which a photograph is attached and are of the opinion that it is genuinely used on Scott U32 entire, cancelled Pony Express San Francisco Oct. 5 via Atchison, Kans. Oct 19 to New York, 1861 use.

For The Expert Committee
Chairman

The Pony Express improved communications between east and west and proved that the central route could be traveled during the winter. It also supported the central route of the transcontinental railroad and kept communication open to California at the beginning of the Civil War.

It is also known for the adventures of its most famous rider, William Cody. He escaped from fifteen Sioux Indians, outriding them on his swift pony for twenty-five miles.

WILLIAM F. CODY (BUFFALO BILL) 1846-1917

William F. Cody (Buffalo Bill)

William F. Cody was born in Scott County, Iowa in 1846. At the age of eight he moved to Kansas with his family. His father died when he was eleven and he started to work as a messenger for different business firms. At the young age of fourteen he rode on a mail route for the Pony Express.

At first, the name Buffalo Bill was a fictional character to symbolize the "Wild West." At the age of twenty-two William Cody was re-christened "Buffalo Bill." Over the years Buffalo Bill had been a trapper, a bullwhacker, a Colorado "Fifty-Niner," a Pony Express rider, a wagon-master, a stagecoach driver, and a soldier in the Civil War.

He is best known for his traveling "Buffalo Bill's Wild West Show." The show portrayed real cowboys and Indians depicting the West. The show spent ten of its thirty years in Europe. It featured the famous woman sharpshooter, Annie Oakley. By the early 1900's Buffalo Bill was probably the most famous and recognizable man in the world.

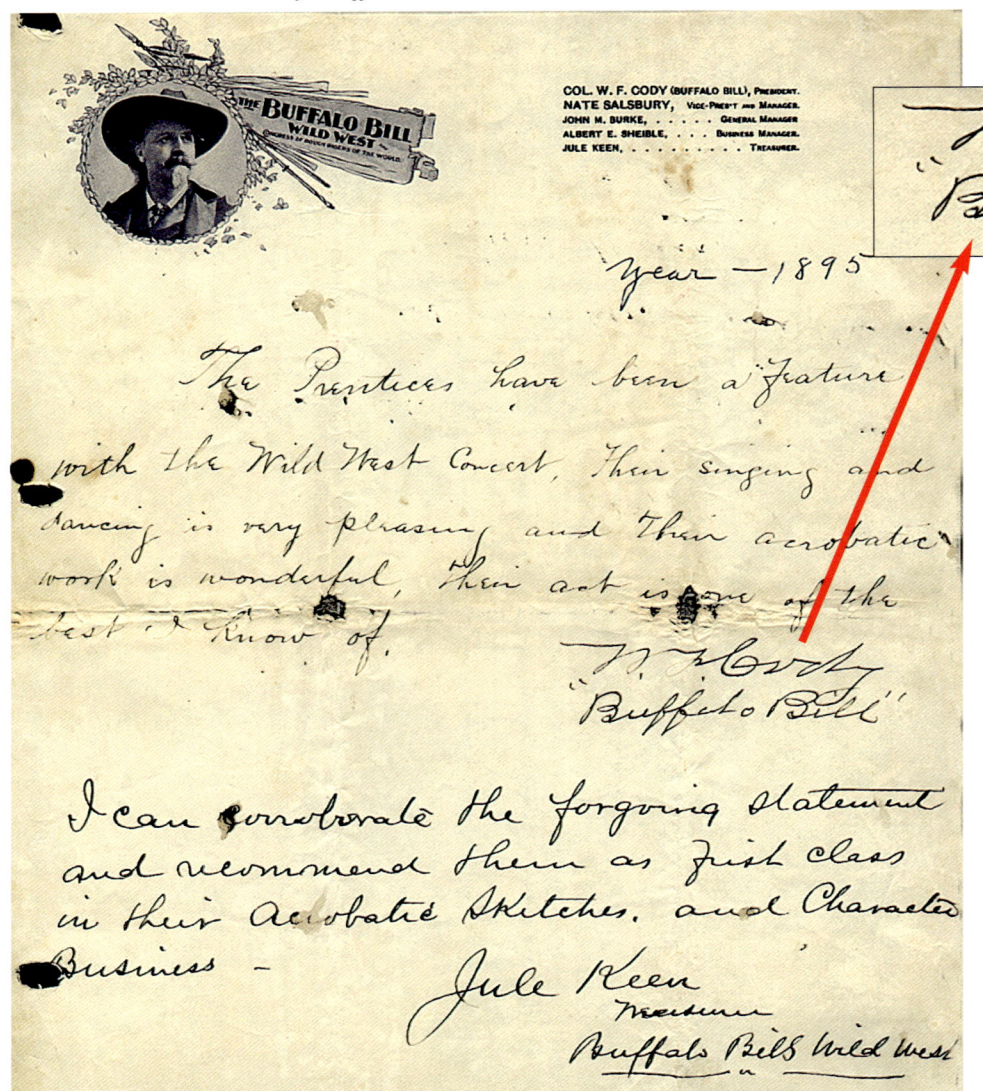

William F. Cody (Buffalo Bill) wrote this letter to the treasurer of his company Julie Keene discussing a new act for the Wild West Show

Another one of Buffalo Bill's significant contributions was of developing the town of Cody, Wyoming. He wanted to develop a western town where old west values and modern technology would exist together. With the help of his friend Teddy Roosevelt two dams were in operation by 1910 to help irrigate the land and the town was developed.

By 1916, Buffalo Bill's health deteriorated and he was faced with ongoing legal battles, contract disputes and financial problems. He died in Denver, Colorado January 10, 1917. His grave is located on Lookout Mountain, near the town of Golden, Colorado.

Left is a portion of a letter written by William F. Cody in September, 1881

Annie Oakley, 1860-1926

Annie Oakley was born Phoebe Ann Moses in Drake County, Ohio. She learned to shoot from her father at the age of eight. She helped support her family by killing game for a local hotel in Cincinnati. Phoebe became famous as one of the world's most accurate shots with the pistol, rifle, and shotgun.

At the age of fifteen she defeated a professional marksman in an exhibition. She subsequently married that marksman, Frank Butler, at the age of sixteen. She then adopted the stage name Annie Oakley, which she was to keep forever. She was called, "Little Miss Sure Shot" by the famous Sioux Indian chief Sitting Bull. She was small in stature, standing only five feet tall.

Annie and Frank toured with Buffalo Bill's Wild West Show for seventeen years. At the age of thirty-one she was injured in a train accident partially paralyzing her, but she continued to tour regularly until her death. Annie Oakley died at the age of sixty-six of pernicious anemia on November 3, 1926.

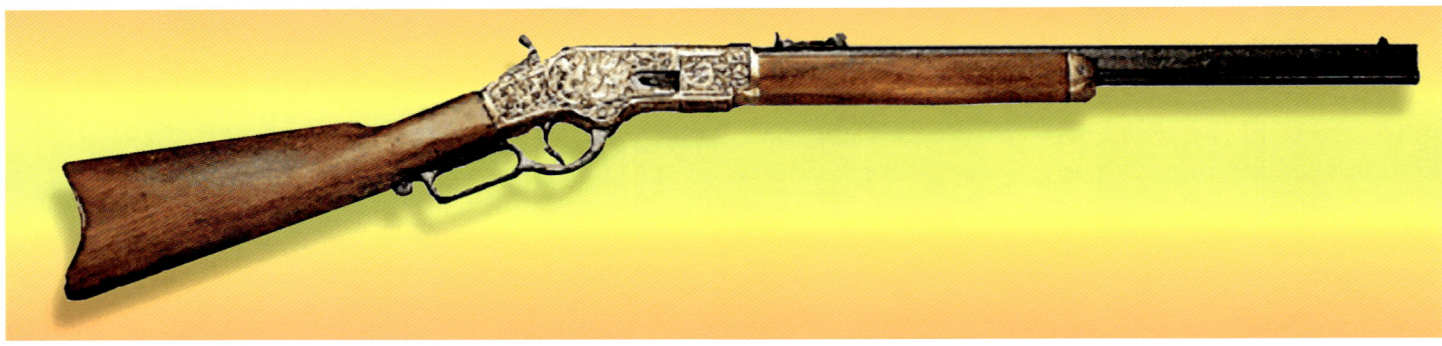

Western style rifle is the type Annie Oakley used in her performance in Buffalo Bill's Wild West Show

Right photo: In 1885 Sitting Bull was allowed to leave the reservation to join Buffalo Bill's Wild West Show, earning $50 a week for riding once around the arena, in addition to whatever he could charge for his autograph and picture. He stayed with the show only four months, unable to tolerate white society any longer. He did manage to shake hands with President Grover Cleveland, which he took as evidence that he was still regarded as a great chief.

Left photo: Annie Oakley also known as "Little Miss Sure Shot"
Photo-Annie Oakley Foundation

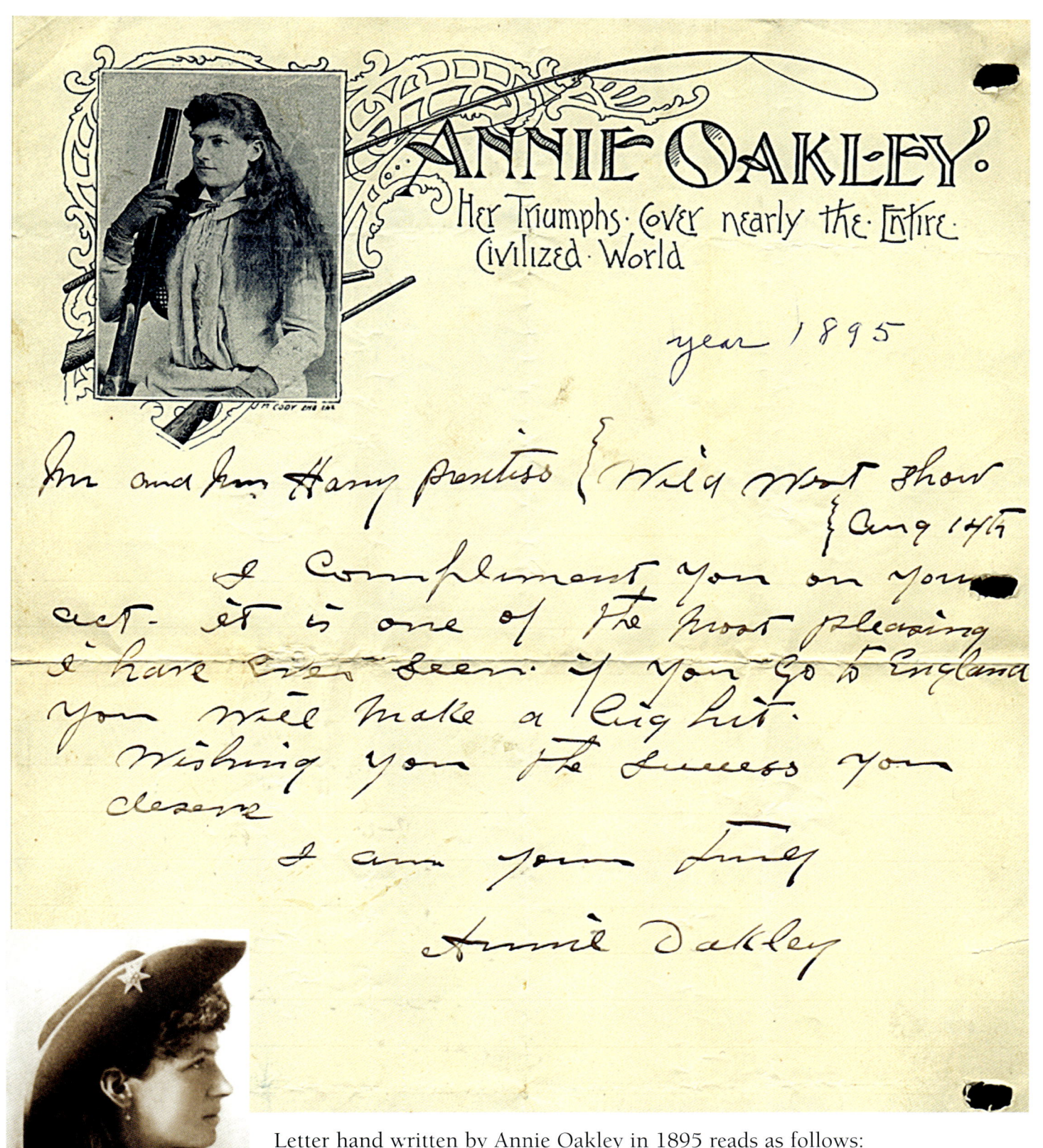

Letter hand written by Annie Oakley in 1895 reads as follows:

Year 1895

Mr. and Mrs Harry Prentiss Wild West Show Aug 14th
    I compliment you on your act. It is one of the most pleasing I have ever seen. If you go to England you will make a big hit. Wishing you the success you deserve.
    I am yours truly
    Annie Oakly

Left photo: Annie Oakley photographed with her many medals won for her sharp shooting
Photo-Annie Oakley Foundation

FREDERIC REMINGTON - 1861-1909

American artist Frederic Remington's extensive collection of paintings and bronze statuettes depicting the American West and the days of the Cowboy during the 1800's are what made him famous in terms of his contribution to 19th century American art.

Furthermore, his statuettes of cowboys and Indians represent a vigorous life in the Old West where he traveled extensively.

Frederic Remington was born in Canton, New York. He studied art at Yale University when he was nineteen years old. His first drawings were published in the university newspaper. His later works of art were action filled paintings, drawings, and sculptures of cowboys and Indians. A well known bronze, "Comin' Through the Rye," finished in 1902 depicts four cowboys on horseback charging at the viewer with happiness. Several of the books he wrote and illustrated are "Pony Tracks" (1895) and "The Way of an Indian" (1906). He died in 1909 having produced over three thousand paintings and sculptures.

My Dear R——

    Glad you are back again at the firing line——. I am going to sand-bag Corlier out of that picture if I can. Don't put him next or he may see me coming ——

    Yours

    Frederic Remington

Chapter III

Legal Tender Notes

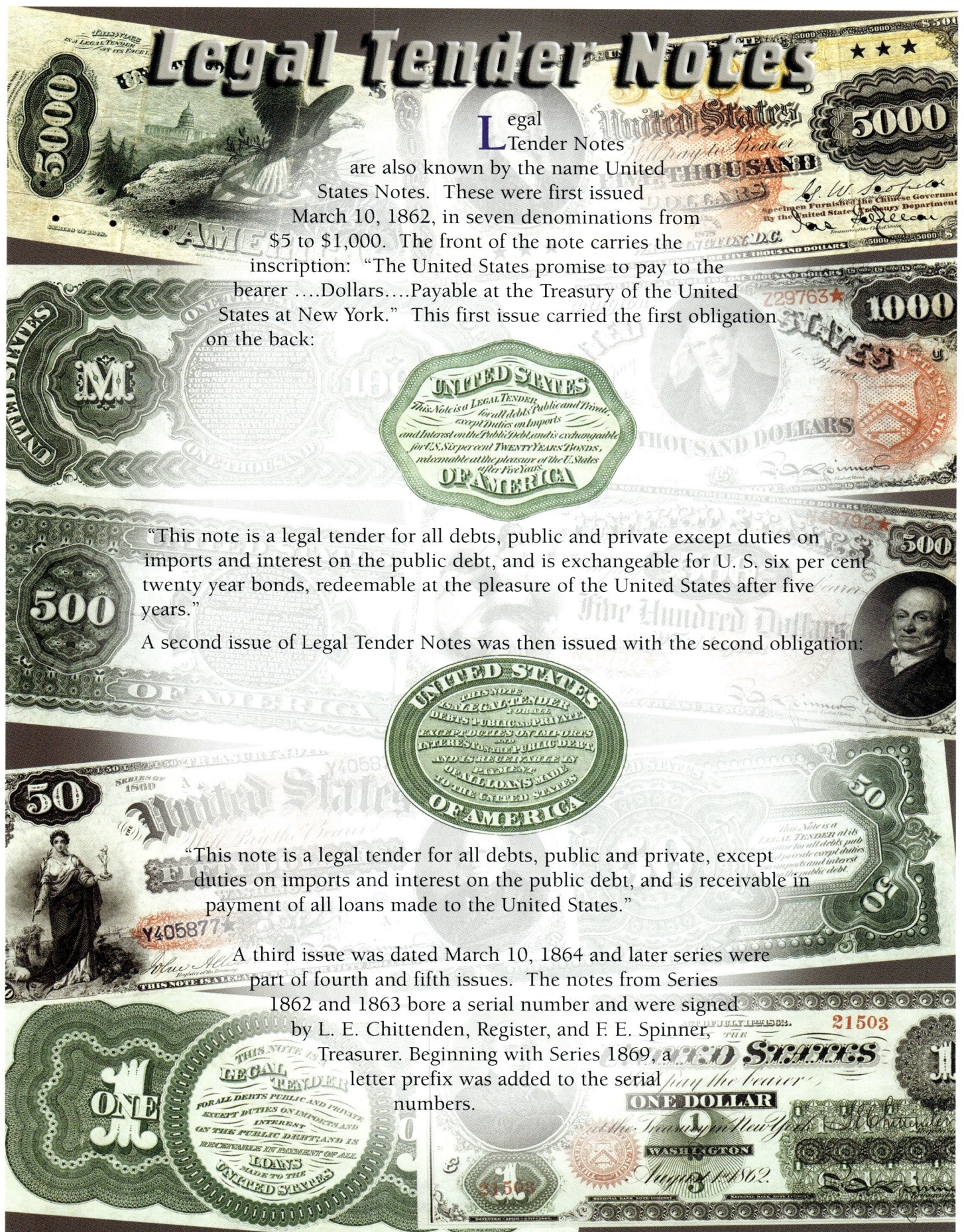

Legal Tender Notes are also known by the name United States Notes. These were first issued March 10, 1862, in seven denominations from $5 to $1,000. The front of the note carries the inscription: "The United States promise to pay to the bearer ….Dollars….Payable at the Treasury of the United States at New York." This first issue carried the first obligation on the back:

"This note is a legal tender for all debts, public and private except duties on imports and interest on the public debt, and is exchangeable for U. S. six per cent twenty year bonds, redeemable at the pleasure of the United States after five years."

A second issue of Legal Tender Notes was then issued with the second obligation:

"This note is a legal tender for all debts, public and private, except duties on imports and interest on the public debt, and is receivable in payment of all loans made to the United States."

A third issue was dated March 10, 1864 and later series were part of fourth and fifth issues. The notes from Series 1862 and 1863 bore a serial number and were signed by L. E. Chittenden, Register, and F. E. Spinner, Treasurer. Beginning with Series 1869, a letter prefix was added to the serial numbers.

ONE DOLLAR LEGAL TENDER NOTES

Salmon P. Chase, Secretary of the Treasury 1861-1864

This was the first one-dollar bill issued by the United States. It was printed by the National Bank Note Company and sent to the Bureau of Engraving and Printing, which cut the printed sheets into individual notes and applied the Treasury Seal. Salmon P. Chase was alive and Secretary of the Treasury when this note was printed; the law later changed in 1866 allowing only deceased people on currency.

Chase was born in New Hampshire in 1808 and graduated from Dartmouth in 1826. He later practiced law and became involved in antislavery and other reform activities. Chase was elected Governor of Ohio in 1855 and 1857 and U.S. Senator in 1860. The Republican Party was formed after the Missouri Compromise and the Kansas-Nebraska Act and Lincoln appointed him Secretary of the Treasury in 1861. He resigned that post in 1864 after irreconcilable differences with Lincoln but was appointed Chief Justice of the Supreme Court later that year and served in that position until his death of a stroke in 1873. Ironically, Chase swore in Andrew Johnson as President after Lincoln's assassination.

Salmon Chase's long antislavery record and party activism led him to be prominently mentioned as a Republican presidential candidate in both 1856 and 1860.
The Frederick Douglass Papers at the Library of Congress presents the papers of the nineteenth-century African-American abolitionist who escaped from slavery and then risked his own freedom by becoming an outspoken antislavery lecturer, writer, and publisher.

TEN THOUSAND DOLLAR FEDERAL RESERVE NOTE
SERIES 1934

Series 1934, Portrait of Salmon P. Chase

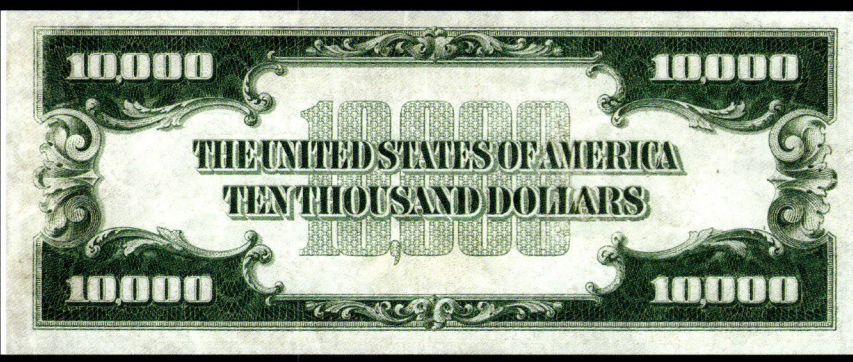

Large denomination notes ($500, $1,000, $5,000, and $10,000) were last printed in 1945 and generally available upon request until the Treasury Department issued an official recall in 1969. When these notes appeared at banks and were returned to the Federal Reserve System, they were forwarded to the Treasury Department for destruction and not re-issued through the banking system.

The official government reason for the elimination of large denomination notes was their diminished and infrequent use due to the widespread availability of checks and credit cards. However, it is quite obvious that elimination of a convenient way for large sums of money to be transported by illegal activities such as money laundering and tax evasion was a major reason for the withdrawal of these beautiful and ornately designed notes that will be forever a part of U. S. history.

Salmon Portland Chase
(13 January 1808 - 7 May 1873)
Source: Harper's Weekly

The Only Complete Set of Rainbow Notes Outside of the U.S. Government Collection

In 1869, all legal tender issues from the $1 to $1,000 denominations were printed on special paper that had a vertical segment of blue color on the obverse interspersed with a large number of silk fibers to deter counterfeiting. The combination of this paper with the red serial numbers, Treasury Seal, and the black main design gave rise to the term "rainbow note." These represent some of the most colorful and popular issues of United States Currency. The $500 and $1,000 notes are unique outside of government holdings and these two notes are needed to complete any type collection of U.S. currency.

One Dollar "Rainbow" Note
Series 1869

After five centuries, Columbus remains as one of the greatest mariners in history, a visionary genius, a national hero, a failed administrator, a naive entrepreneur, and a ruthless and greedy imperialist. He settled for a time in Portugal, where he tried unsuccessfully to enlist support for his project, before moving to Spain. After many difficulties, through a combination of good luck and persuasiveness, he gained the support of the Catholic monarchs, Isabel and Ferdinand.

Christopher Columbus in Sight of Land is the engraving on the left side of the obverse

The First Voyage of Columbus
Painting by Theodore de Bry - 1594

Series 1874, Small Red Seal

This reverse of this design was nicknamed "sawhorse" due to the appearance of the large "X" in the center of the note

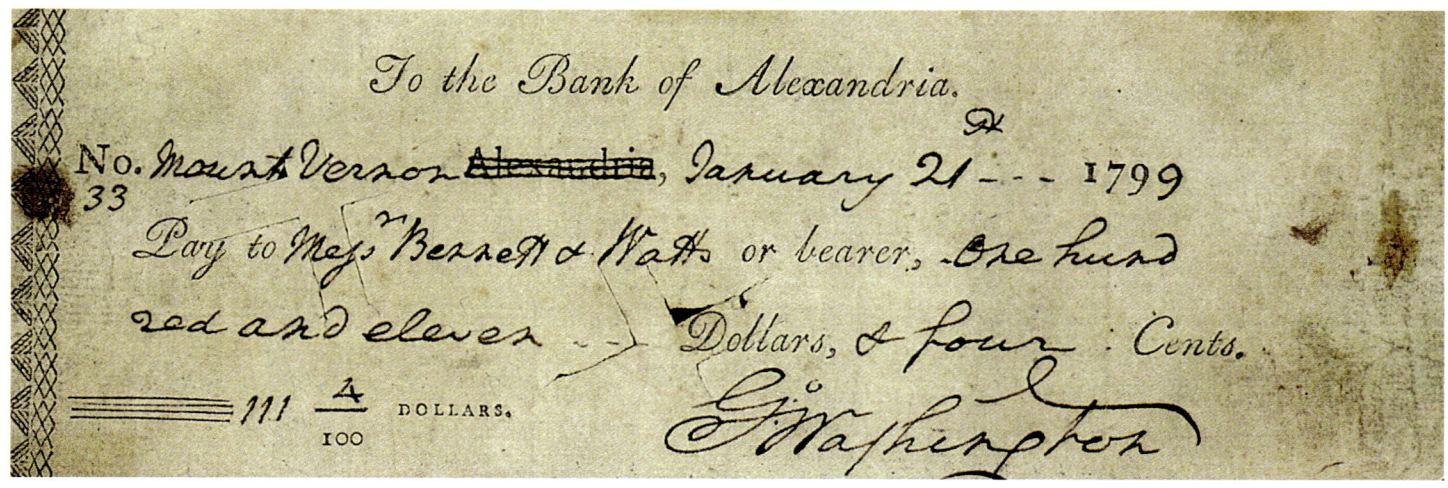

This original check was written and signed by George Washington at Mount Vernon on January 21, 1799. It was made payable to Major Watts for $111.04.

Series 1880, Large Brown Seal

Series 1880, Large Red Spiked Seal

Series 1880, Large Brown Seal

Series 1880, Small Red Scalloped Seal

Series 1917

Series 1923

This was the last large size legal tender note issued before the change to the current small size notes. The portrait of George Washington is the same one used on current one-dollar notes.

*Above: George and Martha Washington at their wedding ceremony
Right: A young George Washington as a soldier
during the French and Indian wars*

Engraved by John Rogers after C.W. Peale, from Prints and Photographs Division, Library of Congress

A Letter Written by George Washington During His Second Term of Office Relative to the Purchase of Oats for Mt. Vernon

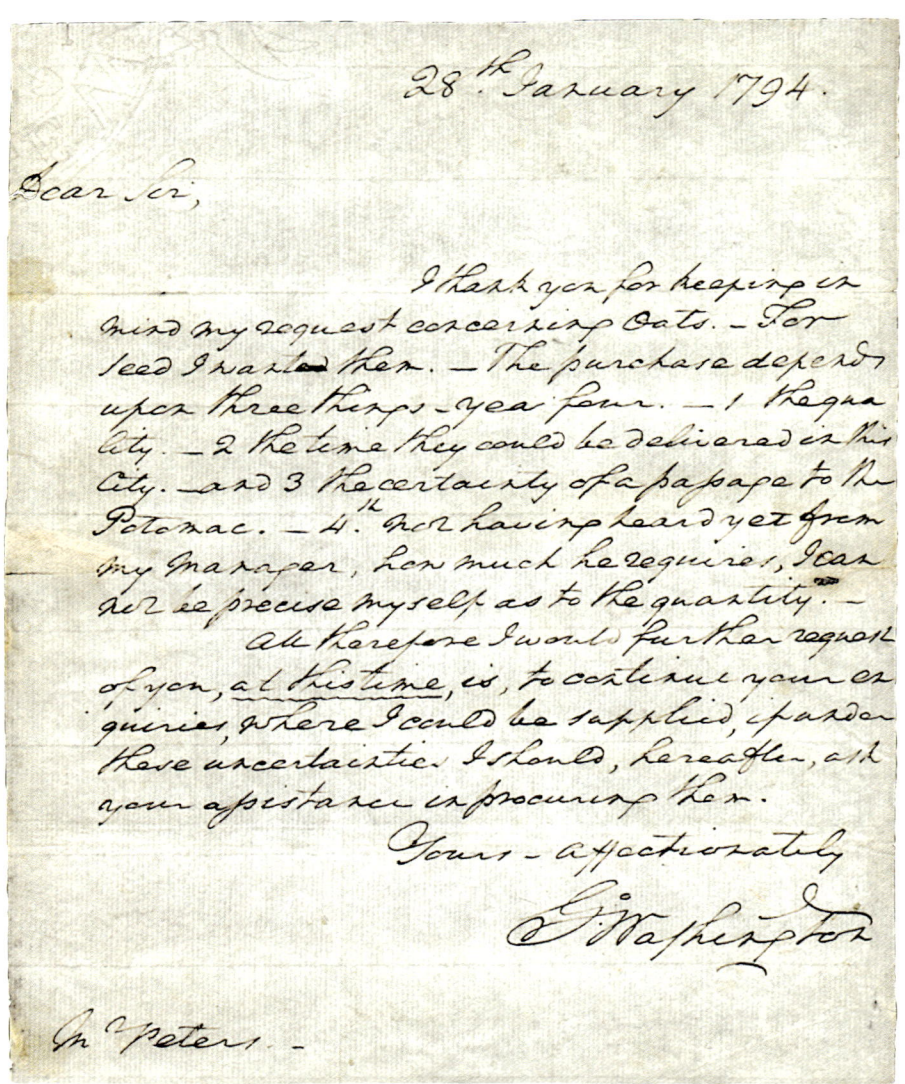

Dear Sir:

I thank you for keeping in mind my request concerning cats – for seed I want them. The purchase depends upon three things – yea four. (1) The quality. (2) The time they should be delivered in this City. (3) The certainty of a passage to the Potomac. (4) Not having heard yet from my Manager, how much he requires, I cannot be precise myself as to the quantity.

All therefore I would further request of you, at this time, is, to continue your inquiries where I could be supplied, if upon these uncertainties I should, hereafter, ask your assistance in procuring them.

                Yours affectionately
                G. Washington

Mr. Peters

Free Frank Signed by George Washington in 1784

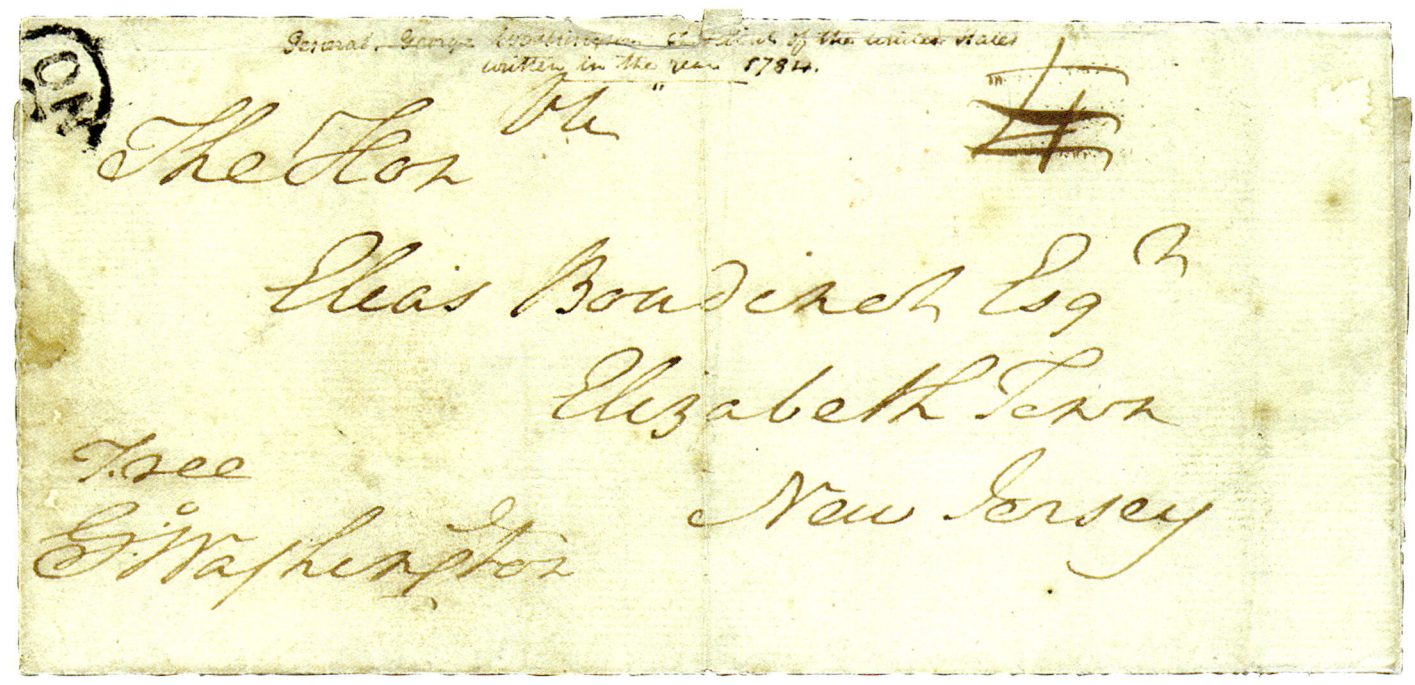

Cover signed by G. Washington and addressed to Elias Boadchek, Esq.

The reverse of this cover reveals a well-preserved and rare example of the Washington family seal. This was embossed onto hot wax and used to prevent tampering of the letter.

TWO DOLLAR LEGAL TENDER NOTES

Portrait of Alexander Hamilton

This note and the one-dollar bill of 1862 were the first notes to show portraits of persons.

This was the first issue of two-dollar notes. They were printed by the National Bank Note Company and are dated August 1, 1862. They were authorized by an act of Congress dated July 11, 1862.

This note is a legal tender for all debts public and private except duties on imports and interest on the public debt; and is receivable in all loans made to the United States.

Did the United States Ever Print a Three-dollar Bill?

The Treasury Department had originally intended to issue on August 1, 1862 legal tender notes in $1, $2, and $3 denominations. The plates for all three were engraved and a common design in all three was a circle to the right of center that had the vertical numbers 1, 2, and 3.

The "1" is in white which was an additional method of identifying the denomination

The "2" is highlighted on this design

Three-dollar bill issued by the State of Florida on December 6, 1861

The decision was made not to print or release the $3 bill. This denomination was used and circulated by various states and banks. All such notes, along with those of other denominations issued by non U. S. Government entities were eventually worthless due to the large number of defaults and are not legal tender, although they are currently popular with collectors.

Two Dollar "Rainbow" Note
Series 1869

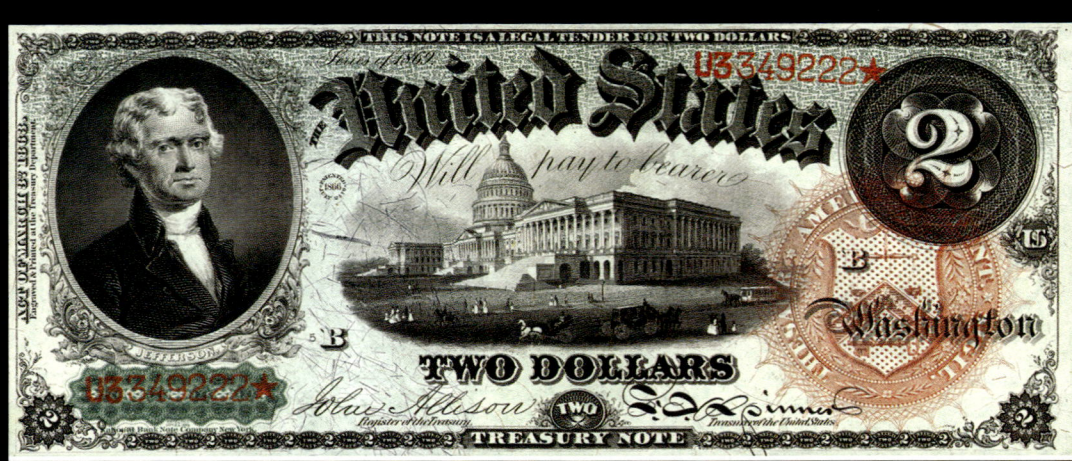

Portrait of Thomas Jefferson, third President of the United States, 1801-1805

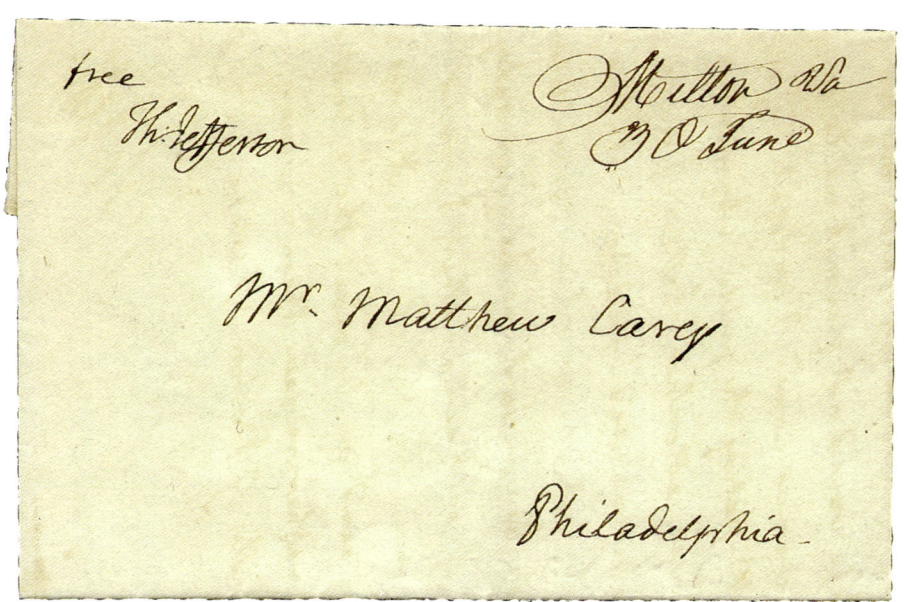

JEFFERSON WRITES TO MATTHEW CAREY AS EX-PRESIDENT JUNE 30, CIRCA 1811-1822

After serving two terms as President, Jefferson retired at his home, Monticello, which he designed and began building in 1770. In his retirement, Jefferson accomplished one of his cherished goals-the creation of the University of Virginia at Charlottesville. Jefferson wrote his own epitaph, which ignores the numerous roles he played in public service, but stated very simply,

"author of the Declaration of Independence, the Statute of Virginia granting religious freedom, and father of the University of Virginia."

This letter is addressed to Matthew Carey in Jefferson's hand. It was posted at Milton, Virginia, an insititutional post office from 1811 to 1822.

Series 1875, Small Red Seal With Rays

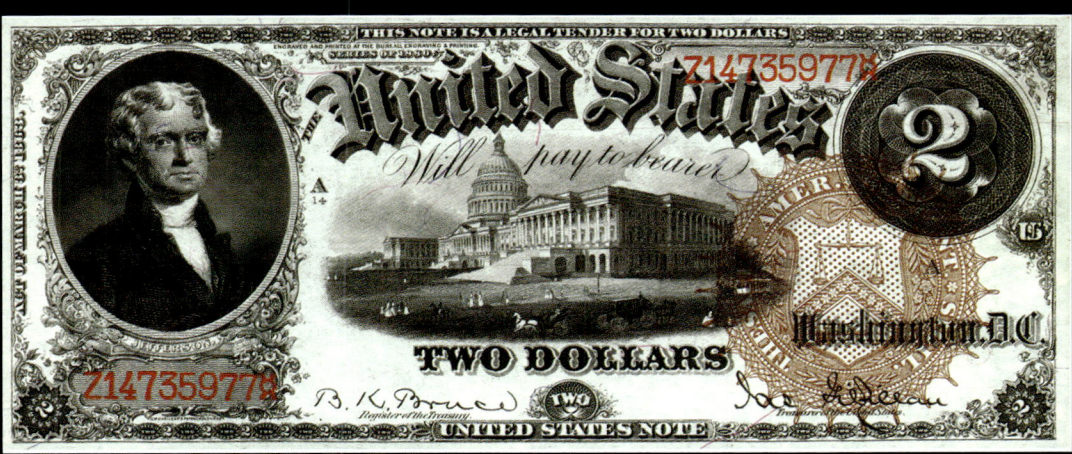

Series 1880, Large Brown Seal with Red Serial Numbers

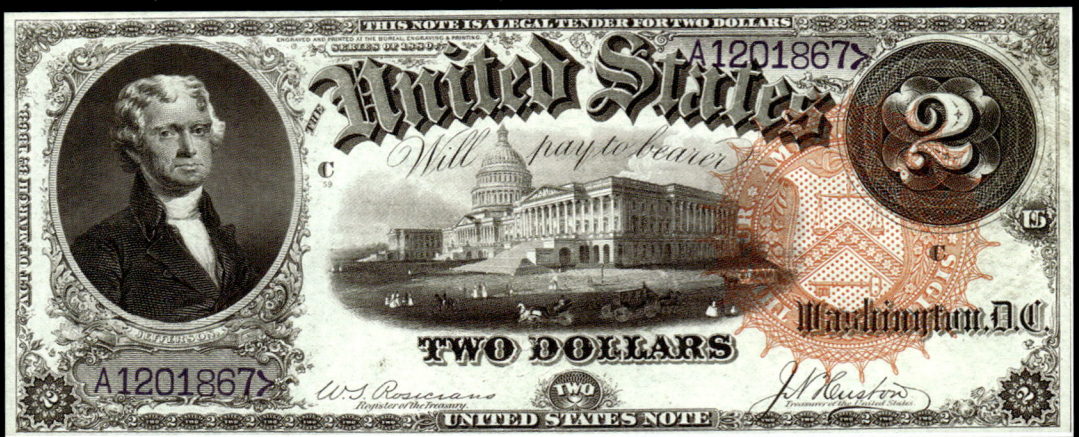

Series 1880, Large Red Seal

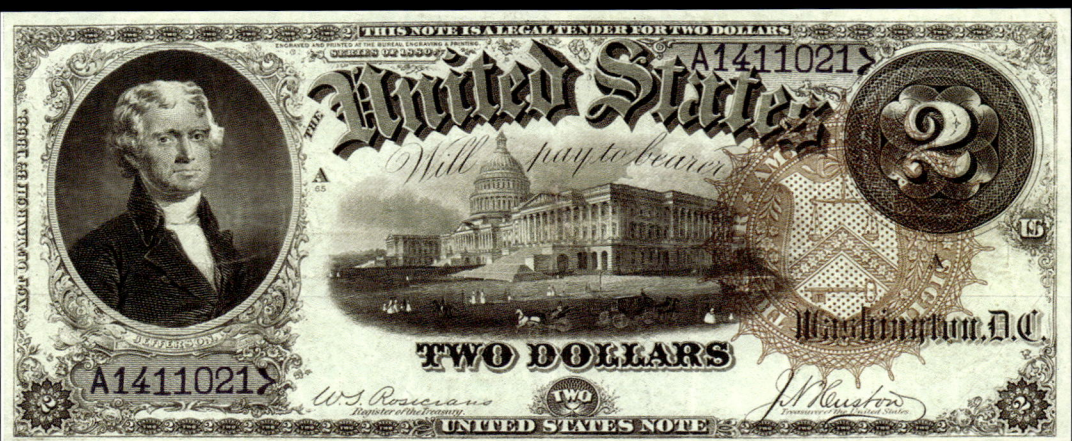

Series 1880, Large Brown Seal with Blue Serial Numbers

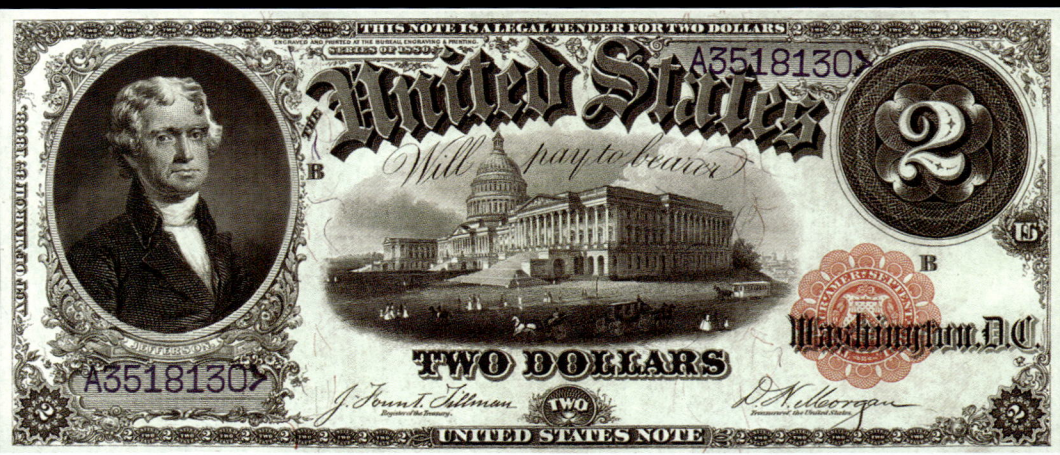

Series 1880, Small Red Scalloped Seal

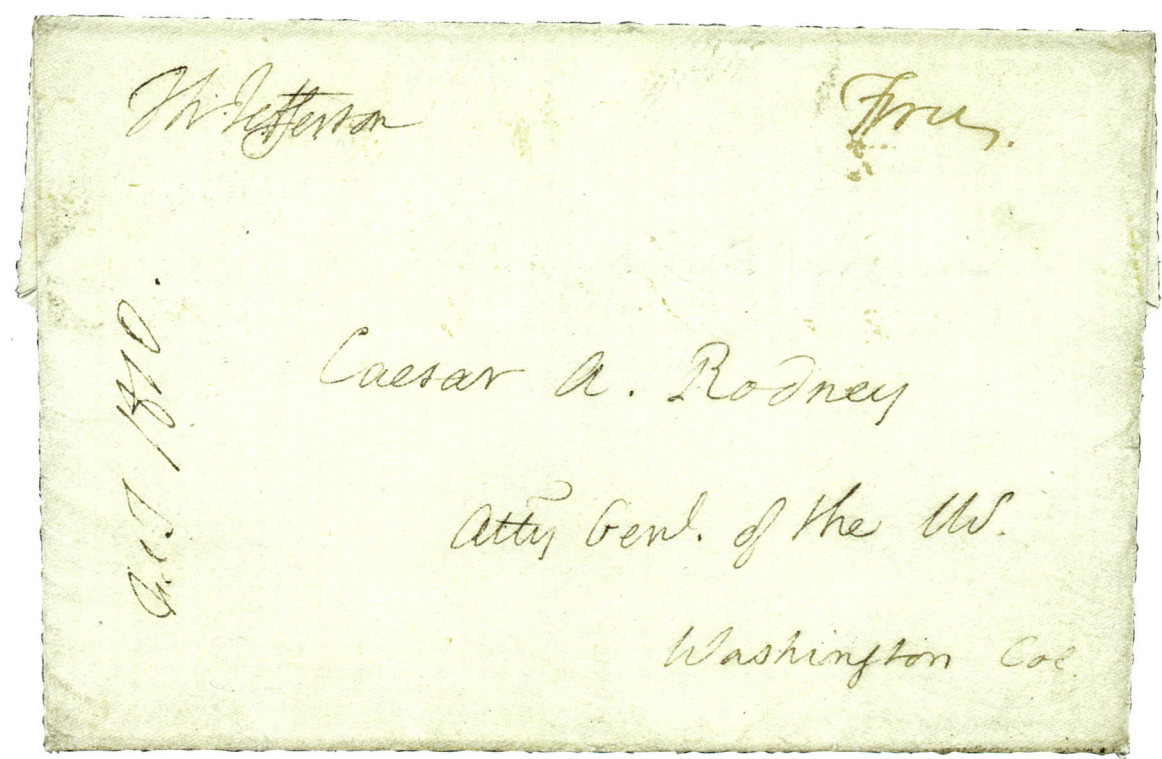

Free frank signed by Thomas Jefferson

The reverse of the two-dollar legal tender note (Series 1963) featured Monticello, the home of Thomas Jefferson.

Monticello is the autobiographical masterpiece of Thomas Jefferson, designed and redesigned and built and rebuilt for more than forty years

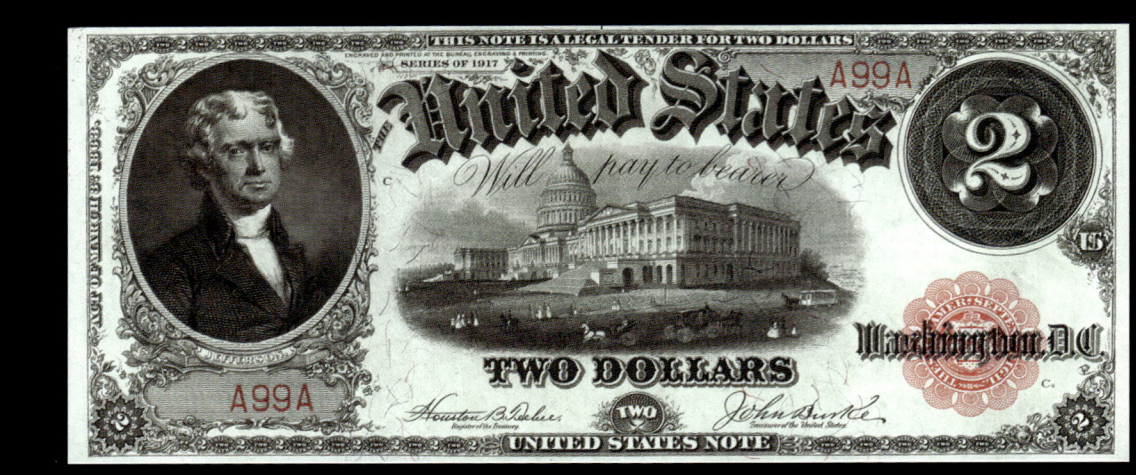

Series 1917—This was the last issue of large size $2 legal tender notes

THOMAS JEFFERSON

Thomas Jefferson - Third President
1801-1809
Photo: Library of Congress

Thomas Jefferson was born in Virginia in 1743. His father was a surveyor and farmer and left him 5,000 acres of land. He studied law at William and Mary. In 1772, Jefferson married Martha Skelton and moved into his home he called Monticello. He was a better writer than speaker and is best known for writing the Declaration of Independence at the age of 33, while he was a member of the Continental Congress.

Jefferson was a reluctant candidate for President in 1796 and lost by only three votes to John Adams. Due to a flaw in the Constitution, he became the Vice-President even though they were opposing each other for President. The most important decision during his presidency was the acquisition of the Louisiana Territory from Napoleon in 1803. The United States was only interested in purchasing New Orleans to assure the right to sail ships down the Mississippi River. However, just before James Monroe was scheduled to arrive in Paris, France unexpectedly sold the Louisiana Territory for $15,000,000. It was the largest single land purchase in U.S. history and added 600 million acres, which became part of the thirteen states. Jefferson died on July 4, 1826, only a few hours before John Adams passed away.

Detail from: Currier and Ives
The Declaration Committee
New York, 1776

Letter signed by John F. Kennedy to Barry Goldwater
Kennedy was born in 1917, the same year the note on the opposite page was issued

THE WHITE HOUSE
WASHINGTON

August 19, 1963

Dear ~~Senator Goldwater~~ Barry:

Mrs. Kennedy and I were deeply moved by your thoughtful remembrance on the loss of our son.

This kind expression of sympathy on the part of you and Mrs. Goldwater meant a great deal to us.

Sincerely,

Honorable Barry Goldwater
United States Senate
Washington, D. C.

On November 22, 1963, when he was hardly past his first thousand days in office, John Fitzgerald Kennedy was killed by an assassin's bullets as his motorcade wound through Dallas, Texas. Kennedy was the youngest man elected President and the youngest President to die in office.

Kennedy's third child, a son named Patrick, died soon after being born prematurely in August, 1963. The lungs were immature and not able to adequately oxygenate the body. This condition is known as hyaline membrane disease. Babies born today with similar conditions would have a much better chance of survival and normal development.

THE WHITE HOUSE

Honorable Barry Goldwater
United States Senate
Washington, D. C.

THE WARREN COMMISSION

One week after Kennedy was assassinated in Dallas, President Johnson established by executive order on November 29, 1963, the appointment of the Warren Commission. It was composed of seven members and was led by the Chief Justice of the Supreme Court, Earl Warren.

EXECUTIVE ORDER
NO. 11130

APPOINTING A COMMISSION TO REPORT UPON THE ASSASSINATION OF PRESIDENT JOHN F. KENNEDY

Pursuant to the authority vested in me as President of the United States, I hereby appoint a Commission to ascertain, evaluate and report upon the facts relating to the assassination of the late President John F. Kennedy and the subsequent violent death of the man charged with the assassination. The Commission shall consist of --

The Chief Justice of the United States, Chairman;

Senator Richard B. Russell;

Senator John Sherman Cooper;

Congressman Hale Boggs;

Congressman Gerald R. Ford;

The Honorable Allen W. Dulles;

The Honorable John J. McCloy.

The purposes of the Commission are to examine the evidence developed by the Federal Bureau of Investigation and any additional evidence that may hereafter come to light or be uncovered by federal or state authorities; to make such further investigation as the Commission finds desirable; to evaluate all the facts and circumstances surrounding such assassination, including the subsequent violent death of the man charged with the assassination, and to report to me its findings and conclusions.

The Commission is empowered to prescribe its own procedures and to employ such assistants as it deems necessary.

Necessary expenses of the Commission may be paid from the "Emergency Fund for the President".

All Executive departments and agencies are directed to furnish the Commission with such facilities, services and cooperation as it may request from time to time.

LYNDON B. JOHNSON

THE WHITE HOUSE,

November 29, 1963.

\# \# \#

This is an original copy of the Executive Order prepared on the White House typewriter. President Johnson and all members of the commission signed it.

The author sent a copy of the Warren Commission Presidential Order to President Gerald Ford for him to authenticate his signature. He was a Congressman in 1963 and is the only surviving member of the Commission.

GERALD R. FORD

June 8, 1994

Dear Dr. Dauer:

It is my authentic signature on the original of the Executive Order appointing the Warren Commission. You forwarded to me a copy of an original signed by President Johnson and all seven members of the Commission.

Frankly, I do not recall whether there was only one original. I do not recall whether each member received a personal copy. If I have one it would be in the Gerald R. Ford Library on the campus of the University of Michigan.

Each member of the Commission received a very limited number of copies of the final report which were signed by President Johnson and each member. My copies have been given to my children and very personal friends.

Sincerely,

Gerald R. Ford

Edward A. Dauer, M.D.
Clinical Associate Professor
University of Miami School of Medicine
Florida Medical Services, Inc.
4850 West Oakland Park Boulevard, Suite 145
Fort Lauderdale, Florida 33313

RANCHO MIRAGE
CALIFORNIA 92270

Gerald R. Ford

Edward A. Dauer, M.D.
Clinical Associate Professor
University of Miami
School of Medicine
Florida Medical Services, Inc.
4850 W. Oakland Park Boulevard
Suite 145
Fort Lauderdale, Florida 33313

MARILYN MONROE
1926-1962

Marilyn Monroe photographed while making the movie Niagara also starring Joseph Cotton

Photos-20th Century Fox

Marilyn Monroe was born in Los Angeles General Hospital with the birth name of Norma Jeane Mortenson. Marilyn never knew the name of her father and her mother was Gladys Monroe.

Immediately after her birth, because of the mental instability of her unmarried mother, Norma Jeane was placed in the foster care of Albert and Ida Bolender. She later stated: "they were terribly strict… they didn't mean any harm…it was their religion. They brought me up harshly."

At the age of eight her mother's friend, Grace McKee, took Norma Jeane to live with her. Grace loved and adored her. Grace told Marilyn at a young age: "Don't worry, Norma Jeane. You're going to be a beautiful girl when you get big…an important woman, a movie star."

When Norma Jeane was fifteen years old she met Jim Dougherty, five years older than her. Grace encouraged the relationship and by the age of sixteen Marilyn Monroe was married to her first husband. Marilyn later stated: "Grace McKee arranged the marriage for me, I never had a choice. There's not much to say about it. They couldn't support me, and they had to work out something. And so I got married."

While Jim Dougherty went overseas with the Merchant Marines, Norma Jeane, at the age of eighteen, when to work in a factory inspecting parachutes. The army began photographing her in a promotion to show women on the assembly line helping the war effort. By the age of nineteen she was known as a "photographers dream" and had already appeared on the cover of thirty-three magazines.

Norma Jeane's marriage was in disarray and she was granted a divorce at the age of twenty. Marilyn later stated: "My marriage didn't make me sad, but it didn't make me happy either. My husband and I hardly spoke to each other. This wasn't because we were angry. We had nothing to say. I was dying of boredom."

Shortly before her divorce, Marilyn selected her mother's family name and became known from then on as Marilyn Monroe. She signed a formal contract with Twentieth Century Fox Studios at the young age of twenty. Marilyn had a minor role in the movie, "Scudda-Hoo! Scudda-Hay," and sang her first song in the movie, "Ladies of the Chorus."

Marilyn Monroe on her way to entertain the troops

At the age of twenty-three she met Johnny Hyde, who worked for the William Morris Agency and he helped jump-start her career. He became her lover and convinced Marilyn to pose nude for a calendar.

Marilyn's acting career took off in the early 1950's with "The Asphalt Jungle," "All about Eve," and "Clash by Night." She received many favorable reviews. New York World – Telegram and Sun wrote in 1952, "a forceful actress, a gifted new star, worthy of all that fantastic press agentry." Among her other films were, "Bus Stop," "Don't Bother to Knock," "Niagara," "Gentlemen Prefer Blondes," "The Seven Year Itch" and "Some Like It Hot." Marilyn Monroe's career as an actress lasted sixteen years. She made twenty-nine films, twenty-four in the first eight years of her career.

By the age of twenty-five Marilyn met baseball legend Joe DiMaggio. He was retired from baseball and thirty- seven years old. Marilyn stated to the press, "I was surprised to be so crazy about Joe. I expected a flashy New York sports type, and instead I met this reserved guy who didn't make a pass at me right away! He treated me like something special. Joe is a very decent man, and he makes other people feel decent, too!"

"I want to grow old without face-lifts...I want to have the courage to be loyal to the face I have made. Sometimes I think it would be easier to avoid old age, to die young, but then you'd never complete your life, would you? You'd never wholly know yourself." Quote by Marilyn Monroe

Early January 1954, Marilyn Monroe and Joe DiMaggio were married. The marriage was doomed from the beginning. Joe wanted Marilyn to stay at home and be a housewife. He was very jealous of Marilyn and her popularity with other men. By the fall of 1954, Joe and Marilyn were divorced. Her spokesperson made the following statement, "As her attorney, I am speaking for her and can only say that the conflict of careers has brought about this regrettable necessity."

In early 1955, Marilyn moved to New York and joined the Actors Studio with Lee Strasberg as her drama coach and director of the studio. She met Arthur Miller and had an affair with him until their marriage in 1956.

By the age of thirty the Millers left for London and Marilyn started on the production of "The Prince and the Showgirl," with Lawrence Olivier. Marilyn returned to Hollywood in the 1960's and started consulting with a prominent psychoanalyst, who prescribed barbiturates and tranquilizers for her. She became very dependent on these "uppers" and "downers." It took her forever to get up and go to work in the mornings. By this time her marriage to Arthur Miller was over. They divorced in January 1961.

Marilyn Monroe had a reported affair with John F. Kennedy and his brother Robert F. Kennedy in late 1961. At the President's birthday party in New York's Madison Square Garden on May 19, 1962, Marilyn sang her now famous "Happy Birthday, Mr. President."

Meanwhile, Marilyn began dating Joe DiMaggio again. A wedding date was set for August 8, 1962. Tragically, Marilyn Monroe was found dead August 5, 1962. Much has been written about the events surrounding her death, and others involvement in it. It was written on her death certificate as an accidental drug overdose. DiMaggio invited no one from Hollywood to Marilyn's funeral, only her close friends and relatives. For over thirty years, Joe DiMaggio sent fresh red roses to her gravesite in Los Angeles.

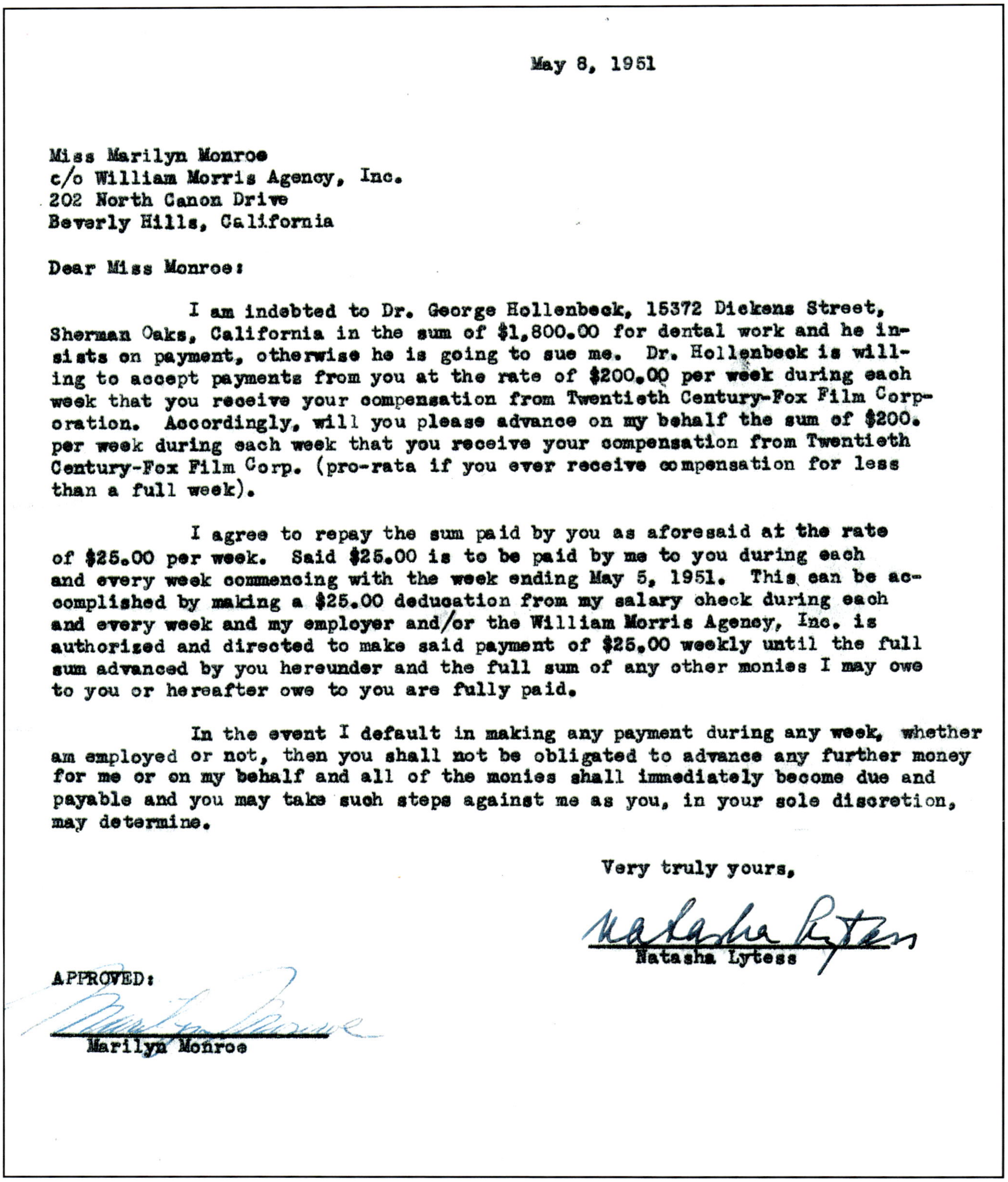

May 8, 1951

Miss Marilyn Monroe
c/o William Morris Agency, Inc.
202 North Canon Drive
Beverly Hills, California

Dear Miss Monroe:

  I am indebted to Dr. George Hollenbeck, 15372 Dickens Street, Sherman Oaks, California in the sum of $1,800.00 for dental work and he insists on payment, otherwise he is going to sue me. Dr. Hollenbeck is willing to accept payments from you at the rate of $200.00 per week during each week that you receive your compensation from Twentieth Century-Fox Film Corporation. Accordingly, will you please advance on my behalf the sum of $200. per week during each week that you receive your compensation from Twentieth Century-Fox Film Corp. (pro-rata if you ever receive compensation for less than a full week).

  I agree to repay the sum paid by you as aforesaid at the rate of $25.00 per week. Said $25.00 is to be paid by me to you during each and every week commencing with the week ending May 5, 1951. This can be accomplished by making a $25.00 deducation from my salary check during each and every week and my employer and/or the William Morris Agency, Inc. is authorized and directed to make said payment of $25.00 weekly until the full sum advanced by you hereunder and the full sum of any other monies I may owe to you or hereafter owe to you are fully paid.

  In the event I default in making any payment during any week, whether am employed or not, then you shall not be obligated to advance any further money for me or on my behalf and all of the monies shall immediately become due and payable and you may take such steps against me as you, in your sole discretion, may determine.

Very truly yours,

Natasha Lytess

APPROVED:

Marilyn Monroe

FIVE DOLLAR LEGAL TENDER NOTES

Series 1862—The obverse is similar to the Demand Note of 1861 with exception of the removal of the words "On Demand" and the presence of the Treasury Seal

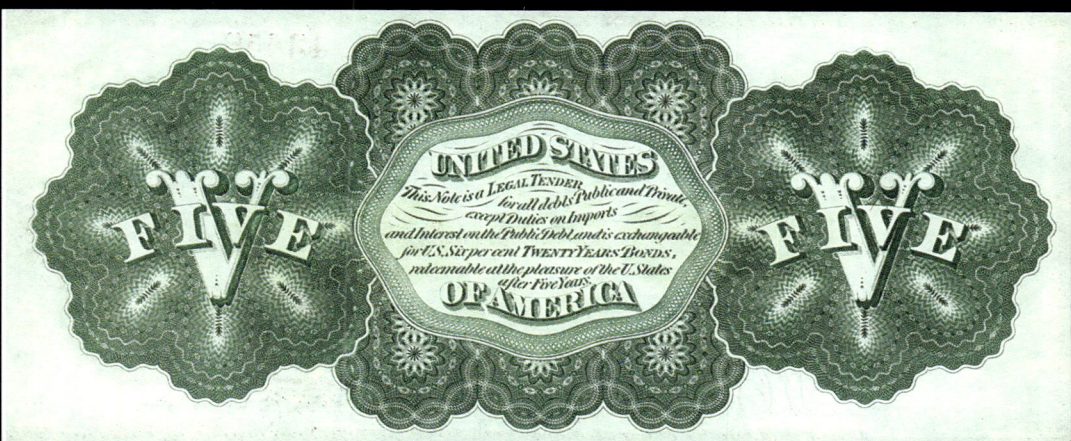

First Obligation Reverse—Printed by the American Bank Note Company

Second Obligation Reverse

Five Dollar "Rainbow" Note
Series 1869

Reverse printed by the American Bank Note Company

Portrait of Andrew Jackson, the seventh President of the United States from 1829-1833.
The engraving in the center represents a pioneer family.

Left: Counterfeiting Warning　　　　　　　　　　　　　　　　Right: Legal Tender Obligation

Series 1878, Small Red Seal With Rays

Series 1880, Large Brown Seal

Series 1880, Large Red Plain Seal

Series 1880, Large Red Seal With Spikes

Series 1880, Large Brown Seal

Military Pension for the War of 1812

Andrew Jackson led American Forces to Victory over the British

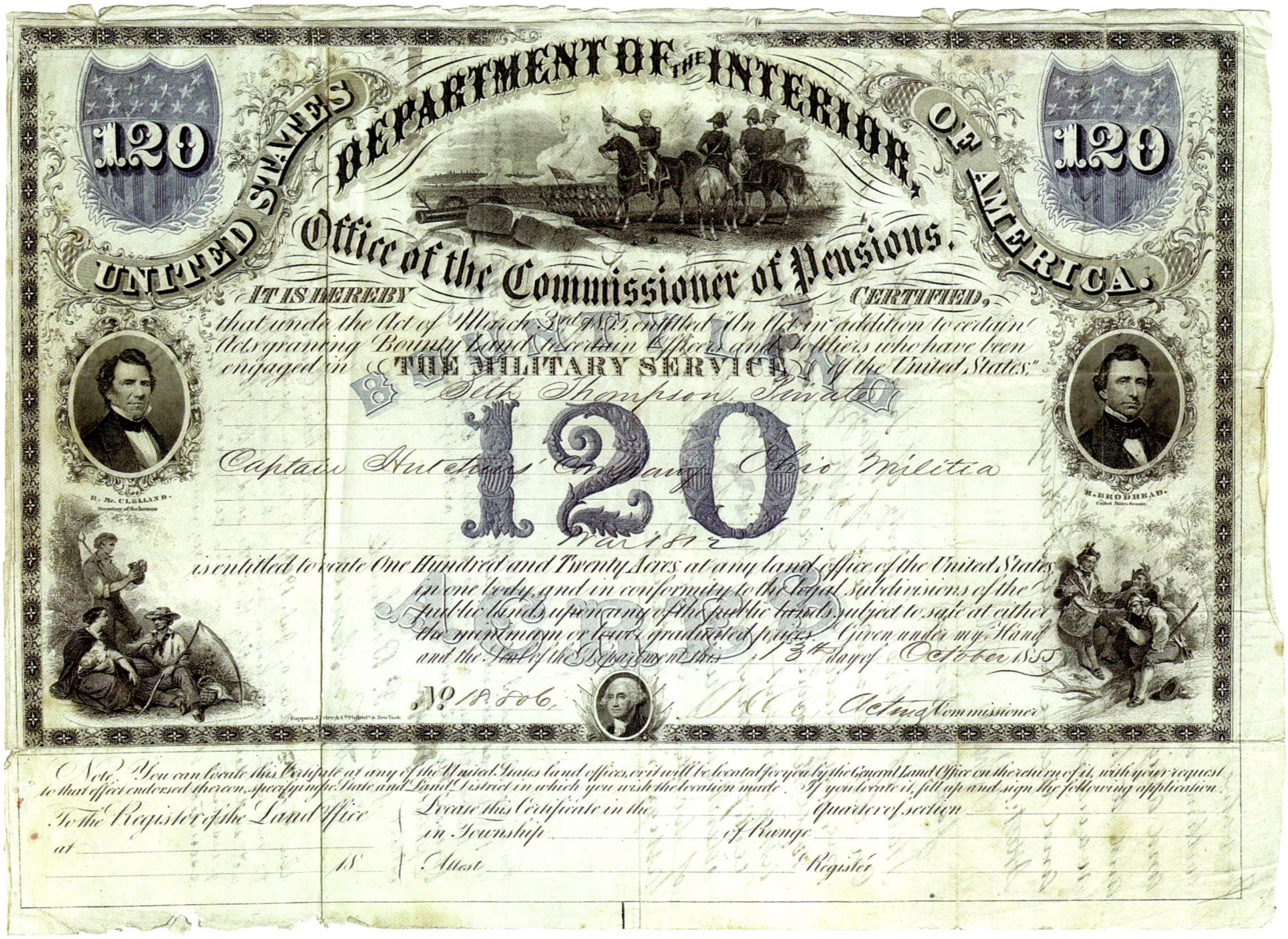

120 UNITED STATES DEPARTMENT OF THE INTERIOR, OF AMERICA. 120

Office of the Commissioner of Pensions.

IT IS HEREBY CERTIFIED, that under the Act of March 3rd 1855, entitled "An Act in addition to certain Acts granting Bounty Land to certain Officers and Soldiers who have been engaged in THE MILITARY SERVICE of the United States."

Seth Thompson, Private

Captain Hutchins' Company Ohio Militia

120

War 1812

is entitled to locate One Hundred and Twenty Acres at any land office of the United States in one body, and in conformity to the legal subdivisions of the public lands, upon any of the public lands subject to sale at either the minimum or lower graduated prices. Given under my Hand and the Seal of the Department this 13th day of October 1855

No. 18,506 Acting Commissioner

R. McCLELLAND, Secretary of the Interior

R. BRODHEAD, United States Senator

Note. You can locate this Certificate at any of the United States land offices, or it will be located for you by the General Land Office on the return of it, with your request to that effect endorsed thereon, specifying the State and Land District in which you wish the location made. If you locate it, fill up and sign the following application.

To the Register of the Land Office at 18 | Locate this Certificate in the Quarter of section in Township of Range | Attest Register

Soldiers who served in the War of 1812 were granted as a pension 120 acres of Federal Land. This original certificate was presented to:

Seth Thompson, Private

Captain Hutchins' Company, Ohio Militia

These are exceedingly rare because they were turned in to the government to claim the land. This perhaps may be the only copy that still exists.

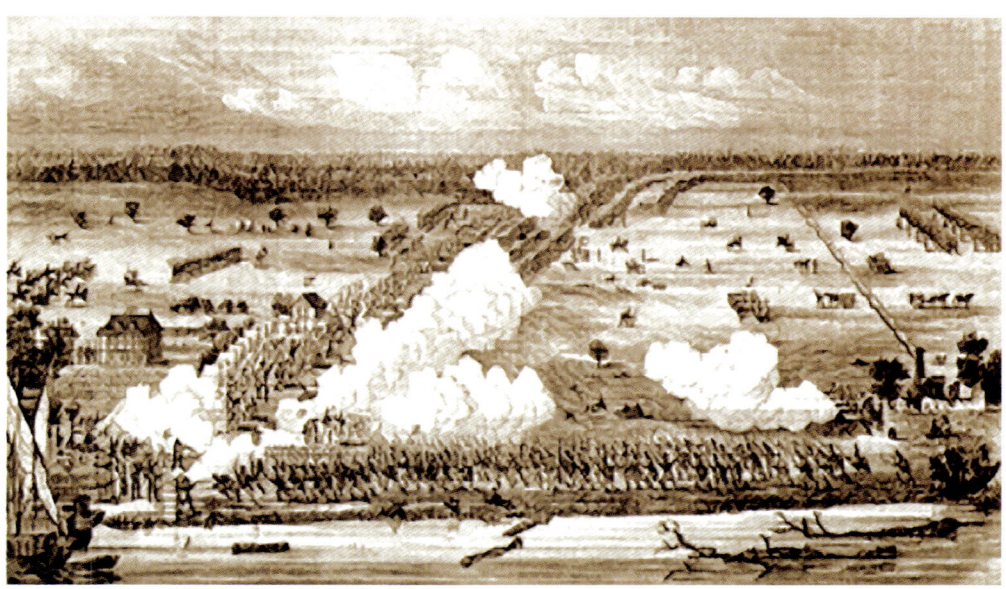

On January 8, 1815, American forces, under General Jackson, decisively defeat the British forces trying to capture New Orleans. The battle, which takes place after the Treaty of Ghent has been signed, is the most decisive American victory of the war.

Written Endorsement Transferring Ownership of the Land to Future Heirs
Written before the Age of Typewriters

For value received, I Seth Thompson Sen., to whom the within warrant No. 18,806 was issued, do hereby sell and assign unto Seth Thompson Jun., of Hartford, and to his heirs and assigns forever, the said warrant, and authorize him to locate the same, and receive a patent therefor.

Attest:
Richard Gates
Joel Miner

Seth Thompson, Sen.

State of Ohio, County of Trumbull.
On this eleventh day of May in the year 1858, before me, personally came Seth Thompson Sen., to me well known, and acknowledged the foregoing assignment to be his act and deed; And I certify that the said Seth Thompson Sen. is the identical person to whom the within certificate of location issued, and who executed the foregoing assignment thereof.

Joel Miner
Justice of the Peace

For value received I Seth Thompson Jun., to whom the within warrant No 18,806 was assigned on the 11th day of May 1858 by Seth Thompson Sen do hereby sell and assign to Mattie McClain and to her heirs and assigns forever the said warrant and authorize her to locate the same and receive a patent therefor

Attest
Sarah P. Bushnell
T. A. Bushnell

Seth Thompson Jun

State of Ohio, County of Trumbull
On this 7th day of July 1904 before me personally came Seth Thompson Jun to me well well known and acknowledged the foregoing assignment to be his act and deed. I certify that the said Seth Thompson Jun. is the identical person to whom the within certificate of location was assigned and who executed the foregoing assignment thereof.

Theo. A. Bushnell
Justice of the Peace

Continuation of Transfer (now typewritten) in 1905 and 1909

No 9005

Rutledge, Pa., Delaware County.

For value received I, Mattie Mc Clain, to whom the attached warrant No. 18,806, was assigned on the 7th day of July, 1904, by Seth Thompson Jun, do hereby sell and assign to R.H. Peale, of Salt Lake City, Utah, and to his heirs and assigns forever the said warrant and I authorize him to locate the same and receive a patent therefor. Said warrant No. 18,806 may be further described as follows, to-wit: It was issued on the 13th day of October 1855 by the Acting Commissioner of Pensions to Seth Thompson, Private, Captain Hutchins' Company Ohio Militia, War of 1812, for 120 acres of land. Said warrant was on the 11th day of May, 1858, assign-ed by Seth Thompson to Seth Thompson Jun.

Attest:
Eliza Y. Hoopes.
N. R. Stackhouse

Mattie McClain

State of Pennsylvania, County of Delaware.

On this 5th day of October, 1909, before me a Justice of the Peace in and for said County and State, personally came Mattie Mc Clain, to me well known, and acknowledged the foregoing assignment to be her free act and deed. I certify that the said Mattie Mc Clain is the identical person to whom the attached certificate of location described in the above assignment was assigned and who executed the foregoing acknowledg--ment thereof.

Paul Hertel
Justice of the Peace
my commission expires March 1911.

"An Act for the Temporary Establishment of the Post Office"

Congress of the United States:

AT THE SECOND SESSION,

Begun and held at the City of New-York, on Monday, the Fourth of January, one thousand seven hundred and ninety.

An ACT *to continue in force for a limited Time, an Act, intituled "An Act for the temporary Establishment of the Post-Office."*

BE it enacted by the SENATE and HOUSE of REPRESENTATIVES of the United States of America in Congress assembled, That the act passed the last session of Congress, intituled "An act for the temporary establishment of the post-office," be, and the same hereby is continued in force until the end of the next session of Congress, and no longer.

FREDERICK AUGUSTUS MUHLENBERG,
Speaker of the House of Representatives.

JOHN ADAMS, *Vice-President of the United States, and President of the Senate.*

APPROVED, August the fourth, 1790.

GEORGE WASHINGTON, *President of the United States.*

(TRUE COPY.)

[signature] *Secretary of State.*

This is the original bill signed by Thomas Jefferson as Secretary of State for the establishment of the Post Office on Jan 4, 1790.

This Act of Congress provided for the temporary renewal of the U.S. Post Office for an additional year. Subsequent bills would renew it and ultimately make the Post Office permanent.

One other original copy is known to exist in the Smithsonian Postal Museum.

Series 1880, Small Red Scalloped Seal

Series 1907, Small Red Scalloped Seal
A red "V" was added to the left side of this note to the right of the portrait.

The above note depicts the early pioneer families that settled the American midwest at the beginning of the 18th century.

This was the era when Andrew Jackson was the seventh President of the United States - 1829 to 1837.

Born in a backwoods settlement in the Carolinas in 1767, Jackson was self educated. He was elected President by popular vote with more votes than any of his predecessors.

As President he sought to act as the direct representative of the common man.

TEN DOLLAR LEGAL TENDER NOTES

Series 1862—The obverse is similar to the Demand Note of 1861 with exception of the removal of the words "On Demand" and the presence of the Treasury Seal

First Obligation Reverse

Second Obligation Reverse

Ten Dollar "Rainbow" Note
Series 1869

On the left is an engraving of Daniel Webster, U.S. Statesman. The design on the right is Pocahantas being presented to the British Royal Family.

The reverse was printed by the National Bank Note Company

This and subsequent notes issued until Series 1880 were commonly called the "Jackass Note." The Eagle appearing on the bottom of the obverse resembled a donkey when it was turned upside down.

Series 1878, Small Red Seal With Rays

The portrait of Daniel Webster is shown on the above $10 note

On the right side of the note is an illustration depicting John Smith and Pocahontas being received by Queen Elizabeth I

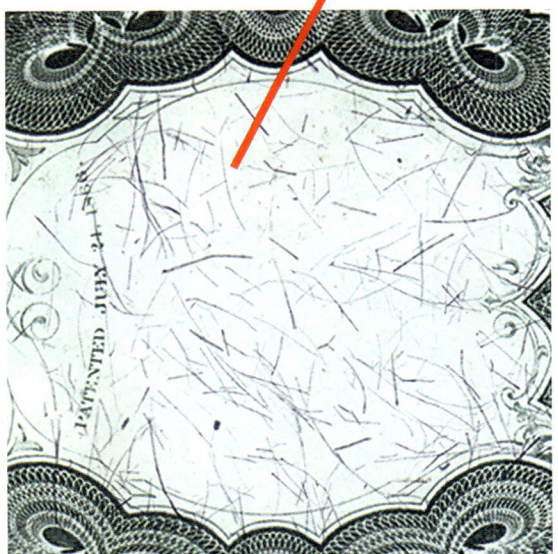

The blank area on the reverse was heavily laden with silk fibers to deter counterfeiters

The intricate geometric lathe design was extremely difficult to duplicate and was an important security feature

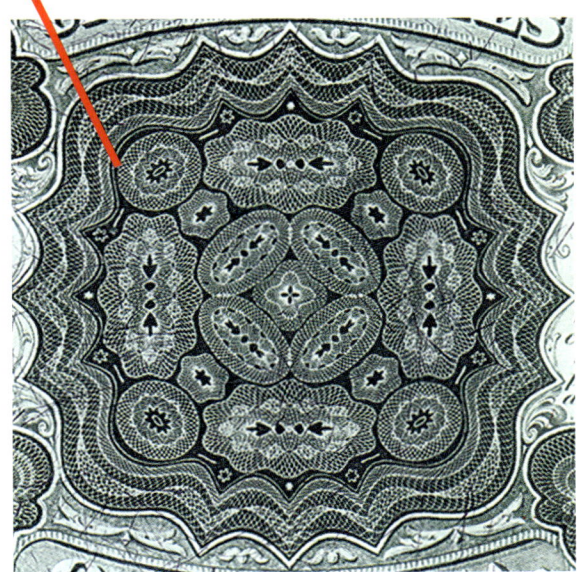

For his contemporaries, Daniel Webster embodied the very spirit of the nation. Webster represented Massachusetts in Congress, argued before the Supreme Court, and eventually served as Secretary of State.

Photo: Mathew Brady Studio Daguerreotype, circa 1849
National Museum of American History
Smithsonian Institution, Washington, D.C.

Daniel Webster House (built 1760) 137 Vaughan Street, Portsmouth, N.H. Webster lived here right after his marriage in 1808 and knew it as the Meserve House. George Meserve had been appointed by the British to collect Portsmouth taxes just as the dreaded Stamp Act was enacted in 1765. Meserve's Portsmouth neighbors burned him in effigy and forced him to resign the position, which he quickly did.

Photo: Portsmouth Library

Series 1880, Large Brown Seal

Series 1880, Large Red Plain Seal

Series 1880, Large Red Seal With Spikes

Series 1880, Large Brown Seal

Series 1880, Small Red Scalloped Seal

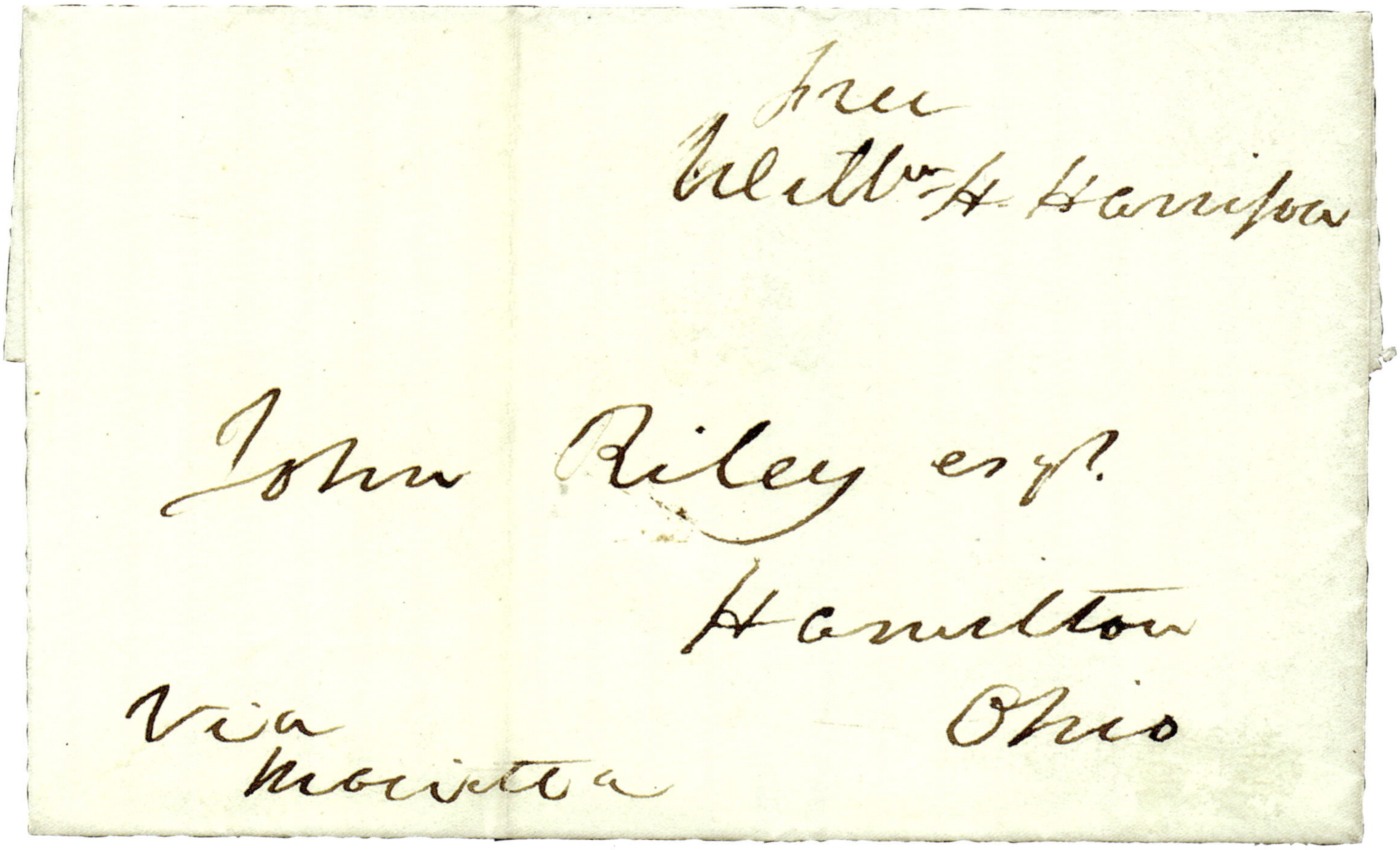

William Henry Harrison
Ninth President of the United States

Free frank signed by Harrison while a member of Congress

William Henry Harrison was born in 1773 in Virginia into an aristocratic plantation home. He began his studies as a medical student in 1791 but then switched to a military career battling the Indians in the Northwest Territory.

He was Governor of the Indiana Territory from 1801 to 1812 and defended the settlers against the Indian chief Tecumseh and his brother Prophet. The battle on Tippecanoe River brought fame to Harrison who also gained fame during the War of 1812.

He won the Presidency in the 1840 election as a candidate of the Whig Party. Harrison died from pneumonia on April 4, 1841, one month after his inauguration speech that lasted for over two hours in a raging snowstorm.

William Henry Harrison, Ninth President of the United States posed for this portrait by Rembrandt Peale in 1814. It hangs in Grouseland, Vincennes, Indiana.

John Tyler, Tenth President of the United States (1841-1845)

John Tyler-Tenth President of the United States-1841-1845

John Tyler was born in Virginia in 1790 and attended law school at the College of William and Mary. He served in the House of Representatives from 1817-1821 and Senate from 1827-1836, voting against most nationalist legislation including internal improvements at federal expense and protective tariffs. Since he was a slave owner, he opposed the Missouri Compromise.

Tyler was a strict constructionist, who believed that federal powers should be limited to those enumerated in the Constitution. His opposition to Andrew Jackson allied him with Daniel Webster and Henry Clay, members of the Whig party. In 1839, the Whig party nominated William Henry Harrison for President and John Tyler as Vice-President, winning the election in 1840. The Whig slogan was "Tippecanoe and Tyler, Too." which stood for nationalism and southern sectionalism. Tippecanoe Creek was the site of a battle between William Henry Harrison and hostile Indians.

Julia Gardiner Tyler
Lived: 1820-1889
Tyler was the first President to marry in office and took his vows in New York on June 26, 1844. The news was then broken to the American people, who greeted it with keen interest, much publicity, and some criticism about the couple's difference in age: 30 years.

Sherwood Forest Plantation was the home of the 10th U.S. President, John Tyler from 1842 until his death in 1862

Harrison died after only thirty days in office, suffering from pneumonia contracted during his two-hour outdoor inauguration speech in the middle of a major snowstorm. Tyler assumed the Presidency, becoming the first Vice President to assume office upon the death of a President. His detractors called him "His Accidency."

His administration enacted positive legislation such as the "Log-Cabin Bill," a law allowing a settler to purchase 160 acres of federal land for $1.25 per acre, and the annexation of Texas in 1845. Although his strong support of states' rights strengthened the Presidency, it increased sectional feeling that ultimately led to the secession of the South.

John Tyler retired to his Virginia plantation in 1845 and was chairman of a peace convention, which unsuccessfully attempted to avoid the Civil War. He died on Jan 18, 1862, before taking his seat as a member of the Confederate House of Representatives.

The "Bison" Note
Series 1901

Portraits of Meriwether Lewis and William Clark

Allegorical figure of Columbia

The buffalo in the center of the note was also used as the model for the reverse of the Indian head nickel, minted from 1913 until 1938. This note is a very popular and beautiful design, commonly called the "Bison" note due to the central vignette of the buffalo.

The great American bison is a truly magnificent animal. It is the largest land mammal in North America since the end of the Ice Age. Estimates of the pre-European herd size vary from 30,000,000 to 70,000,000 animals and they ranged over most of North America.

The first Buffalo nickels were struck in 1913, and pictured Black Diamond standing on a mound above the words "Five Cents."

Lewis and Clark

Meriwether Lewis (1774-1809) *William Clark (1770-1838)*

On February 28, 1803, President Thomas Jefferson won approval from Congress for an endeavor that would become one of America's greatest stories of adventure. Twenty-five hundred dollars was appropriated to fund a small expeditionary group, whose mission was to explore the uncharted West. It would be led by Jefferson's secretary, Meriwether Lewis, and Lewis' friend, William Clark.

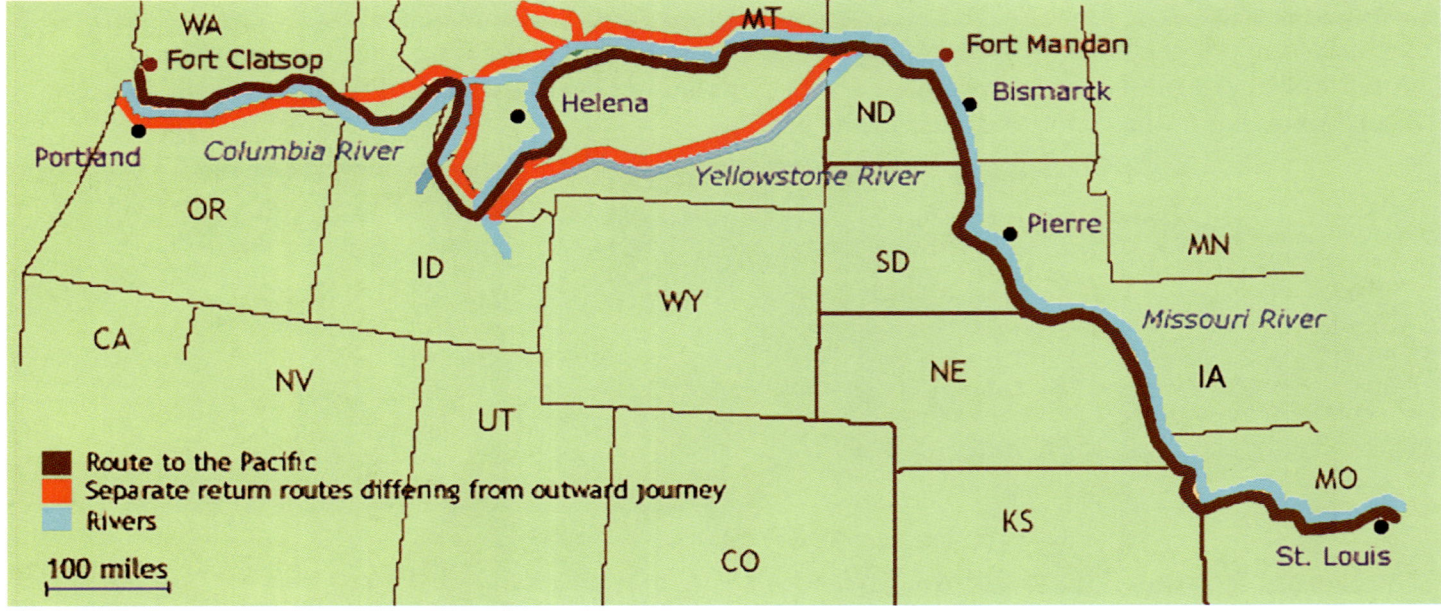

The expedition traveled the arteries of the continent, the Missouri and Columbia rivers, and it crossed the nation's backbone, the Rocky Mountains. Now, nearly 200 years later, America has begun a national pilgrimage following the steps of Meriwether Lewis, William Clark and the Corps of Discovery.

The last of the large size ten-dollar notes has the same portrait of Andrew Jackson that was used on the small size twenty dollar notes

Andrew Jackson was born in South Carolina on March 15, 1767, the third son of parents who moved from Ireland. He served as a courier in the Revolutionary War at the age of thirteen, and later attended law school. His political career began in 1796 as the first representative to Congress from Tennessee and Senator in 1797. Jackson's military fame came from his victory at the Battle of New Orleans on January 8, 1815. This was the last battle of the war of 1812 and the British suffered over 2,000 casualties with U.S. forces reporting six dead and twelve wounded.

Prior to this battle he earned the nickname "Old Hickory" due to his leadership and efficiency in marching his men during a strenuous march from Mississippi back to Tennessee.

In 1829, Jackson was successful in his bid for the Presidency after an earlier defeat and served until 1837. John Calhoun was Vice-President during his first term but was replaced by Martin Van Buren who was elected President after Jackson left office to return to his home, The Hermitage, near Tennessee. His later political efforts were involved in annexation of Texas and the opposition of Van Buren caused Jackson to support Polk for the Presidency in 1844. Andrew Jackson died at his home on June 8, 1845.

The above image is of a crowd that descended on the White House to celebrate Jackson's victory in 1828. It is now hanging in the Capitol rotunda.

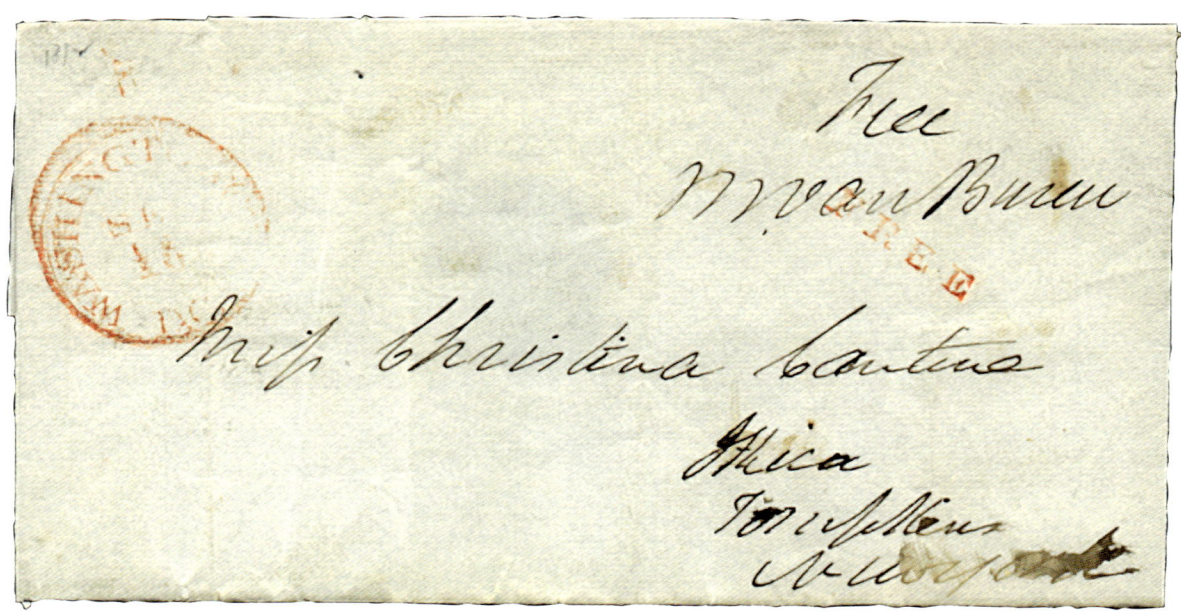

Free frank signed by Martin Van Buren, 8th President of the United States

Free frank signed by James Polk, 11th President of the United States

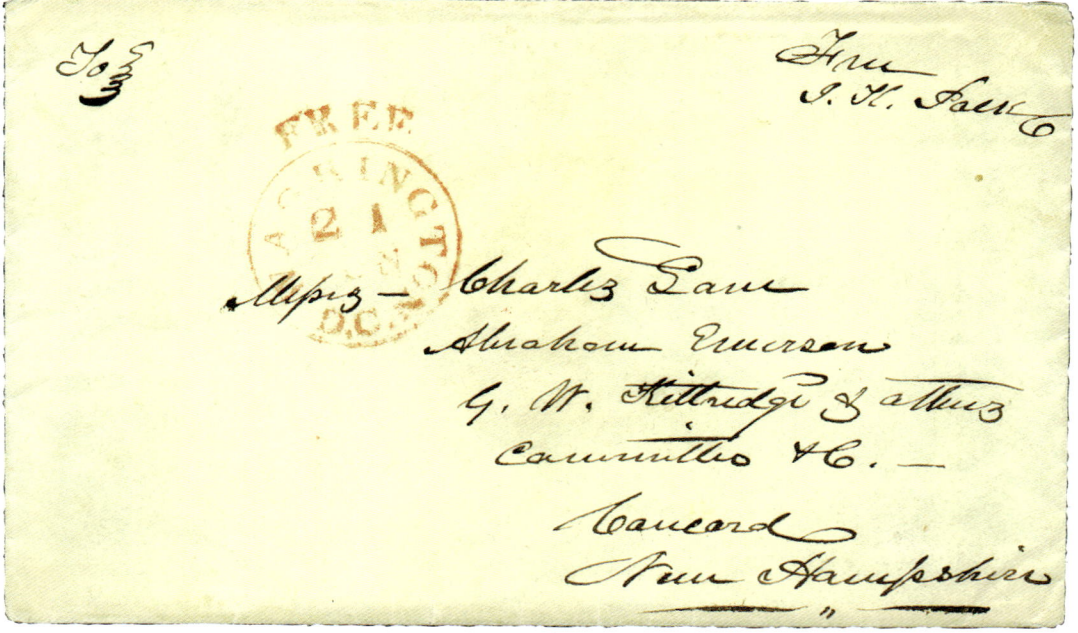

94

This document signed by Andrew Jackson as President, provided safe passage of a 389 ton merchant ship "TO PASS with her Company Passengers, Goods and Merchandise without any hindrance, seizure or molestation…"

TWENTY DOLLAR LEGAL TENDER NOTES

Series 1862—The obverse is similar to the Demand Note of 1861 with exception of removal of the words "On Demand" and the presence of the Treasury Seal

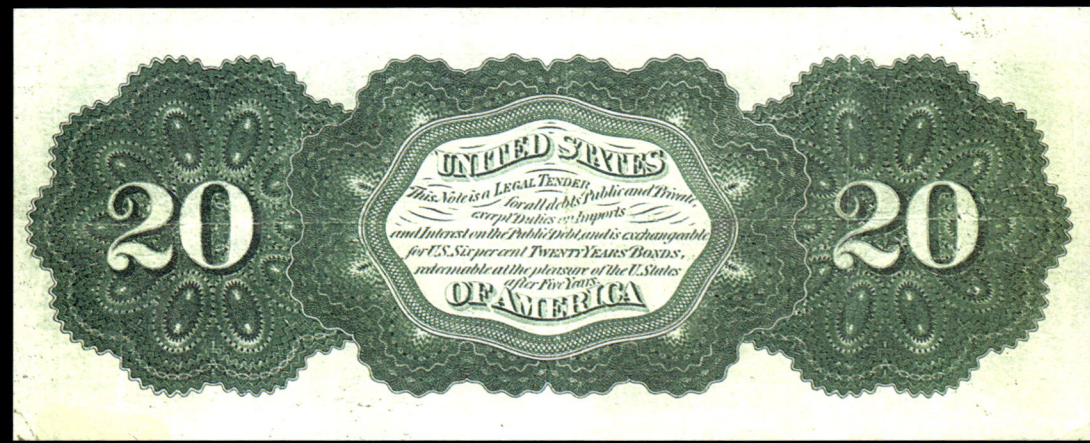

First Obligation Reverse

Second Obligation Reverse

Twenty Dollar "Rainbow" Note
Series 1869

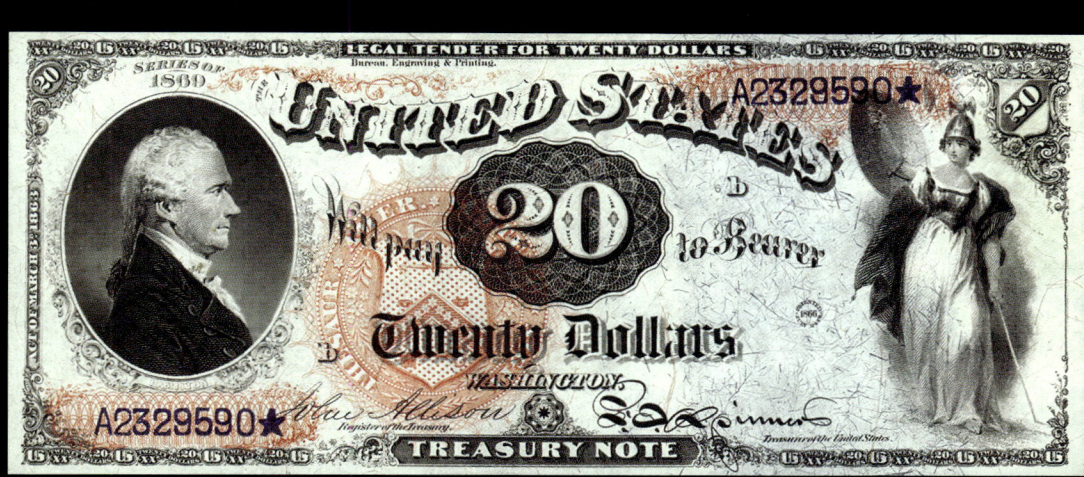

Portrait of Alexander Hamilton on the left
The figure on the right is representative of Victory holding a sword and shield

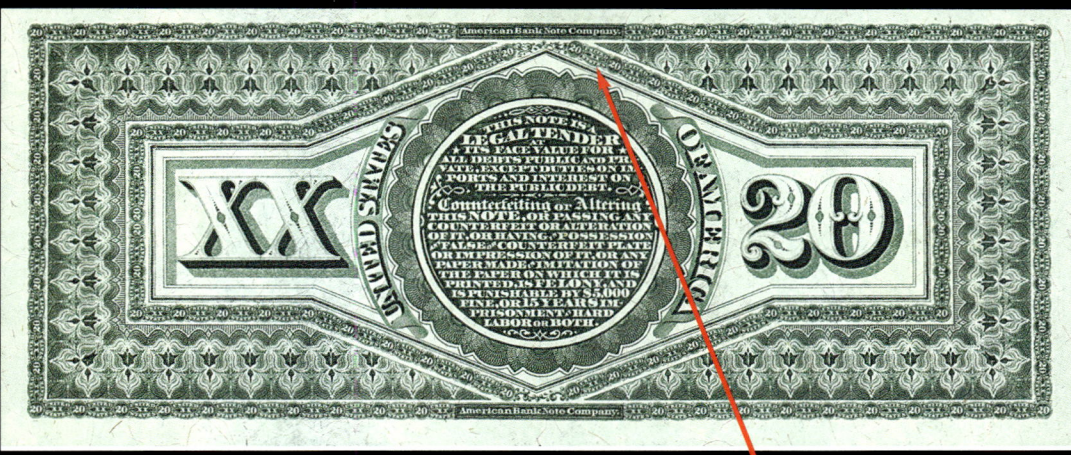

Note: The Arabic numeral 20 and Roman Numeral XX are each repeated over 100 times around the borders on the reverse of the note

Series 1878, Small Red With Rays

Series 1880, Large Brown Seal

Series 1880, Large Red Plain Seal

Series 1880, Large Red Seal with Spikes

Alexander Hamilton illustrated on the twenty dollar note

Perhaps nothing contributed more to the formation of Alexander Hamilton's political outlook than his experience at Valley Forge. General Washington and his forces were wintered at the desolate, but easily defendable encampment near Philadelphia.

Hamilton did some hard thinking about the American political situation. While he helplessly watched soldiers starve at Valley Forge, there was increased talk of a plot to overthrow Washington. A conspiracy was eventually rooted out, and crushed by a solid core of loyal Washington supporters. Eventually, Hamilton came to the conclusion that Congress was too preoccupied with state interests, and began forming his opinions about a strong central government.

Famous painting of Washington crossing the Delaware from Valley Forge

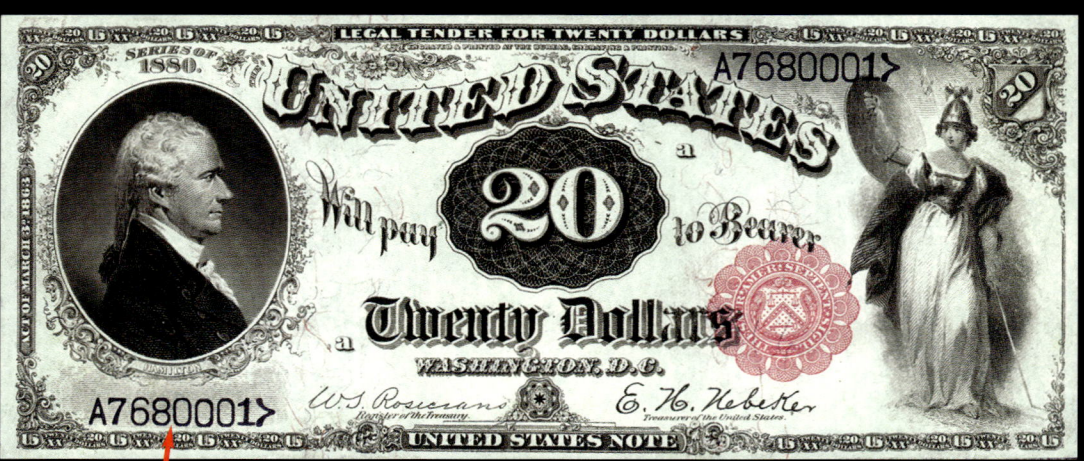

Series 1880, Small Red Scalloped Seal Blue Serial Numbers

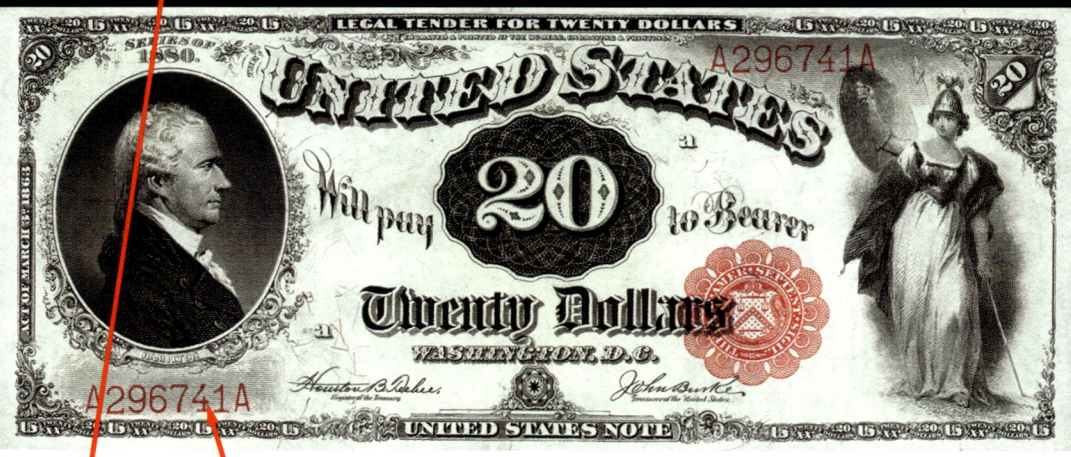

Series 1880, Small Red Scalloped Seal
Red Serial Numbers

Note blue serial numbers with red scalloped seal

Note red serial numbers with small red scalloped seal

Allegorical figure illustrated on the obverse of the 1880 twenty dollar note

THOMAS EDISON, 1847-1931

Thomas Alva Edison-the wizard of Menlo Park
Photos-Library of Congress

Thomas Alva Edison was born February 11, 1847 in Milan, Ohio. He was the seventh and last child of Samuel Edison, a jack- of - all trades, and Nancy Elliot Edison, a teacher. When Edison was seven years old, his family moved to Port Huron, Michigan after his father was hired as a carpenter at the Fort Gratiot military post.

At an early age he had hearing problems and had trouble following his school-work. His attendance was very poor at school. However, he became an excellent reader at the age of ten. Around the age of twelve he set up a laboratory in an empty freight car where he worked as a train-boy on the Grand Trunk Railway. He also began printing a weekly newspaper, which he named the Grand Trunk Herald. It was circulated to 400 railroad employees.

While working for the Grand Trunk Railway an event changed the life of Thomas Edison forever. A station official's son had fallen down onto the tracks of an oncoming train and Thomas saved the boy's life. For his heroism, the boy's father began to teach Thomas how to use the telegraph.

From the age of fifteen to twenty-one Edison worked as a roving telegrapher around the United States. He developed a telegraphic repeating machine that made it possible to transmit messages automatically. At the age of twenty-one he joined Western Union Telegraph Company in Boston.

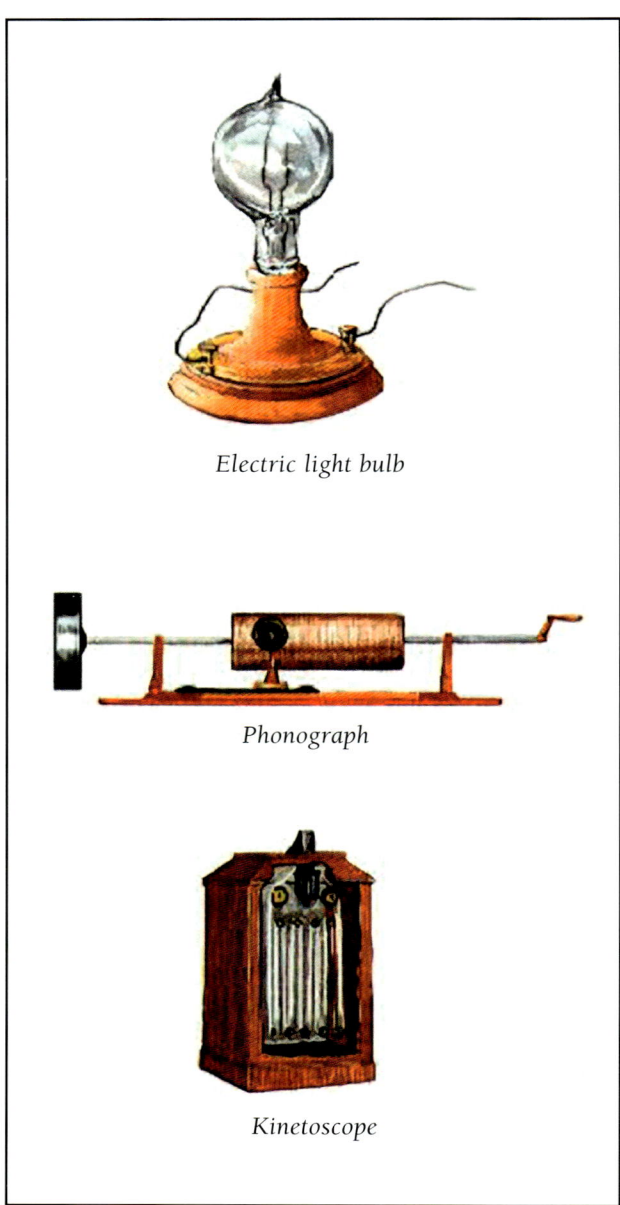

Electric light bulb

Phonograph

Kinetoscope

camera, the electric generator, the electric–powered train, a cement mixer, the dictaphone, and a duplicating machine.

Thomas Edison married Mary Stilwell at the age of twenty-three and they had three children. At the age of thirty-seven Edison's wife died unexpectedly and he was left to care for the young children. Two years later, he married Mina Miller, the daughter of an inventor, manufacturer, and philanthropist. They had three children together. His oldest son from this marriage went on to become Secretary of the Navy and eventually Governor of New Jersey. Both of Edison's wives complained that he spent entirely too much time in his laboratory and was not home with his family.

Thomas Alva Edison died at the age of eighty-four in West Orange, New Jersey. At the time of his death he was trying to invent a method of making synthetic rubber from goldenrod plants. Many of his inventions and laboratory buildings are preserved in Greenfield Village, Detroit, Michigan thanks to the friendship he had with Henry Ford.

By the age of twenty-two he was a full time inventor and entrepreneur. With only three months of formal education he has changed the lives of millions of people with such inventions as the electric light, the phonograph, the Edison Universal Stock Printer, the automatic telegraph, the kinetoscope, the Edison storage battery, the electric pen, the mimeograph, the microtasimeter and the first talking moving pictures. Edison patented 1,093 inventions in his lifetime. He also improved on the inventions of others. He made improvements on the stock ticker, the telephone, the typewriter, the motion picture, the

Edison and a model demonstrating the Ediphone in the West Orange lab's library, July 20, 1914
Smithsonian

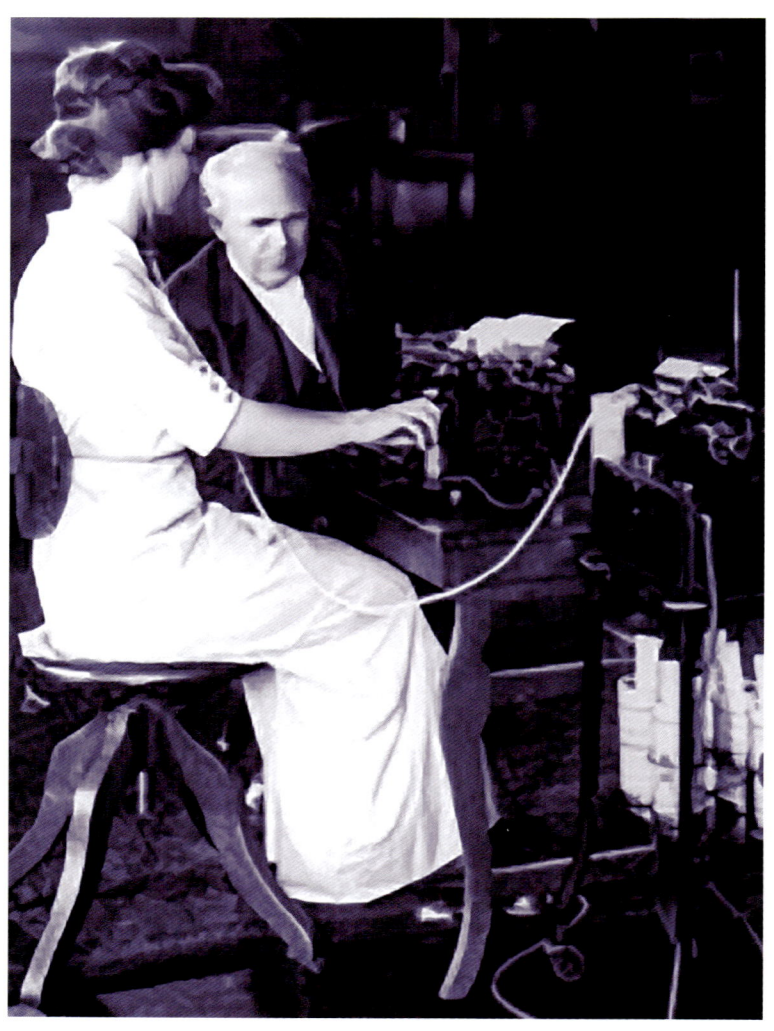

Cable Address "Edison, New York"

From the Laboratory of Thomas A. Edison, Orange, N.J.

October 29, 1925.

Miss Mildred B. Schmidt,
Lahaska, Bucks County,
Pennsylvania.

Dear Miss Schmidt:

I greatly appreciate the courtesy which prompted you to write me such a nice letter, and I want to thank you for your complimentary remarks and the good wishes which you kindly sent me.

Yours very truly,

Thos A Edison.

Ediphoned:H

FIFTY DOLLAR LEGAL TENDER NOTES

Series 1862, Portrait of Alexander Hamilton

This is the first issue of $50 notes, which were printed by the National Bank Note Company. This issue and others of 1862 and 1863 were frequently counterfeited.

This note has the first obligation reverse. The paper used on the first issue of legal tender notes was very thin and did not hold up during the normal wear and tear of everyday use. Notes in high-grade condition of the higher denominations are rare and seldom seen.

Portrait of Alexander Hamilton by John Trumbull (c. 1806)

Alexander Hamilton was born in 1757 on the Island of Nevis, in the Leeward group, British West Indies. He was the illegitimate son of a common-law marriage between a poor itinerant Scottish merchant of aristocratic descent and an English-French Huguenot mother who was a planter's daughter.

When the new American government got under way in 1789, Hamilton won the position of Secretary of the Treasury. He began at once to place the nation's disorganized finances on a sound footing.

Meanwhile, when Jefferson and Aaron Burr tied in Presidential electoral votes in 1800, Hamilton threw valuable support to Jefferson. That same year, Burr, taking offense at remarks he believed to have originated with Hamilton, challenged him to a duel, which took place at present Weehawken, NJ, on July 11. Mortally wounded, Hamilton died the next day. He was in his late forties at death. He was buried in Trinity Churchyard in New York City.

Series 1863, Printed by the American Bank Note Company and the National Bank Note Company

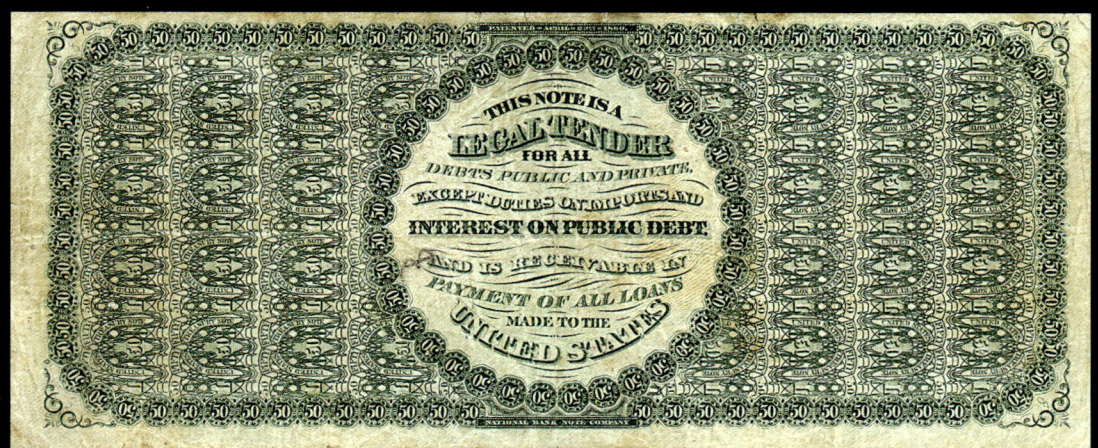

This reverse features the second obligation reverse

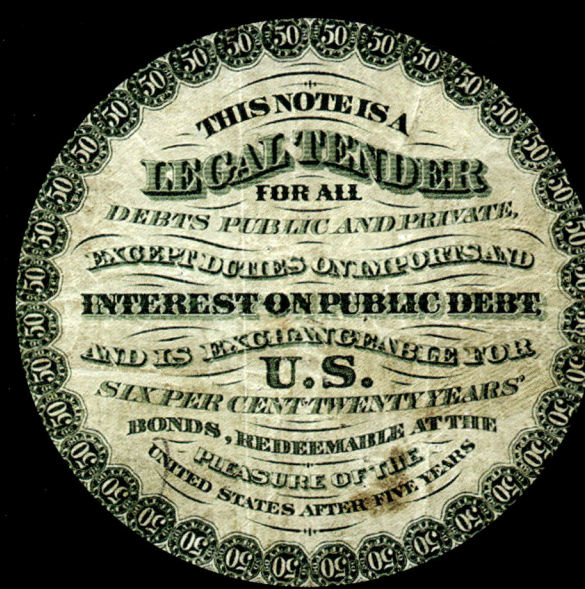

First obligation Second obligation

Henry Clay was Secretary of State in the Administration of John Quincy Adams

Clay is best known for his support of the Missouri Compromise in 1820. When Missouri applied for statehood in 1819, there was a bitter debate in Congress whether the territories arising from the 1804 Louisiana Purchase should be admitted as free states or slave states. The dispute was resolved with the northern part of Massachusetts split to form Maine, a new free state. Missouri was admitted as a slave state, thus maintaining the balance of twelve free states and twelve slave states.

He also played a vital role in the compromise of 1850 that ended for eleven years the threat of civil war over the issue of slavery in the western territories. The new territories of New Mexico, Arizona, Utah, and Nevada would be organized without mention of slavery. California would be admitted as a free state and although slavery would still be permitted in Washington, D.C., the trading of slaves in the nation's capital would be prohibited.

Portrait of Henry Clay painted by Henry F. Darby - (1829 - 1897)

Woman holding Mercury-an allegorical figure on the left of the $50.00 Rainbow Note

Fifty Dollar "Rainbow" Note
Series 1869

Head of Henry Clay-- (1777-1852)
On the left is an allegorical figure of a woman holding a laurel branch and a statue of Mercury

Henry Clay was Secretary of State in the administration of John Quincy Adams from 1825-1829. He ran three times unsuccessfully for President in 1824, 1832, and 1844. The 1844 election was lost due to his failure to support the annexation of Texas, costing him the important Southern vote. Clay also served as a U. S. Senator and Congressman. His ability to facilitate compromise in bitter political conflicts earned him the nickname "The Great Pacificator."

During his first term in Congress in 1811, he was known as a "war hawk" and was one of the politicians who helped bring about the War of 1812 with England. Clay was selected as one of the commissioners representing the U.S. in the drafting of the Treaty of Ghent, which ended the war in 1814.

Henry Clay tried three times for the presidency as a candidate of the Democratic-Republican and the Whig Party in 1844

Photo from the Senate website

1869 Issue of U.S. Postage

One cent—Benjamin Franklin

Two cent—Pony Express

Three cent—Early Locomotive

Six cent—George Washington

Ten cent—Shield and Eagle

Twelve cent—Steamship Adriatic

The same year of the issuance of the "rainbow" notes was also the first pictorial issue of U.S. postage stamps. From 1847 until 1869, all of the U.S. stamps merely featured different style portraits of Benjamin Franklin, George Washington, Thomas Jefferson, and Andrew Jackson.

Plaque at Montgomery and Merchant Streets - San Francisco

An early locomotive of the Chicago and Northwestern RR - circa 1900

Fifteen cent—Landing of Columbus

Twenty four cent—Signing of the Declaration of Independence

Thirty cent—Shield, Eagle, and Flags

Ninety cent—Abraham Lincoln

This series of stamps was printed by the National Bank Note Company and they were square in design. Although they were extremely beautiful, colorful, and well engraved, the stamps were not popular with the public and were replaced within one year. The fifteen through ninety cent denominations were the first U.S. stamps printed in two colors.

*Portrait of Benjamin Franklin
Engraved by J. Thomson, 1805
From an Original Picture by J.A. Duplessis*

SS "Adriatic" left Sydney for England but had to be returned to port after it's stern was damaged by ice

*Pictured above is a rare and scarce complete sheet of 150 of the 1869 three-cent pictorial stamp.
All stamps are unused with the original gum and never hinged.*

Franklin served his nation as a statesman, scientist, and public leader
Statue at the Franklin Institute in Philadelphia

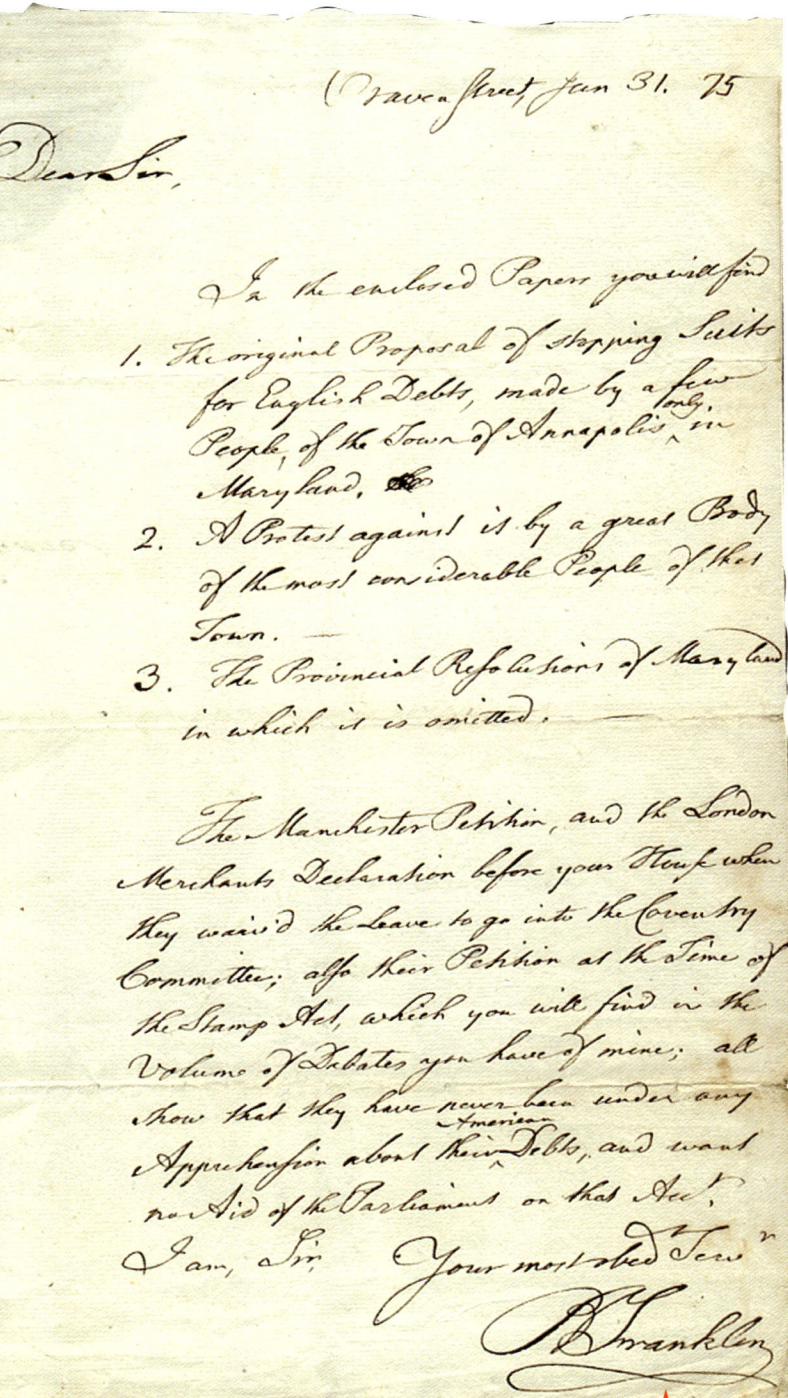

Letter from Benjamin Franklin to David Hartley, written from Craven Street on the 31st of January 1775.

Dear Sir,
   In the enclosed papers you will find

1. The original proposal of stopping suits for English debts, made by a few people, of the town in Annapolis only in Maryland.

2. A protest against it by a great body of the most considerable people of that town.

3. The Provincial Resolutions of Maryland in which it is omitted.

The Manchester Petition, and the London Merchants Declaration before your house when they wanted the leave to go into the Coventry Committee; also their petition at the time of the Stamp Act, which you will find in the volume of debates you have of mine; all show that they have never been under any apprehension about their American debts, and want no aid of the Parliament on this account.

I am, Sir,

                        Your most obedient Servant,

                        B. Franklin

Benjamin Franklin's signature from the letter

Series 1874, Portrait of Benjamin Franklin
On the right is an allegorical figure of Liberty holding a sword and shield.
Her crown includes the words "E Pluribus Unum."

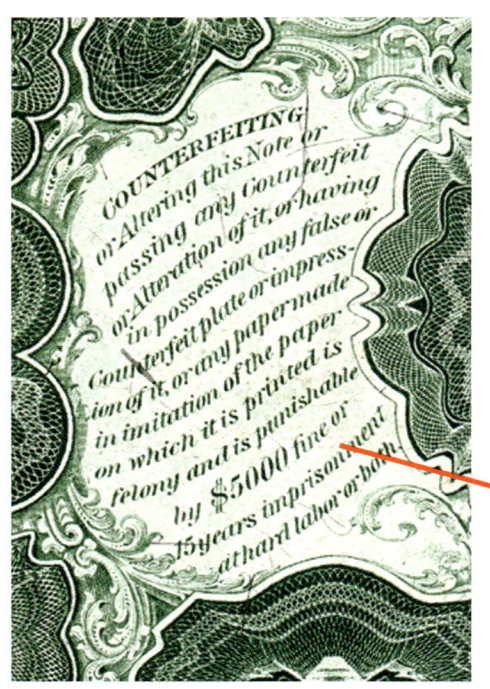

Note: The words E Pluribus Unum on Miss Liberty's crown

Wording on the reverse of the 1874 fifty dollar note

COUNTERFEITING
or Altering this Note or passing any counterfeit or Alteration of it, or having in possession any false or Counterfeit plate or impression of it, or any paper on which it is printed is felony and is punishable by $5000 fine or 15 years imprisonment at hard labor or both.

E PLURIBUS UNUM - Out of Many, One

E Pluribus Unum is part of the Great Seal of the United States and was chosen by the Great Seal Committee in 1776. It is a Latin term that means "out of many, one." This signifies the unification of the original thirteen colonies into a unified country.

Other parts of the obverse of the Great Seal include the thirteen stripes representing the states, thirteen stars forming a single constellation, and thirteen arrows in a bundle representing great strength held in an eagle's left talon. An olive branch, symbolizing the power of peace, is held by the right talon.

The pyramid signifying strength and duration

The Great Seal shown on the right side of the one dollar bill

The reverse side of the Great Seal features an unfinished pyramid signifying strength and duration. It was first used on the reverse of the one dollar bill in 1935 and still is in use today. The "eye" at the summit or apex of the pyramid and the motto "Annuit Coeptis" (He [God] has favored our undertakings) refers to the frequent interventions of Providence in favor of the American cause.

The date, MDCCLXXVI, is the year the Declaration of Independence was signed. The words under it, "Novus Ordo Seclorum" translates into "A new order of the ages." This signifies the beginning of the United States in 1776.

The Great Seal is still used today to seal official U.S. documents approximately 2,000 to 3,000 times per year. The actual sealing is done by an officer of the Department of State's Presidential Appointments Staff. It is impressed on documents such as instruments of ratifications of treaties, appointment commissions of ambassadors, and letters of communication from the President of the United States written to heads of foreign governments.

Series 1880, Large Brown Seal

Series 1880, Large Red Seal

Series 1880, Large Red Spiked Seal

Series 1880, Large Brown Seal

Series 1880, Small Red Scalloped Seal

ONE HUNDRED DOLLAR LEGAL TENDER NOTES

Series 1862, Printed by the American Bank Note Company

First obligation

This is the very first year $100 bills were printed. Adjusted for inflation, the purchasing power of this denomination was enormous at the time. The American Eagle appeared for the first time on this note.

The Eagle, Our National Emblem:

An eagle with outspread wings appears on the backs of our gold coins, the silver dollar, the half dollar, the quarter, and for the first time on the obverse of the 1862 $100 bill. The eagle's appearance on the great seal of the United States represents freedom.

Series 1863

Second Obligation

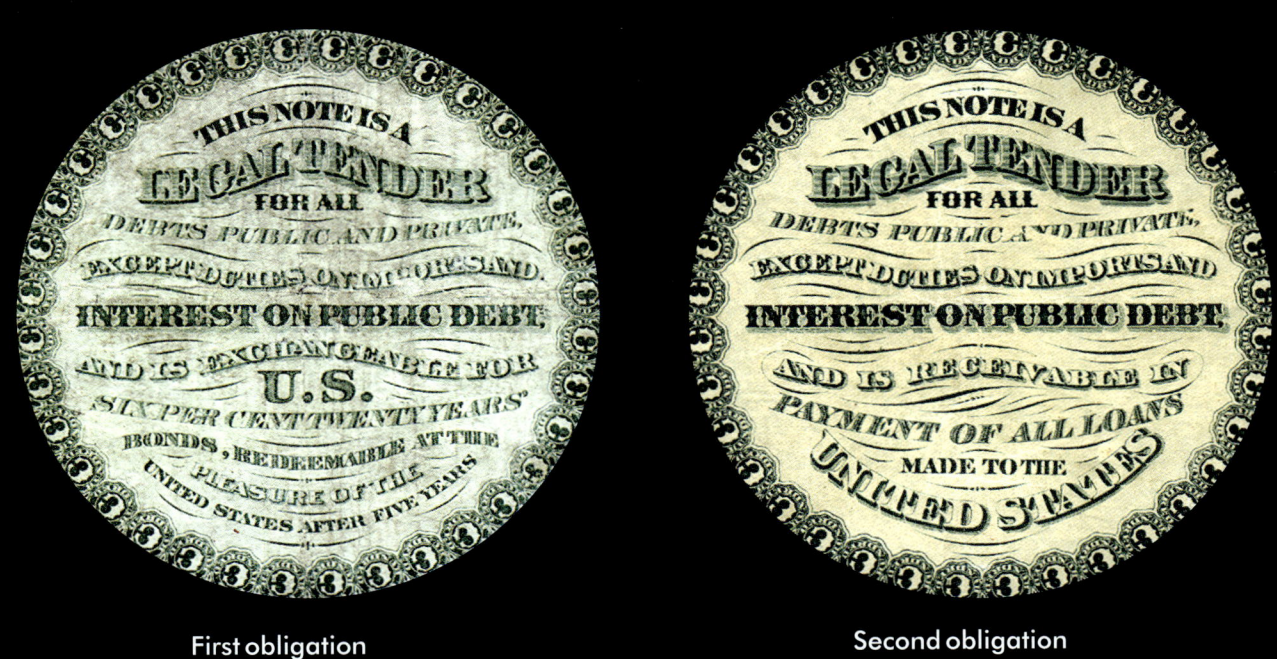

First obligation　　　　　　　　　　　　Second obligation

One Hundred Dollar "Rainbow" Note
Series 1869

Portrait of Abraham Lincoln. The figure on the right is an allegorical figure representing Architecture

This is the beautiful and popular "rainbow note," very popular with currency collectors. A total of seventeen copies are known to exist in private collections. Six more are permanently part of government and private museum collections.

By the simplest definition, architecture is the design of forms, buildings and other living spaces. But it is much more. It is the expression of the architect, of his thoughts in his creation. It is not simply construction, the piling of stones or the spanning of spaces with concrete or steel girders. It is the intelligent design of forms and spaces that in themselves express an idea. In the nineteenth century, architecture was important in a young America and so it was therefore depicted on the one hundred dollar note of 1869.

Series 1875, Small Red Seal with Rays

Series 1880, Large Brown Seal

Series 1880, Small Red Scalloped Seal

Counterfeiting warning on the reverse of the 1880 one hundred dollar note

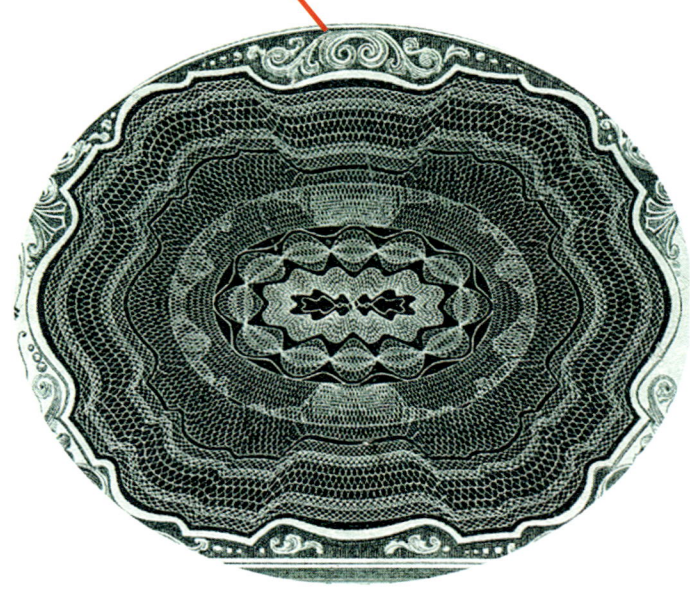

Finely engraved pattern designed to make it extremely difficult to counterfeit

Series 1880, Large Red Plain Seal

Series 1880, Large Red Spiked Seal

Thomas (Tad) Lincoln, the youngest child of Mary and Abraham. Thomas, was born on April 4, 1853, in the Lincoln home in Springfield. He was named after Lincoln's father, Thomas, but, Abraham nicknamed him "Tad," short for "Tadpole," apparently because of his appearance as an infant. Tad was inventive in thinking up mischief and he became rather famous for his pranks, which he often carried out with the help of his older brother Willie. Tad died on July 15, 1871, at the age of 18, about six years after the assassination of his father. His death was a great loss to his mother, because she had depended upon him for love, companionship, and understanding after Abraham's death.

Shown left is Lincoln reading to his son Tad
Photo: National Archives

This letter was written by Abraham Lincoln while President on Executive Mansion (White House) stationery

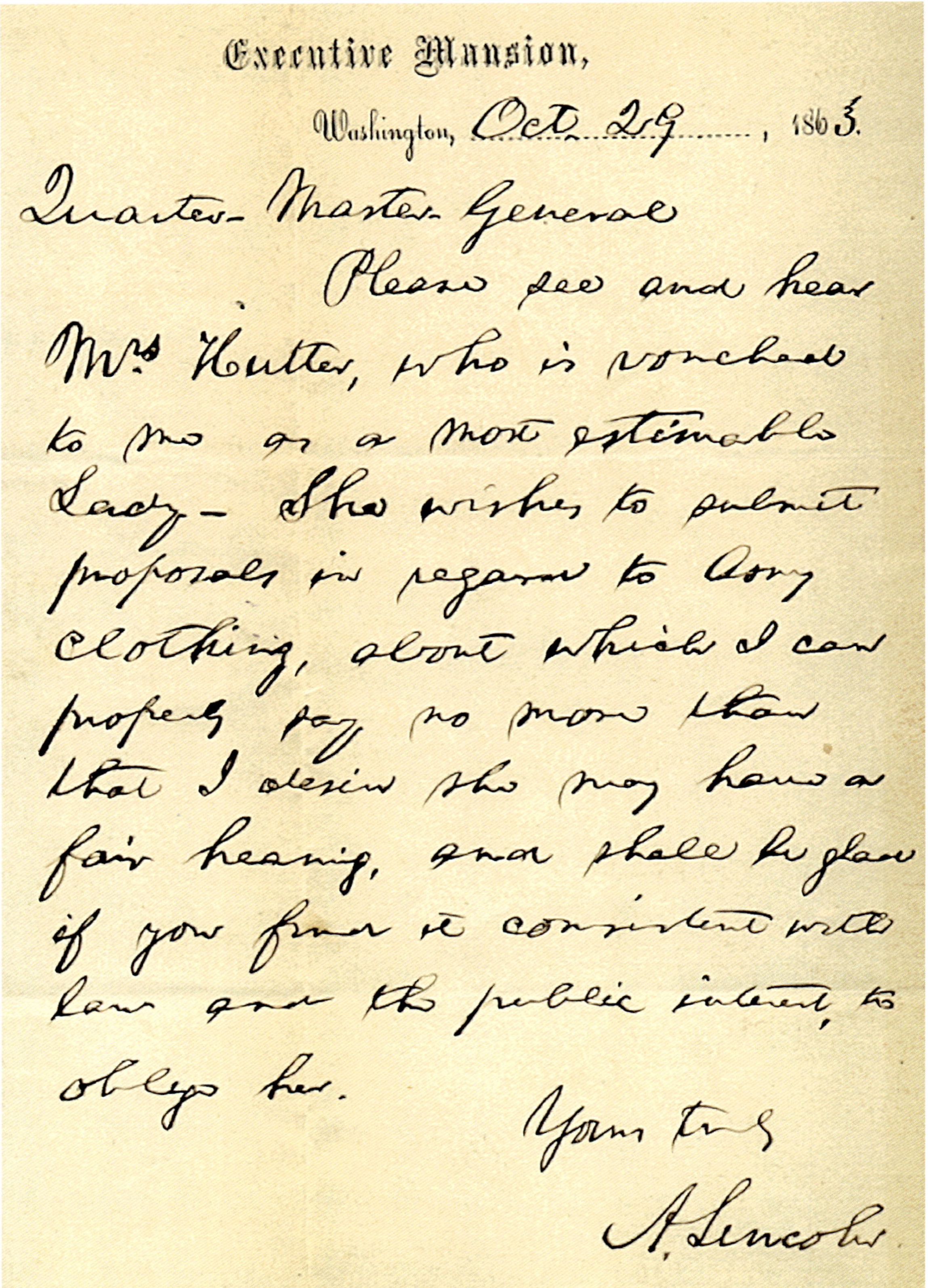

Executive Mansion,

Washington, Oct. 29, 1863.

Quarter-Master General

Please see and hear Mrs Hutter, who is vouched to me as a most estimable Lady— She wishes to submit proposals in regard to Army clothing, about which I can properly say no more than that I desire she may have a fair hearing, and shall be glad if you find it consistent with law and the public interest, to oblige her.

Yours truly

A. Lincoln

Oct. 29, 1863

Quarter Master General

Please see and hear Mrs. Hutter, who is vouched to me as a most estimable lady—She wishes to submit proposals in regards to army clothing, about which I can properly say no more than that I desire she may have a fair hearing, and shall be glad if you find it consistent with law and the public intent, to oblige her.

Yours truly

A. Lincoln

The Oat Bin Hoard
as told by Dean Oakes

The farm in Missouri where the "Oat Bin Hoard" was discovered

Author's Note: I am grateful to Mr. Dean Oakes, a prominent and knowledgeable currency dealer for supplying me with the picture and text for this section of the book. Mr. Oakes was influential in the development of my collection and was the first dealer I worked with in the 1970's. (E.D.)

The Oat Bin Hoard was brought to numismatic attention by Howard Carter, M.D. "Doc" Carter lived in a suburb of Kansas City but had his practice in the small town of Hamilton, Missouri. He also bought a small bank in Kingston, Missouri and carried on the duties as president. In this position he became known to many fellow bankers as someone to contact if old types of currency were found in an estate.

Dr. Carter received a call from a fellow banker in 1966 about a cash hoard that had just been brought in to the bank. Some of the bills were so worn that they would have to be turned in "if the Federal Reserve would even take them." Doc related to me that he seldom cancelled appointments but that morning he did. He assured the banker he would be at his bank later in the day and he would help determine which notes should be kept and which should be turned in. "Some of the notes were very old if indeed real and some had a smell to them," were the closing remarks of that conversation, I was told. I'm sure Dr. Carter was as amazed as many of us who later looked at the notes that were in this accumulation of old "horse blanket" bills.

Photograph of Oat Field in the Midwest United States

Doc told me that when he arrived at the bank he was greeted and taken to a back room where, on a table, were various small to large stacks of currency. At first glance, he noted some were new and these were National Bank Notes. Other notes were dirty and almost oval in shape from wear. Lying on the table beside the older bills was a money belt, quite hard and still in a round shape. One flap was off and stitching was coming undone from long term use. "Where did you find this stuff?"

123

The Oat Bin Hoard continued

The building on the farm where the "Oat Bin Hoard" was discovered in 1966. It has since been torn down.

The banker related that last week one of the men they had hired to clean up the farmstead of an estate they were settling had brought this money in. Most of the buildings on the farm were falling down and the men were going through and cleaning anything of use out of there. A few sheds had been pushed over and burned. They had been working on a building built to hold small bins of grain and one bin was full of oats. It looked as though it had been there a number of years from the appearance of the grain. They were scooping the oats out by hand onto a wagon and as they were working one fellow hit something with a scoop, and pulling oats away from it, saw that it was a large crock with a lid still on it He tipped the crock over and as the oats spilled out they found a large glass jar (three to five gallon size) with a wide top. It was full of what looked like rolls of paper, but it was U.S. paper money, some over one hundred years old.

The jar also contained an old money belt, well worn and containing more bills than it was designed to hold. Having so many bills in the belt resulted in the outside notes, five or six deep, being worn into an oval from the friction of the leather against the paper. The two men brought the money to the banker with the explanation, "Look what we found in that old oat bin at the farm."

THE OAT BIN HOARD HAD BEEN DISCOVERED. Dr. Carter never told me what he paid for the $40,000 face value of the notes, but I'm sure it was only a small percentage over face as some notes had to be redeemed because of their poor condition. The $500 Gallatin and $1000 Morris U.S. notes of 1862 were the key notes in the hoard and are both unique. They were described by Dr. Carter as having good color and were in fine to very fine condition. He valued them at three times face value in 1967; after I bought them, they were sold for $5,000 and $10,000 in 1975.

FIVE HUNDRED DOLLAR SERIES 1862
FIRST OBLIGATION BACK, FROM THE "OAT BIN HOARD"

The above note is unique and is even missing from the U. S. Government collection. It is the first issue of $500 legal tender notes and was discovered in the Oat Bin Hoard (see previous page). The portrait is Albert Gallatin, an early American Statesman born in Switzerland in 1761.

ALBERT GALLATIN, 1761-1849

Albert Gallatin

Albert Gallatin was an immigrant from Geneva, Switzerland. He moved to the United States in 1780. He lived for a brief time in Boston and Virginia before making his home on the Pennsylvania frontier. During the days of the Whiskey Rebellion, the first great test of the power of the Federal Government, Gallatin played a leading role. He was much more moderate than many, and advocated against breaking with the government.

He was elected U.S. Senator from Pennsylvania in 1793. President Jefferson appointed him Secretary of the Treasury in 1801 and he administered the financial affairs of the U.S. for the next twelve years.

Free frank on Treasury Department stationery signed by Albert Gallatin

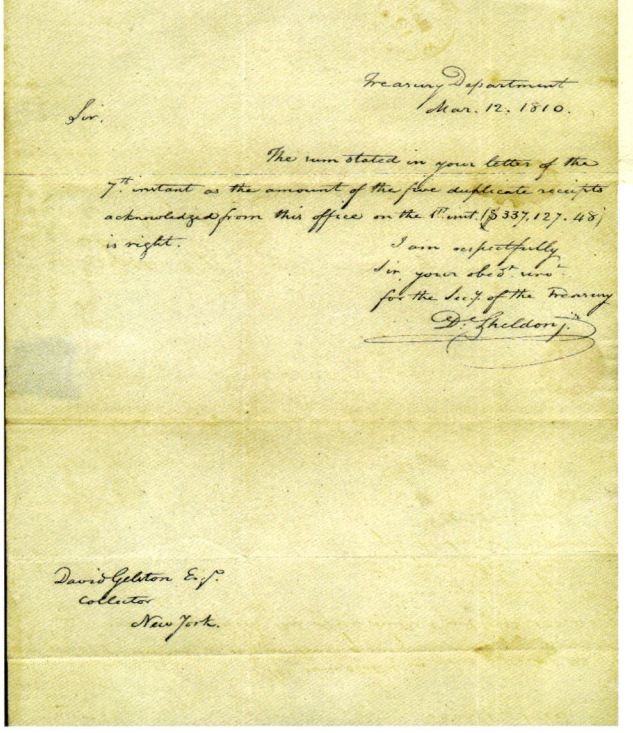
Letter from the envelope shown above

As Secretary of the Treasury, Albert Gallatin found the resources to buy the Louisiana Purchase and for its exploration, and to build the roads and canals to help a young nation survive and thrive. Before and after this, he was intimately involved in important political events such as the Treaty of Ghent.

In 1816, he was appointed Minister to France by President James Madison and lived overseas for the next seven years, returning to the United States in 1823. He became Minister to England in 1826 and finally returned to the United States in 1829. He retired from public service and became the President of the National Bank of New York.

Five Hundred Dollar "Rainbow" Note
Series 1869

This is the only specimen known that is available to collectors. Two other notes are permanently part of U.S. Government collections. This design featuring the portrait of John Quincy Adams, sixth President of the United States, was rapidly withdrawn from circulation due to an abundance of counterfeits. There are several counterfeits still known to exist today. The figure on the left is an allegorical representation of "Justice" seated.

John Quincy Adams was the first President who was the son of a President. John Quincy Adams in many respects paralleled the career as well as the temperament and viewpoints of his illustrious father. Born in Braintree, Massachusetts, in 1767, he watched the Battle of Bunker Hill from the top of Penn's Hill above the family farm. As secretary to his father in Europe, he became an accomplished linguist and assiduous diarist.

John Quincy Adams
Sixth President of the United States

Serving under President Monroe, Adams was one of America's great Secretaries of State, arranging with England for the joint occupation of the Oregon country and obtaining from Spain the cession of the Floridas. He formulated with the President the Monroe Doctrine.

In the political tradition of the early 19th century, Adams as Secretary of State was considered the political heir to the Presidency. But the old ways of choosing a President were giving way in 1824 before the clamor for a popular choice.

Upon becoming President, Adams appointed Clay as Secretary of State. Jackson and his angry followers charged that a "corrupt bargain" had taken place and immediately began their campaign to wrest the Presidency from Adams in 1828.

John Quincy Adams - Free Franks

John Quincy Adams as former President and member of Congress (1829 - 1848) writes to Reverend Calvin Colton in New York City (left).

After he was defeated for a second presidential term, he was persuaded to run for Congress and was elected for nine consecutive terms starting in 1830 until his death in 1848.

John Adams was a strong anti-slavery advocate and he voiced his opinion often as a member of Congress. Notice the shaky handwriting on both free franks. This indicates they were written later in his life, probably not long before his death. Both of these folded covers bear the hand of Adams. The cover on the right is written by Adams as a member of Congress to the Reverend Nathan Lord, President of Dartmouth College.

Free frank written by John Adams (father of John Quincy Adams) and mailed from Trenton, N.J.

John Adams was the first President to live in the White House. He and his wife moved into the mansion in 1800 before it was finished.

The White House, a watercolor by Benjamin Henry Latrobe - 1807 (Library of Congress)

The First Father & Son who became Presidents

THE FATHER - John Adams

John Adams
Second President 1797-1801

Learned and thoughtful, John Adams was more remarkable as a political philosopher than as a politician. "People and nations are forged in the fires of adversity," he said, doubtless thinking of his own as well as the American experience.

Adams was born in the Massachusetts Bay Colony in 1735. A Harvard-educated lawyer, he early became identified with the patriot cause; a delegate to the First and Second Continental Congresses, he led in the movement for independence.

During the Revolutionary War Adams served in France and Holland in diplomatic roles, and helped negotiate the treaty of peace. From 1785 to 1788 he was minister to the Court of St. James, returning to be elected Vice President under George Washington.

When Adams became President, the war between the French and British was causing great difficulties for the United States on the high seas and intense partisanship among contending factions within the Nation.

After his presidency, Adams retired to his farm in Quincy. Here he penned his elaborate letters to Thomas Jefferson. On July 4, 1826, he whispered his last words: "Thomas Jefferson survives." But Jefferson had died at Monticello a few hours earlier.

THE SON - John Quincy Adams

John Quincy Adams
Sixth President 1825-1829

The first President who was the son of a President, John Quincy Adams in many respects paralleled the career as well as the temperament and viewpoints of his illustrious father. Born in Braintree, Massachusetts, in 1767, he watched the Battle of Bunker Hill from the top of Penn's Hill above the family farm.

The campaign of 1828, in which his Jacksonian opponents charged him with corruption and public plunder, was an ordeal Adams did not easily bear. After his defeat he returned to Massachusetts, expecting to spend the remainder of his life enjoying his farm and his books.

Unexpectedly, in 1830, the Plymouth district elected him to the House of Representatives, and there for the remainder of his life he served as a powerful leader. Above all, he fought against circumscription of civil liberties.

In 1836 southern Congressmen passed a "gag rule" providing that the House automatically table petitions against slavery. Adams tirelessly fought the rule for eight years until finally he obtained its repeal.

In 1848, he collapsed on the floor of the House from a stroke and was carried to the Speaker's Room, where two days later he died. He was buried-as were his father, mother, and wife-at First Parish Church in Quincy. To the end, "Old Man Eloquent" had fought for what he considered right.

The Second Father & Son who became Presidents

George Herbert Walker Bush

George Bush brought to the White House a dedication to traditional American values and a determination to direct them toward making the United States "a kinder and gentler nation."

Coming from a family with a tradition of public service, George Herbert Walker Bush felt the responsibility to make his contribution both in time of war and in peace. Born in Milton, Massachusetts, on June 12, 1924, he became a student leader at Phillips Academy in Andover. On his 18th birthday he enlisted in the armed forces. The youngest pilot in the Navy when he received his wings, he flew 58 combat missions during World War II. On one mission over the Pacific as a torpedo bomber pilot he was shot down by Japanese antiaircraft fire and was rescued from the water by a U. S. submarine. He was awarded the Distinguished Flying Cross for bravery in action.

George Herbert Walker Bush Forty-First President 1989-1993

President Bush with Allison, Joanne and Edward Dauer in 1986 (while Vice-President)

President Bush with Allison Dauer at the White House, March, 2002, celebrating the National Championships of the University Of Miami football and baseball teams

Who is the real President?

131

Five Hundred Dollar
Series 1874

Portrait of Major General Joseph King Mansfield
The figure on the left is an allegorical representation of Victory.
There are two large red "D's" on either side of a red "500" on the bottom of the note

The reverse was printed by the Columbian Bank Note Company. 56,000 notes of this series were printed and only five specimens are known to exist, two of them part of government collections.

On the morning of September 17, 1862, a Civil War battle was unfolding on a forty-acre cornfield, in Sharpsburg, Maryland, now known as the "The Battle of Antietam," one of the Civil War's bloodiest. An estimated casualty count of 22,720 men occurred within a four-hour period of time. With guns firing and cannons thundering, the result became an orgy of death. The 12th Massachusetts lost 224 of 334 men in a matter of minutes. An hour later Union troops under General Joseph Mansfield counterattacked and by 9 o'clock had regained some of the lost ground. General Mansfield was promoted posthumously to Major General on March 12, 1863, retroactive to July 18, 1862.

The "Bloody" cornfield today where the Battle of Antietam was fought on September 17, 1862

132

Five Hundred Dollar
Series 1880

Small Red Scalloped Seal
This is the only example of the Bruce and Roberts signature in a private collection. Four other copies are in government collections

Major General Mansfield was born in Connecticut in 1803 and graduated from West Point in 1822. He served as Chief Military Engineer of the U.S. Army during the Mexican War under General Taylor. He was promoted rapidly from the rank of Captain to Colonel for gallant service and bravery.

Mansfield was then appointed by Jefferson Davis, the U.S. Secretary of War, as Inspector General of frontier posts. When the Civil War began he was promoted to Brigadier General and was commander of the twelfth Army two days before the Battle of Antietam. He was mortally wounded in that battle and died September 18, 1862.

Major General Joseph King Mansfield
1803 - 1862

ONE THOUSAND DOLLAR SERIES 1863
SECOND OBLIGATION REVERSE, FROM THE "OAT BIN HOARD"

Photo-U.S. government

The above banknote is also unique and was discovered in the Oat bin hoard. Although it is dated 1863, it has a script date of 1862. The portrait is of Robert Morris, a signer of the Declaration of Independence and Superintendent of Finance from 1781-1784. Morris is also featured on the ten dollar silver certificates of 1878 and 1880.

Robert Morris was a native of Lancashire, England, where he was born January, 1733. The massacre at Lexington during April, 1775, seems to have decided the mind of Mr. Morris as to the unalterable course which he would adopt in respect to England. Mr. Morris was elected by the legislature of Pennsylvania as a delegate to the second Congress that met at Philadelphia.

ONE THOUSAND DOLLAR SERIES 1863
SECOND OBLIGATION REVERSE

This note has a script date and act date of 1863. Only two examples are known to exist and both are in AU (almost uncirculated) condition and reside in private collections. The other example (Serial Number 99202) was sold at public auction in December, 1998, for $451,000.

Robert Morris
The man who financed the American Revolution

Robert Morris

Thomas Paine, Patrick Henry, Thomas Jefferson, Benjamin Franklin, and George Washington are the most famous heroes of the American Revolution, but it wouldn't have turned out successfully without Robert Morris.

A signer of the Declaration of Independence, the Articles of Confederation and the Constitution, Morris was a Philadelphia merchant who raised money, often from his own pocket, so that George Washington could feed, clothe and pay his restless soldiers. Morris made it possible for Washington to take his troops to Yorktown, Virginia where he defeated British General Charles Cornwallis, winning the Revolutionary War.

The massacre at Lexington, April, 1775 seems to have decided the mind of Mr. Morris, as to the unalterable course which he would adopt in respect to England. The news of this battle reached Philadelphia four days after its occurrence.

On the third of November, 1775, Mr. Morris was elected, by the legislature of Pennsylvania, a delegate to the second congress that met at Philadelphia. A few weeks after he had taken his seat, he was added to the secret committee of that body, which had been formed by a resolve of the preceding Congress, (1775) and whose duty it was to contract for the importation of arms, ammunition, sulphur, and saltpetre, and to export produce on the public account, to pay for the same.

While attending to the duties of their appointment, Mr. Morris received a letter from Gen. Washington, then with his army on the Delaware, opposite Trenton. In this letter, he communicated to Mr. Morris his distressed state, in consequence of the want of money. The sum he needed was ten thousand dollars, which was essentially necessary to enable him to obtain such intelligence of the movement and position of the enemy, as would authorize him to act offensively. To Mr. Morris, Gen. Washington now looked, to assist him in raising the money.

On December 30, 1786, the Pennsylvania Assembly named him as a delegate to the Constitutional Convention. Although he faithfully attended all the meetings, he didn't participate much in the debates. He supported ratification of the Constitution and served a term as U.S. Senator from Pennsylvania.

He used his shipping fortune to buy land throughout the Union, and by 1795 he had acquired over 6 million acres. The mortgages and taxes were more than he could pay. Creditors had him arrested, and he was sentenced to Philadelphia debtor's prison. Humiliated and broke, he died on May 7, 1806. It was a sad end for the practical man who had done so much to help America achieve independence.

The signing of the Declaration of Independence, July 4, 1776

John Hancock 1737—1793
Representing Massachusetts at the Continental Congress
Born: January 12, 1737 in Braintree (Quincy), Mass.
Education: Graduated Harvard College (Merchant.)
Work: Elected to the Boston Assembly, 1766; Delegate to, and President of, the Provincial Congress of Massachusetts, circa 1773; Elected to Continental Congress, 1774; Elected President of the Continental Congress, 1775; Member of Massachusetts state Constitutional Convention, elected Governor of Massachusetts, through 1793.
Died: October 8, 1793.

This document signed by John Hancock, as Governor of Massachusetts, is to Phineas Jones. It is his appointment as major in the militia of the Commonwealth of Massachusetts.

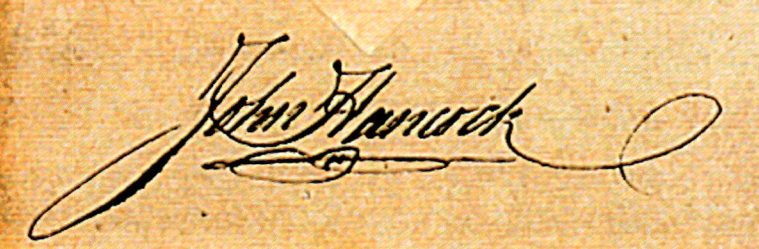

One Thousand Dollar "Rainbow" Note
Series 1869

The seated figure on the left is Christopher Columbus

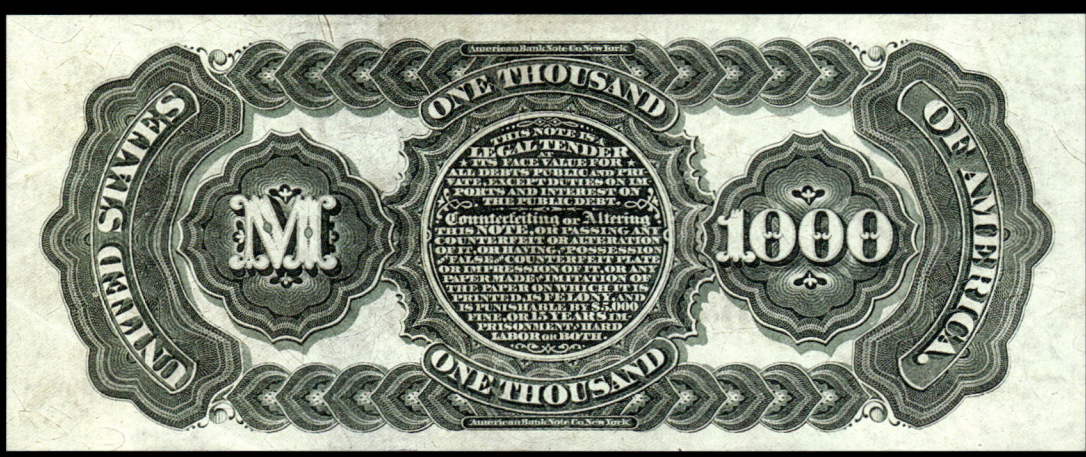

This is the highest denomination of the beautiful and desirable "rainbow notes" of 1869. 87,100 notes were originally printed and only two are known to exist. The note pictured above is the only example available to collectors and has never been publicly sold at auction. The other copy is part of the permanent collection of the Federal Reserve Bank of Chicago.

In order to open the country west of the Appalachian Mountains to settlers and to offer a cheap and safe way to carry produce to market, in 1808, Governor of New York, Dewitt Clinton, proposed the construction of a canal. However, it was not until July 4, 1817 that Governor Clinton finally broke ground for the construction of the canal. In those early days, it was often sarcastically referred to as "Clinton's Big Ditch." When finally completed on October 26, 1825, it was the engineering marvel of its day.

View of Erie Canal painted by John William Hill, 1829

One Thousand Dollar
Series 1880

This is one of only three issues of $1,000 notes printed with the "$" sign. The other two examples are the 1907-1922 $1,000 gold certificates and the 1918 $1,000 Federal Reserve notes.

DeWitt Clinton was born in New York and attended Columbia University, graduating as an attorney. He was elected to the U.S. Senate in 1802 and resigned after just one year in office to become mayor of New York City. He was appointed a member of the commission in 1810 that built the Erie Canal. The success of this venture led to his election as Governor of New York for two terms from 1817-23. In 1825, he was elected for a third term but died in Albany on February 11, 1828.

DeWitt Clinton (1769-1828). He was elected a U.S. Senator from New York in 1802 but resigned after being elected mayor of New York City in 1803 and Governor of New York for three terms.

President William Jefferson Clinton
(No relation to Dewitt Clinton)

Joanne Dauer with President Clinton at the Miami home of Sylvester Stallone

Sylvester Stallone sold his home in Miami on Bayshore Drive near Coconut Grove shortly after this picture dewas taken

Coconut Grove, Florida - 1922

Coconut Grove Florida

1922 March 10

In response to your request for my autograph I have much pleasure in handing it to you hereon.

Yours sincerely,

Alexander Graham Bell

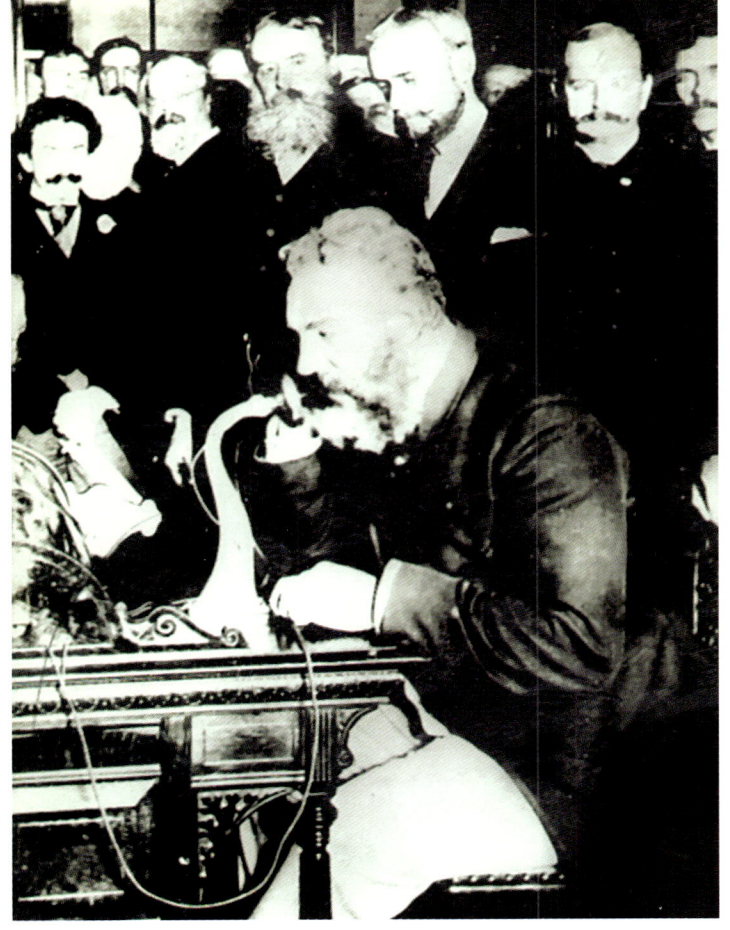

Alexander Graham Bell moved to Ontario, Canada, from Scotland to escape the scourge of tuberculosis. He began his career as an inventor in Boston. In his later life, he resided in Baddeck, Nova Scotia, but liked to spend the winters in Coconut Grove.

This is the only known picture ever taken of Alexander Graham Bell (1847-1922) next to a telephone. This photo was taken at the Centennial Exhibition in Philadelphia on June 25, 1876. This was also the same day that Custer was defeated at the Battle of the Little Big Horn. The Exhibition was organized to celebrate the one hundred year anniversary of the signing of the Declaration of Independence. The telephone was the star attraction and was the first public appearance of the invention that would be the most valuable invention ever patented.

FIVE THOUSAND DOLLAR SERIES 1878

Portrait of James Madison, fourth President of the United States, 1809-1813

All specimens of the $5,000 and $10,000 legal tender notes of 1878 have been redeemed and destroyed by the Treasury Department. The note above is a specimen furnished to the Chinese Government. Proof or specimen notes are usually either printed on cardboard or have a blank reverse. This note is printed on both sides and on legitimate currency paper. It is thus highly desired by collectors and it is the only surviving example of this design.

Five Thousand Dollar Federal Reserve Note
Series 1934

This is the same portrait of James Madison that was used on the $5,000 large size legal tender note issued in 1878, shown on the previous page.

These, as all issues of U. S. currency issued since 1861, are still legal tender today but their rarity makes them highly desirable for collectors. All large denomination notes up to the $10,000 value have recently become very popular with highly paid professional athletes. This increased demand has caused these notes to be worth many multiples of their face value, especially in crisp uncirculated condition such as the example illustrated above.

In Congress, Madison helped frame the Bill of Rights and enact the first revenue legislation. Out of his leadership in opposition to Hamilton's financial proposals, which he felt would unduly bestow wealth and power upon northern financiers, came the development of the Republican, or Jeffersonian Party.

Photo -The Library of Congress

JAMES MADISON
Fourth President of the United States

James Madison

At his inauguration, James Madison, a small man, appeared old and worn. Washington Irving described him as "but a withered little apple-John." But whatever his deficiencies in charm, Madison's wife Dolley compensated for them with her warmth and gaiety. She was the toast of Washington.

When he was first introduced to Dolley Payne Todd by his friend Aaron Burr, he was immediately smitten. The exhuberant Dolley was a bright contrast to Madison's quiet image.

Born in 1751, Madison was brought up in Orange County, Virginia, and attended Princeton (then called the College of New Jersey). A student of history and government, well-read in law, he participated in the framing of the Virginia Constitution in 1776, served in the Continental Congress, and was a leader in the Virginia Assembly.

When delegates to the Constitutional Convention assembled at Philadelphia, the thirty-six year old Madison took frequent and emphatic part in the debates. Madison made a major contribution to the ratification of the Constitution by writing, with Alexander Hamilton and John Jay, the Federalist essays. In later years, he was referred to as the "Father of the Constitution."

Reverend William B. Sprague, one of the earliest collectors of autographs received this letter from Dolley Madison on November 20, 1835. The signature on the free frank indicated Madison's poor health. He died just seven months later in 1836.

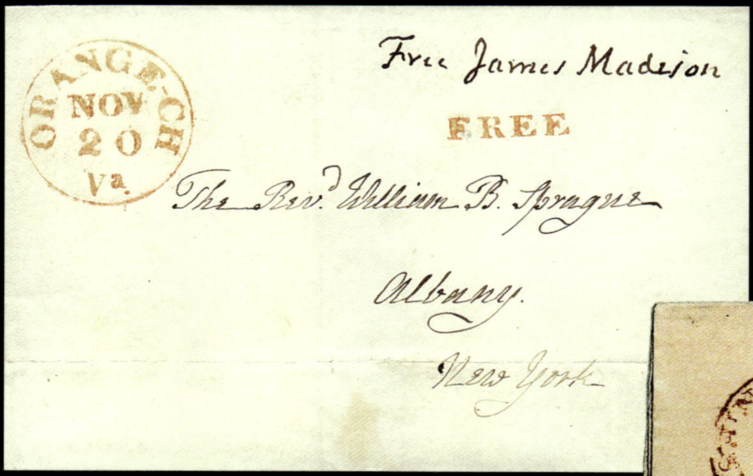

Free frank signed by James Madison

Free frank signed by Dolley Madison as "D.P. Madison"

Chapter IV

SILVER CERTIFICATES

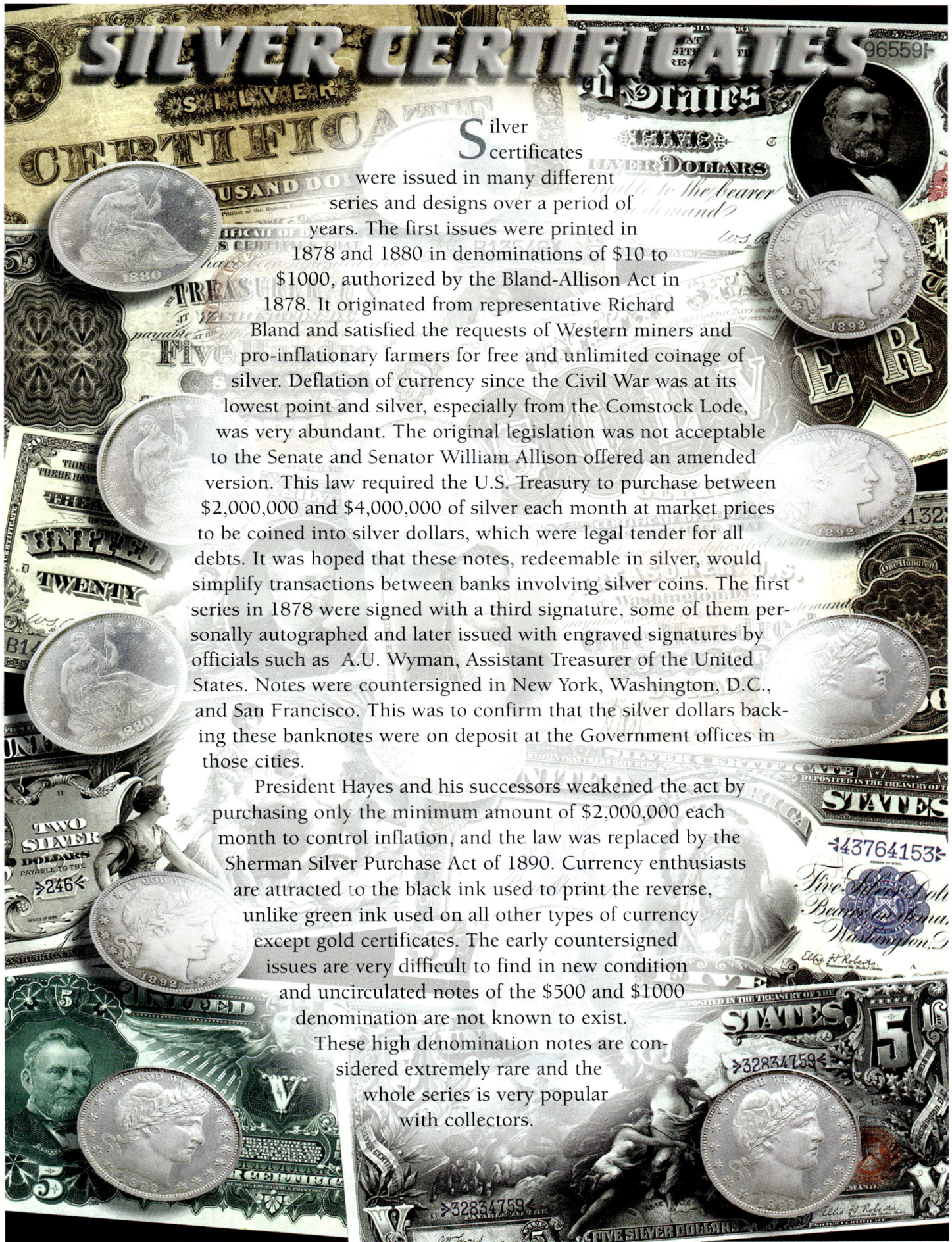

Silver certificates were issued in many different series and designs over a period of years. The first issues were printed in 1878 and 1880 in denominations of $10 to $1000, authorized by the Bland-Allison Act in 1878. It originated from representative Richard Bland and satisfied the requests of Western miners and pro-inflationary farmers for free and unlimited coinage of silver. Deflation of currency since the Civil War was at its lowest point and silver, especially from the Comstock Lode, was very abundant. The original legislation was not acceptable to the Senate and Senator William Allison offered an amended version. This law required the U.S. Treasury to purchase between $2,000,000 and $4,000,000 of silver each month at market prices to be coined into silver dollars, which were legal tender for all debts. It was hoped that these notes, redeemable in silver, would simplify transactions between banks involving silver coins. The first series in 1878 were signed with a third signature, some of them personally autographed and later issued with engraved signatures by officials such as A.U. Wyman, Assistant Treasurer of the United States. Notes were countersigned in New York, Washington, D.C., and San Francisco. This was to confirm that the silver dollars backing these banknotes were on deposit at the Government offices in those cities.

President Hayes and his successors weakened the act by purchasing only the minimum amount of $2,000,000 each month to control inflation, and the law was replaced by the Sherman Silver Purchase Act of 1890. Currency enthusiasts are attracted to the black ink used to print the reverse, unlike green ink used on all other types of currency except gold certificates. The early countersigned issues are very difficult to find in new condition and uncirculated notes of the $500 and $1000 denomination are not known to exist. These high denomination notes are considered extremely rare and the whole series is very popular with collectors.

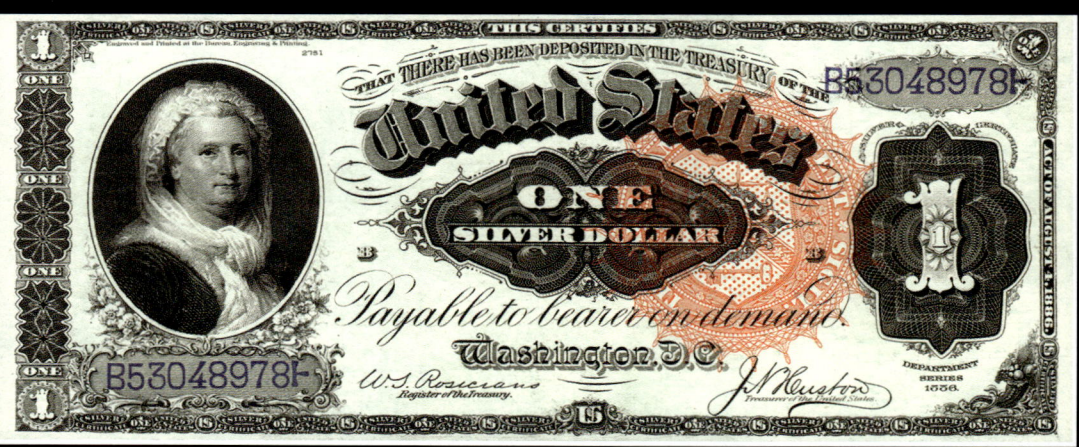

Martha Dandridge was widowed eight years after being married to a wealthy landowner, Daniel Parke Custis. She met George Washington, a Colonel in the Virginia militia at a dance in Williamsburg. Washington was a planter and surveyor and was transformed into a wealthy landowner when he married Martha on January 6, 1759.

Martha Washington is the only woman whose portrait appeared on U.S. Currency. The native American, Pocahontas, is featured as part of a painting showing her baptism on the back of the twenty dollar National Bank Notes, issued from 1863 to 1882.

One, two, and five dollar silver certificates were first printed in 1886, halfway through the first term of President Grover Cleveland. Cleveland was both the 22nd and 24th President of the United States, the only person ever to be elected to non-consecutive terms. He studied law in Buffalo where he became Mayor in 1882 and was elected Governor of New York in 1883. He was an honest and able politician but ran the Nation as if it was any big city that needed to be cleaned up.

His personal life was not always admirable. He was involved with unsavory characters, was present at a few brawls, and spent late nights at bars. He also admitted to fathering an illegitimate child. During his first term, he married his 23 year old ward, Frances Folson, in the White House.

The Native American Pocahontas died shortly after this portrait was painted in 1616-she is shown on the back of $20 National Currency notes issued from 1863 to 1882

Grover Cleveland - 1837-1908

Letter from Grover Cleveland

Photo-Library of Congress

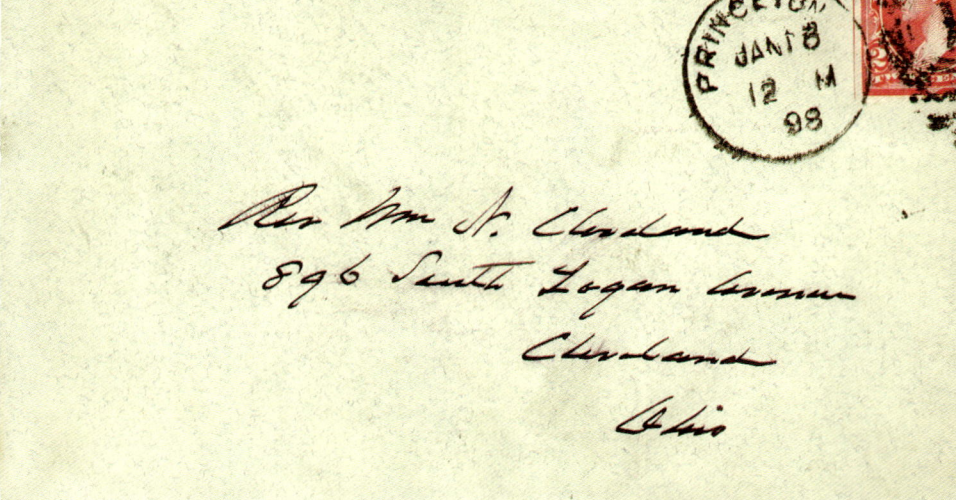

This letter above was handwritten by Grover Cleveland to his brother, Reverend William Cleveland. He sent him a check for sixty dollars and talked about the family. Letters handwritten by Presidents and signed by them are popular with collectors.

The envelope on the left shows a postmark of Princeton, Jan 18, 1898 and uses a two cent regular issue postage stamp in use during that time

President Grover Cleveland's administration is best known for adding thousands of jobs to the Civil Service System, attempting to stop the annexation of Hawaii, and undergoing violent labor unrest. He also vetoed two thirds of the bills passed by Congress. During his term the Statue of Liberty was dedicated in 1886, the Interstate Commerce Act was passed by Congress in 1887, and the Panic of 1893 resulted in the repeal of the Sherman Silver Purchase Act. Geronimo, the last of the Indian Chiefs to surrender, was sent to a reservation in Florida.

The Statue of Liberty was dedicated in 1886 during Cleveland's first term

Geronimo - the last of the great Indian Chiefs

World Columbian Exposition
The 1893 Chicago World's Fair

The Chicago World's Fair of 1893 was not only a celebration of America and the new technology of the industrial revolution, but was also a celebration of the 400th anniversary of the discovery of America by Christopher Columbus

The theme of the Chicago World's Fair was the four hundredth anniversary of the discovery of America by Christopher Columbus. The fair was also a reflection and celebration of American culture and society and was a showcase for the future. It was the last and the greatest of the nineteenth century world's fairs. The dedication day was Oct 26, 1892, it was officially opened on May 1, 1893, by President Grover Cleveland and closed October 30, 1893. There were 21.5 million tickets sold and admission was fifty cents for adults and twenty-five cents for children. The cost of construction was over thirty million dollars.

President Grover Cleveland, 24th President of the United States opened the Exposition on May 1, 1893

Photo Library of Congress

As everyone knows, Columbus had three ships on his first voyage-the Niña, the Pinta, and the Santa Maria. This ancient woodcut illustrates Columbus leaving Spain for his historic voyage.

The Ferris Wheel, one of the most exciting attractions, was first introduced at the 1893 Chicago World's Fair. This amazing ride was created by George Ferris, a Pennsylvania bridge builder.

While the 1889 Paris Exposition was known for the Eiffel Tower, the Chicago fair was known for the introduction of the Ferris Wheel, built by George Ferris, a Pennsylvania bridge builder. It was the engineering highlight of the exposition and held thirty-six wooden cars that carried sixty people at a cost of fifty cents per ride. The wheel had a diameter of 250 feet, was supported by two 140 foot steel towers, and its 45 foot axle was the largest piece of forged steel in the world. It was also used in the St. Louis World's fair in 1901 and was scrapped in 1906. Other famous innovations were the first elevated electric railway, and the introduction of Cracker Jacks, Aunt Jemima Syrup, cream of wheat, shredded wheat, Pabst beer, Juicy Fruit Gum, the hamburger, and diet soda.

Right is a reproduction of a poster that was placed all over Chicago in 1892 and 1893 to advertise the upcoming Worlds Fair and Exposition

The following photographs are from Chicago and Philadelphia, and from "Glimpses of the World's Fair Through a Camera," produced in Chicago, in 1893.

Left: Replicas of Columbus' Caravels built for the Columbian Exposition

A view of the fair from the north-east

The official logo "Miss Columbia" for the 1893 Chicago Worlds Fair

Right: A view of the Columbian Exposition from the south court

Original Admission Tickets
To the World's Columbian Exposition

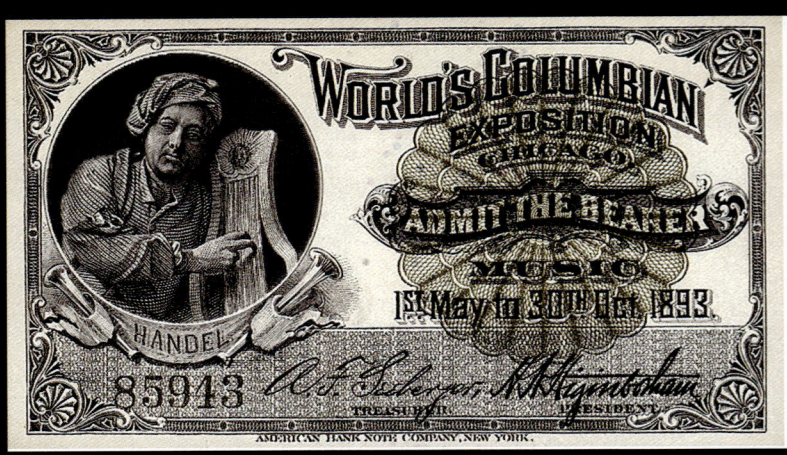

The Commemorative Stamps of 1893
Christopher Columbus - Admiral of the Ocean Seas

Sebastiano del Piombo painted this portrait of Columbus thirteen years after his death

Perhaps the most famous explorer we celebrate today is Christopher Columbus. Born in Genoa, Italy, in 1451 to a weaver, young Columbus first went to sea at the age of fourteen. As a young man, he settled in Portugal and married a woman of noble background. After his wife's death in 1485, Columbus and his young son, Diego moved to Spain. Like all learned men of his time, Columbus knew the world was round. He theorized that since the earth was a sphere, a ship could eventually reach the Far East from the opposite direction. He thought to establish trade routes to Asia in this manner. The fifteenth-century Europeans were not aware of the South and North American continents during this timeframe. Mapmakers did not show an accurate picture and no one knew there was a Pacific Ocean.

The stamps on the following pages were issued as commemoratives in 1892 to celebrate the 400th anniversary of the discoveries of Columbus.

One cent—Columbus in Sight of Land from a Painting by William Powell; 449,195,550 Stamps Printed

Two cent—Columbus Landing on Guanahani—from a Painting by Vanderlyn in the U.S. Capitol Rotunda; 1,464,588,750 Stamps Printed

Three cent—The Flagship of Columbus, the Santa Maria—from an Old Spanish Engraving; 11,501,250 Stamps Printed

Four cent—The Fleet of Columbus, the Nina, Pinta, and Santa Maria—from an Old Spanish Engraving; 19,181,550 Stamps Printed

From an exhibit at the Library of Congress - Washington, D.C.

Columbus approached the Portuguese king and the Spanish monarchs to obtain a grant to explore possible trade routes to the west. After initially turning him down, King Ferdinand and Queen Isabella reconsidered once the Moors had been successfully expelled from Spain in 1492.

Five cent—*Columbus Soliciting Aid from Isabella—from a Painting by Brozik in the Metropolitan Museum of Art in New York; 35,248,250 Stamps Printed*

Six cent—*Columbus Welcomed at Barcelona—from the Bronze Doors of the U.S. Capitol in Washington by Randolph Rogers; 4,707,550 Stamps Printed*

Eight cent—*Columbus Restored to Favor—from a Painting by Francesco Jover; 10,656,550 Stamps Printed*

Ten cent—*Columbus Presenting Natives—from a Painting by Luigi Gregori at Notre Dame University; 16,516,950 Stamps Printed*

Fifteen cent—*Columbus Announcing his Discovery—from a Painting by R. Baloca in Spain; 1,576,950 Stamps Printed*

Thirty cent—*Columbus at La Rabida—from a Painting by R. Maso; 617,250 Stamps Printed*

Columbus promised to bring back gold, spices, and silks from the Far East, to spread Christianity, and to lead an expedition to China. In return, Columbus asked for and got the hereditary title "admiral of the ocean seas" and became governor of all discovered lands.

Columbus soliciting aid from Isabella—from a painting by Brozik in the Metropolitan Museum of Art in New York-reproduced on the 5¢ stamp

Fifty cent—*Recall of Columbus—from a Painting by Augustus G. Heaton in the U.S. Capitol; 243,750 Stamps Printed*

One dollar—*Isabella Pledging her Jewels— from a Painting by Munoz Degrain in Madrid; 55,050 Stamps Printed*

Two dollar—*Columbus in Chains; from a Painting by K. Leutze, Germantown, Pennsylvania, 45,550 Stamps Printed*

Three dollar—*Columbus Describing his Third Voyage; from a Painting by Francesco Jover, 27,650 Stamps Printed*

Four dollar—*Queen Isabella and Columbus; Isabella from a Painting in Madrid, Columbus by Lotto, 26,350 Stamps Printed*

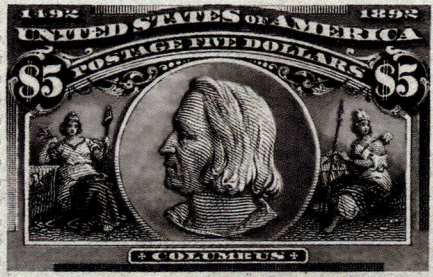

Five dollar—*Columbus; from a Cast of the U.S. Commemorative Half Dollar of 1892, 27,350 Stamps Printed*

The $1.00 Isabella pledging her jewels, part of the only known complete set of sheets of 100 commemorative stamps of the 1893 Columbian Exposition

To commemorate this event, the United States issued its first series of commemorative stamps. Fifteen different values from one cent to five dollars were issued on January 2, 1893. The eight-cent value was not originally planned and was later issued on March 3, 1893.

They were printed by the American Bank Note Company on unwatermarked paper in plates of 200 subjects. They were sold to the general public in sheets of 100 stamps. The one dollar sheet is unique. The two dollar through five dollar denominations do not exist in sheets and only exist in small multiples.

The only known complete set of sheets of one hundred was the centerpiece of the Smithsonian National Postal Museum's "Columbus' Voyage of Discovery" exhibit in Washington, D.C. It was shown for one year ending March 15, 2002.

The document on the right is a press release issued from the Smithsonian Postal Museum announcing the upcoming exhibition of the rare Columbian Exposition stamps to open March 23, 2001

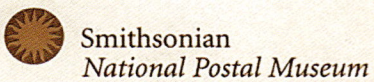

Smithsonian National Postal Museum

News

Office of Public Affairs

Feb. 28, 2001

Media only: Kristin Carvell at (202) 786-2120
Public: (202) 357-2991
Web site: http://www.si.edu/postal

NATIONAL POSTAL MUSEUM TO DISPLAY RARE "COLUMBIAN" STAMPS

In an unusual new exhibit, the Smithsonian Institution's National Postal Museum will feature rare full sheets of the Columbian Exposition stamps, in denominations from the one-cent to the one-dollar. The exhibition will mark the first time the sheets have been displayed together. "Columbus' Voyage of Discovery" opens March 8 and will remain on display until June 1, 2001.

The new exhibit includes 12 sheets of 100 stamps each of the now legendary 1893 Columbian issues, including what is believed to be the only surviving example of a sheet of the one-dollar denomination, "Isabella Pledging Her Jewels." The sheets are from the private collection of Joanne and Edward A. Dauer, M.D., of Fort Lauderdale, Fla. The collection was assembled with the assistance of Harry Hagendorf from the Columbian Stamp Co. of Scarsdale, N.Y.

The Columbian Exposition issues are considered among the most important, and admired, stamps to be issued by the U.S. Postal Service. The first true U.S. commemoratives, the Columbians were nearly twice the width of previous postage stamps to accommodate the scenes in Columbus' life they depicted. They were also the last U.S. stamps to be printed in the 19th century by a private printer, the American Banknote Co. The following year, the Bureau of Engraving and Printing took over stamp production for the Post Office Department. No sheets above the one-dollar denomination are believed to have survived.

The National Postal Museum showcases the largest, most comprehensive collection of stamps, philatelic materials, and postal history artifacts in the world. The free-admission museum, open daily from 10 a.m. to 5:30 p.m., is wheelchair-accessible. Gallery guide tapes are available for visually impaired visitors at the Visitor Information Desk.

####

On March 23, 2001, The Smithsonian Institution, National Postal Museum invited the authors to exhibit their collection of "Columbus' Voyage of Discovery: The Columbian Series of 1893" of rare stamps at the Smithsonian Postal Museum. The exhibition was shown for one year from March, 2001 until March 2002. The centerpiece of the show was the unique sheet of one hundred of the $1.00 stamp illustrated on the postcard on page 161. This postcard is sold in the museum gift shop.

'Isabella Pledging Her Jewels'
from the unique sheet of one hundred,
collection of Dr. Edward A. and Joanne Dauer

Right: The invitation for the opening ceremony, March 23, 2001

Left: The back of the official postcard from the opening, March 23, 2001

The postcard shown was the "Official Souvenir Postal" for the Worlds Columbian Exposition of 1893. It contained a message from President Harrison inviting the world to celebrate the 400th anniversary of the discovery of America by Christopher Columbus in 1492.

Right: The front of the official postcard

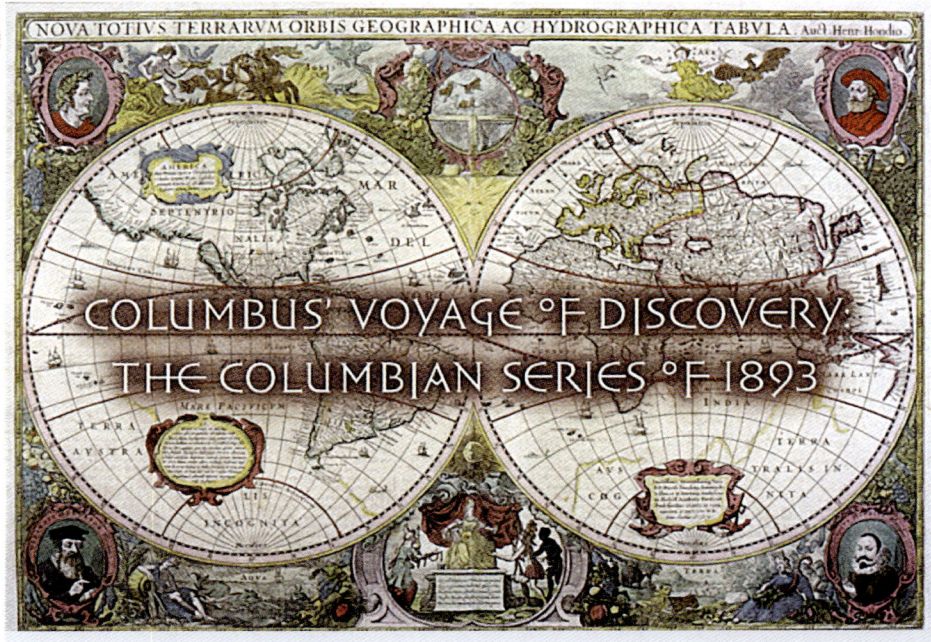

Opening the Exhibition at the Postal Museum

Joanne and Edward Dauer presenting the opening remarks

At the opening of the exhibit, the authors, Joanne and Dr. Dauer were invited to say a few words about this amazing exhibition of their one-of-a-kind rare series of stamps commemorating the 400th anniversary of the discovery of America at the great Chicago Exposition of 1893. The collection was on display at the museum until March 15, 2002.

Donna Shalala, president of the University of Miami accompanied the Dauers from Miami to the opening of the exhibition, meeting Dr. Miguel Bretos, the acting curator.

Dr. Lew Temares, Dean of the College of Engineering, Donna Shalala, President of the University of Miami and Karen Dudley with Dr. Edward Dauer

Dr. Miguel Bretos with Donna Shalala and Dr. Edward Dauer

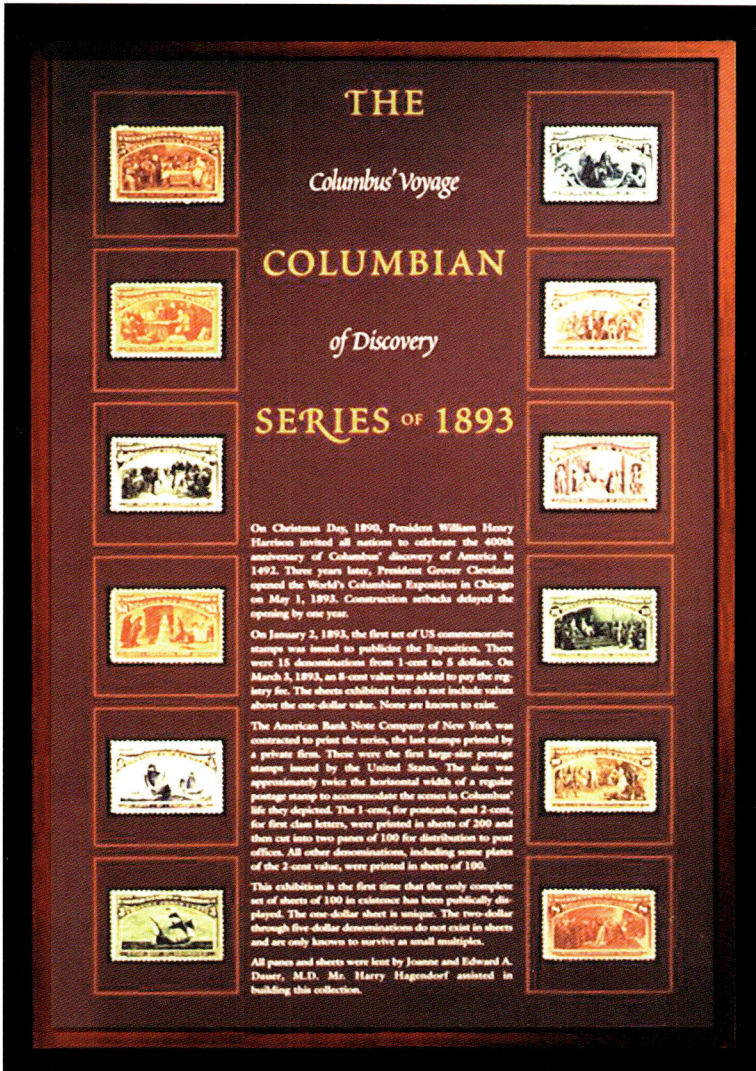

The Introduction Plaque to the Exhibit

The plaque displayed on the left was prepared for the exhibition and displayed at the opening ceremony, March 23, 2001 at the Smithsonian Postal Museum. The inscription reads as follows:

The Columbus' Voyage COLUMBIAN of Discovery SERIES OF 1893

On Christmas day, 1890, President William Henry Harrison invited all nations to celebrate the 400th anniversary of Columbus' discovery of America in 1492. Three years later, President Grover Cleveland opened the World's Columbian Exposition in Chicago on May 1, 1993. Construction setbacks delayed the opening by one year.

On January 2, 1893, the first set of commemorative stamps was issued to publicize the Exposition. There were 15 denominations from 1-cent to 5 dollars. On March 3, 1893, an 8-cent value was added to pay the registry fee. The sheets exhibited here do not include values over the one-dollar value. None are known to exist.

The American Bank Note of New York was contracted to print the series, the last stamps printed by a private firm. These were the first large size postage stamps issued by the United States. The size was approximately twice the horizontal width of a regular postage stamp to accommodate the scenes in Columbus' life they depicted. The one-cent for postcards, and 2-cent for first class letters, were printed on sheets of 200 and then cut into two pieces of 100 for distribution to post offices. All other denominations, including some plates of the 2-cent value, were printed in sheets of 100.

The exhibition is the first time that the only sheet of 100 in existence has been publicly displayed. The one-dollar sheet is unique. The two-dollar through five-dollar denominations do not exist in sheets and are only known to survive at small multiples.

All pieces and sheets were lent by Dr. Edward and Joanne Dauer. Mr. Harry Hagendorf assisted in building this collection.

 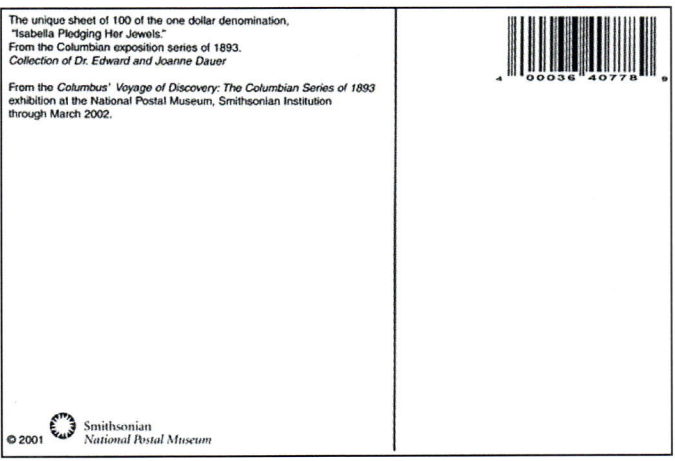

Postcard showing the front and back faces was issued by the Smithsonian for the Exhibition and Sold in the Museum Gift Shop

The Educational Notes

Three ornately engraved silver certificates were issued in 1896 in the denominations of one, two, and five dollars. Since they featured themes related to history and science, they were soon given the name "Educational Notes." They are truly the most beautiful engravings ever to appear on any currency note. The series was short lived and was discontinued in 1899.

"History Instructing Youth"—To the right is the Constitution; the Washington Monument and the Capitol are in the background. Names of famous Americans are in wreaths around the border.

The reverse features the heads of George and Martha Washington. Ornate, allegorical figures appear on the upper corners.

1899 One Dollar Silver Certificates

Commonly known as the "black eagle" note, this design replaced the educational series of 1896. An eagle in the center of the note is over the heads of Presidents Lincoln and Grant.

Date above Serial Number

Date below Serial Number

Date to right of Seal

1923 Silver Certificate

This is the last year of the large size one dollar silver certificate. The obverse very closely resembles the modern silver certificate which was replaced by the Federal Reserve Note in 1963.

Warren G. Harding
29th President of the United States

Warren G. Harding
1865-1923

Warren G. Harding, the twenty-ninth President of the United States, only served from 1921 to 1923 when he died in San Francisco of a heart attack. He was known for eliminating wartime controls and slashing taxes. Harding also established a Federal budget system, restored protective trade tariffs, and imposed strict limitations upon immigration.

Letter written by Harding while serving as President

THE WHITE HOUSE
WASHINGTON

January 25, 1923.

My dear Porter:

Thank you for yours of January 18th, and the copy of the golf magazine to which you refer.

Mrs. Harding continues to improve in health and we are counting quite confidently on going to Florida in March. It is possible that I will have the pleasure of greeting you at that time.

Very truly yours,

Warren G. Harding

Mr. Arthur F. Porter,
Box 32,
Washington, D. C.

Madame Marie Curie
Discoverer of Radium

*Madame Marie Curie
1867-1934*

Marie Sklodowska, as she was known before marriage, was and still is today the world's most famous woman scientist. With her husband Pierre and French physicist Henri Becquerel, she pioneered the study of radioactivity. Marie was born in Warsaw in 1867. Both her parents were teachers who believed in the importance of education.

She studied mathematics and physics at the Sorbonne in Paris when she met Pierre Curie in 1894 and married him in 1895. While Roentgen invented the X-ray tube in 1895, Becquerel in 1896 realized that uranium gave off similar invisible radiation.

Marie discovered two new elements: radium and polonium (named for her native Poland), and she was the first to use the term radioactive to describe elements that give off radiations as their nuclei break down. She and her husband shared the 1903 Nobel Prize in Physics with Becquerel for the discovery of radioactive elements. Not only was she the first woman to win a Nobel Prize, but in 1911 she was awarded a second Nobel Prize in chemistry, for her work on radium and radium compounds.

Pierre died in 1906, run over by a horse-drawn cart. Marie suffered from chronic radiation sickness and died on July 4, 1934, from pernicious anemia caused by overexposure to radiation.

Marie was ten years old when her mother died in May 1878. As an adult Marie remembered it as "the first great sorrow of my life, which threw me into a profound depression."

The attention that English scientists paid to the Curies' work helped make them household names in that country, as in this famous caricature, "Radium," from the popular British periodical Vanity Fair.

Left: The International symbol for Radioactivity

M. Curie

Marie Curie made her first visit to America in 1921. Scientific friends in the United States raised $100,000 to purchase for her one gram of pure radium, vitally needed for her continued research. In this famous photograph which she personally autographed, she is in Washington, D.C. with her daughter receiving the gold key to the box of radium from President Harding.

Left: Pierre and Marie Curie, working in their laboratory. Photo taken circa 1905.

Two Dollar Notes of 1886

Winfield Scott Hancock, a famous Union general during the Civil War, was named after Winfield Scott, General-in-Chief of the Army from 1841-1848 and 1855-1861. Hancock began his service as a captain and assistant quartermaster and quickly rose to the rank of major general, serving in such famous battles as Antietam, Fredericksburg, and Gettysburg. He was forced out of the army in 1866 by Grant, who objected to his lenient treatment of the South.

General Winfield Scott Hancock (1824-1886)

1891 Silver Certificate
William Windom, Secretary of the Treasury - 1881 to 1884 and 1889 to 1891

William Windom was nominated by President James A. Garfield to be the 33rd Secretary of the Treasury, serving from March 8, 1881 until November 13, 1884. He was later nominated by President Benjamin Harrison to be the 39th Secretary of the Treasury, serving from March 7, 1889 until January 29, 1891. Before joining the Treasury Department, he served as Congressman from Minnesota from 1859 to 1869. Windom was a strong supporter of President Lincoln and later the Radical Republicans.

Treasury Library Files

1896 Two Dollar Educational Note

Shown on the back of the two dollar educational note are the portraits of two of America's greatest inventors: Samuel F. B. Morse, inventor of the Morse code communication system, and Robert Fulton, mistakenly credited with the invention of the steamboat. Fulton's achievements in the introduction of steam-navigation were by no means the best or highest measures of his genius. He was an inventor, and a great one; but he did not invent the steamboat, or, so far as is known, any part of it. The grand achievement of Fulton was the direction of an enterprise which resulted in the production by Watt and his partners in Great Britain, and by Brown in New York, of a steamboat that could give commercial returns in its actual daily operation, and the institution of a "line" of boats between New York and Albany. He was a prophet, inasmuch as he foresaw the outcome of this grand revolution, in which he was so active a participant and agent; but he has been recognized neither as prophet nor as statesman, both of which he was, but as the inventor of the steamboat - which he was not.

Samuel Finley Breese Morse developed the "Morse code" an electronic alphabet that could carry messages. A line was constructed between Baltimore and Washington and the first message, sent May 24, 1844 was "WHAT HATH GOD WROUGHT."

Robert Fulton

Samuel F.B. Morse

170

1899 Two Dollar Note

The two dollar note of 1899 is one of many that feature the portrait of George Washington. He is surrounded by mythical figures representing Mechanics and Agriculture.

Every tractor in use today incorporates essential features and components developed and refined by 19th Century pioneering companies. Without their contributions to the mechanization of agriculture, modern farming techniques would be yet unrealized. Indeed, their role in farm mechanization changed forever the lives of North Dakota farmers and farmers across the United States.
Photos-Library of Congress

Five Dollar Silver Certificate Series 1886

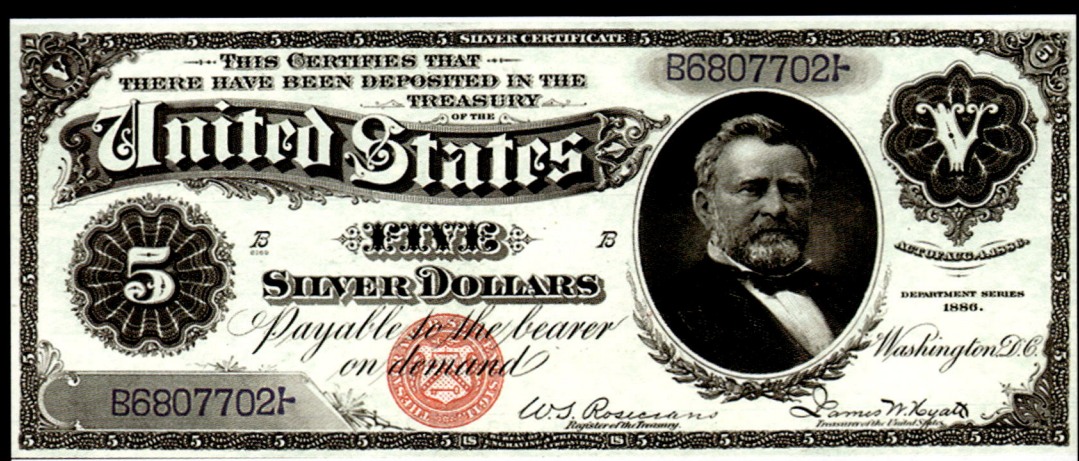

Engraving of Ulysses S. Grant, General of the Union Army during the Civil War and President of the United States from 1869-1873.
The back prominently features five silver dollars, the center coin is dated 1886.

Ulysses S. Grant, Eighteenth President of the United States, was born in 1822, the son of a tanner. He went to West Point against his father's wishes and was an average student, graduating in the middle of his class. His military experience included serving with General Zachary Taylor during the Mexican War. Taylor was the Twelfth President of the United States from 1849 to 1850.

1886

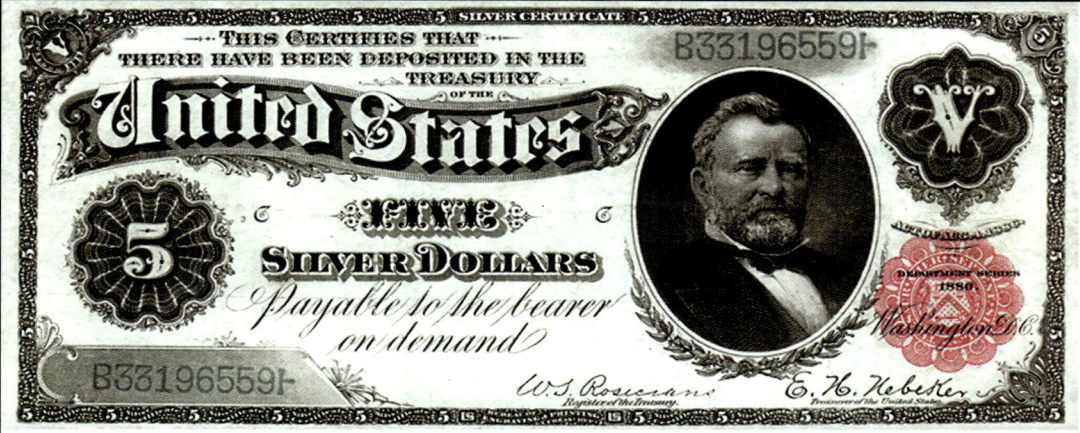

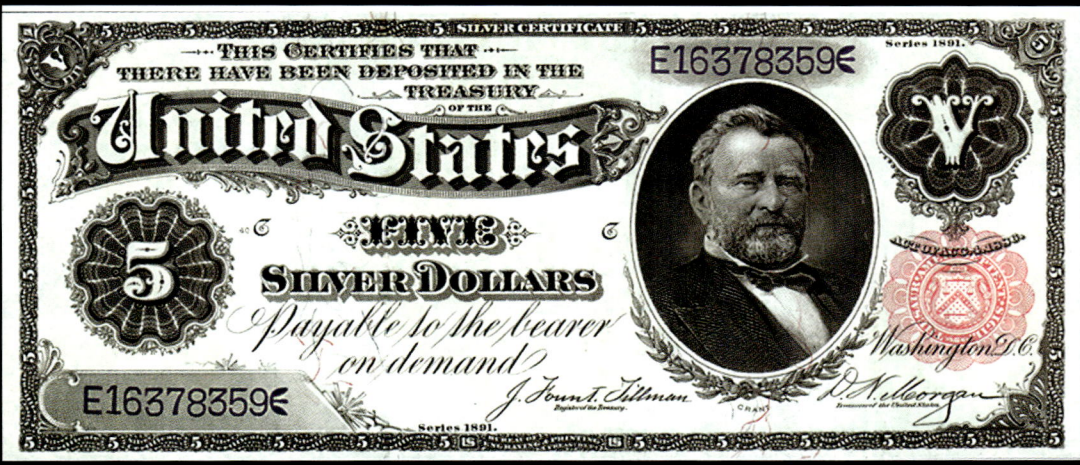
1891

> I hereby authorize and direct the Secretary of State to affix the Seal of the United States to a Warrant for the pardon of Patrick Kelly, dated this day, and signed by me; and for so doing this shall be his warrant.
>
> U.S. Grant
>
> Washington 21st December, 1872.

Above: Pardon signed by Grant for Patrick Kelly

Above: Zachary Taylor 1784-1850

Below: Free frank of Zachary Taylor

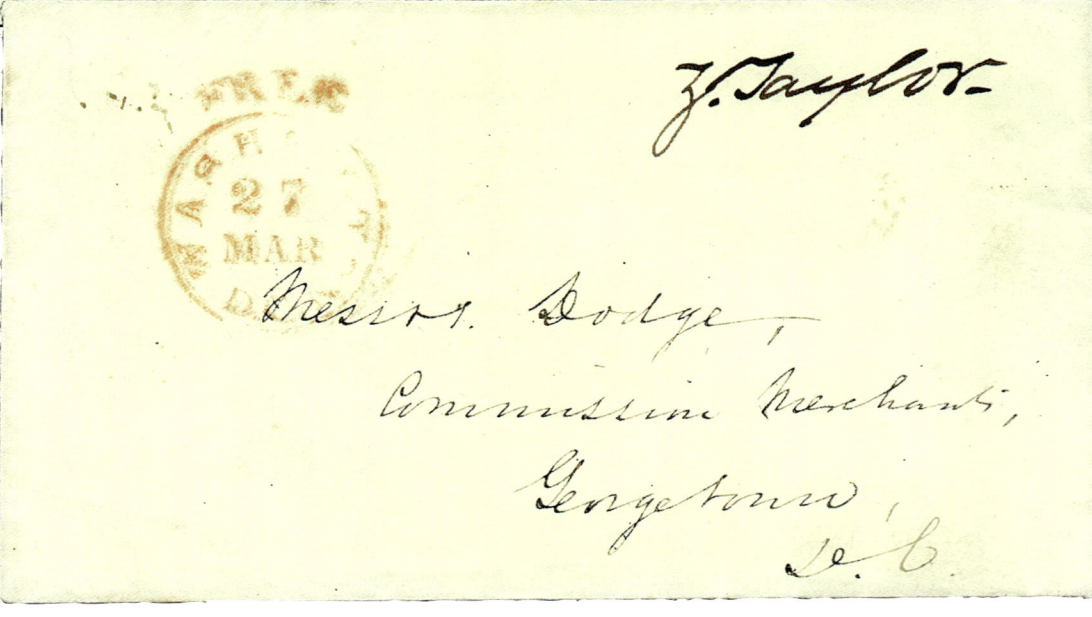

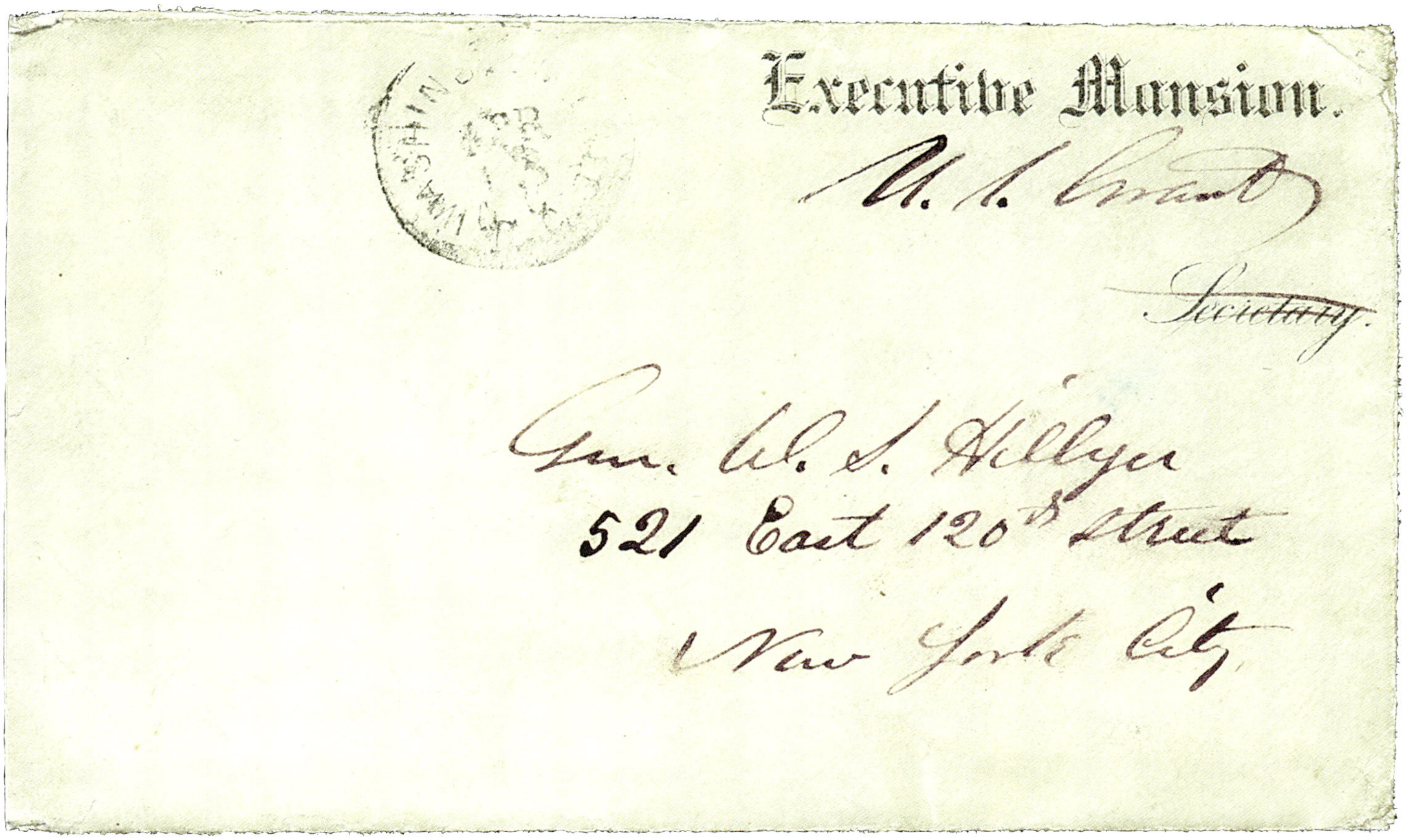

This free frank was signed by Grant while he was President. It is on Executive Mansion (old term for The White House) stationery.

Grant was best known for his role as General of the Army during the Civil War. The battle of Vicksburg, Mississippi, effectively cut the Confederacy in half and broke the Confederate hold on Chattanooga. Lincoln appointed him General-in-Chief in March, 1864. On April 9, 1865, at Appomattox Court House, Lee surrendered to Grant.

Grant was first elected President in 1869, the American people hoping for an end to the turmoil of the Civil War reconstruction. After the retirement from his second term in 1877, he became a partner in a financial firm that filed for bankruptcy. He wrote an autobiography to pay off his debts and earned $450,000. He died of throat cancer after completing his last page in 1885.

Sam Houston

Sam Houston was born in Virginia on March 2, 1793. He moved to Tennessee as a youth and spent much time with the Cherokee Indians, learning their culture and language. He later joined the army and fought against the British during the War of 1812.

After leaving the army in 1818, he attended law school and began his political career by successfully winning a Congressional seat representing Tennessee in 1823. In 1827, he was elected Governor of Tennessee.

Houston moved to Texas in 1832 and was one of fifty-five delegates to the "Convention of 1833" which met at San Felipe. Texans demanded a reduction in tariffs, lifting of restrictions on immigration to Mexico, funding of schools, the formation of a separate state of Texas within the Republic of Mexico, and a Texas Constitution. The refusal of Mexico to accept these terms led to the war of independence between Texas and Mexico.

He was elected commander-in-chief of the Texas army and took control of the military after the fall of the Alamo. General Santa Anna was defeated at the battle of San Jacinto on April 21, 1836, leading to the formation of the Republic of Texas and the election of Houston as the first President of Texas.

Texas was admitted as a state in 1845 and Houston was elected Senator and later Governor. He was removed from office in March, 1861, due to his failure to support the secession of Texas from the Union. He died July 26, 1863, at the age of seventy.

November 1839 — The Texas Congress met for the first time in Austin, the frontier site selected this flag for the capital of the Republic.

Sam Houston as President of the Republic of Texas signed this document. It is a land grant to Gonsalvo H. G. Woods and is signed in Austin, Texas on February 5, 1842. ("…and the year of the Independence of said Republic, the sixth.")

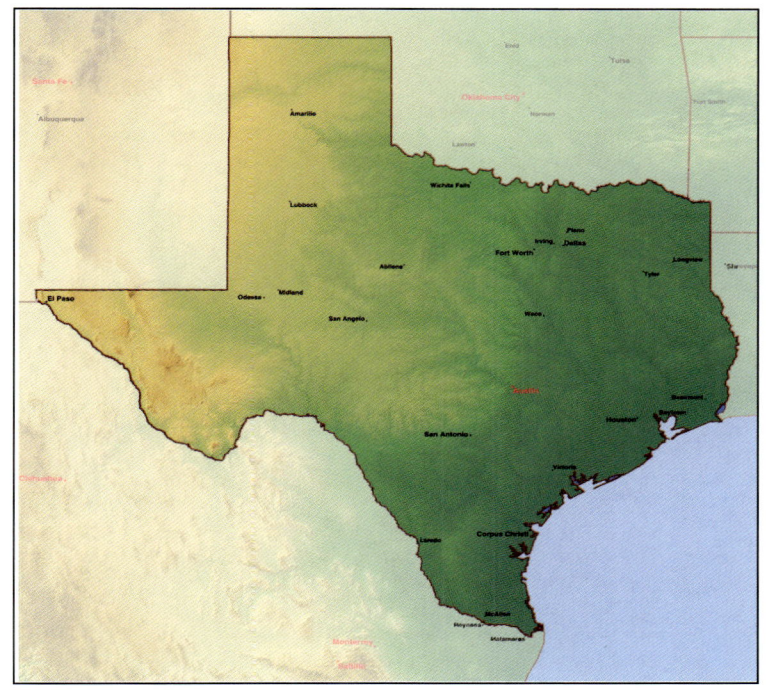

DAVID "DAVY" CROCKETT, 1786-1836
Frontiersman, Politician, Hero

David "Davy" Crockett was born in Greene County, Tennessee. His father was a tavern owner. "Davy" was known for playing hooky from school and did not learn to read or write until the age of eighteen. He was an avid hunter and known as a backwoods bragger.

Crockett was a successful politician. He started in local government and was elected three terms to the United States Congress. In his run for a fourth term he was defeated by a narrow margin.

He moved to Texas to renew his political career and to become a wealthy land agent. He found himself with 189 men in The Battle of the Alamo fighting for the independence of Texas from Mexico. On March 16, 1836 the Mexicans stormed the Alamo and killed all the Texans, including "Davy" Crockett.

David (Davy) Crockett, frontiersman, congressman, and defender of the Alamo

Crockett died in battle of the Alamo on March 16, 1836

Davy Crockett's birthplace in Greene County, Tennessee

Free frank signed by Davy Crockett as a member of Congress from Tennessee, one of two free franks known to exist

FRANKLIN PIERCE, 1804-1869
14th President of the United States

Franklin Pierce was born in Hillsboro, New Hampshire. He studied law under the Governor of New Hampshire and entered politics at the age of twenty-four. He was elected to the New Hampshire House of Representatives and eventually became Speaker of the House. At the age of thirty-three he became the youngest United States Senator from New Hampshire. He was elected fourteenth President of the United States at the age of forty-eight.

Two months before Franklin Pierce took office there was a tragedy in his family. His eleven-year old son died in a train accident. Mrs. Pierce remained the "very picture of melancholy" throughout her husband's presidency. She also suffered from tuberculosis.

After his presidency, the Pierce family went abroad to try to improve her health. She died shortly after their return. Franklin Pierce died six years later in 1869 at the age of sixty-five. He is buried in the Old North Cemetery in Concord, New Hampshire.

Fourteenth President
1853-1857
Married to Jane Means Appleton Pierce

Franklin Pierce's gravesite in Concord, New Hampshire

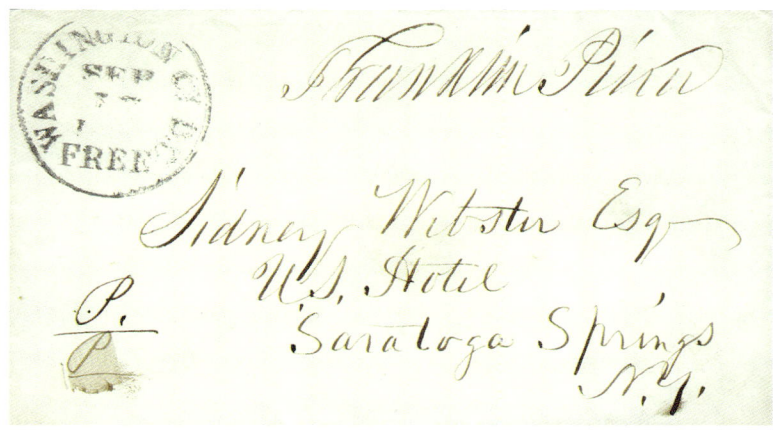

Cover addressed by Franklin Pierce to Sidney Webster Esq. in Saratoga Springs, N.Y.

The Franklin Pierce Homestead is maintained and operated by the Hillsboro Historical Society

Five Dollar Educational Note of 1896

This is the third and final note of the educational series. The engraving depicts electricity as the dominant force of the world. There was a public outcry over the depiction of a bare female breast, and that in part caused the entire series of notes to be prematurely withdrawn from circulation, replaced by the 1899 series of notes.

Reverse features the heads of Ulysses S. Grant and Philip Sheridan, Union Generals during the Civil War.

About the same time that these notes were being released to the public in the United States, Wilhelm Conrad Roentgen had discovered x-rays while experimenting with the Crookes tube at the University of Würzburg in Germany.

Wilhelm Conrad Roentgen - 1845 to 1923

Wilhelm Conrad Roentgen, the scientist who discovered X-Rays on November 8, 1895

Wilhelm Conrad Roentgen, German physicist, discovered x-rays, and won the first Nobel Prize in physics in 1901. Roentgen's discovery of X rays was a momentous advance for physics and medicine.

Roentgen was born in Lennep, Germany, and grew up in the Netherlands. He earned a mechanical engineering degree at the Federal Institute of Technology in Zürich, Switzerland, in 1868 and a Ph.D. degree in physics at the University of Zürich in 1869. Roentgen worked as a laboratory assistant at the University of Würzburg in Germany from 1868 to 1872 and at the University of Strasbourg in Germany from 1872 to 1874. He began teaching physics in 1874, starting at the University of Strasbourg, then moving to the Agricultural Academy in Hohenheim, Germany, in 1875, and back to Strasbourg in 1876. In 1879 he became a professor of physics at the University of Giessen in Germany, where he remained until 1888, when he became professor of physics and director of the Physical Institute at the University of Würzburg. He accepted a position as professor of physics and director of the Physical Science Institute at the University of Munich in 1899 and taught there until his retirement in 1920.

Photograph of Roengten's research laboratory at the Physical Institute of the University of Würzburg, Germany

The first X-Ray ever taken, the hand of Bertha, Roentgen's wife, was produced on November 8, 1895. Her wedding ring is shown on the radiograph.

Roentgen's first public demonstration of X-rays painted by Robert Alan Thom. In the painting, Roentgen speaks to the audience while Kölliker's hand is exposed to the rays.

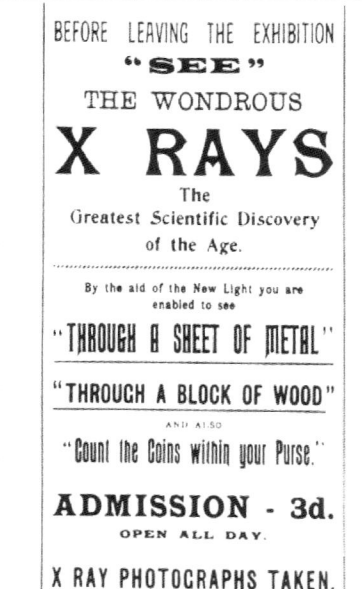

Broadsheet advertisements in 1896 announced a demonstration of X-rays at the Crystal Palace Exhibition in London.

The news of Roentgen's discovery spread quickly. As early as February, 1896, X-rays were being used clinically in the United States.

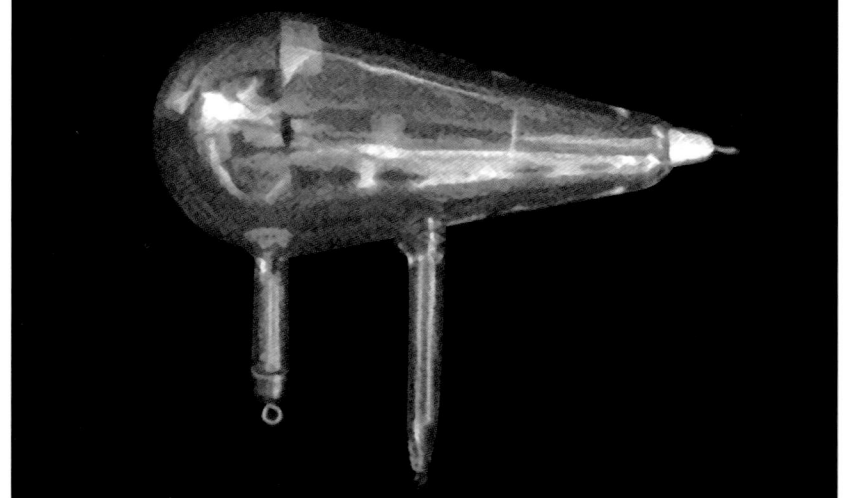

Roentgen concluded that a new type of ray emitted from the tube, passed through the covering and cast shadows of solid objects. The rays passed through most substances, including the soft tissue of the body, but left the bones and most metals visible.

Early fluoroscope (1896). A quick way to test the x-rays being produced was to place the hand between the vacuum tube and the fluorescent screen

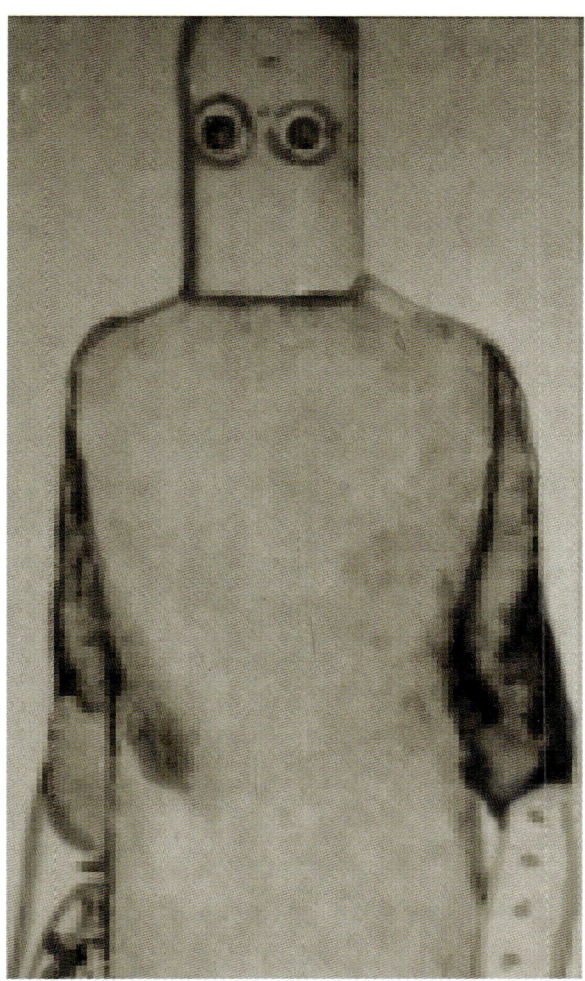

When the dangers of radiation were finally understood by the medical profession, this lead lined hood and coat became the standard uniform for radiologists and technologists in the 1920's.

On November 8, 1895, at the University of Würzburg, Roentgen made an accidental discovery. Roentgen's attention was drawn to a glowing fluorescent screen on a nearby table. Roentgen immediately determined that the fluorescence was caused by invisible rays originating from the partially evacuated glass Hittorf-Crookes tube he was using to study cathode rays (i.e., electrons). Surprisingly, these mysterious rays penetrated the opaque black paper wrapped around the tube. Roentgen had discovered X-rays, a momentous event that instantly revolutionized the field of physics and medicine. However, prior to his first formal correspondence to the University Physical-Medical Society, Roentgen spent two months thoroughly investigating the properties of X-rays. Silvanus Thompson complained that Roentgen left "little for others to do beyond elaborating his work." For his discovery, Roentgen

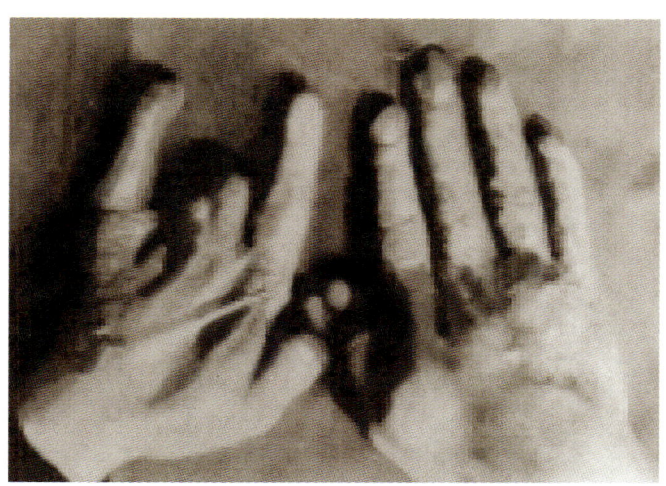

The damage to the hands from chronic radiation exposure. This is what happened to the people who looked at their hands under fluoroscopy.

received the first Nobel Prize in physics in 1901. When later asked what his thoughts were at the moment of his discovery, he replied "I didn't think, I investigated." It was the crowning achievement in a career beset by more than its share of difficulties. As a student in Holland, Roentgen was expelled from the Utrecht Technical School for a prank committed by another student. Even after receiving a doctorate, his lack of a diploma initially prevented him from obtaining a position at the University of Würzburg. He even was accused of having stolen the discovery of X-rays by those who failed to observe them. Nevertheless, Roentgen was a brilliant experimentalist who never sought honors or financial profit for his research. He rejected a title (i.e., von Roentgen) that would have provided entry into the German nobility, and donated the money he received from the Nobel Prize to his University. Roentgen did accept the honorary degree of Doctor of Medicine offered to him by the medical faculty of his own University of Würzburg. However, he refused to take out any patents in order that the world could freely benefit from his work. At the time of his death, Roentgen was nearly bankrupt from the inflation that followed WW I.

Historical information courtesy of the United States Environmental Protection Agency

1899 FIVE DOLLAR SILVER CERTIFICATE
Portrait of Running Antelope (Ta-to-ka-in-han-ka)

This is the first and only time that an American Indian has been featured on U.S. Currency. His authentic headdress had three upright feathers, which projected too high on the first design of the note. A Pawnee war bonnet was borrowed from the Smithsonian, but he refused to pose with it since it belonged to a rival tribe. The bonnet was put on the head of an employee of the Bureau of Engraving and Printing and photographed; then cut out and added to the portrait of Running Antelope. The Indian was a member of the Uncpapa or Hunkpapa Sioux tribe and he is commonly referred to as "Chief Onepapa."

A portrait of Running Antelope shown with the Pawnee war bonnet in this photo doctored by the Bureau of Engraving and Printing

Running Antelope with the authentic headdress of 3 upright feathers

1923 FIVE DOLLAR SILVER CERTIFICATE

This is the last issuance of large size silver five dollar certificates, in production from 1923 to 1927. It is commonly referred to as the "Porthole" note because of the circular design around Lincoln's portrait.

On the right a letter signed by Abraham Lincoln while President appointing George Harrington to serve as Acting Secretary of the Treasury during the temporary absence of Salmon P. Chase. Letters signed by Lincoln are rare with his first name spelled out. Most signatures known to exist are "A. Lincoln."

Photo-the last portrait of Lincoln, taken by Gardner on April 10, 1865

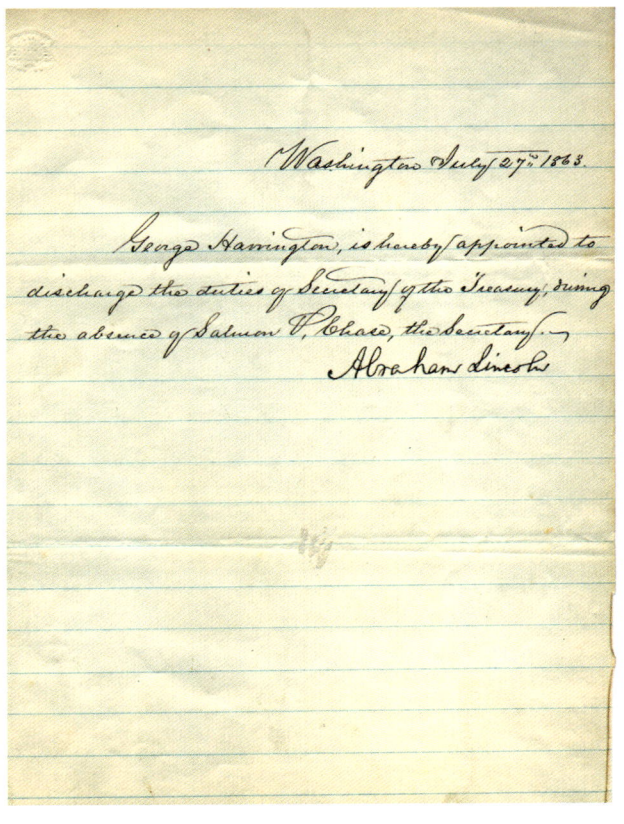

TEN DOLLAR SILVER CERTIFICATES

The first issue of silver certificates were the $10 notes of 1878. Notes printed in that series from $10 to $1000 were countersigned with a third signature; some of them were signed by hand and the rest by machine. The second half of series 1880 and later issues had only two signatures.

Countersigned by J. C. Hopper

Countersigned by A. U. Wyman

Countersigned by T. Hillhouse

These notes feature the portrait of Robert Morris, one of the signers of the Declaration of Independence. He was also Superintendent of Finance from 1781 to 1784.

Large Brown Seal

Large Red Seal

1886 Ten Dollar Silver Certificates

Small Red Seal

Large Red Seal

Thomas Hendricks - U.S. Vice President

Thomas Hendricks was born in Zanesville, Ohio, in 1819. He was elected to Congress in 1851 and became a U.S. Senator from 1863-1869. He was elected Governor of Indiana in 1872; in 1884, he was chosen as Grover Cleveland's running mate. He died nine months after his inauguration as Vice-President. Because of the appearance of the frame around his portrait and his death in public office, this is commonly referred to as the "Tombstone Note."

Thomas Hendricks

Grover Cleveland

Large Brown Seal, Series 1886

Small red, scalloped seal, Series 1886

Small red, scalloped seal, Series 1891

Series 1908, blue seal

The note above is from the last series of large size ten dollar silver certificates, printed in 1908. That was also the year that Henry Ford (1863-1947) first developed the Model T automobile. Over seventeen million were built from 1908 until 1928 when it was replaced by the Model A. Its low price of $850 allowed the average working family to afford an automobile and made the Ford Motor Company the largest automobile producer in the world. The inexpensive standardized design and use of the assembly line resulted in a low production cost.

Henry Ford and his Model T circa 1908
Photo - courtesy Ford Museum

The Ford factory Model T assembly line
Photo - courtesy Ford Museum

Left: Personally autographed photo of Henry Ford from the author's collection. The inscription on the photo reads as follows:

FORD, HENRY (1863-1947), Photograph signed ("Henry Ford"), n.p., n.d. {circa 1921}. 240 x 175 mm. (9-3/8" x 7") including margin beneath signature worn (slightly affecting signature); matted. A half-length, formal portrait of the inventor of the Model T (1913), smiling slightly into the camera, signed in the lower margin.

manufacture automobile tires in 1896. He formed the Firestone Tire and Rubber Company in 1900. His ocean-front winter home was on Miami Beach, currently the site of the Fountainbleau Hotel.

Harvey Firestone - 1868-1930

Autographed photo of Harvey Firestone and Henry Ford in Old Town San Diego, 1912. (Below, lower left) Harvey Firestone (1868-1930) was an American industrialist who began to

Model T Ford   *Model A Ford*

Henry Ford and Harvey Firestone - circa 1912
from the author's collection

A replica of a 1930's garage complete with a 1934 Ford gasoline tanker truck from the Dauer Museum of Classic Cars, Sunrise, Florida

Captain Stephen Decatur
American Naval Commander during the War of 1812

Countersigned by A.U. Wyman, Series 1878

Countersigned by T. Hillhouse, Series 1878

These notes on the following three pages feature the portrait of Captain Stephen Decatur, American Naval Commander during the War of 1812. He was born in Maryland on January 5, 1779 and joined the U.S. Navy in 1798. Decatur became famous by leading a daring entry into the harbor of Tripoli in 1804 to destroy a U.S. ship that had been captured. He escaped and only one sailor under his command was wounded, amid the rapid firing and falling shot of 141 guns. His success won him a promotion to Captain and the Sword of Honor from Congress.

Decatur captured the "Macedonian" during the War of 1812 and was also the commander of a squadron of ships blockaded by the British in New York Harbor. After the war of 1812 ended, he was commander of the naval squadron that rescued captured Americans and Europeans from the pirates operating out of Algiers, Tunis, and Tripoli. The Barbary Powers ended all hostilities and signed a peace treaty in 1815.

Stephen Decatur - 1779-1820
Painting by Robert Hinkley - 1884

Twenty Dollar Silver Certificates

Series 1878 and 1880—Triple Signatures

Countersigned by J. C. Hopper—One of three notes known, Series 1878

Countersigned by T. Hillhouse, Series 1878—The only note that exists outside of the U.S. Government

Large Brown Seal

Small Red Seal

Series 1886-Portrait of Daniel Manning
Secretary of the Treasury during the Cleveland Presidency

Large Red Seal, Allegorical figures representing Agriculture and Industry

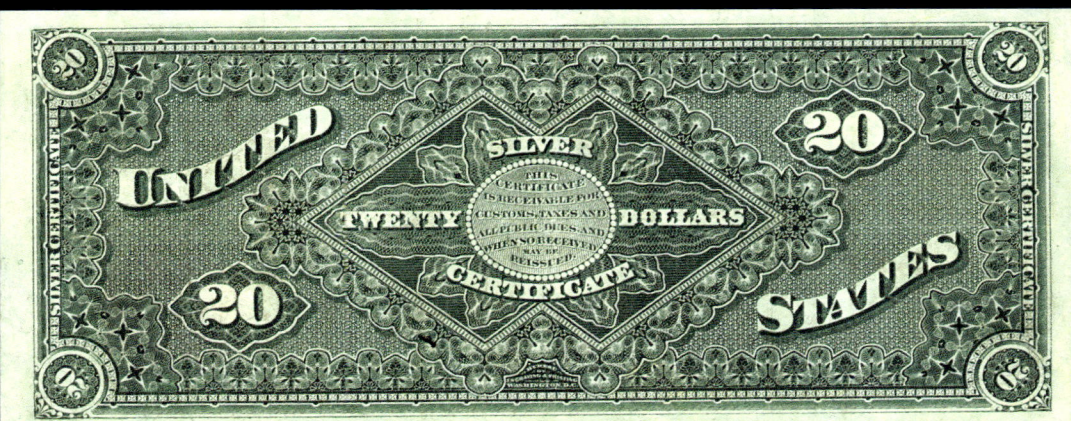

These are commonly referred to as "diamond backs" due to the design on the reverse

Large Brown Seal

Daniel Manning continued

President Grover Cleveland appointed Daniel Manning (1831-1887) Secretary of the Treasury in 1885. The pressing issue of the period was government currency, specifically, how much currency should be in circulation and whether it should be backed by gold or silver.

Conservative Eastern financiers urged a currency backed by gold, while Western speculators, in need of a large, more plentiful money supply to build railroads and businesses on the frontier, wanted a currency backed by readily available silver.

Daniel Manning - 1885–1887
Courtesy – Secretary of the Treasury-office of the Curator

Small Red Seal

Small Red Seal, Series 1891

Manning advocated a compromise currency based on both gold and silver which would be redeemable in gold. He stated that "every dollar note shall be the representative certificate of a coin dollar actually in the Treasury and payable on demand; a currency in which our monetary unit coined in gold ... and its equivalent coined in silver-shall not be suffered to part company." In the international arena, Manning began work on what eventually became the McKinley Tariff of 1890, which significantly lowered customs duties. He resigned from the cabinet in 1887 due to ill health.

During President Grover Cleveland's first term and when the "Series 1886" notes were issued, the Statue of Liberty was dedicated by President Cleveland on October 28, 1886, in New York

Blue Seal

Fifty Dollar Silver Certificates
Portrait of Edward Everett - Secretary of State during the Fillmore Presidency

Series 1878, Triple Signature, Countersigned by A.U. Wyman
This is the finest of three known specimens, one of them is part of the collection of the
Federal Reserve Bank of San Francisco

Edward Everett was born at Dorchester, Massachusetts, in 1794, and was an American statesman and orator. He was called to the ministry of the Unitarian Church in Boston and also taught Greek at Harvard, from which he graduated at the age of seventeen. His service to the United States included ten years as a member of the House of Representatives, Governor of Massachusetts and ambassador to Great Britain. He became Secretary of State during the Fillmore adminstration, after the death of his close friend, Daniel Webster. The purchase of Mount Vernon was made possible by his successful campaign to raise over one hundred thousand dollars.

Edward Everett - 1794-1865
Courtesy – Secretary of the Treasury-office of the Curator

"L" Under Seal, Series 1880

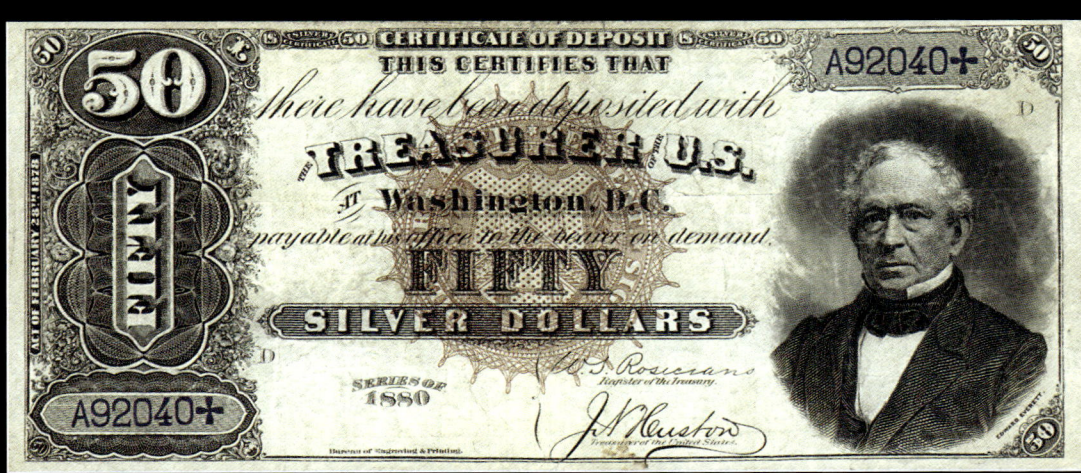

Large Brown Seal

Small Red Seal, Series 1880

Small Red Seal, Series 1891

Edward Everett was appointed Secretary of State in the Fillmore administration on March 3, 1853. Millard Fillmore, the 13th President of the United States in his rise from a log cabin to wealth and the White House, demonstrated that through methodical industry and some competence, an uninspiring man could make the American dream come true.

In 1823 he was admitted to the bar; seven years later he moved his law practice to Buffalo. As an associate of the Whig politician Thurlow Weed, Fillmore held state office and for eight years was a member of the House of Representatives. In 1848, while Comptroller of New York, he was elected Vice President.

Millard Fillmore Thirteenth President 1850-1853
Photo-U.S. Government Archives –The White House

Millard Fillmore addressed this free frank cover to a Reverend, Doctor Sprague of Albany, New York

Blue Seal

As Vice President, Fillmore presided over the Senate in capable fashion. The senators generally bowed to his admonitions, but Seward, who had been elected to the Senate in January 1849, regarded him with unrelenting hostility. A bitter struggle over patronage in New York State developed between the two men. Seward won President Taylor's confidence, and his control over the New York State appointments became virtually complete. Seward and Fillmore also differed over the proper method of dealing with the slavery crisis. Fillmore favored the Compromise of 1850, but Seward opposed it as granting too much to the South and supported Taylor's plan for the prompt admission of California and possibly New Mexico as states.

The compromise made little progress during the spring and early summer of 1850, but on July 9, Taylor died, and Fillmore became president of the United States. His choice of Daniel Webster as Secretary of State and John J. Crittenden as Attorney General indicated his pro-compromise stand, and his message to Congress (Aug. 6, 1850) proposed indemnification of Texas for surrendering its claim to New Mexican territory.

Millard Fillmore built this house in the early 1820's and lived in it with his wife, Abigail from 1826-1830. Today, the house is maintained by the Aurora Historical Society.

ONE HUNDRED DOLLAR SILVER CERTIFICATES
James Monroe, fifth President of the United States, 1817-1825

Series 1878, Triple Signature Countersigned by A. U. Wyman
Extremely rare and one of only two available to collectors. Four examples are permanently impounded in museums and government holdings.

James Monroe
Fifth President of the United States - 1817-1825
Photo-U.S. Government Archives –The White House

James Monroe was born in Westmoreland County, Virginia, in 1758. Monroe attended the College of William and Mary, fought with distinction in the Continental Army, and practiced law in Fredericksburg, Virginia.

On New Year's Day, 1825, at the last of his annual White House receptions, President James Monroe made a pleasing impression upon a Virginia lady who shook his hand:
"He is tall and well formed. His dress plain and in the old style.... His manner was quiet and dignified. From the frank, honest expression of his eye ... I think he well deserves the encomium passed upon him by the great Jefferson, who said, 'Monroe was so honest that if you turned his soul inside out there would not be a spot on it.' "

As a youthful politician, he joined the anti-Federalists in the Virginia Convention which ratified the Constitution, and in 1790, an advocate of Jeffersonian policies, was elected United States Senator. As Minister to France in 1794-1796, he displayed strong sympathies for the French cause; later, with Robert R. Livingston, he helped negotiate the Louisiana Purchase.

His ambition and energy, together with the backing of President Madison, made him the Republican choice for the Presidency in 1816. With little Federalist opposition, he easily won re-election in 1820.

An amended bill for gradually eliminating slavery in Missouri precipitated two years of bitter debate in Congress. The Missouri Compromise bill resolved the struggle, pairing Missouri as a slave state with Maine, a free state, and barring slavery north and west of Missouri forever.

Large "C" Below Seal, Series 1880

James Monroe, fifth President of the United States, 1817-1825

In foreign affairs Monroe proclaimed the fundamental policy that bears his name, responding to the threat that the more conservative governments in Europe might try to aid Spain in winning back her former Latin American colonies. Monroe did not begin formally to recognize the young sister republics until 1822, after ascertaining that Congress would vote appropriations for diplomatic missions. He and Secretary of State John Quincy Adams wished to avoid trouble with Spain until it had ceded the Floridas, as was done in 1821.

"... the American continents," he stated, "by the free and independent condition which they have assumed and maintain, are henceforth not to be considered as subjects for future colonization by any European Power." Some twenty years after Monroe died in 1831, this became known as the Monroe Doctrine.

*The James Monroe Museum and Memorial Library
Fredericksburg, Virginia*
Courtesy of the James Monroe Museum and Memorial Library, Fredericksburg, Virginia.

Series 1880

Series 1891

FREE FRANK OF JAMES MONROE
AS PRESIDENT (1817-1825)

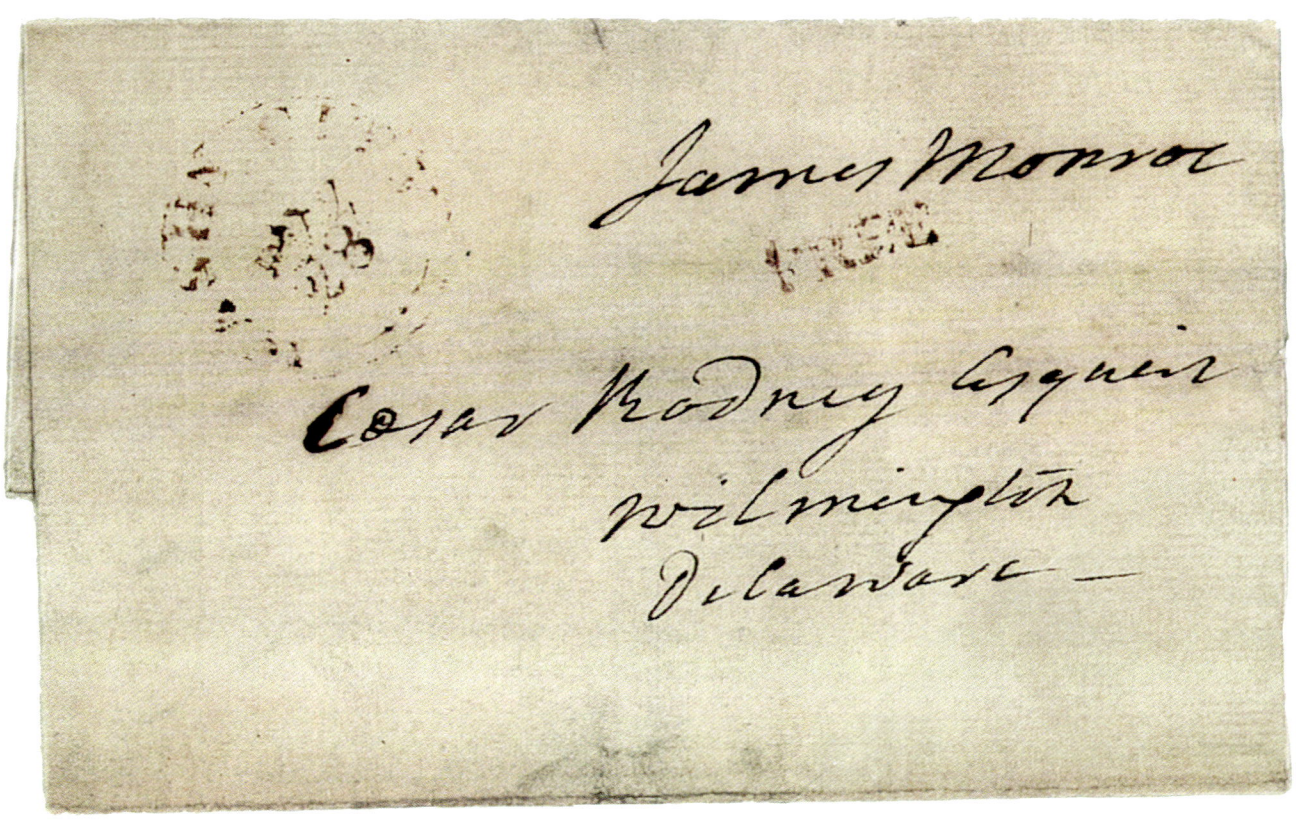

Monroe writes a letter as President in 1820 to Caesar Rodney, one of the signers of the Declaration of Independence

The election of James Monroe to the Presidency in 1816 marked the death of the Federalist Party. The third Republican to win office, Monroe was unopposed in his bid for a second term. Only one electoral vote, cast by a Federalist-turned-Republican, kept Monroe from unanimously winning the election of 1820.

During his administration the major events were the Seminole War, the acquisition of Florida from Spain, the Missouri Compromise, the Cumberland Road Bill veto, and the enunciation of U.S. foreign policy in the form of the Monroe Doctrine. This last act of his administration established the U.S. policy of non-intervention in European political affairs, except when the U.S. sovereignty was threatened.

This cover is entirely addressed in Monroe's own hand and bears his signature in the upper right corner. The style of his handwriting is consistent with other examples known to exist that were written around 1820.

*James Monroe
Fifth President of the United States-1817-1825*

205

FIVE HUNDRED DOLLAR SILVER CERTIFICATE
Charles Sumner, 1811-1874, U.S. Senator from Massachusetts

Series 1880

A total of five notes of this signature combination exist, three of them permanently part of museum collections. Only this and one other example are available to collectors.

Charles Sumner

January 6, 1811 - March 11, 1874

Source: History of Congress, 1867-69, Vol.I

Note the beautiful engravings on the obverse of the five hundred dollar silver certificate of cherubs and other figures imbedded into the numerals "500"

Series 1880

*The above note is the only example of this signature combination available to collectors.
One other note is part of the collection of the Federal Reserve Bank of San Francisco.*

On May 22, 1856, the "world's greatest deliberative body" became a combat zone. In one of the Senate's most dramatic and deeply ominous moments, a House member entered the chamber and beat a senator into unconsciousness.

The inspiration for this clash came three days earlier when Senator Charles Sumner, a Massachusetts antislavery Republican, addressed the Senate on the explosive issue of whether Kansas should be admitted to the Union as a slave or a free state. Sumner directed his fire at two Democratic senators, Stephen Douglas and South Carolina's Andrew Butler. Representative Preston Brooks was Butler's South Carolina kinsman. Armed with a light cane of the type used to discipline unruly dogs, he entered the old chamber after the Senate had adjourned and found Sumner. Moving quickly, Brooks slammed his gold-topped cane onto the unsuspecting Sumner's head.

Bleeding profusely, Sumner was carried to a committee room. Brooks walked coolly out of the chamber without being detained by the shocked onlookers. Overnight, both men became regional heroes.

Sumner, after a slow recovery, returned to the Senate, where he remained for another eighteen years. The nation, suffering from the breakdown of reasoned discourse that this event symbolized, plunged toward the catastrophe of civil war.

Charles Sumner became a leader of the anti-slavery forces in the U.S. Senate. During the Civil War, he introduced the 13th Amendment to the Senate in 1864 and was a strong supporter of emancipation. During Reconstruction, he supported the bill that became the Civil Rights Act of 1875, which was later overturned by the Supreme Court in 1883.

The Caning of Senator Charles Sumner-by Preston Brooks May 22, 1856

One Thousand Dollar Silver Certificate-Series 1880
William L. Marcy, 1786-1857

Series 1880

This is one of only two notes available to collectors. Three other examples are permanently part of the collections in the Smithsonian and Federal Reserve Banks of Chicago and San Francisco.

In the second decade of the nineteenth century, William L. Marcy joined Martin Van Buren, Benjamin F. Butler, Samuel J. Tilden, and other New York politicians in a group known as the "Holy Alliance" or the "Albany Regency." In 1829, Governor Van Buren appointed Marcy to the New York State Supreme Court, a post he left in 1831 for the United States Senate. Marcy returned to New York as Governor in 1833, serving three terms. After Van Buren became President in 1840, Marcy became a familiar figure in Washington, serving as Secretary of War under James K. Polk and Secretary of State under Franklin Pierce.

William L. Marcy - 1786 - 1857
Matthew Brady photograph

Another Example of Allegorical Figures
Contributing to the Design - From the $1,000 Silver Certificate

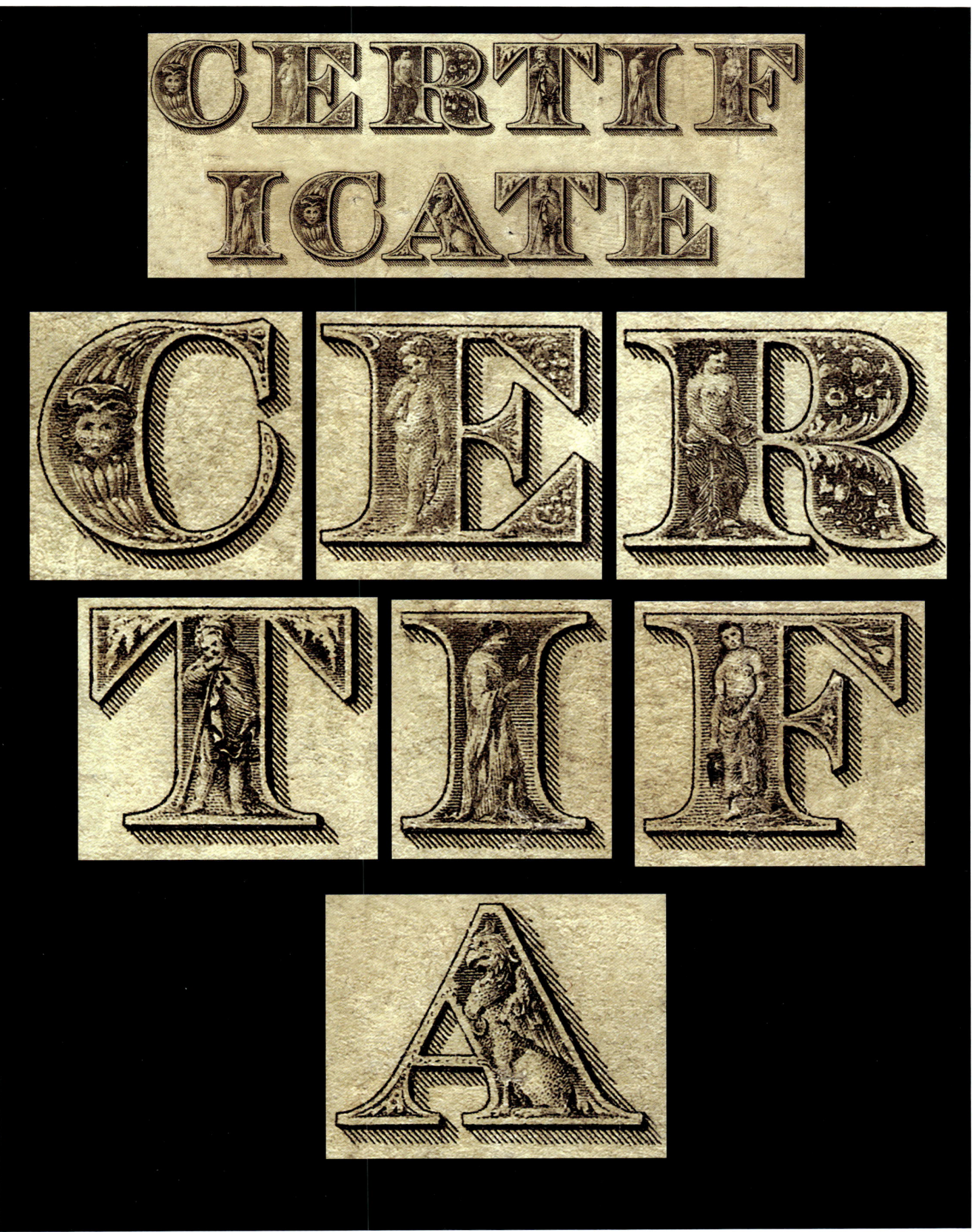

The "Marcy Note" 1891 One Thousand Dollar Silver Certificate - Part of The Triple Crown of American Currency

This is one of three notes featured on the cover, which together represent the most sought after, and desirable banknotes in existence. This is unique in private hands and was part of the Amon Carter Collection. Another example is permanently impounded in the Smithsonian, forever unavailable to collectors.

Chapter V

TREASURY OR COIN NOTES

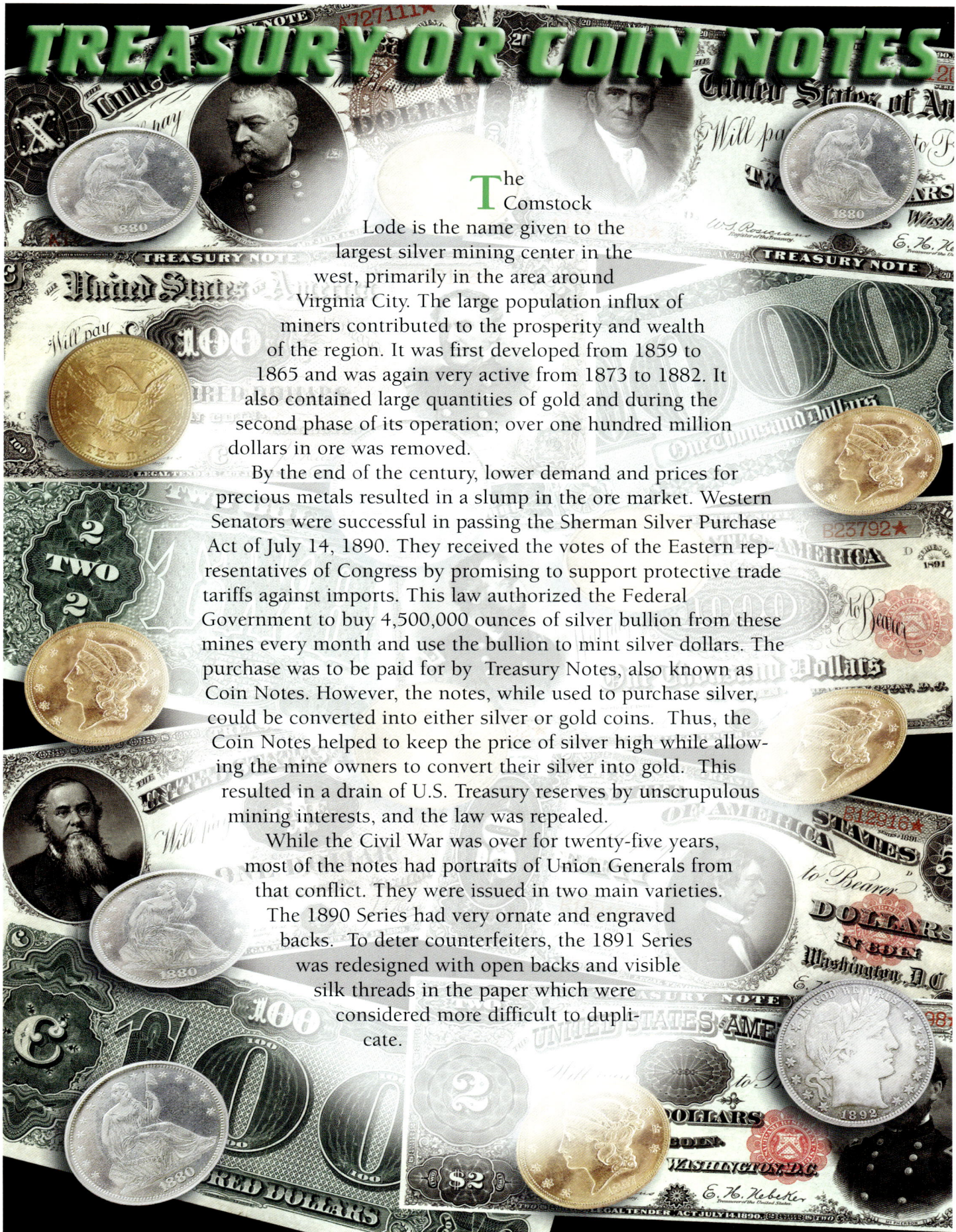

The Comstock Lode is the name given to the largest silver mining center in the west, primarily in the area around Virginia City. The large population influx of miners contributed to the prosperity and wealth of the region. It was first developed from 1859 to 1865 and was again very active from 1873 to 1882. It also contained large quantities of gold and during the second phase of its operation; over one hundred million dollars in ore was removed.

By the end of the century, lower demand and prices for precious metals resulted in a slump in the ore market. Western Senators were successful in passing the Sherman Silver Purchase Act of July 14, 1890. They received the votes of the Eastern representatives of Congress by promising to support protective trade tariffs against imports. This law authorized the Federal Government to buy 4,500,000 ounces of silver bullion from these mines every month and use the bullion to mint silver dollars. The purchase was to be paid for by Treasury Notes, also known as Coin Notes. However, the notes, while used to purchase silver, could be converted into either silver or gold coins. Thus, the Coin Notes helped to keep the price of silver high while allowing the mine owners to convert their silver into gold. This resulted in a drain of U.S. Treasury reserves by unscrupulous mining interests, and the law was repealed.

While the Civil War was over for twenty-five years, most of the notes had portraits of Union Generals from that conflict. They were issued in two main varieties. The 1890 Series had very ornate and engraved backs. To deter counterfeiters, the 1891 Series was redesigned with open backs and visible silk threads in the paper which were considered more difficult to duplicate.

The Comstock silver lode found near Virginia City

The notes by definition were a short-lived series, and the presence of circulating silver certificates at the same time lessened their need. They are highly desired by collectors today and are considered rare in denominations of $50 and above.

Edwin M. Stanton is featured on the $1 note and was the Secretary of War under Presidents Lincoln and Johnson. President James Buchanan appointed Stanton Attorney General in 1860, and Lincoln made him Secretary of War two years later.

Prospectors working the Comstock Lode near old Virginia City

With the advent of the steam locomotives, moving heavy loads became easier for the mining companies and very profitable for the railroads

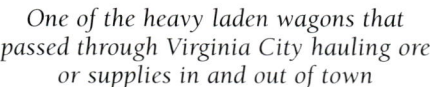

Looking over Virginia City shows a bustling mining town before many of the buildings disappeared - circa 1890

One of the heavy laden wagons that passed through Virginia City hauling ore or supplies in and out of town

Edwin M. Stanton
Secretary of War under Presidents Lincoln and Johnson

    Stanton was not popular in the war office and Lincoln did not like him very well. Stanton was outspoken and made many enemies. But he was an able manager and gained a reputation for efficiency.

    When Andrew Johnson became President, he and Stanton clashed repeatedly over the treatment of the South. Stanton cooperated with Johnson's enemies in congress, and when Johnson removed Stanton from office, the House of Representatives impeached the President. Johnson was acquitted by one vote and Stanton left office in May, 1868. The next year, President Ulysses S. Grant appointed Stanton to the Supreme Court, but Stanton died four days later.

Andrew Johnson as President (1865-1869)

George T. Brown, Sergeant-at-Arms of the Senate serving the sommons on President Johnson - Harper's Weekly August 24, 1867

The Congress controlled by the Republicans opposed Lincoln's plan of reconstruction for three main reasons: the readmission of Southern representatives would shift the balance of power to the Democrats; the Lincoln policy promoted lenient and humane treatment of citizens of the South, who the Republicans felt should be punished; and the newly organized Southern states did not give political rights to the black population.

During his first two years as President, Johnson and his opponents waged a bitter campaign over reconstruction. The feud resulted in numerous vetoes and congressional overrides, culminating in the Tenure of Office Act passed by Congress in 1867 to weaken the President's executive powers.

Finally, in 1868, Congress proceeded with impeachment charges against Johnson, based largely on his disregard of the Tenure of Office Act by discharging Secretary of War Edwin M. Stanton on February 21, 1868.

The Tenure of Office Act was repealed in 1887. In 1926, the Supreme Court ruled, in Myers vs. U.S., that it was unconstitutional even though it was repealed forty years earlier. That case dealt with the ability of Congress to limit the power of the President to remove a Postmaster.

Free Frank Signed by Johnson as President

Seventeenth President
1865-1869
Married to Eliza McCardle Johnson

Born in Raleigh, North Carolina, in 1808, Johnson grew up in poverty. He was apprenticed to a tailor but ran away. As a boy he opened a tailor shop in Greeneville, Tennessee, married Eliza McCardle, and participated in debates at the local academy. After Lincoln's death, President Johnson proceeded to reconstruct the former Confederate States while Congress was not in session in 1865. He pardoned all who would take an oath of allegiance, but he required leaders and men of wealth to obtain special Presidential pardons.

Photo-Library of Congress

Andrew Johnson as President signed this cover on June 10, 1867. It was addressed to Henry Stanbery, Attorney General in Johnson's Cabinet.

Andrew Johnson, a Southern Democrat, was thrust into the Presidency by the murder of Abraham Lincoln and faced the challenging task of reuniting the country and dealing with reconstruction. He had protested his colleagues' decision to secede and was faced with partisanship politics being waged by the Northern Republican Congress.

The Congress felt Johnson was a representation of the South Democrats they opposed and would not tolerate his objective of implementing Lincoln's plan for restoration of the South after the Civil War. Henry Stanbery, as Attorney General, played a major role in Johnson's defense before his trial in the Senate.

The Impeachment Trial of President Andrew Johnson

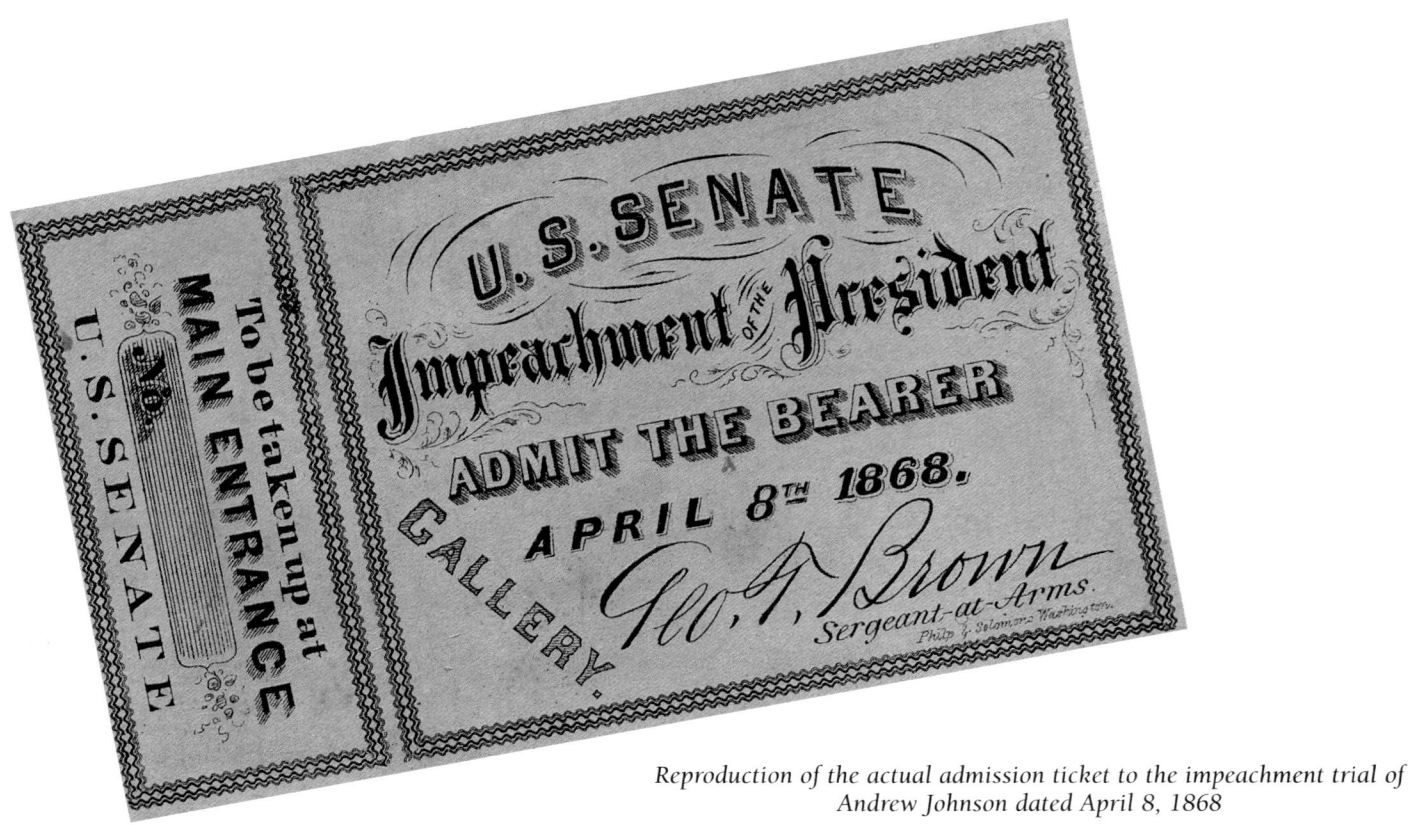

Reproduction of the actual admission ticket to the impeachment trial of Andrew Johnson dated April 8, 1868

President Andrew Johnson's impeachment trial ran from March 13 to May 26, 1868. Johnson did not appear at the trial.

General James McPherson

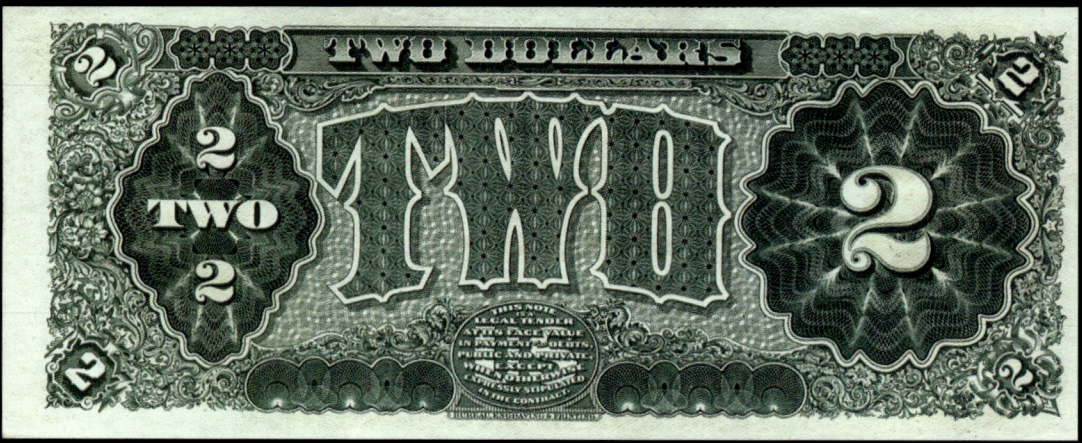

The battle of Vicksburg

General James McPherson was a Union Army general and hero during the battle of Vicksburg. The Vicksburg campaign was waged from March 29 to July 4, 1863. It included battles in west-central Mississippi at Port Gibson, Raymond, Jackson, Champion Hill, Big Black River and 47 days of Union siege operations against Confederate forces defending the City of Vicksburg. Located high on the bluffs, Vicksburg was a fortress guarding the Mississippi River. It was known as "The Gibraltar of the Confederacy." Its surrender on July 4, 1863, coupled with the fall of Port Hudson, Louisiana, divided the South, and gave the North undisputed control of the Mississippi River.

At the time of the Civil War, the Mississippi River was the single most important economic feature of the continent-the very lifeblood of America. Upon the secession of the southern states, Confederate forces closed the river to navigation, which threatened to strangle northern commercial interests. President

Abraham Lincoln told his civil and military leaders, "See what a lot of land these fellows hold, of which Vicksburg is the key! The war can never be brought to a close until that key is in our pocket....We can take all the northern ports of the Confederacy, and they can defy us from Vicksburg."

In the spring of 1863, Major General Ulysses S. Grant launched his Union Army of Tennessee on a campaign to pocket Vicksburg and provide Mr. Lincoln with the key to victory. Grant realized that Vicksburg could not be taken by storm and decided to lay siege to the city. Slowly, his army established a line of works around the beleaguered city and cut Vicksburg off from supply and communications with the outside world.

Undaunted by his failure on the 19th and realizing that he had been too hasty, Grant made a more thorough reconnaissance, then he ordered another assault. Early on the morning of May 22, Union artillery opened fire and for four hours bombarded the city's defenses. At 10:00 the guns fell silent and Union infantry was thrown forward along a three-mile front. Sherman attacked once again down the Graveyard Road, McPherson in the center along the Jackson Road, and McClernand on the south along the Baldwin Ferry Road and astride the Southern Railroad of Mississippi.

General McPherson along the Jackson road attacking Confederate positions

The U.S. Flag is raised over the Courthouse in Vicksburg after the surrender. At 10 a.m., on July 4, white flags were again displayed from the Confederate works and the brave men in gray marched out of their entrenchment.

This section of the Rodney Road has changed little since the days of the Civil War. Imagine if you will, soldiers marching down this road tightly packed in columns of four.

General George H. Thomas

The Battle of Chickamauga

General George H. Thomas

The Battle of Chickamauga was fought over three days in September 1863. The Union General William Rosecrans consolidated his forces scattered in Tennessee and Georgia and forced the Confederate General Braxton Bragg's army out of Chattanooga. Bragg was determined to reoccupy Chattanooga and decided to meet a part of Rosecran's army, defeat them, and then move back into the city. General Bragg headed north, intending to meet and beat the Union forces.

On the second day, his cavalry and infantry fought against the Union, armed with Spencer repeating rifles. Fighting began in earnest on the morning of the third day, and Bragg's men destroyed many units but did not break the Union line. The scene of the battle was one neither General Bragg's nor General Rosecrans wanted to fight. The battlefield was a very dense forest with few open fields in northwestern Georgia. The next day, General George H. Thomas took over command of Union troops from General Rosecrans and began consolidating forces on Horseshoe Ridge and Snodgrass Hill. He found his troops still on the field with less than one half of his Army. He formed his troops closely and was successful in resisting the Confederate troops for over six hours. General Thomas placed himself against a rock and refused to be driven from the field. There was no finer victory than General George H. Thomas at the Battle of Chickamauga. This was when General Thomas became known as "The Rock of Chickamauga."

Between 1890 and 1899 the Congress of the United States authorized the establishment of the first four military parks: Chickamauga and Chattanooga, Shiloh, Gettysburg, and Vicksburg. The first and largest of these, and the one upon which the establishment and development of most other national military and historical parks was based, was Chickamauga and Chattanooga.

Dr. Richard J. Gatling

Above: Dr. Richard J Gatling invented one of the first successful machine guns.

Dr. Richard Jordan Gatling, a medical doctor with numerous patents in farm equipment to his credit, devised the famous Model 1862 "Revolving Battery Gun," now simply referred to as the Gatling gun. Although Dr. Gatling was not the first person to manufacture a multi-fire weapon, he was the first to produce a reliable, rapid fire, "machine gun." The rest, as they say, is history.

The Gatling gun was a hand-crank-operated weapon, comprised of six barrels revolving around a central shaft. The original gun was actually designed to fire the standard military issue, 58 caliber paper cartridge of the day. The paper cartridge was placed inside a steel or brass chamber with percussion nipple on the back end, just like muzzle loading rifles and pistols of the time. The cartridges were gravity-fed through a hopper mounted on the top of the gun. Six cam-operated bolts alternately wedged, fired, and dropped the bullets, which were contained in steel chambers. Gatling used the six barrels to partially cool the gun during firing. Since the gun was capable of firing six hundred rounds a minute, each barrel fired one hundred rounds per minute.

Major General Benjamin F. Butler purchased twelve, model 1862, Gatling guns for $1,000 each, in 1863 and employed them successfully at the battle of Petersburg.

As an interesting side note, what we see in movies today and usually displayed or shot is not the original model 1862. Most probably, it is a model 1873 or a later version.

In January of 1865, Gatling proposed his improved model 1865 gun to the United States Government, which was subsequently tested by the Ordnance Department. This model was adopted officially in 1866. After receiving government approval, Gatling began to sell his guns throughout the world, where they achieved world-wide fame. Twenty-five countries, twenty-nine calibers, and fifty-five years later, the hand-crank Gatling gun was finally retired from United States military service, just prior to the U.S. entry into World War I.

The Gatling gun was the first quick-firing machine gun developed in the United States. Patented in 1862, it was used only to a limited extent during the Civil War. Improved models became standard equipment for the U.S. Army and Navy during the Spanish American War.

The Gatling Gun

 Even then, it remained deployed into the middle 1920's stateside. Tucked away in storage for over thirty years, an original model 1883 in 45-70 caliber, was able to successfully fire 5,600 rounds per minute by hooking it up to an electric motor. This ultimately became the forerunner of today's Vulcan system capable of firing 6,000 rounds per minute of 20mm cannon shells.

All in all, the 1862 Gatling gun is one of the greatest design achievements in military armament ever created, ranking up with breech loading weapons and metallic cartridges in significance to modern warfare.

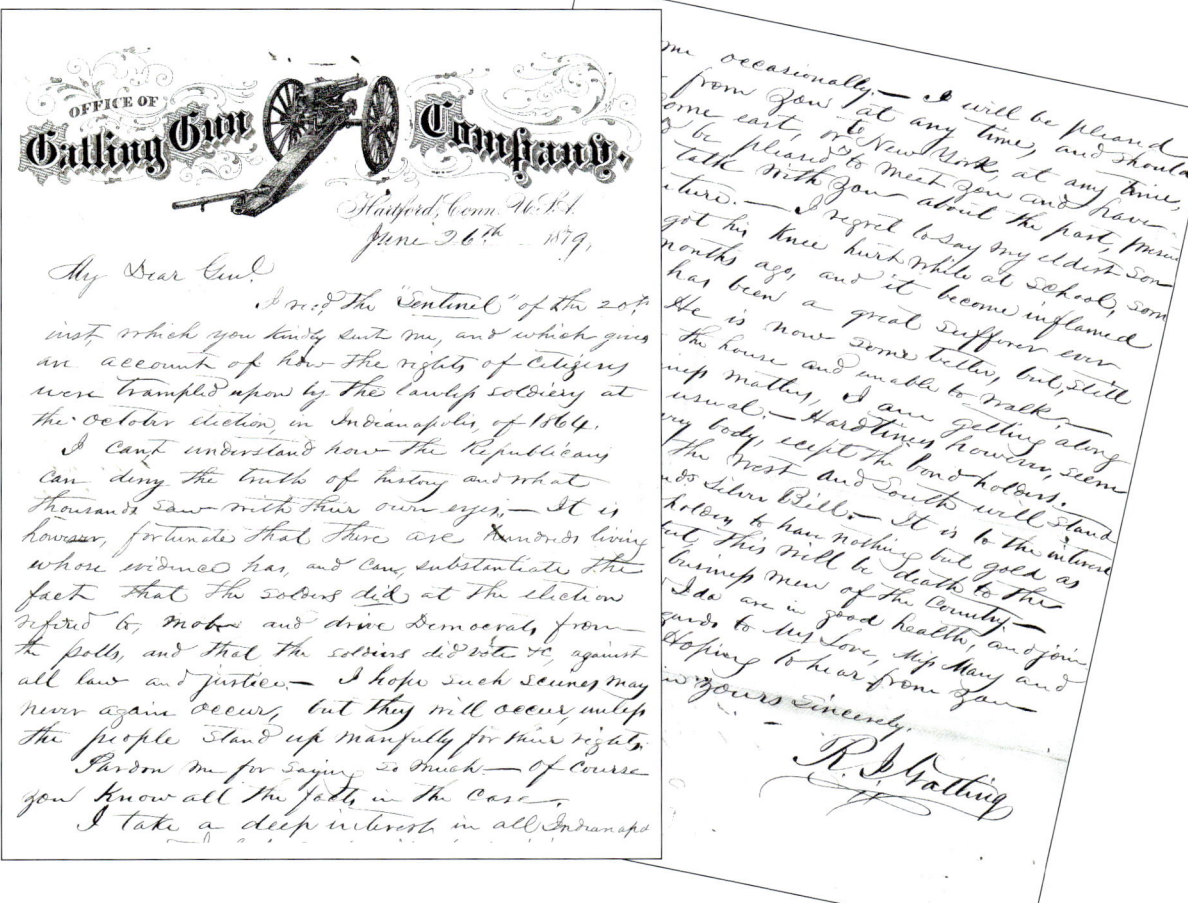

Right: Letter written by Gatling in June 1879 to his friend in Indianapolis discussing the election of 1864.

Close-up of Dr. Gatling's actual signature

The Gatling gun, one of the earliest forms of functional machines guns, was used during the Spanish American War, both on land and at sea. The use of the Gatling gun during the War is most well-known from its use in the assault on San Juan Hill.

General George Armstrong Custer

One of the most chronicled events in the history of the American West was the famous Battle of the Little Big Horn, otherwise known as Custer's Last Stand.

Traveling up Rosebud Creek at noon, General Custer split his command into three battalions. Major Reno, in command of the first group, was directed to attack the southern most end of the village. Captain Benteen, in command of the second group, was directed to explore the area in a southwesterly direction, and to "pitch into anything that he might find." Captain McDougall was assigned to the next group to guard the pack train while Custer took the remaining troops, to make a frontal attack on the encampment.

It was hot that day, the temperature hovering near 100 degrees; the thin blue line of cavalry troops moved slowly in a northwesterly direction. They were confident being led by the golden haired "Boy General," the man who never sounded a retreat, and their victory was certain. With the sun past noon, the Seventh Cavalry and General George Armstrong Custer moved forward to their appointment with glory, and death. The intent of the plan was to prevent the escape of the Indians by having the slower-moving infantry and Custer's fast-riding cavalry reach the Little Big Horn around the same time. General Alfred H. Terry had offered to send the Gatling gun detachment, but Custer refused, believing it would slow him down. Within a short period of time, Custer and his troops were annihilated by the full might of an estimated 5,000 Lakota Sioux and Cheyenne Indians, who were led by Chief Sitting Bull and Chief Crazy Horse.

Four days later, the other two battalions of the regiment were rescued by supporting cavalry troops under the command of Generals Terry and Gibbon.

In search for survivors of Custer's forces, not one of the over two hundred troopers under Custer's command was found alive. Five members of the Custer family were killed at the "Battle of the Little Big Horn;" General George A. Custer, his brother Captain Tom Custer, brother-in-law Captain James Calhoun, younger brother Boston, and nephew Autie Reed.

Note signed by Custer sent to an unidentified senior officer. It reads:
"Head Quarters Cavalry February 16, 1865
Respectfully forwarded attention invited to the endorsement of Brig. Gen Gibbs Commanding 1st Cavalry Div. which is recommended."
G.A. Custer
Brevat Major General Commanding

Crazy Horse boasted that he would never allow the white man's camera to "steal his shadow." No fully authenticated image of him exists, although several photographs have been published purporting to be him. It bears a fascinating resemblance to written descriptions of Crazy Horse. Is this Crazy Horse? You decide.

Custer, as he appeared at the Battle of Little Big Horn on June 25, 1876, was described by the last white people to see him alive as "prematurely bald at age thirty-six." His famous blond locks had been cropped short. He wore buckskin breeches and had his buckskin coat strapped to his saddle. His shirt was a version of a "fireman's shirt" made of lightweight wool and trimmed on the collar and cuffs with white tape. Crossed cavalry sabers with a seven above were embroidered in silver on his collar; and the shirt had mother-of-

Custer (3rd from left) his officers and their wives pose before the beginning of the campaign. Many would not return.

General Terry had offered to send the Gatling gun detachment, but Custer refused, believing it would slow him down. What a different history might have been written if he had brought those Gatling guns to the Little Bighorn.

pearl buttons. Custer wore his trademark red silk cravat, which was also worn by most of the officers and men in imitation of their commander. At his waist, he wore a canvas cartridge belt, containing rounds for his Remington Sporting rifle, a knife in a beaded scabbard, and a holstered Webley's Royal Irish Constabulary revolver with white handles and a lanyard ring. A binocular case hung from a strap around his neck. Also with him was the buckskin coat he wore at the Battle of the Washita and his personal campaign banner. Major General George Armstrong Custer was one of the more colorful characters in U.S. military history.

Biography: George Armstrong Custer, Lieutenant Colonel. Born on December 5, 1839, in New Rumley, Ohio, the son of Emanuel Henry (born December 10, 1806 – died November 17, 1892), and Maria Ward Kirkpatrick Custer (born May 31, 1807 – died January 13, 1882). He attended the Military Academy from July 1, 1857 to June 24, 1861, graduating 34 in his class of 34 as the 1966th academy graduate.

The battlefield of the Little Big Horn as it appears today

General Philip H. Sheridan

John and Mary Sheridan, Philip Henry Sheridan's parents, came to America in 1830 at the urging of John's uncle, Thomas Gainor, living in Albany, New York. John and Mary were second cousins from County Caven, Ireland. Before leaving Ireland the couple had two children, Patrick H. and Rosa. Rosa died aboard ship and was buried at sea. Philip Henry was born March 6, 1831. His birthplace is still a mystery. There are no records available in New York, Boston, Massachusetts (where their ship landed), or Ohio. Philip at various times claimed all three places. He arrived with his parents in Somerset, Ohio as a babe-in-arms and spent his childhood there. The Sheridan family soon increased in size by the births of Mary, Michael, and John L. Sheridan. Sheridan attended school in Ohio until the age of fourteen, at which time he went to work for various businessmen, notably Fink and Dittoe.

Right: Civil War photo of General Sheridan
Library of Congress

General Philip H. Sheridan
(continued)

In 1848 Congressman Thomas Ritchie, who knew both Philip Sheridan and his father, obtained an appointment to West Point for Sheridan. In 1851, his third year at West Point, he was suspended for a year for fighting with a fellow cadet. Sheridan graduated thirty-fourth in a class of fifty-two in July 1853, and was assigned to the First Infantry at Fort Duncan, Texas, as a Second Lieutenant. In 1855 he was transferred to the fourth Infantry in the Pacific Northwest. April 1856, he was assigned to duty at the Grand Ronde Indian Reservation in Yamhill County, Oregon, and was promoted to First Lieutenant.

After the start of the Civil War, April 4, 1861 Sheridan was promoted to Captain and in September of 1861, was called east to St. Louis for duty with the Union Armies of the West, the first step in his journey to greatness. He was assigned to supply under General Hallick but eventually convinced him he would be of better service in the field. Sheridan was reassigned to General Curtis who was preparing to drive the Confederates out of southern Missouri. At this point, Sheridan later met up with General William T. Sherman, and was recommended by Sherman to be given command of one of Ohio's volunteer regiments, but was turned down. Later, General Gordon Granger requested Sheridan be given command of the 2nd Michigan Cavalry vacated by Granger's promotion. Sheridan was accepted and jumped from Captain to Colonel overnight.

Two months later Sheridan was stationed at a forward post near Booneville, Mississippi. The Confederates pressed forward with 5,000 to 6,000 troopers to wipe out Sheridan's annoying outpost of only 827 men. Sheridan was equipped with repeating rifles and pistols which gave him some advantage, but in repelling the enemy he proved his military genius. By loading troops on a train and discharging them noisily at Booneville, silently marching them back up track and reloading and discharging them time and again, he deceived Confederate General Chalmers into thinking he was being reinforced.

Sheridan was promoted to Captain just after the start of the Civil War

Civil War photo from the Matthew Brady Collection showing General Sheridan in his camp during the Battle of Chattanooga

Above: This statue is considered one of the most dramatic in D.C. and was designed by Borglum, who was more famous for conceiving of and executing the presidential memorials at Mount Rushmore.

Sheridan's assignment under General Rosecrans at Murfreesboro on Stones River south of Nashville, Tennessee played an important part in holding back the Confederates under General Bragg. In later years Grant stated that in this battle, Sheridan saved Rosecran's army. He should have also included the help he gave to General George H. Thomas at the Battle of Chickamauga. It was principally for Sheridan's services at Stones River that Thomas was promoted in April, 1863 to Major General.

During the battles of Chickamauga, Missionary Ridge, and Lookout Mountain, near Chattanooga, Tennessee, Sheridan fought with Generals Grant and Sherman. Sheridan's division was one of the main forces that swept to the top of Missionary Ridge, and with his division he pursued the enemy and captured equipment and prisoners.

On March 12, 1864 General Grant was appointed General-in-Chief of the Union Armies; he soon called Sheridan to join him in Washington. Here Sheridan was appointed Chief of Cavalry, Army of the Potomac. As aides-de-camp, Sheridan chose his brother Michael and Lieutenant T. Moore; Captain James W. Forsyth, an old friend, was a staff officer. Sheridan's main area of operation was the Shenandoah Valley. Here he contested General Early's Confederate troops, destroyed crops which were the breadbasket of the Confederate army, defeated and killed General J.E.B. Stuart (famous cavalry leader of the south) and eventually, in the battle of Cedar Creek, drove Early out of the valley. As the war neared its end, Sheridan was the leader in forcing General Lee out of his Petersburg, Virginia defenses and eventually cutting off his retreat at Appomattox Court House.

Signed portrait from the Library of Congress

Left to right: Wesley Merritt, David McM. Gregg, Sheridan, Henry E. Davies (standing), James H. Wilson, and Alfred Torbert.

At the end of the war Sheridan was sent to Texas to maintain peace with Mexico. Napoleon III had installed Maximilian and Carlota to the throne of Mexico. By maneuvering and threats he was able to instill peace and force France to withdraw their claims. After serving some time in New Orleans, Louisiana, as head of Reconstruction, he was relieved after much controversy and was ordered to take command of the Department of the Missouri in September 1867. Here he was ordered to subdue the Indians and place them on reservations. Several treaties were drawn up, few of which were kept due to the white man's encroachment on the Indian reservations.

In 1869, after Grant became president, General Sherman became General of the Army, and Sheridan was appointed lieutenant general with his headquarters in Chicago. In this capacity Sheridan traveled throughout the west, and with this knowledge he was later instrumental in having Yellowstone declared a national park. He also went to Europe as an observer with Prussia in the French and Prussian War. Returning to Chicago he presided over the Great Chicago Fire of October 7th-8th 1871. He brought troops into the city to stop looters and directed fire fighting and reconstruction.

On June 3, 1875, Sheridan married Miss Irene Rucker, the youngest daughter of General Daniel H. Rucker. She was twenty-two years younger than Sheridan. The couple had four children – Mary, Irene and Louise (twins), and Philip Henry Jr. None of the girls married. Philip Jr. married and had a son, Philip II. Lieutenant General Sheridan assumed the nation's highest military office at the comparative youthful age of fifty-two. In 1887 he had built a summer cottage in Nonquit, Massachusetts overlooking Martha's Vineyard. The next year he suffered a series of heart attacks. Congress revived the grade of full General and Sheridan was given his fourth star by President Grover Cleveland. He was the fourth man in United States history to be so honored. (Washington, Grant, Sherman, and Sheridan) At 10:30 p.m., Sunday, August 5, 1888, Philip Henry Sheridan passed away at Nonquit, Massachusetts. He lay in state at St. Matthew's Church in Washington, D.C., and was laid to rest in Arlington National Cemetery on August 11th. General Sheridan's father and mother, brothers Patrick and John, and sister Mary are buried in Holy Trinity Cemetery in Somerset, Ohio. Brother Michael, who was Sheridan's aide during the Civil War, is also buried in Arlington National Cemetery.

The Sheridan Gate At Arlington National Cemetery

Sheridan's tombstone at Arlington National Cemetery

Chief Justice John Marshall

The Marshalls had long before decided that John was to be a lawyer. The last time of formal education came in 1780 during a six week stay at William and Mary College where he attended the law lectures of George Wythe. James Madison was President of the college at that time, and it has been reported that Marshall took a course in philosophy from him. When Cornwallis occupied Williamsburg in June of 1781, he made the president's house his headquarters.

John Marshall joined the Culpeper Minute Men and was chosen Lieutenant. Both he and his father were at a number of the battles well-known even today, such as Great Bridge (also called "the little Bunker Hill" because of the tremendous loss of British lives and no loss for the Americans), Brandywine, Germantown (the last two serious defeats for the Americans), Monmouth, and ending, for John, with a dashing episode as a member of a detail from the Light Infantry of Virginia under the command of Major Henry Lee.

Head of the Supreme Court - 1801-1835

President Adams asked him to become an Associate Justice of the Supreme Court but Marshall refused. In 1799 he ran for a seat in the House of Representatives and won. His close alliance with President Adams continued and in 1800 Adams appointed him Secretary of State. In January, 1801, after loosing his re-election bid to Jefferson, Adams appointed Marshall Chief Justice of the United States, making him the fourth one. Marshall continued as Secretary of State for the remaining two months of Adam's term.

The federal courts were under a sustained and determined attack by President Jefferson and the Republican Party, who wished to bring the courts under the domination of the executive branch. Marshall's opinion in Marbury v. Madison showed his intellectual and moral force and foreshadowed the views he would express in later decisions. Throughout his tenure with the court, he was deeply concerned with preserving private property rights, the enhancement of the prestige and power of the court, and the establishment of a strong central federal power.

The force and persuasiveness of Marshall's constitutional interpretations became most apparent after 1811. From that time until his death in 1835, most future Chief Justices found themselves in agreement with his important decisions.

John Marshall, fourth Chief Justice of the United States, established the Supreme Court's power to review legislative acts

William H. Seward
Secretary of State - 1860-1869

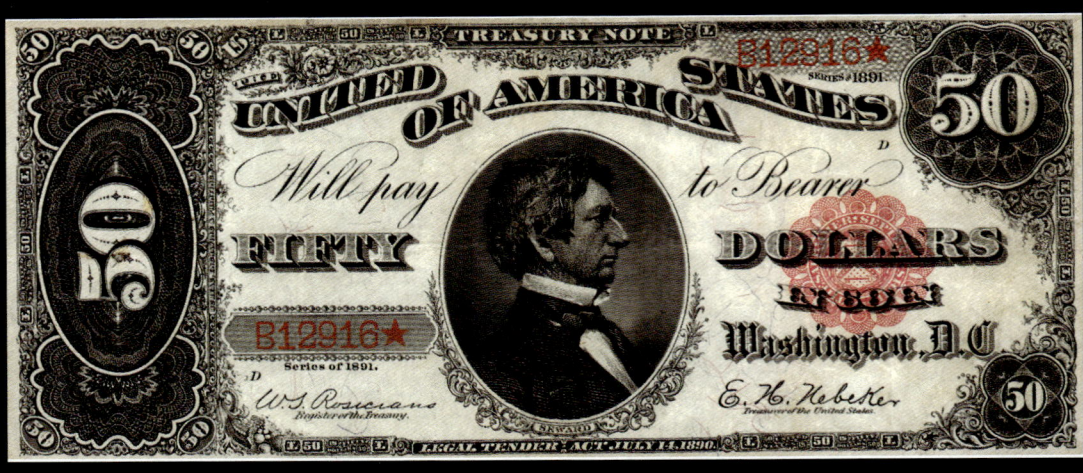

William H. Seward Famous Brady photo

Born in New York State in 1801, Seward attended local schools before entering Union College at the age of fifteen. After graduating from Union in 1820, he read law and was admitted to the bar in 1823. Seward naturally gravitated into politics. He served as state senator and, in 1838, won his first term as Governor. He was re-elected in 1840. However, he stirred controversy and antagonized some anti-foreign and anti-Catholic elements of the Whig party when he supported the demands of Catholics to have their children taught in public schools by teachers speaking the same language and sharing the same faith. His humanitarianism was also evident in his increasing interest in antislavery.

During the 1850s, as the slavery issue intensified, Seward initially tried to keep the Whig party alive, but by the end of 1855, he joined the newly organized Republican party..

Failing to get the Republican nomination at Chicago in 1860, Seward campaigned extensively in the North for Lincoln. His prominence in the party led Lincoln to offer Seward the chief position in the cabinet, secretary of state. It was in 1867, while serving in Johnson's administration, that he became the key figure in the purchase of the Alaskan Territory. During this administration, the United States purchased the Alaska Territory from Russia for $7,200,000.00. But at the time it was mockingly called "Seward's Folly" and "Seward's icebox!"

The Alaska purchase - 1867

Florence Nightingale - the Lady with the Lamp
Helped Establish Military Hospitals during the Civil War

Florence Nightingale - Photo – Florence Nightingale Museum London, England

Florence Nightingale (1820-1910) was born in Florence, Italy to wealthy British landowner parents.

Florence rejected the choice of husbands by her parents. At the age of thirty-one she went to Germany to become a nurse.

Florence was known as the "Lady with the Lamp" by the British soldiers during the Crimean War. She wrote numerous letters to British military officials demanding bandages, supplies and better health conditions for the wounded soldiers. At night, her lamp burned as she walked the four miles of corridors to care for the sick and wounded. She was truly the founder of the nursing profession.

During the Civil War (1861-1865) the United States sought Florence Nightingales advice for setting up their military hospitals. She implemented a nursing schedule for the care of the wounded and also set forth the schedule for the kitchen work and the diets of the soldiers.

She was a national heroine in 1856 upon her return to England. She published two books, Notes on Hospital (1859) and Notes on Nursing (1859) to promote her reforms in military hospitals.

In later life Florence Nightingale went completely blind and was an invalid. She had to receive full time nursing care. She died at the age of ninety.

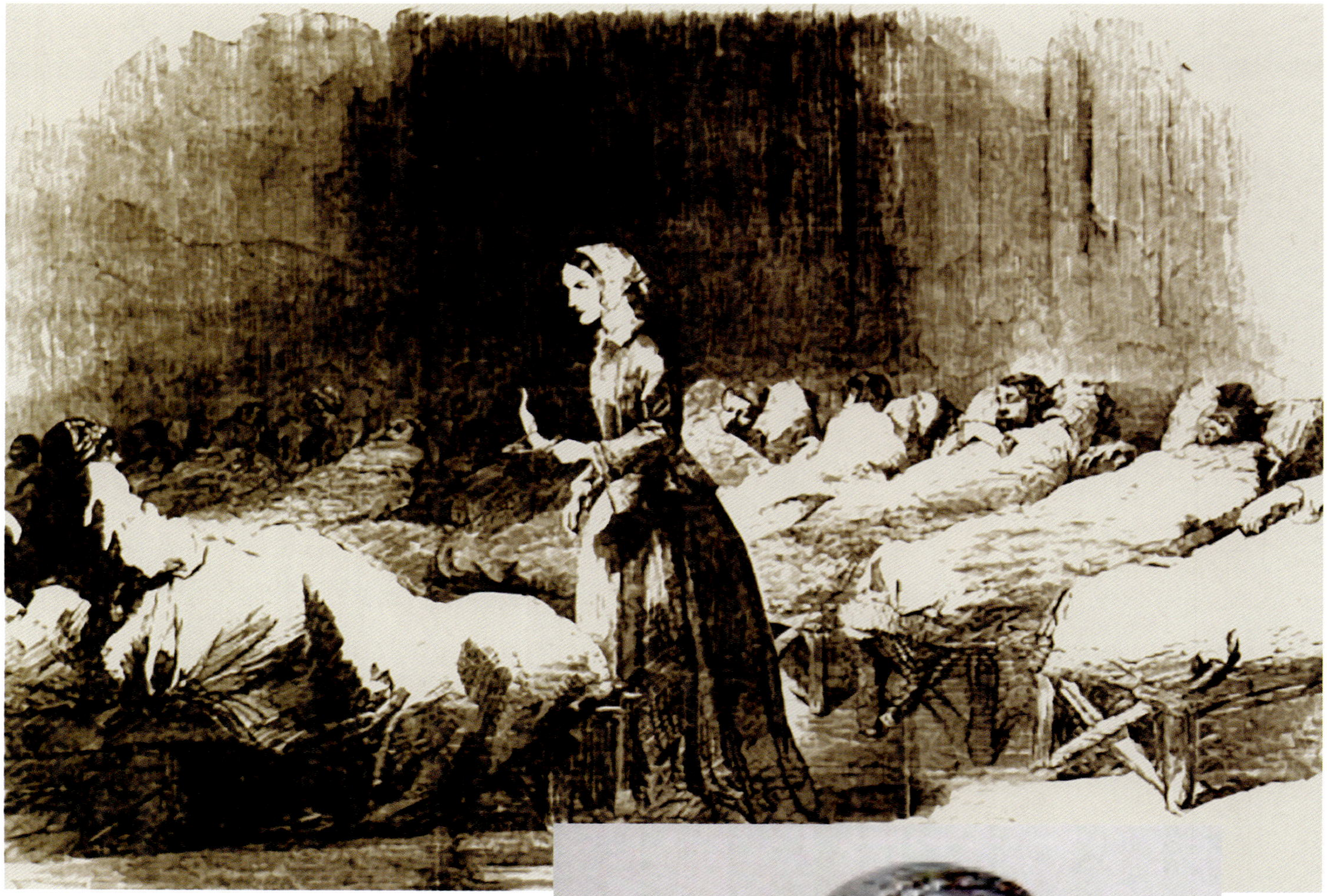

Florence Nightingale continued

Above: Florence Nightingale, the "Lady with the Lamp," tending to wounded soldiers during the Crimean war.
From the Illustrated London News – 24th February, 1855

Right: Statue of Florence Nightingale in the entrance of the Flornce Nightingale Museum
Photo – Florence Nightingale Museum, London, England

Admiral David Glasgow Farragut
Civil War hero

Farragut Career Academy in Chicago, Illinois, is named after a naval officer whose Spanish heritage includes a generation of sea fighters.

David Glasgow Farragut was born near Knoxville, Tennessee on July 5, 1801. His father, Jorge Farragut, a hero of the American revolution, was born on the Spanish Island of Minorca. David's mother, Elizabeth Shine, was the daughter of Irish and Scotch pioneers, who distinguished themselves in the history of the revolution as well.

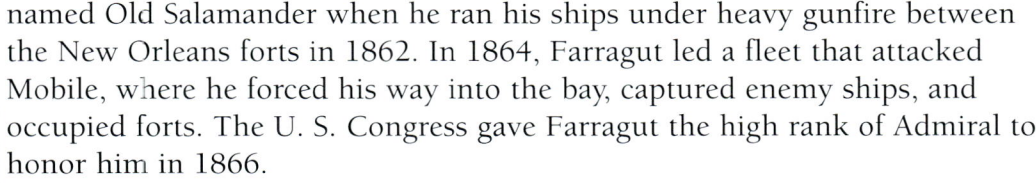

Following in the footsteps of his parents, David Farragut became a senior naval officer at the out break of the Civil War. He was nicknamed Old Salamander when he ran his ships under heavy gunfire between the New Orleans forts in 1862. In 1864, Farragut led a fleet that attacked Mobile, where he forced his way into the bay, captured enemy ships, and occupied forts. The U. S. Congress gave Farragut the high rank of Admiral to honor him in 1866.

David Farragut won fame with the battle cry, "Damn the torpedoes! Full speed ahead!"

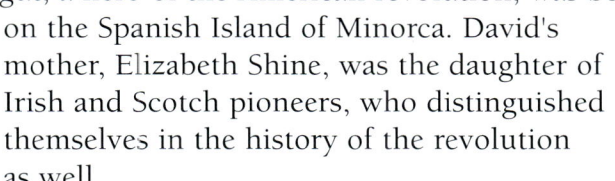

A statue of Admiral Farragut was erected in the heart of our nation's capital known as Farragut Square. It remains a lasting tribute to the most distinguished naval officer of the Civil War.

Admiral David Glasgow Farragut
The Watermelon Note

The one hundred dollar note shown above is the famous "Watermelon" note. This has been so named because of the unusual shape of the zeros which are shaped like a watermelon.

General George Gordon Meade
Commander of the victorious Union Army at Gettysburg

This Grand "Watermelon" note is one of only three by type that exist in private collections and is extremely rare. The last time a similar note was sold at public auction was December, 1998 for a price of $792,000.

George Gordon Meade (1815-72), was an American army officer, born in Cádiz, Spain, and educated at the U.S. Military Academy. He joined the Union forces at the outbreak of the American Civil War, participating in the defense of Washington, D.C., in 1861. As a Major General of volunteers, he fought at the Battle of Chancellorsville in 1863 and shortly thereafter was appointed Commander of the Army of the Potomac. In July 1863, in the battle that is considered the turning point of the war, he defeated the Confederate forces at Gettysburg, Pennsylvania. He continued as Commander of the Army of the Potomac, working closely with General Ulysses S. Grant, until the end of the war. Promoted to Major General in the regular army in 1864, Meade commanded various military departments in the U.S.

The Battle of Gettysburg painting from the Library of Congress

General George Gordon Meade

Although this is the 1891 open back $1,000 note and does not show the watermelons, it is much rarer and is the only surviving example known to exist in a private collection. It has changed ownership privately several times since its origin from the Grinnell collection, where it was sold at auction nearly sixty years ago. It is well-centered and in crisp uncirculated condition.

Meade was Grant's subordinate, although nominally in command of the Army of the Potomac until the end. He fought in the army through the Wilderness, Spotsylvania, Cold Harbor, and the long months in front of Petersburg. He was finally rewarded with the grade of Major General, U.S.Army, after both W. T. Sherman and Philip Sheridan, the latter his subordinate, had received their appointments.

At the close of the war, he was assigned to the command of departments and divisions in the East and South. He was in charge of the Military Division of the Atlantic, headquarters at Philadelphia, when he died on November 6, 1872, from pneumonia. He is buried in Laurel Hill Cemetery, Philadelphia.

General George Meade depicted at the battle of Gettysburg, hanging in the Library of Congress

The Matthew Brady photo showing the slaughter after the battle of Gettysburg

Chapter VI
Federal Reserve Bank Notes

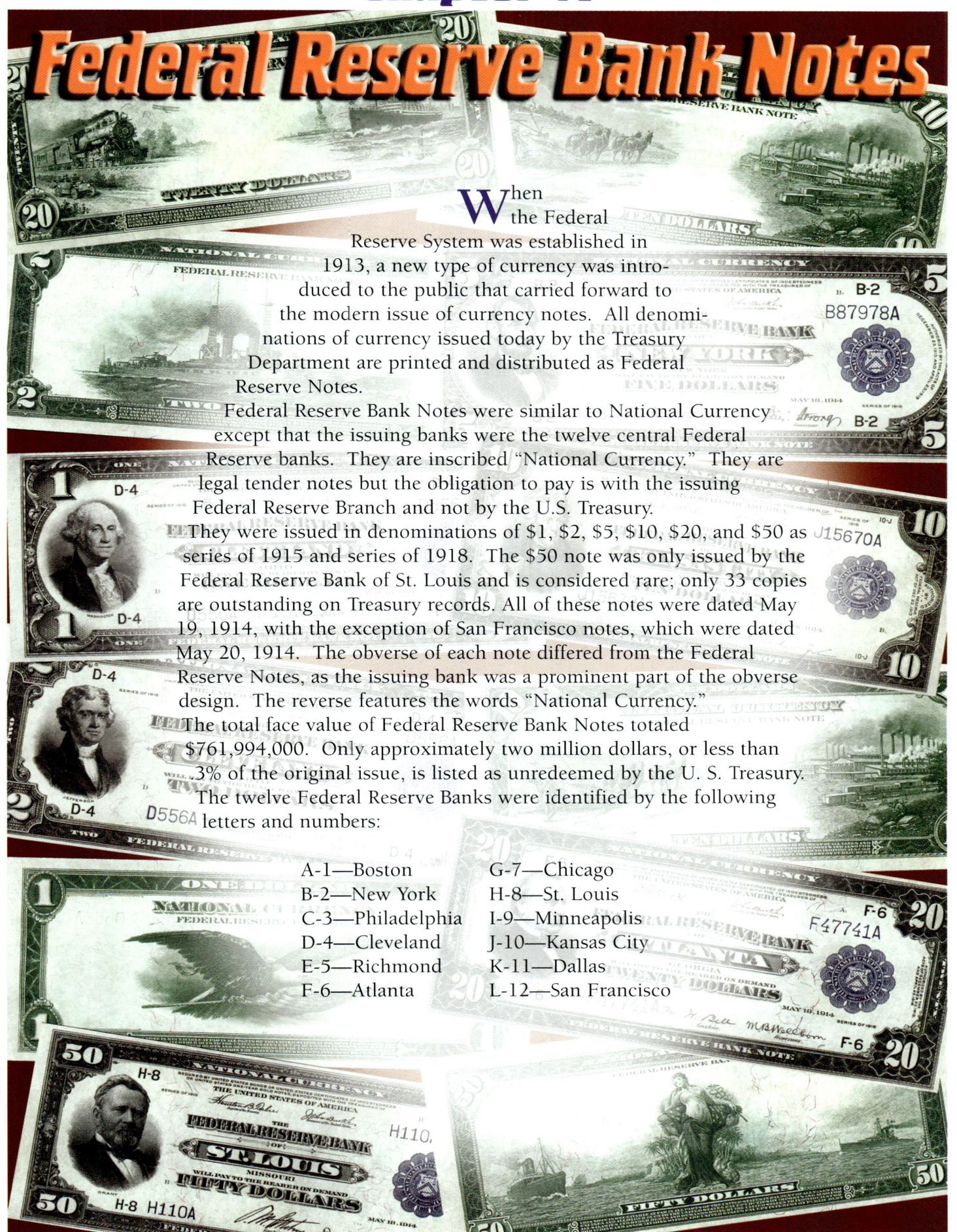

When the Federal Reserve System was established in 1913, a new type of currency was introduced to the public that carried forward to the modern issue of currency notes. All denominations of currency issued today by the Treasury Department are printed and distributed as Federal Reserve Notes.

Federal Reserve Bank Notes were similar to National Currency except that the issuing banks were the twelve central Federal Reserve banks. They are inscribed "National Currency." They are legal tender notes but the obligation to pay is with the issuing Federal Reserve Branch and not by the U.S. Treasury.

They were issued in denominations of $1, $2, $5, $10, $20, and $50 as series of 1915 and series of 1918. The $50 note was only issued by the Federal Reserve Bank of St. Louis and is considered rare; only 33 copies are outstanding on Treasury records. All of these notes were dated May 19, 1914, with the exception of San Francisco notes, which were dated May 20, 1914. The obverse of each note differed from the Federal Reserve Notes, as the issuing bank was a prominent part of the obverse design. The reverse features the words "National Currency."

The total face value of Federal Reserve Bank Notes totaled $761,994,000. Only approximately two million dollars, or less than 3% of the original issue, is listed as unredeemed by the U. S. Treasury.

The twelve Federal Reserve Banks were identified by the following letters and numbers:

A-1—Boston   G-7—Chicago
B-2—New York   H-8—St. Louis
C-3—Philadelphia I-9—Minneapolis
D-4—Cleveland   J-10—Kansas City
E-5—Richmond   K-11—Dallas
F-6—Atlanta   L-12—San Francisco

FEDERAL RESERVE BANK NOTES
SERIES OF 1915 AND 1918

One Dollar Note
Portrait of George Washington

Bald eagle perched on the American Flag

Only three percent of Federal Reserve bank notes issued in 1915 and 1918 are still outstanding on Treasury records. Many of these notes are undoubtedly gone forever-destroyed during World War I, burned in fires and airplane crashes, or lost on the bottom of the sea. All of the notes featured in this section were never used and are in crisp uncirculated condition.

On June 28, in Sarajevo, Gavrilo Princip (a Slav nationalist) assassinated Archduke Franz Ferdinand, heir to the throne of the Austro-Hungarian Empire. Austria-Hungary blamed Serbia for the killing and because Europe was linked by a series of diplomatic alliances - Austria-Hungary/Germany/Italy (Central Powers) and Britain/France/Russia (Triple Entente/Allied forces) - the affair escalated into full-scale war.

The 16th Irish and 36th Ulster June-1917

Tending the wounded of the 1st Lancashire Fusliers. 1-July-1916

Military Pension for World War I

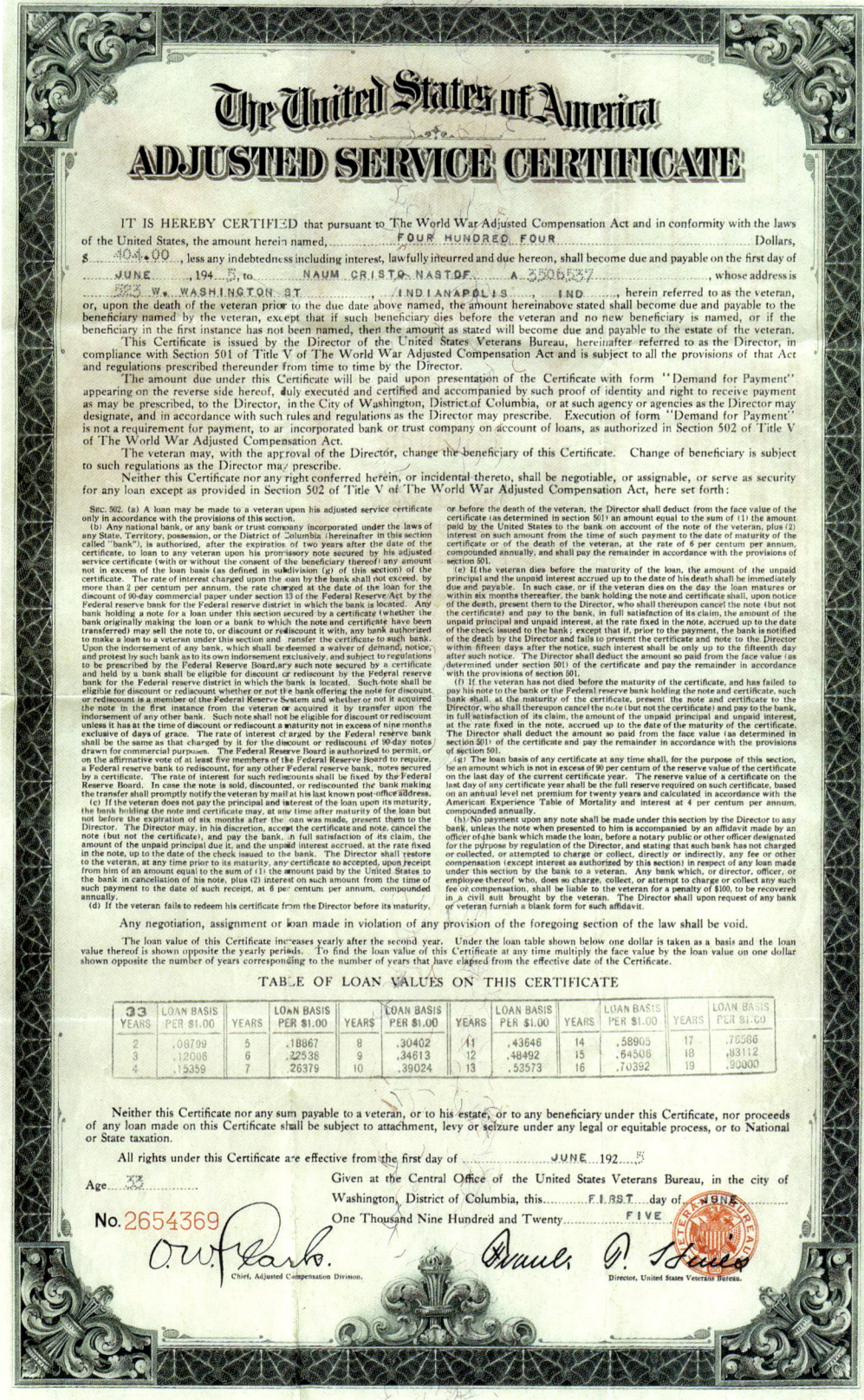

Soldiers who served in World War I were provided an "Adjusted Service Certificate." This certificate represented a pension that was worth $404 and could be redeemed in June, 1945. This certificate was issued in 1925 and could be used as collateral for loans. It is printed on currency paper by the Bureau of Engraving and Printing. Because they had to be presented to be redeemed, this may be one of very few examples that exist today.

The front of the World War I Adjusted Compensation Act Document

"UNCLE SAM NEEDS YOU"
Famous World War I poster calling for recruits to join up to fight in the European war

Two Dollar Note
Portrait of Thomas Jefferson

Engraving on the reverse shows the type of battleship used in the United States Navy in 1914

The U.S.S. Maine continued extensive east coast operations until late 1897. Then the ship prepared for a voyage to Havana, Cuba, to show the flag and to protect American citizens in the event of violence in the Spanish struggle with the revolutionary forces in Cuba.

Arriving January 25, the Maine anchored in the center of the port, remained on vigilant watch, allowed no liberty, and took extra precautions against sabotage. The battleship suddenly sank without warning from an explosion in Havana Harbor in 1898. This marked the beginning of the Spanish American War.

The U.S.S. Maine was of a similar design, shown on the reverse of the note. While members of Congress used the words "Remember the Maine" to justify the declaration of war against Spain, many historians believe now that the explosion in the powder magazine was accidental and not the result of sabotage or hostile action.

Out of 350 officers and men on board that night (4 officers were ashore), 252 were dead or missing.

U.S.S. Maine sank in Havana Harbor
February 15, 1898

The above photo is that of a lithograph published in 1898. The original painting is by F.N. Atwood and was painted in 1895.

Five Dollar Note
Portrait of Abraham Lincoln

The engraving on the right depicts the first landing of the Pilgrims in America. The scene on the left is representative of the first sighting of land (San Salvador) by Christopher Columbus in 1492.

Rare free frank signed "A. Lincoln"

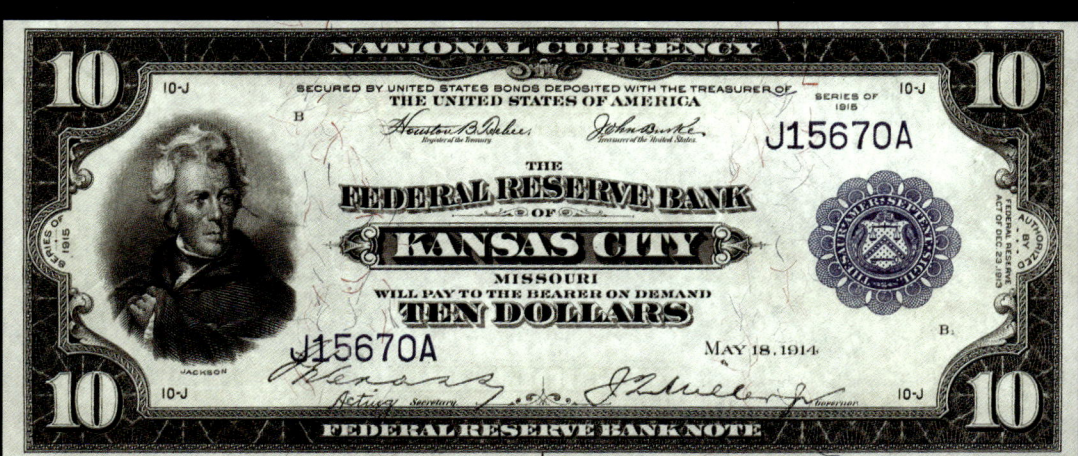

Ten Dollar Note
Portrait of Andrew Jackson—This is the same engraving used on the small size $20 Federal Reserve Note that was printed from 1928 until recently replaced by the "big head" $20 bill

Midwest farming scene and a modern industrial facility

Free frank of Andrew Jackson written entirely in his hand while President (1829-1837). The postmark "City of Washington," in red ink, was used between 1832 and 1835. It is addressed to James Brown, Philadelphia.

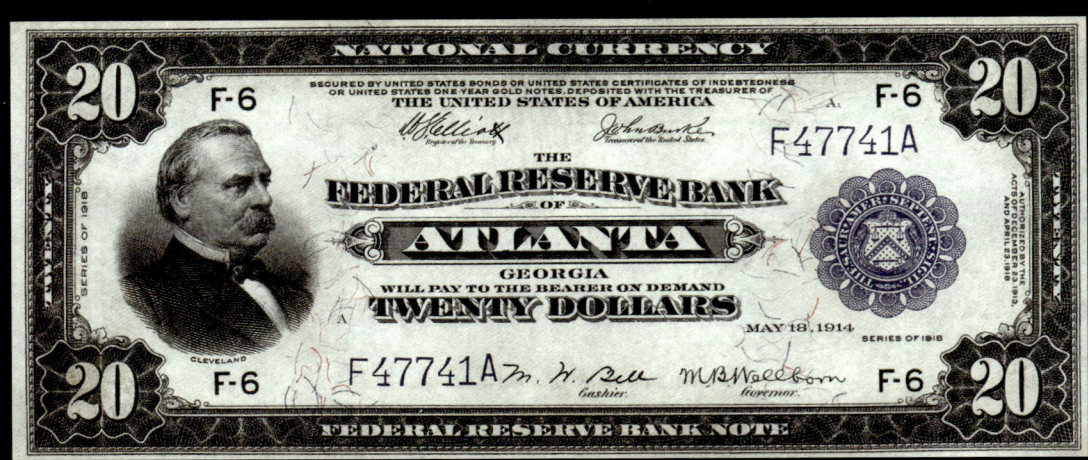

Twenty Dollar Note
Portrait of Grover Cleveland—The only President to be elected to non-successive four year terms. This is the same portrait that was later used on the small size $1000 bills printed from 1928 until 1945.

The reverse illustrates forms of transportation during the early 1900's. An automobile is seen next to a steam train and an ocean liner similar to the Titanic is seen adjacent to the Statue of Liberty.

Early transportation has enabled people to quickly travel from one end of the country to the other. It gave mobility to the military and it has saved countless lives. Today almost everyone owns at least one. It is a modern marvel, which has made the world smaller. What is this marvel that people need and take for granted? It is the automobile. The car is a tool for getting from one place to another in the shortest possible time. The invention of the internal combustion engine in 1878, which used gasoline, made the car a more practical means of transportation. The automobile is not a modern invention as many people think; the early cars were steam-powered.

Early steam locomotive - circa 1900

Early automobile - circa 1900

ONE THOUSAND DOLLAR GOLD CERTIFICATE
SERIES 1928

Series 1928 $1,000 Gold Certificate with the same portrait of Grover Cleveland that was used on the first issue of $20 Federal Reserve Notes.

This design was printed from 1928 until 1933, when President Roosevelt and Congress enacted legislation removing the United States from the Gold Standard. This note is the same size as currently printed notes.

Gold certificates were illegal to possess after 1933, and their presence even in collections made them subject to confiscation and destruction by the Treasury Department. This was the first and only time since 1861 that an issue of U. S. currency became illegal to own. That restriction was lifted in 1964 and all issues of gold certificates once again became legal tender.

By 1935 the Nation had achieved some measure of recovery from The Great Depression, but businessmen and bankers were turning more and more against Roosevelt's New Deal program. They feared his experiments, were appalled because he had taken the Nation off the gold standard and allowed deficits in the budget, and disliked the concessions to labor. Roosevelt responded with a new program of reform: Social Security, heavier taxes on the wealthy, new controls over banks and public utilities, and an enormous work relief program for the unemployed.

Franklin D. Roosevelt-Thirty-Second President - 1933-1945
Photo, The White House

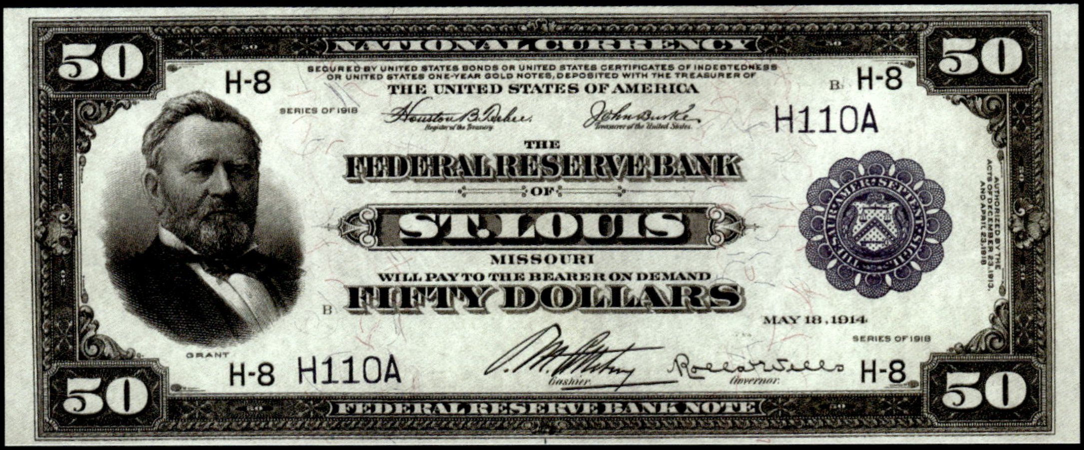

Fifty Dollar Note
Portrait of U.S. Grant, 18th President of the United States

The reverse depicts an allegorical representation of the Panama Canal, which opened on August 15, 1914. The cost of construction of $375,000,000 was a huge sum of money at that time and included $100,000,000 paid to the Government of Panama.

Official inauguration ceremonies were planned to coincide with the opening of the Panama Pacific Exhibition in San Francisco, a world's fair type show. However, the sudden advent of World War I forced the cancellation of the festivities.

The opening of the waterway to world commerce on August 15, 1914, represented the realization of an heroic dream of over 400 years. The 50 miles across the isthmus were among the hardest ever won by human ingenuity. The average time spent in transit from port to port is approximately 8-10 hours. Until Lake Mead was formed by the building of the Hoover Dam, Gatun Lake at the canal was the largest artificial body of water in the world.
Photo-Panama Canal Authority

Woodrow Wilson, 1856-1924
He was Elected President in 1913, the Year the Federal Reserve System was established

Woodrow (Thomas) Wilson was born in Staunton, Virginia December 28, 1856. His father, Joseph Ruggles Wilson was the pastor of the Presbyterian Church in Virginia. When Wilson was fourteen he moved with his family to Columbia, South Carolina where his father accepted a professorship at the Columbia Theological Seminary.

At the age of seventeen Wilson entered Davidson College in North Carolina and two years later, he entered the College of New Jersey, now Princeton University. While at Princeton he fell in love with history, became a great debater, and wrote various college magazines.

Wanting to become a statesman, Wilson entered the Law School of the University of Virginia at the age of twenty-three. He withdrew the following year after a physical breakdown. Two years later after taking a home study course he was admitted to the bar. He opened a law practice in Atlanta, but did not prosper. In desperation, he entered Johns Hopkins University in Baltimore at the age of twenty-seven to become a teacher. He married Ellen Louise Axson two years later and they happily brought up three daughters. He received his doctorate at the age of thirty.

After Wilson's marriage to Ellen Wilson he accepted an associate professorship of history at Bryn Mawr College outside Philadelphia. He was not happy at this all women's college and left within three years to teach at Wesleyan University in Connecticut. He enjoyed tremendous success there and was the coach of one of the most successful football teams in school history.

Twenty-Eighth President
1913-1921
Married to Ellen Louise Axson Wilson and to
Edith Bolling Galt Wilson

He was honored when Princeton University offered him a professorship two years later. He remained at Princeton 12 years and published numerous books and essays. He lectured regularly at Johns Hopkins and was offered at least seven times the presidency of many major universities. When the Board of Trustees of Princeton fired their President in 1902, Wilson was the first layman chosen to be President.

He served as President of Princeton University for eight years from 1902-1910. Wilson resigned on Oct. 20,1910 to campaign for governor of New Jersey. He was elected by the largest majority of votes by a Democrat in New Jersey. As governor he changed the state from one of the most conservative states into one of the most progressive.

By 1911 reforms in New Jersey brought Wilson national attention. He was the Democratic parties nominee for President of the United States. He won the election in 1913 and served his first term until 1917. Mrs. Wilson became ill in the White House and died in 1914. The President was so saddened by her death that he nearly lost all interest in living. Seven months later he met the widow of a Washington jeweler. He fell in love with Edith Bolling Galt and married her nine months later. She was a most devoted and caring wife to the President.

Wilson proclaimed the neutrality of the United States in his first term as President. During his second term he was elected by a narrow margin and served his term from 1917-1921. On April 6, 1917 Congress passed a resolution declaring war on Germany. President Wilson was a great leader during the war and fought for a peace treaty for all the European nations.

On a speaking tour throughout the Midwest, Wilson collapsed from fatigue and had a nervous breakdown. He suffered a stroke at the age of sixty-three while still President. He did not give up his presidency, but the Cabinet met and carried on much of the routine work of the government during his illness. He died in his sleep at the age of sixty-eight. He is buried in Washington Cathedral in Washington, D.C.

Each year thousands still visit the final home of the twenty-eighth President. The house remains for us today as it was when he lived here, a place for insightful reflection on his career as educator, social reformer, and world statesman.

Letter Written by Woodrow Wilson on October 5, 1902

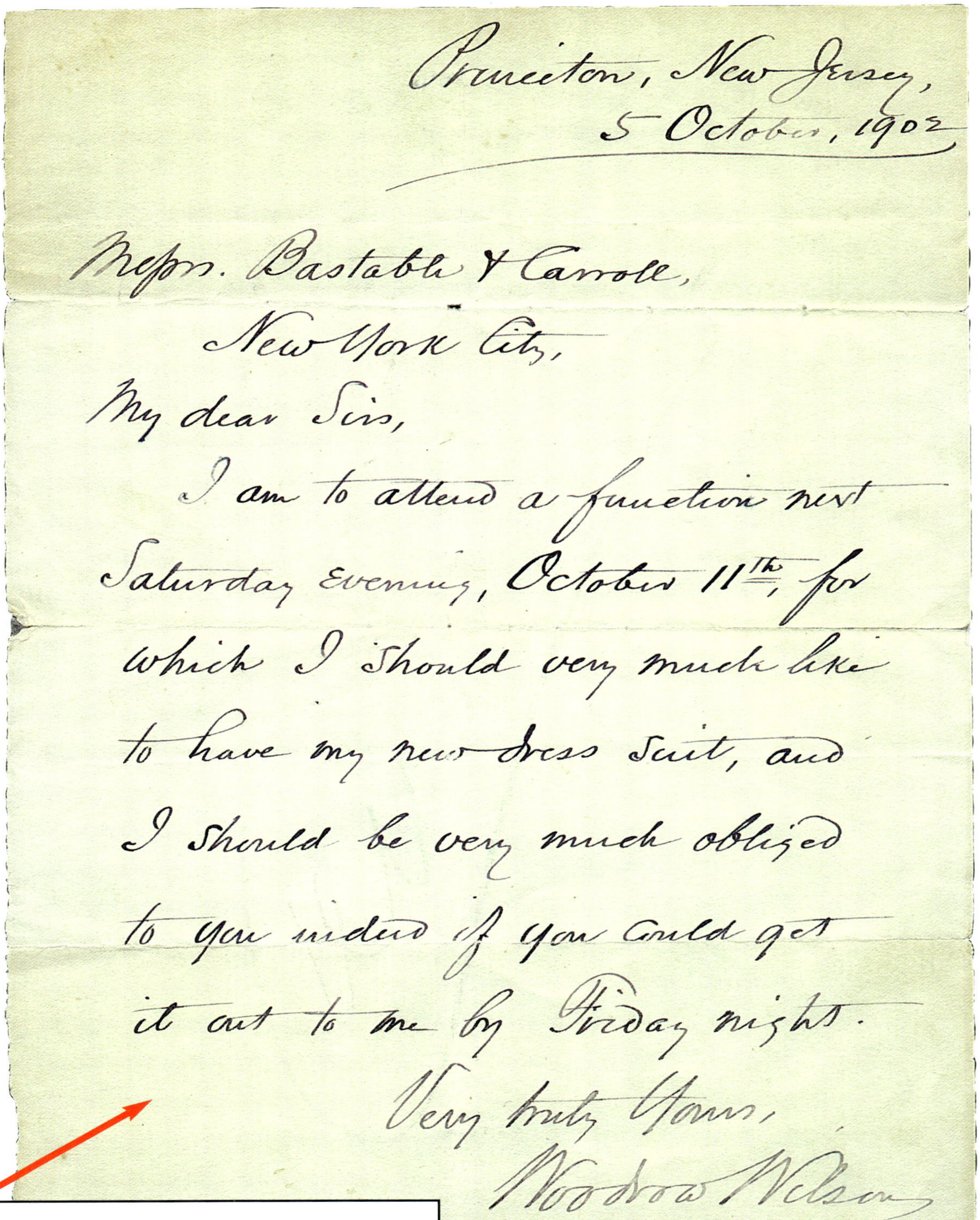
Princeton, New Jersey,
5 October, 1902

Messrs. Bastable & Carroll,
New York City,

My dear Sirs,

I am to attend a function next Saturday evening, October 11th, for which I should very much like to have my new dress suit, and I should be very much obliged to you indeed if you could get it out to me by Friday night.

Very truly Yours,
Woodrow Wilson

Princeton, New Jersey
5 October 1902

Mssrs. Bastable and Carroll
New York City

My Dear Sirs,

I am to attend a function next Saturday evening, October 11th, for which I should very much like to have my new dress suit, and I should be very much obliged to you indeed if you could get it out to me by Friday night.

Very truly yours,
Woodrow Wilson

U.S. Treasury Bearer Bond 4-1/4 % dated October 24, 1918
Signed by Woodrow Wilson

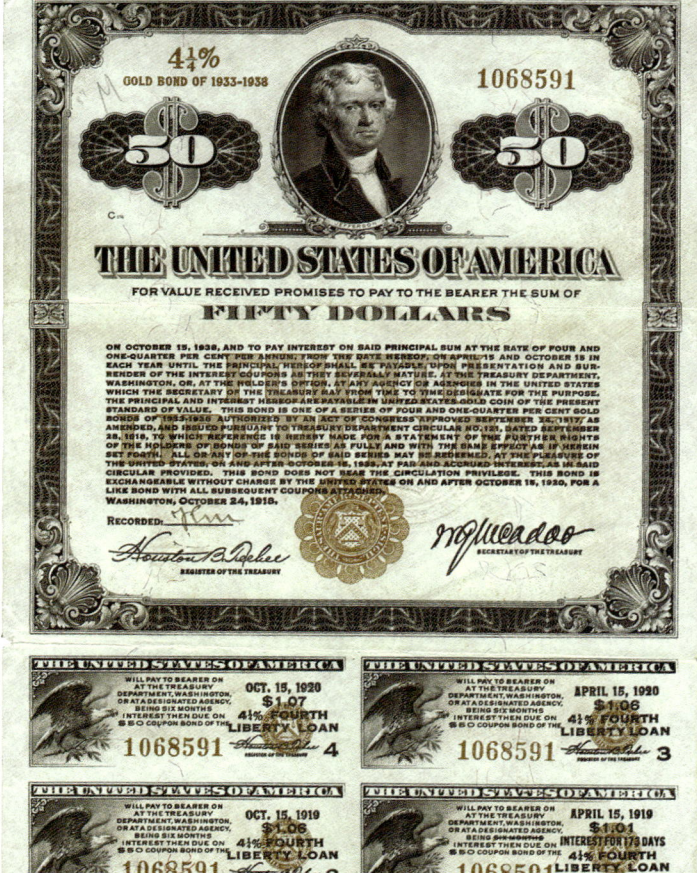

This U.S. Government Bond, issued to help finance the debt incurred during World War I, had a final redemption date of 1938, but was callable in 1933.

Interest was paid semi-annually by the cutting and submission of coupons to the Treasury Department. The first four coupons on this bond are still attached. It is still valid for redemption today at its face value plus the uncut coupons. It was probably saved because of the autograph by Wilson.

Bearer bonds are rare and considered very desirable by collectors.

The History of Joe's Stone Crab
"The First Established Eating Place on Miami Beach" - 1913

Joe's Stone Crab restaurant in the 1950's

Author's Note: We would like to thank Susan Nowling, Millinda Sinnreich and Stephen Sawitz (Joe's Stone Crab owner) for supplying us with the pictures and text for this section of the book. The historical information and the editing of the story was greatly appreciated. J.D. E.D.

In the early 1900's Miami Beach was a wild tangle of mangroves, snakes, alligators, mosquitoes and flamingos. The beach was inhabited by the Tequesta Indians, enterprising wreck seekers, Seminole Indians, and a runaway group of slaves to name a few.

This area of Florida was too wild for high society from the Midwest and Upper East Coast until a well-connected society woman from the Midwest named Julia Tuttle persuaded Henry Flagler, the owner of Standard Oil, to extend his railroad to Miami in order to build a community of luxury hotels for the upper crust.

In 1913, the progressive vision of John Collins and Carl Fisher, two of the movers and shakers in Miami, was the impetus behind the first bridge to connect the small city of Miami to Miami Beach. Before the new Collins Bridge was constructed, the only transportation was the ferry. The bridge offered tourists an expedient way to squander the day on the white sandy shores of the pristine and turquoise waters of the Atlantic Ocean.

Meanwhile, Joseph Weiss, an Hungarian immigrant living in New York, was sent on doctor's orders to seek a healthier atmosphere for his problematic asthma. He initially lodged in Miami, which did not help the condition; so, he tried living on the beach. Advantageously, the asthma cleared and the history of Joe's began to unfold.

Palm Beach society started to visit Miami Beach via the railroad. Although the two society's, Palm Beach (old money) and Miami (new crass money) mixed like vinegar and oil, they had two things in common; they loved basking on Miami Beach, and they loved the food at Joe's Seafood Restaurant.

Joe & Jennie Weiss' first restaurant on Miami Beach - circa 1913

Joe Weiss' first restaurant opened in 1913 as a lunch stand at Smith's Bathing Casino, not far from where Joe's Stone Crab is today. Soon after Joe opened his doors, he sent for his wife Jennie and their high-spirited son, Jesse, to join him.

Joe's Stone Crab uses the year 1913 to mark its anniversary, as this is the actual date that Joe Weiss opened his first restaurant and his dream began to unfold.

In 1918, Joe and Jennie had accumulated a small sum and purchased a meager bungalow on Biscayne Street (now called South Pointe Drive). The couple moved into the back and set up the front as a restaurant. Eight tables were all they could fit. Part of this original bungalow is within the structure of Joe's Stone Crab today.

The population of the beach at this time was approximately 644 people and Collins Avenue was a dirt road. Can you even imagine it? Yet Joe knew he owned one of the only restaurants on the beach and that there was a reason to stick it out. And he was right on the money.

Founder Joseph Weiss-opened his first restaurant, Joe's Seafood Restaurant, in 1913

Miami Beach began enjoying the title of "America's Winter Playground." During the short twelve-week winter season, Miami Beach would attract the rich and the famous. These high rollers came to gamble at the racetracks, enjoy the tropical breezes, and load up on seafood. Miami Beach had an unwritten law that if it was all in fun, the betting and bookies and liquor, and whatever other lewd behavior was exhibited; the law basically looked the other way. These tourists were stimulating the beach's economy. Joe's Seafood Restaurant was popular and well-known for their shore dinners and seafood, but not for stone crabs. In fact, this local delicacy had not yet been discovered.

The stone crab, in the words of Damon Runyon, "is an ornery looking critter that hangs out around the Florida Keys and nowhere else in the world, and has a shell harder than a landlord's heart." The stone crabs were innocently added to the menu in 1921 when Jim Allison of Indianapolis, built a seaquarium and invited a Harvard ichthyologist (marine biologist in today's language) to travel to Miami Beach and professionally explore the marine life in the area. A group of researchers stopped in at Joe's with a burlap bag loaded with these critters so prevalent in Biscayne Bay, and asked Joe if they might be edible. After a few culinary conversations about how to cook these rock hard crabs, the stone crab craze began.

In 1925, the Miami Beach boom was in full swing. The developers were bulldozing and dredging mangroves and sand to put up luxury hotels on the beach, and the railroad could not get the supplies to Miami fast enough. But, by 1926 the city was feeling the effects of a shaky stock market and a bear economy.

The morning of Sept 17,1926, the newspaper assured its readers that the hurricane brewing in the Atlantic would miss Miami. Close to midnight of that same day, the killer hurricane had changed its path and veered towards Miami for a direct hit that no one was prepared for.

The famous Joe's Stone Crab neon sign which has welcomed hundreds of famous people from Madonna to Mohammed Ali

A la Carte

COCKTAILS

Tomato Juice	.25
Stone Crab	.75
Fresh Shrimp	.50
Florida Lobster	.40
Oyster	.40
Fresh Fruit	.35

RELISHES

Mixed Pickles	.25
Sweet Pickles	.25
Dill Pickles	.25
Sliced Tomatoes	.25
Celery	.35
Queen Olives	.35
Ripe Olives	.35
Stuffed Olives	.35
Stuffed Celery	.60

SOUPS

Spring Vegetable	.25
Cream of Tomato	.25

FISH AND SEA FOOD IN SEASON

Pompano	1.50
Stone Crabs	2.25
Frog Legs, Tartar	1.50
Florida Lobster	1.00
Scallops with Bacon	1.00
Fried Shrimp, Tartar Sauce	1.00
Shrimp Creole	1.00
Fried Oysters	1.00
Stewed Oysters	.60
Salt Water Trout	.75
Spanish Mackerel	.75
Kingfish	.75

STEAKS—CHOPS—CHICKEN

Single T-Bone Steak	1.75
Single T-Bone Steak, Extra Thick	2.00
Porterhouse Steak (for two)	4.00
Single Tenderloin Steak	1.75
Broiled Lamb Chops	1.00
Veal Cutlet	1.00
Half Spring Chicken, Broiled or Fried	1.00
Half Fried Chicken, Maryland Style	1.25

Early menu from Joe's Seafood Restaurant-circa 1930's

This killer storm ripped through Miami with a vengeance. When it was all over, the storm had damaged or destroyed every building in Miami's business district, plus the beach hotels and casinos were battered and surrounded by standing water.

Hundreds died and thousands were injured. The whole city had to be rebuilt. The aftermath scared away many of the winter tourists for years to come. There were some lean years ahead for Joe's and the rest of the damaged entertainment spots on Miami Beach.

In 1921 you could order five stone crab claws with coleslaw and potatoes for $1.25. (Why so much?) Coffee was a dime. Through the years, the restaurant honed their culinary skills to include creamed spinach, hash browns, grilled tomatoes, and extraordinary key lime pie. Later, in the 60's the pie was swiftly added to the menu, because a reporter from up North bragged about a slice of key lime pie he devoured at Joe's, and at the time Joe's served only apple pie. The column was well-read and the Weiss' knew they had to quickly get this pie on the menu. So in keeping with this family's entrepreneurial spirit, a remarkable key lime pie recipe was created and on the menu the very next day.

Joe's Stone Crab today is the largest wholesaler of stone crab claws in the United States. If you have not eaten at Joe's Stone Crab, you really have not been to Miami Beach. Long lines and three-hour waits do not deter the hungry fans of this famous and delectable landmark. Back in Jesse's days, the story goes, that a bird flew into the dining room through an open door in the kitchen; a diner remarked about the bird to Jesse, and he wisecracked that the bird must have tipped the Maitre'd in order to get such a good seat in the dining room so quickly!

What Joe and Jennie Weiss began has been carried forward through five generations of the Weiss family. The restaurant was handed down to their only child, Jesse Weiss, who was branded as a character, scoundrel, a womanizer, and a gambler. It was Grace, the fifth and seventh of his six wives, (Yes! He married Grace twice.) that kept the restaurant running properly. It was Jesse that gave the restaurant its panache. This bigger than life and bold man built relationships with the powerful, the rich, the famous, and the regular "Joe" on the street.

They all called Jesse their "buddy." The most important person in Jesse's life was his daughter, Jo Ann. In the late sixties, Jo Ann and her husband at the time, Irwin "Say" Sawitz ran the show at Joe's. Jo Ann is solely responsible for creating many of the landmark recipes and running the restaurant like the well-oiled machine that it is today.

Today Jesse's grandson, Stephen Sawitz, might greet you while he is handling the day-to-day operations, of this huge business. Steve enjoys keeping his family's restaurant in the limelight and ensuring the same incredible service and quality Joe's is famous for. Between Steve, his mother and a staff of 300, Joe's Stone Crab keeps the customers happy and coming back for more.

Today the number of meals served are pretty impressive. In the 2001-2002 season, which runs from October through May, Joe's served on average, 15,000 pounds of stone crabs per week. Joe's has shipped over 11,000 orders of stone crabs, cracked 491,962 pounds, shredded 63,321 pounds of cabbage for their famous coleslaw, poured 21,312 quarts of cream for their popular creamed spinach, squeezed 122,100 key limes for those original key lime pies and served over 10,000 gallons of Joe's mustard sauce. Unbelievable numbers, for an entirely family-owned restaurant with such meager beginnings!

Jo Ann Bass-the former Jo Ann Weiss

Stephen Sawitz, Joe's Stone Crab owner and manager

There have been so many celebrities who have gone through the doors of Joe's. You could go into Joe's and if lucky, sneak a peek at Al Capone, J. Edgar Hoover, Arthur Godfrey, Guy Lombardo, Phil Donahue, Phyllis Diller, Mickey Spillane, Milton Berle, Princess Caroline of Monaco, The Duke and Duchess of Windsor, Sophie Tucker, Damon Runyon, Gloria Swanson, Will Rogers, Amelia Earhart, Joseph Kennedy, and countless others. All were considered friends of Jesse's. They all enjoyed his rogue-like personality.

This is Joe's Stone Crab restaurant in the 1980's. A hallmark of the City of Miami Beach.

Left to right: Donna Shalala, President of the University of Miami, Larry King, Joanne Dauer, Lauren Dauer, Dr. Eddie Dauer and Marc Dauer

Today, Steve Sawitz entertains a host of celebrities as they visit Miami, many of them renting the entire restaurant for private parties. Don't be surprised if you see Steve hanging at the front entry, talking to the likes of Larry King, President Donna Shalala, Cameron Diaz, Madonna, Sting, Don Johnson, Al Pacino, the late Dick Schapp, his son Jeremy, and Mohammed Ali.

Sports figures from the pro teams in town, and the coaches from the University of Miami, Larry & Dianna Coker, Jim & Denise Morris have all frequented Joe's. George & Barbara Bush, George W., and Jeb Bush have all visited Joe's. Bill Clinton has entertained guests, and Cindy Crawford has made this stunning restaurant even more beautiful.

University of Miami head coaches Jim Morris (baseball) with his wife Denise and Larry Coker (football) with his wife Dianna

Count on Joe's not to stand still. Even at the level of success and notoriety they have enjoyed thus far, Joe's has even more to offer. The Weiss family is in the midst of mass-producing their famous mustard sauce and making it available to every dinner table in the nation. And after that, there will be other Joe's delicacies available to the general market. So, if you can't come to Joe's…Joe's will come to you!

You can consider yourself lucky if you are one of the three hundred employees that make their livings at Joe's. This is a group of people that have served this restaurant and have treated each other as one big family. Many have worked at Joe's for ten or twenty years or more. You can feel that camaraderie from the valet stand and throughout your very unique dining experience. Next time you visit Joe's, ask your server about his/her job. Just be certain to order your meal first or they might pull up a chair and tell you how wonderful their lives are, and why Joe's is the reason.

Just ask any of the servers that work at Joe's Stone Crab, and they'll tell you what a great place it is.
Left to right: Cathy, Eddie, Janine, Lowell, Diane, Jorge

This historic restaurant, registered as a Hallmark, of the City of Miami Beach, is a living legend that offers you a glimpse into the Miami Beach scene yesterday, today, and tomorrow.

Who's that with Aunt Rose? Why that's President Bill Clinton and Eddie Rolle in the background. Photograph taken at Joe's Stone Crab Restaurant.

Joe's Stone Crab as it appears today from it's original building on South Pointe Drive

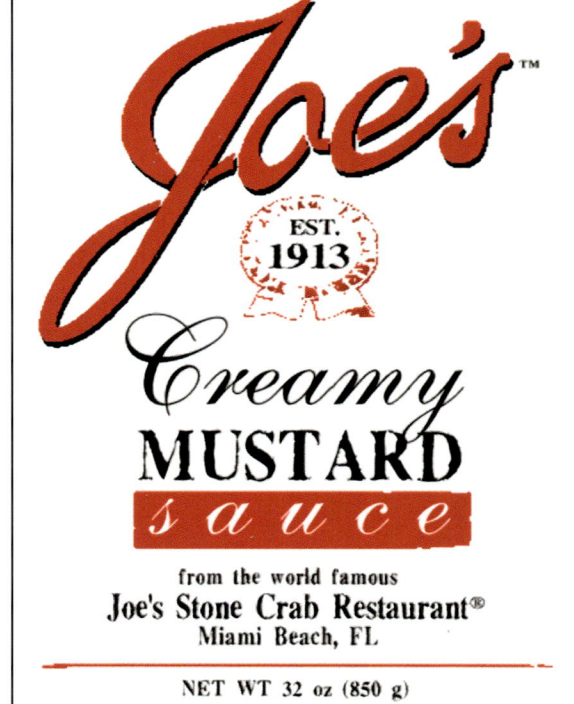

The famous Joe's Stone Crab mustard sauce will soon be sold in supermarkets throughout the nation

Author Joanne Dauer and Steve Sawitz examine the first proofs of the book as Steve suggests some editorial changes

Chapter VII
Federal Reserve Notes

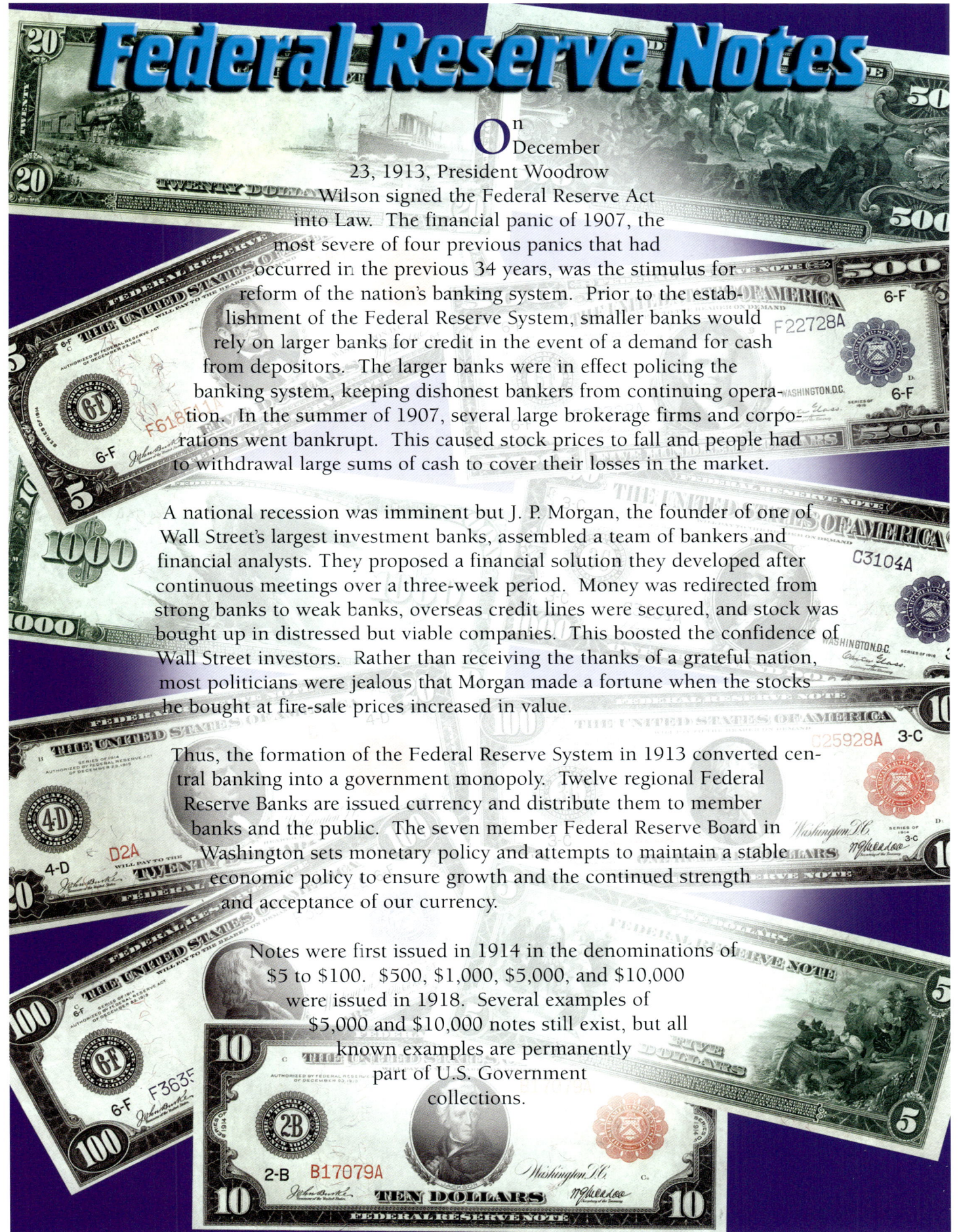

On December 23, 1913, President Woodrow Wilson signed the Federal Reserve Act into Law. The financial panic of 1907, the most severe of four previous panics that had occurred in the previous 34 years, was the stimulus for reform of the nation's banking system. Prior to the establishment of the Federal Reserve System, smaller banks would rely on larger banks for credit in the event of a demand for cash from depositors. The larger banks were in effect policing the banking system, keeping dishonest bankers from continuing operation. In the summer of 1907, several large brokerage firms and corporations went bankrupt. This caused stock prices to fall and people had to withdrawal large sums of cash to cover their losses in the market.

A national recession was imminent but J. P. Morgan, the founder of one of Wall Street's largest investment banks, assembled a team of bankers and financial analysts. They proposed a financial solution they developed after continuous meetings over a three-week period. Money was redirected from strong banks to weak banks, overseas credit lines were secured, and stock was bought up in distressed but viable companies. This boosted the confidence of Wall Street investors. Rather than receiving the thanks of a grateful nation, most politicians were jealous that Morgan made a fortune when the stocks he bought at fire-sale prices increased in value.

Thus, the formation of the Federal Reserve System in 1913 converted central banking into a government monopoly. Twelve regional Federal Reserve Banks are issued currency and distribute them to member banks and the public. The seven member Federal Reserve Board in Washington sets monetary policy and attempts to maintain a stable economic policy to ensure growth and the continued strength and acceptance of our currency.

Notes were first issued in 1914 in the denominations of $5 to $100. $500, $1,000, $5,000, and $10,000 were issued in 1918. Several examples of $5,000 and $10,000 notes still exist, but all known examples are permanently part of U.S. Government collections.

FEDERAL RESERVE NOTES
Series 1914—Five Dollar Notes

The reverse of this series is similar to the Federal Reserve Bank Notes but are missing the words "National Currency" and "Bank"

These seals and serial numbers were initially printed in red ink and then later blue ink which was supplied by Germany. Following the onset of World War I, the supplies were disrupted but a suitable substitute made in the United States was developed.

Series 1914 - Ten Dollar Notes

Series 1914 - Twenty Dollar Notes

Series 1914 - Fifty Dollar Notes

Series 1914-One Hundred Dollar Notes

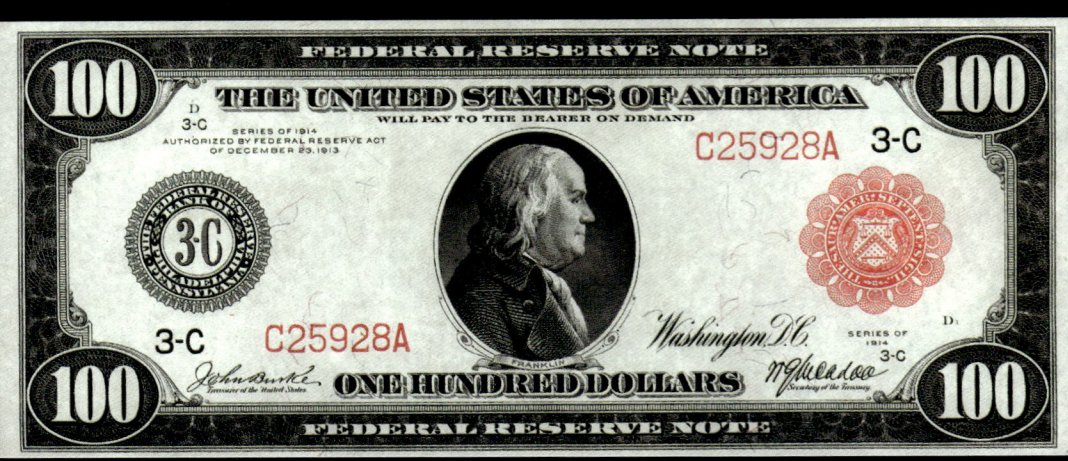

Five allegorical figures from mythology
The God Mercury is on the right wearing his winged helmet and sandals

Mercury-The Messenger of the Gods

The Romans called this God "Hermes." "Mercury" was the name used by the Greeks. He was the messenger of the Gods and also the guide to the Underworld. His father was Zeus, King of the Gods, and his mother was a mountain nymph.

Mercury is always seen wearing sandals with wings. These allowed him to fly and to move with great speed. His helmet, also containing wings, made him invisible and contributed to his stealthness.

He carried a caduceus or staff, which was his symbol as divine messenger. It was originally made of a willow wand entwined with ribbons. Mythology states that he intervened between two fighting snakes, and they then twined themselves together in peace on his staff. This caduceus has evolved into the modern symbol of medicine and healing.

Series 1918 - Five Hundred Dollar Note

This is the same portrait of John Marshall, fourth Chief Justice of the Supreme Court, that appears on the $20 Treasury Notes of 1890 and 1891

The reverse design features a painting of De Soto discovering the Mississippi

Spanish explorer, Hernando De Soto, discovered the Mississippi River and is also known for his exploration of Cuba and conquest of the Incas. De Soto had heard from the Indians of a great northern sea which he believed to be the Pacific Ocean and a shortcut to China. He died on the return trip back from the Mississippi in 1541 at the age of forty-one, and his crew burned his body to prevent the Indians from desecrating it.

1562 Map of Spanish North America - Diego Gutiérrez
acquired by the Library of Congress in 1949

Hernando De Soto

De Soto fighting the Indians

Drawings from a 16th century Spanish history book by Herrera found in Winsor

Series 1918 - One Thousand Dollar Note

Head of Alexander Hamilton

The Flag and American Eagle

Alexander Hamilton illustrated on the one thousand dollar bill

This is one of three designs of the $1,000 bill to include the "$" sign. The other two are the $1,000 gold certificates of 1907-22 and the $1,000 legal tender note of 1880.

The $500, $1,000, $5,000, and $10,000 denominations were first issued in 1918. Although examples of the $5,000 and $10,000 notes exist in U. S. Government collections, there are no known copies that exist in the public domain and thus they are unavailable to collectors.

Alexander Hamilton
(1757-1804) founding father, first Secretary of the Treasury, advocate of strong national government, member of the Continental Congress and Constitutional Convention, co-author of the Federalist Papers, proposed Bank of the U. S., helped create Federalist Party, died in a duel with rival Aaron Burr.

CORRESPONDENCE FROM THE TITANIC

The Year Before the Federal Reserve Act Became Law

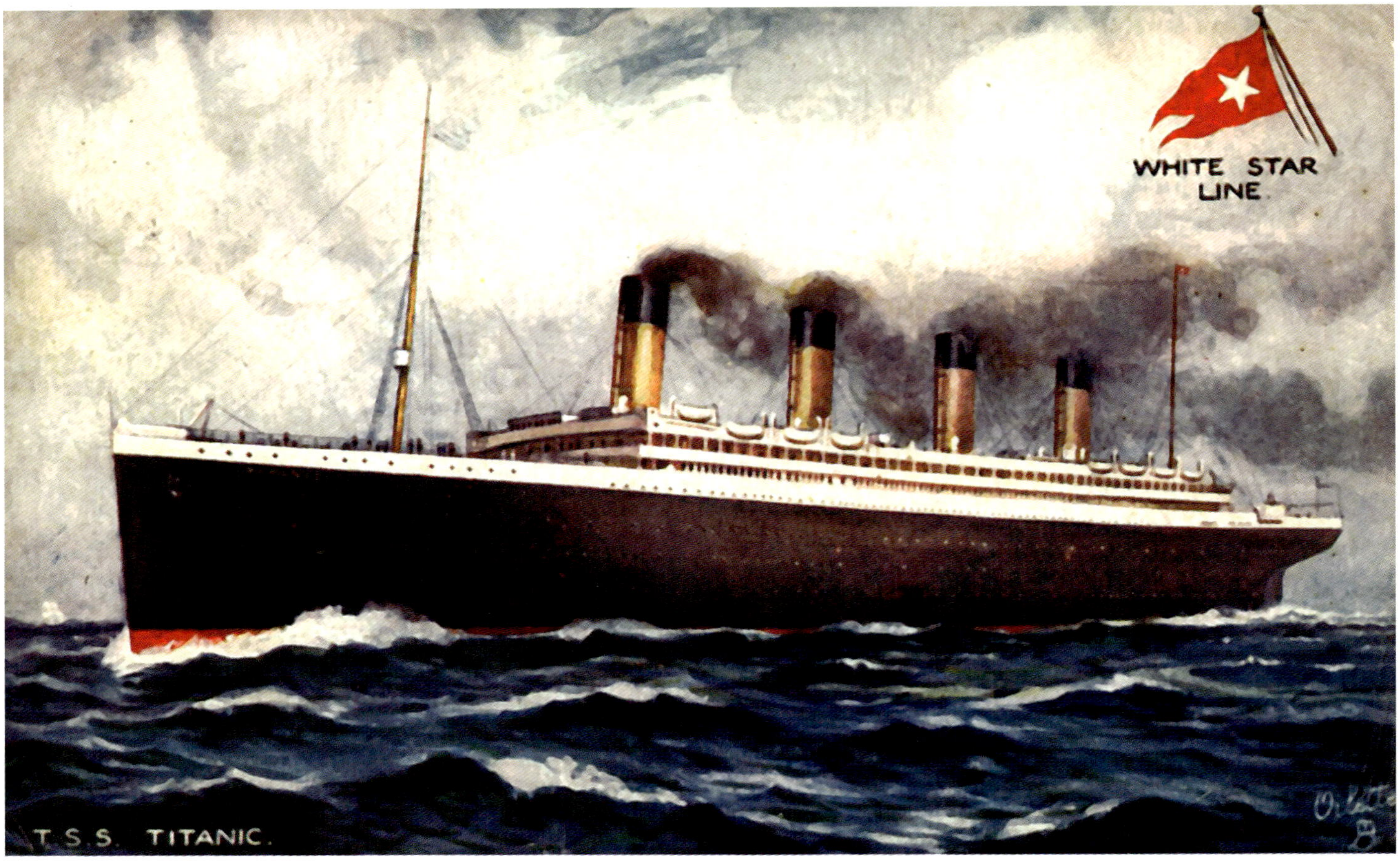

The front side of this rare postcard written on the Titanic on April 10, 1912. It was mailed at Queenstown, Ireland.

Just one year prior to the development of the Federal Reserve System in 1913, the most famous maritime disaster in history took over fifteen hundred lives. At approximately 11:40 p.m. on April 14, 1912, the Titanic struck an iceberg in the North Atlantic and sunk several hours later during the early hours of April 15, 1912.

№ 160 274

THE ROYAL PHILATELIC SOCIETY
LONDON

41, Devonshire Place,
London, W1N 1PE

Meeting of 24 FEB 1993

In the OPINION of The **EXPERT COMMITTEE** the item submitted as

Great Britain ; 1912 **S.G. No.** 339
½d green – two – used on picture postcard of "Titanic" – with Transatlantic Post Office obliteration of 10 Apr. 1912 – is genuine

Observations

Chairman

Submitted by Gilbert M. Roderick.

This certificate of authenticity is from the Royal Philatelic Society, which examined the Titanic postcard. It states:

"Great Britain, 1912 1/2D green—two used on picture postcard of 'Titanic'—with transatlantic post office obliteration of 10 Apr, 1912—is genuine."

This Illustrated Postcard was Mailed at Queenstown, Ireland 3 Days Before the Disaster

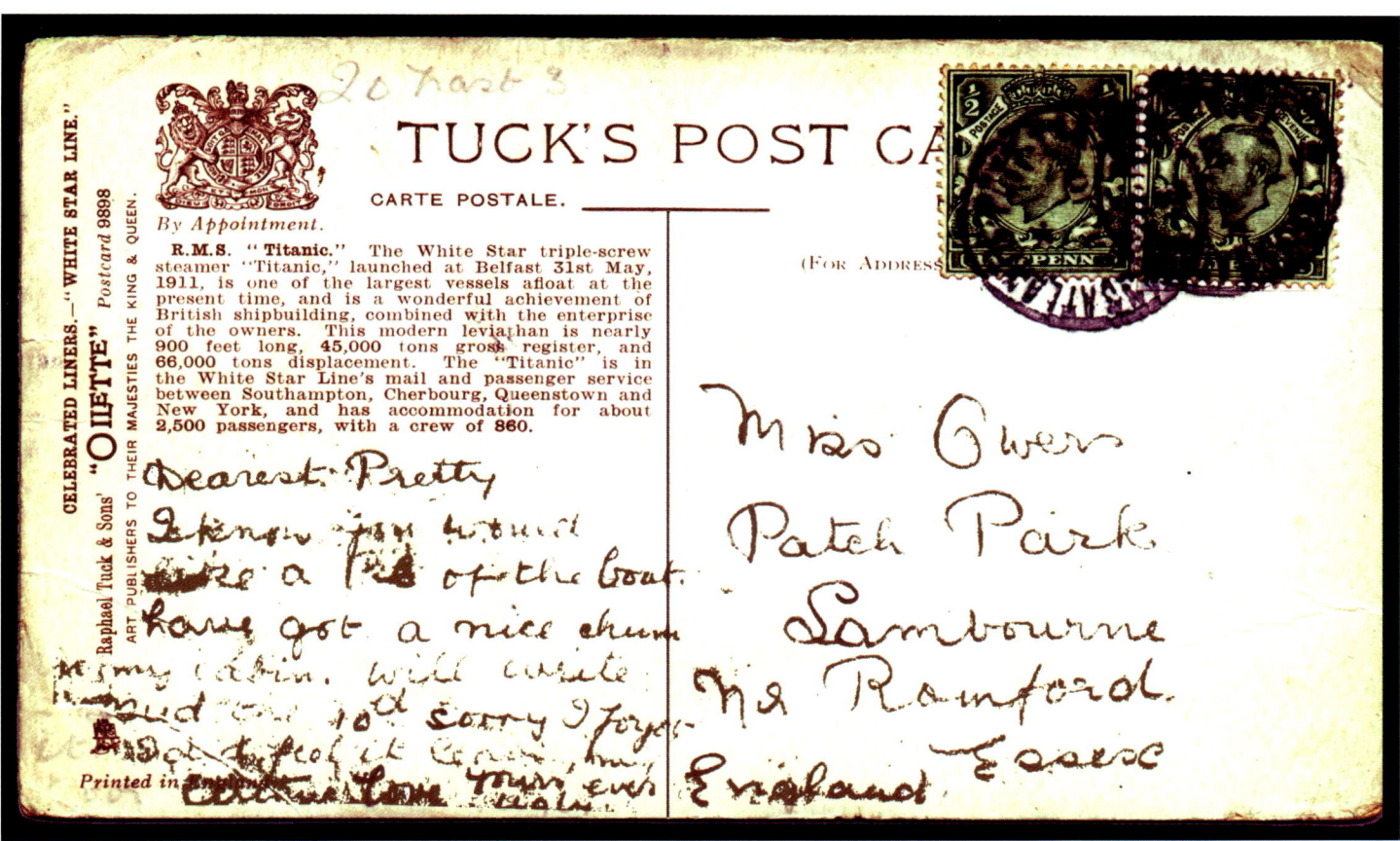

The message side of the postcard is addressed to Miss Gwen, Patch Park, Lambourne, Nr. Romford, Essex, England.
The written text reads as follows: →

"Dearest Pretty, I know you would like a pc of the boat. Have a nice chum in my cabin. Will write around the 10th. Sorry I forgot it. I did it leaving my one true. Love yours ever, Ugly."

September 6, 1869 was the date that Thomas Henry Ismay founded the Oceanic Steam Navigation Company, which became known as the White Star Line. The R.M.S. Titanic, when launched at Belfast on May 31st, 1911, was one of the largest vessels afloat at the time, weighing 45,000 tons and nearly 900 feet long. The Titanic embarked on its maiden voyage from Southhampton, England on April 10, 1912 at 12:15 p.m. The vessel docked at Cherbourg, France, at 6:35 p.m. to take on passengers and mail. She departed at 8:10 p.m. for Queenstown, Ireland, arriving on April 11th around noon. Additional passengers and 194 mail sacks were loaded on the ship for the voyage to New York.

The postcard illustrated above is one of the few surviving examples known to exist. It was written on the Titanic and was sent ashore at Queenstown. It bears two Great Britain one half penny stamps of George V tied by two cancellations: "Transatlantic Post Office, April 10, 1912."

EXTREMELY RARE SURVIVNG LETTER WRITTEN ON BOARD THE TITANIC ON WHITE STAR WATERMARKED STATIONERY AND ALSO MAILED FROM QUEENSTOWN, IRELAND

This letter was written by Mrs. A. Pritchard, age 33, a stewardess who was born in London. It is composed of four pages with a centerfold and only the first page is illustrated. She joined the crew of the Titanic on April 6, 1912 and received monthly wages of 3 pounds, 10 shillings. She was rescued on lifeboat 11 which had a capacity of 65 passengers (but carried only an estimated 55 or 60) from the starboard side of the Titanic at approximately 1:30 A.M., April 15, 1912, an hour before the ship sank.

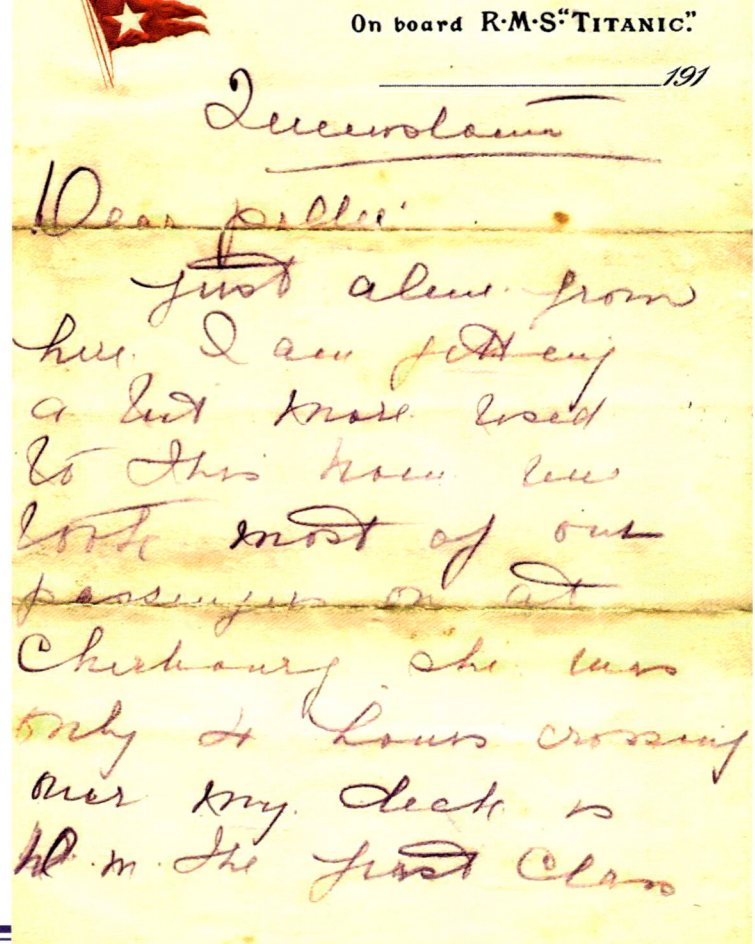

The above photo is a White Star Line envelope used by passengers on the Titanic and her sister ship the Olympic

The text on the letter, one of four pages, was written by Mrs. A. Pritchard, a stewardess who was on board and reads as follows:

Dear Pollie,

Just a line from here. I am getting a bit more used to this now. We took most of our passengers on at Cherbourg. She was only 4 hours crossing over. My deck is D.M., the first class, but I have to go such a way to the pantry. As I am writing this the band is playing. Just outside my room is the reception room. They play there 4 to 5 and 9 to 10. I hope my darling will keep well. I would give anything to kiss her dear little face now. It seems so hard to have to leave her dear smile. I never thought I should come to this. It is a very cruel world when one has to be parted from their only child for want of money. Now dear I will close with fond love. Kiss my darling for me and take care of her from Alice. Tell Olive to buck up and be good at figures as there are lots of jobs lady cashiers here in the restaurant and two ladies attendants for the Turkish baths. Do write to me so I get it at Plymouth on my way home. Address it
   Mrs. Pritchard, Stewardess
   R.M.S. Titanic
   White Star Line
   Plymouth

And let me know how daddy is.

"Not even God himself could sink this ship"
Comment of a White Star employee about the Titanic

Sea post clerk Oscar Scott Woody

Oscar Scott Woody was one of five Postmasters working on the Titanic with four other assistants to safeguard the mail. Sea mail was taken very seriously and was an important souce of revenue for steamship companies. The Edwardian era was the high point of International Sea Postal Service. The sea postal clerks were highly skilled and respected workers, frequently sorting as many as 60,000 letters per day. The Titanic carried a total of 3,364 bags of mail; approximately 200 bags contained registered mail.

The night of April 14, 1912, when they were celebrating O.S. Woody's 44th birthday, the mail clerks knew something was wrong when the Titanic collided with an iceberg. They moved as many of the 200 registered mail bags to the top deck as possible to keep the mail dry, but eventually found themselves in the cold water, none of them able to secure a place in a lifeboat.

The lifejackets of that era were made of cork and kept the upper torso completely dry and out of the water. In the suit Woody was wearing that night were several facing slips with the Titanic postmark and his name. These were placed on bundles of mail to indicate their final destination. Each facing slip had the clerk's name on them to assist in tracing sorting errors. In addition to several facing slips (which were kept dry by the life vest), he had the keys to the mailroom, his letter of appointment, pocket watch, and other personal effects. They were recovered from his body and given to his widow Leila, who resided in Washington, D.C.

In his 1912 Annual Report Postmaster General Hitchcock made this commendation for the clerks' heroic efforts:

> **About a quarter of an hour after the collision the opening or lower room in the sea post office was found to be practically filled with water and the sacks in it adrift. The clerks were seen in the sorting room above, closing sacks and preparing to take on deck all the mail available. The last reports concerning their actions show that they were engaged in this work and in carrying the sacks up on deck to the last moment.**

Courtesy—Smithsonian Postal Museum

This Ingersoll/Midgett pocket watch belonged to Oscar Scott Woody. It is corroded from immersion in sea water following the sinking of R.M.S. Titanic.
Courtesy—Smithsonian Postal Museum-On loan from the Miotell Collection of San Francisco through W. John Miottel, Jr

> **"As the situation became more desperate they (the postal clerks) appealed to the vessel's stewards to assist them in carrying the valuable mail to the upper deck. They continued in this work until the last. Every one of them was lost."**
> Newspaper Report, April 20, 1912

Off duty, Woody was a devoted Mason. Two Masonic dues cards were found on his body following the sinking of Titanic.

Courtesy—Smithsonian Postal Museum-On loan from the Grand Lodge of Ancient Free and Accepted Masons of Maryland

Oscar Woody's widow donated his personal effects to the Grand Lodge of Masons in Maryland. They were stored in the attic for over eighty years until they were "re-discovered" after the movie "Titanic" was released in 1997. The facing slip illustrated below is one of the actual ones from the Titanic and forever will be part of a memorable moment of United States history.

Courtesy—Smithsonian Postal Museum

> **I urged them to leave their work. They shook their heads and continued at their work. It might have been an inrush of water later that cut off their escape, or it may have been the explosion. I saw them no more.**
> *Albert Theissinger talking about the postal clerks aboard the Titanic Theissinger was a steward aboard R.M.S. Titanic and a survivor.*

This Masonic pocket knife was also found on Woody's body following the sinking

Courtesy—Smithsonian Postal Museum-On loan from the Grand Lodge of Ancient Free and Accepted Masons of Maryland

Small stain from contact with sea water

Picture of facing slip discovered after the movie "Titanic" is one of the actual ones from the Titanic

On the Olympic and Titanic, first-class passengers were surrounded by the most lavish possible appointments, including the magnificent grand staircase

A throng gathered near Cunard's New York Pier hoping to catch a glimpse of Titanic's survivors arriving aboard the Carpathia

Courtesy—Library of Congress

First-class reception room of the Titanic, published in The Shipbuilder, 1911 National Archives-Northeast Region, New York City, records of District Courts of the United States

Courtesy - National Archives and Records Administration

The original postcard on the left was printed after the disaster and bore the following text:

S.S. Titanic

Largest in the world. Cost $10,000,000. 882 feet 6 inches in length; displacement, 66,000 tons. Sailed April 10th, 1912 from Southampton on her maiden trip. Struck an iceberg on the night of April 15 and sank with a loss of life of more than 1,500.

Another commemorative postcard contains the following text:

OCEAN LINER TITANIC-LARGEST STEAMER IN THE WORLD
Sunk by iceberg on maiden trip off Halifax, April 15, 1912; 1600 people drowned. Length, 882 feet; breadth, 92 feet; number of steel decks, 11; watertight bulkheads, 15; passengers accommodated, 2,500; crew, 860, 860 tonnage registered, 45,000; tonnage displacement, 66,000; cost, $7,500,000

Lifeboat photographed from the R.M.S. Carpathia, which rescued the 705 survivors

The Titanic's surviving wireless opertator, Harold Bride, had to be carried down Carpathia's gangway, his severely frostbitten and smashed feet swathed in bandages

WHO FIRST RECEIVED THE TELEGRAPHIC SIGNAL?
THE FIRST VESSEL TO USE S.O.S AS THE INTERNATIONAL DISTRESS CALL WAS THE TITANIC!

David Sarnoff – photo courtesy of the David Sarnoff Research Center

David Sarnoff was born in Russia in 1891 and immigrated to New York City in 1900. At age fifteen he bought a telegraph key and learned Morse code. After being hired as an office boy for the Marconi Wireless Telegraph Co. of America, he became a junior telegraph operator in 1908.

On the evening of April 14, 1912, Sarnoff was working at the Marconi station atop Wanamaker's department store in New York City and was the first person to pick up the message relayed from ships at sea: "S.S. Titanic ran into iceberg, sinking fast." He remained at his post for the next seventy-two hours, giving the world the first authentic news of the disaster and the names of survivors.

In 1915, he proposed an idea for a "radio music box" at a time when radio was primarily used by ships and amateur radio operators. After World War I, the Radio Corporation of America (RCA) was formed by General Electric (GE) to absorb Marconi's U.S. assets (including him). In 1921 he was appointed the general manager of RCA and produced the first commercial sports broadcast—the Jack Dempsey—Georges Carpentier fight.

He created NBC, the first radio network, in 1926 and was named RCA president in 1930. Sarnoff introduced the first TV broadcast to the U.S.—a telecast from the 1939 World's fair in New York City. He told the crowd of curious viewers **"Now we add sight to sound."**

Lee de Forest - The Father of the Radio

The development of radio and television would not have been possible without the invention of the triode vacuum tube by Lee de Forest in 1906. He added a third electrode (to the existing anode and cathode) which allowed the "audion tube" to both rectify and amplify. This meant electronic circuits would finally be commercially feasible. Right is a letter signed by Dr. de Forest.

In the 1950's, in the above photo, de Forest posed with his 1920 Oscillion transmitter of the kind he constructed and installed for another early broadcast pioneer, WWJ, the Detroit News station

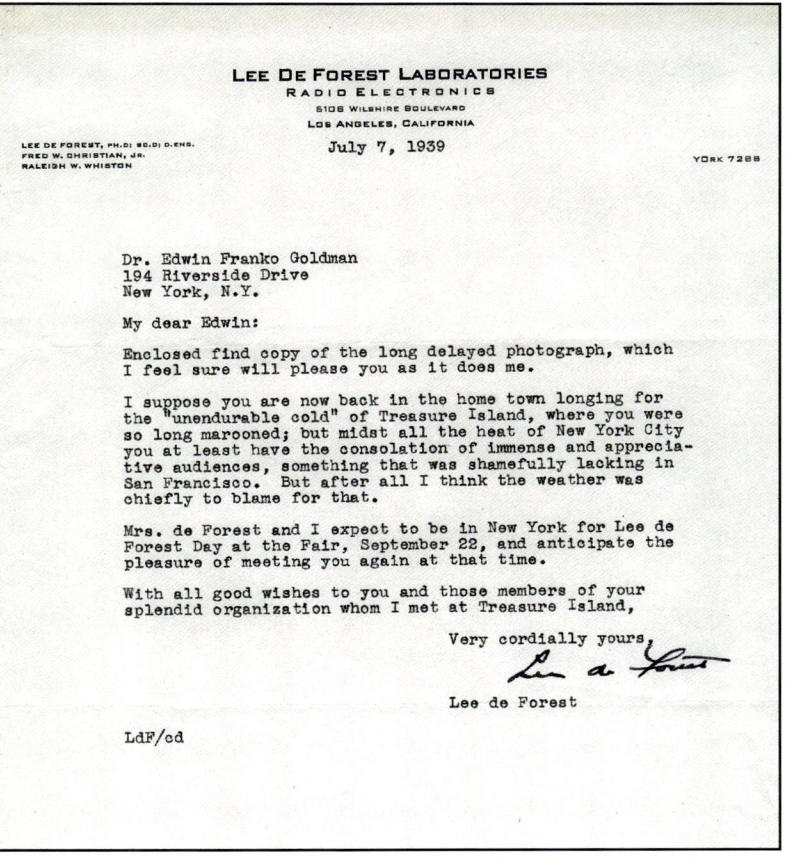

This letter was written by Lee de Forest to his friend Edwin Goldman in July, 1939, talking about his upcoming visit to the 1939 World's Fair at Lake Success, New York for Lee de Forest day

WHY DID THE STEEL HULL FAIL?

Modern science has provided the answer as to why the strongest steel available in 1912 failed to protect the Titanic from the fatal damage caused by the iceberg. A portion of the steel was recovered from the ocean floor and examined under a scanning electron microscope. The use of x-ray spectroscopic analysis revealed a very high sulphur content in the steel.

Dr. Edward Dauer operating the scanning electron microscope at the University of Miami. The picture on the screen is the weld joint on an intracoronary angioplasty stent. The SEM is used to design and investigate the strength and performance of this and other invasive biomedical devices.

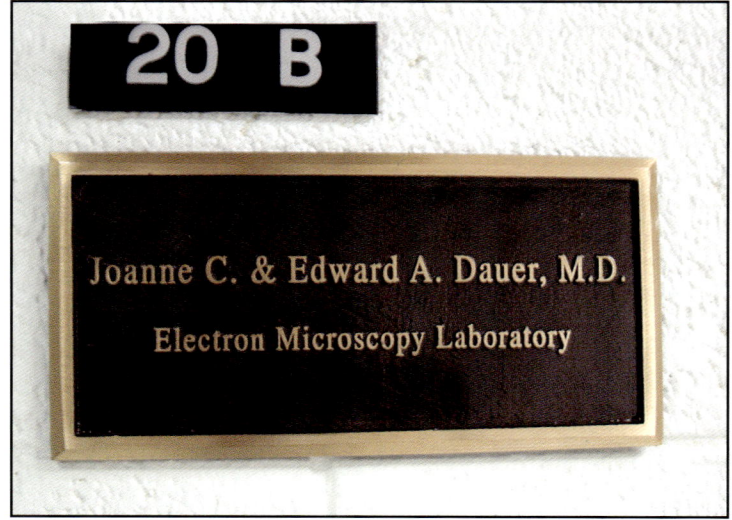

Entrance to the electron microscope laboratories at the University of Miami (Florida)

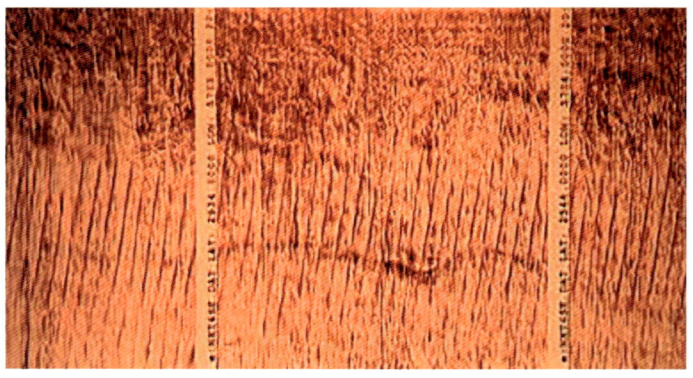

Sonar imaging allowed this first look at the actual damage to the Titanic's hull laying under the mud. Instead of the gaping gash, acoustic technology revealed six narrow openings caused by the Titanic's collision with the iceberg. These openings, like the one shown in the photo were responsible for her sinking.

Dr. Jeff Prince, Director of the electron microscope laboratories at the University of Miami, Department of Biology with the transmission electron microscope

Author's note: Thanks to Dr. Prince for his help in editing this book

Although this was normal for steel produced during that era, the high sulphur content is now known to have caused the steel to become very brittle in cold temperatures. This caused an unexpected weakness that was not taken into consideration during design and construction of the ship. If the steel were produced with less sulphur (as per the standards of today), the hull would not have been pierced by the iceberg but merely deformed.

Serving more than five million people as the only academic medical center in South Florida, the University of Miami School of Medicine has earned international acclaim for research, clinical care, and biomedical innovations.

Right: photo of elemental analysis of paint of black pigment found on a cave wall picture, performed by an electron microscope

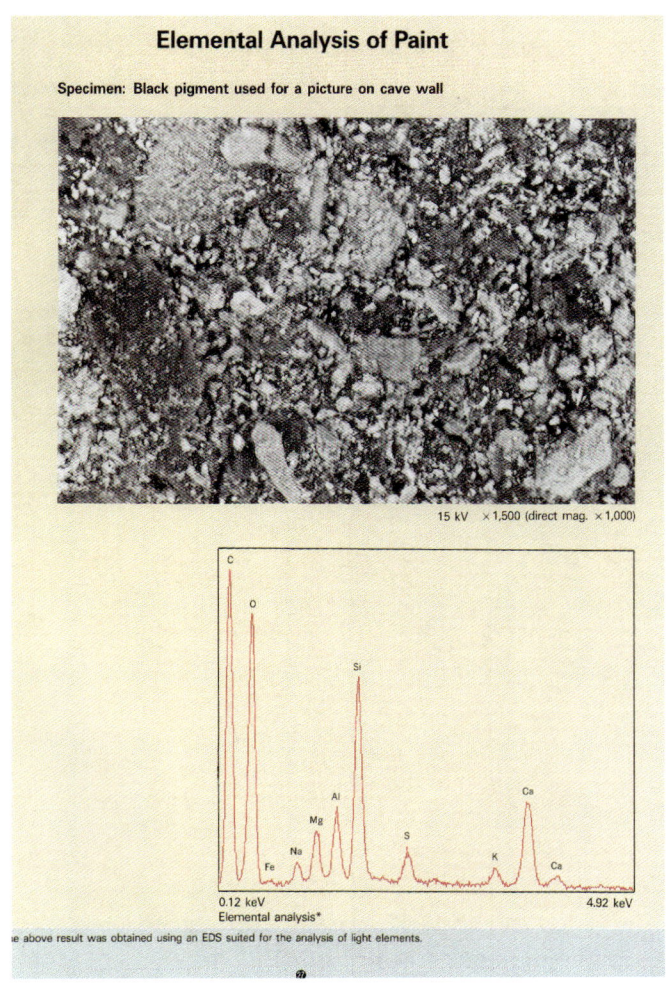

277

Letter Written by T. E. Lawrence - "Lawrence of Arabia"

16 VIII 22

Dear Mrs. Philly

This will be another inconclusive letter. We decided to invite Abdulla. Then a question rose of Feisal's coming home. Two would be too many: so Abdulla's invitation is held up pending the decision of the Irak business.

I think Abdulla will win: & he will probably be asked for about Sept. 10-20: & to stay perhaps 3 weeks.

Herbert Samuel suggested first that your man shouldn't come with him, for fear lest the province go to smash meanwhile. We wired back & he has weakened on this. I think that they will be asked to come together: but when & if ?   No one can say for the moment – but the point must be settled in the next fortnight. Winston's being away holds everything up ten days.

Yours very truly

T E Lawrence

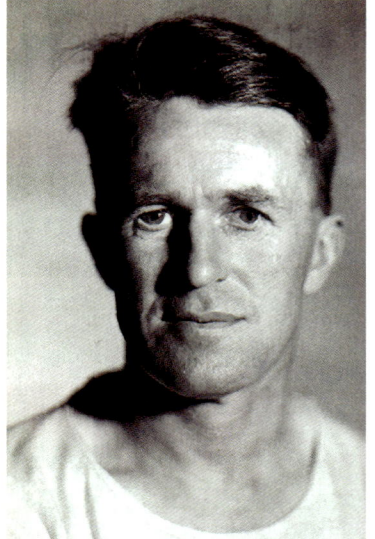

T. E. Lawrence (Lawrence of Arabia)
British Soldier and Author

1888 - 1935

"All men dream, but not equally. Those who dream by night in the dusty recesses of their minds wake in the day to find that it was vanity: but the dreamers of the day are dangerous men, for they may act their dream with open eyes, to make it possible."

JENNY
The most famous stamp error in existence

The stamp issued for use on the world's first airmail service was put on sale May 13, 1918. It was a 24-cent stamp picturing a Curtiss Jenny mail biplane and was printed in two colors. The number on the body of the plane was 38262, the number of the plane that made the first mail flight out of Washington, D.C.

Each pane of the stamps was printed by hand on a "spider press," similar to the type used to print currency. They were produced in sheets of one hundred stamps. The border or frame was printed first in red ink followed by the plane in blue ink. This second printing required the sheets to be manually removed and reinserted into the press after the plates were changed and re-inked in blue.

Unused copy of the "inverted Jenny," position #50, purchased by the author from Sonny Hagendorf, owner of Columbian Stamp Company. This stamp was originally part of a vertical pair sold from the 27th sale of the Colonel Edward H.R.Green collection on April 23, 1946 for $2,300.

The Spider press used to print the Jenny stamps
Photo-Courtesy, Bureau of Engraving and Printing

The "Jenny" was nicknamed after air pioneer Glenn H. Curtiss combined the best features of his "J" model and his own designed "N" model to create the "JN." The models ordered for the mail service was the JN-4H, capable of hauling 200 pounds of mail.

The Curtiss Jenny similar to the one pictured, disembarked from Washington D.C. on May 15, 1918. The trip to New York City was expected to take three hours, two hours shorter than the train. Franklin Delano Roosevelt, Assistant Secretary of the Navy and a stamp collector, was there along with Woodrow Wilson and other dignitaries.

George Boyle, a very young lieutenant, took off at 11:46 a.m. with 5,500 letters and the map to New York strapped to his leg. Boyle headed south instead of north, and crash landed in Waldorf, Maryland, 20 miles south of his take-off point. The plane was found UPSIDE DOWN in a field, just like the plane in the inverted Jenny.

Lieutenant Boyle's ill-fated flight after crashing in a field in Maryland. His later report described how he lost his way after leaving Washington, D.C.

Photo from The Christian Herald, June 12, 1918

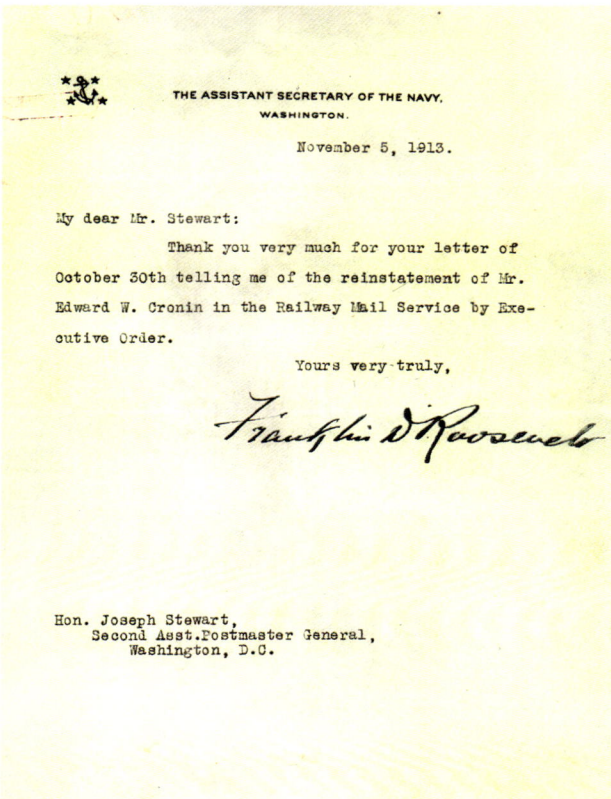

Two letters written by Franklin Delano Roosevelt. Left is a letter written on November, 1913 while he was Assistant Secretary of the Navy; right is a letter written in April of 1936, while he was the President of the United States.

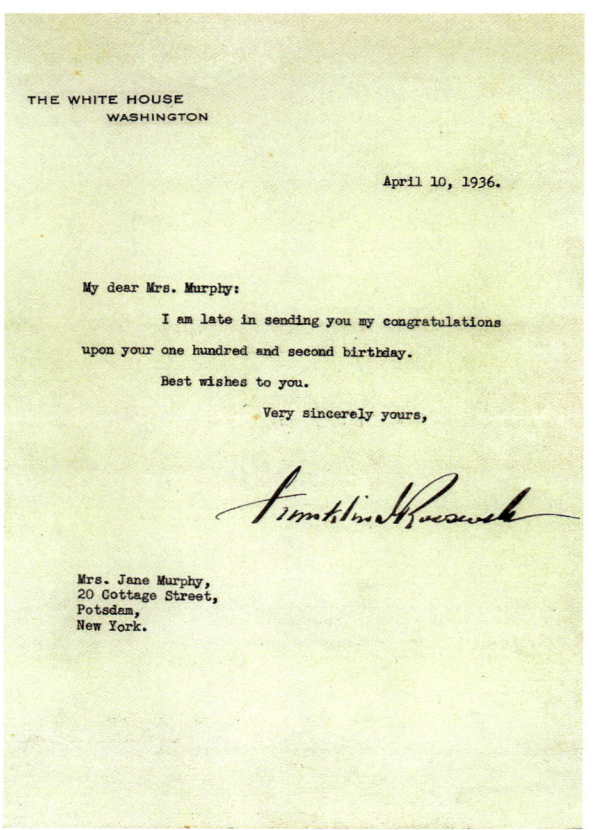

The Discovery of the Jenny

William T. Robey

William Robey was born April 21, 1889 and worked as a cashier at a Washington, D.C. stockbroker, W.B. Hibbs and Company. He was also a serious stamp collector and supplemented his meager income buying and selling stamps to help support his infant daughter and wife. Robey was aware of the possibility of the new airmail stamp being accidentally printed with the center inverted. He went to the post office at 1319 New York Avenue since it was only six blocks from his job. When he left home in the morning, he told his wife that he wanted to go to the post office before work, because "I have a strange feeling there's going to be a mistake."

The sheets he examined on his first visit to the post office were poorly centered, so Robey returned at noon and asked the same clerk if he had received any more stamps. The clerk reached down and pulled out one sheet of one hundred stamps with the blue plane printed upside down. Robey's "heart stood still." …"A thrill that comes once in a lifetime."

Robey without hesitation gave the clerk $24 for the sheet of stamps, showed him the error, and then inquired "Give me another one like the one I just bought." Robey left the post office in great haste when the clerk slammed the window shut.

The post office on New York Avenue in Washington D.C. where William T. Robey was sold the Jenny invert

Photo from The D.C. public library

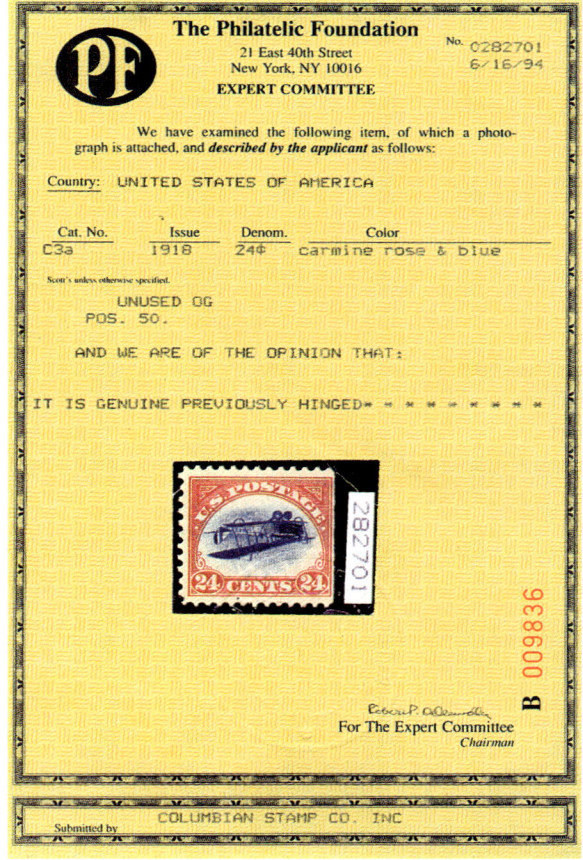

Philatelic Foundation certificate of authenticity for the Jenny invert

The Sale of the Sheet

Envelope this letter was sent in

The clerk was later interviewed by a newspaper reporter who asked him why he sold the sheet with such an obvious error. The clerk replied, "How was I to know the thing was upside down? I never saw an airplane before." Robey was soon visited by postal inspectors but since the stamps were legally purchased over the counter, they were unable to force him to return the error sheet.

Robey mistakenly believed that the stamps were printed in panes of 400 and thought that three other sheets may be already in other collectors hands, thereby lowering the value of his sheet. He wanted to sell the sheet as quickly as possible but wanted to obtain the highest price. The first offer of $500 from a dealer was not enough money. He sent this letter to Elliott Perry, a stamp dealer he had worked with in the past. It was postmarked 8 A.M. on May 15, 1918.

Letter sent to Perry by Robey dated May 15, 1918. "Did you receive my telegram. I have secured a sheet of 100 with inverted center, The only one in existence at this date. Are you interested?"

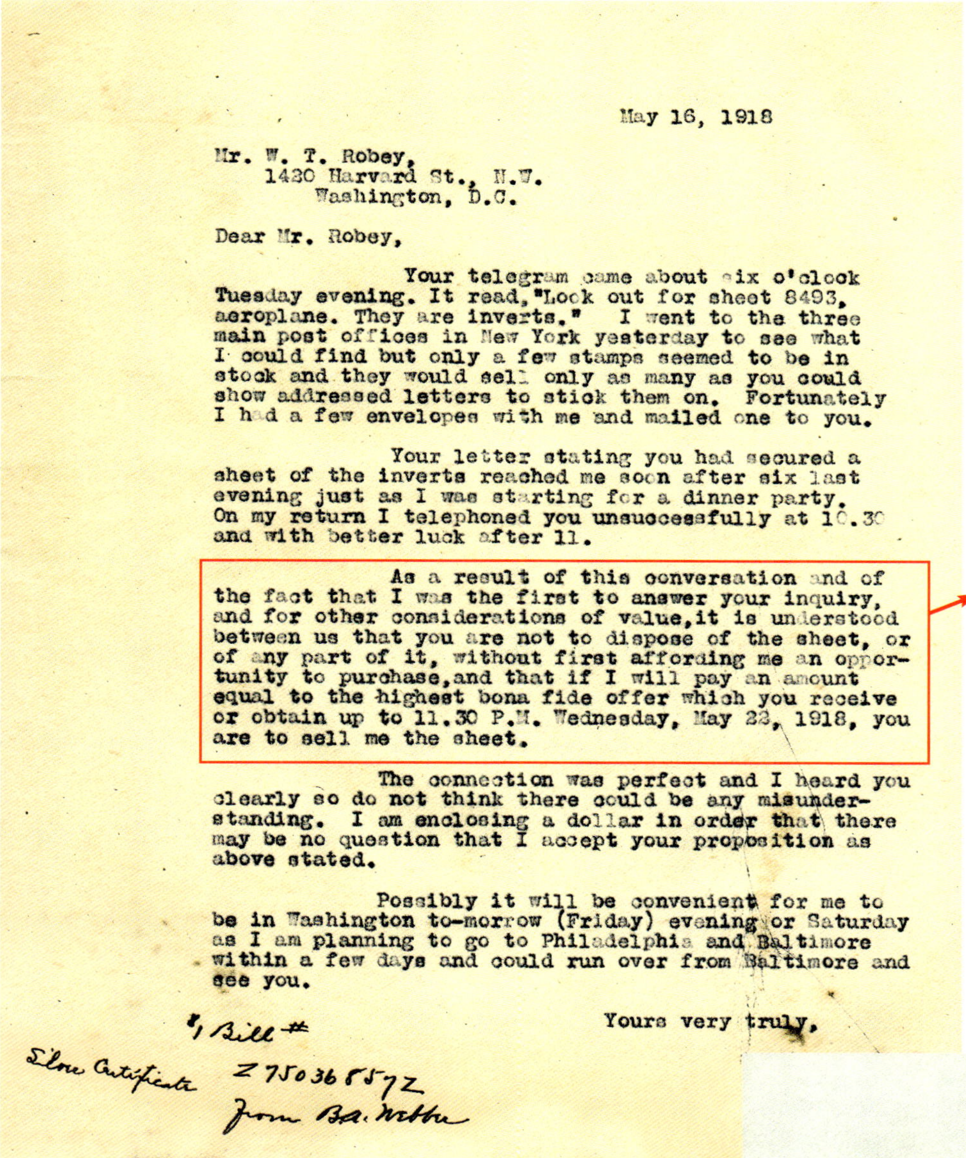

May 16, 1918

Mr. W. T. Robey,
1420 Harvard St., N.W.
Washington, D.C.

Dear Mr. Robey,

    Your telegram came about six o'clock Tuesday evening. It read, "Look out for sheet 8493, aeroplane. They are inverts." I went to the three main post offices in New York yesterday to see what I could find but only a few stamps seemed to be in stock and they would sell only as many as you could show addressed letters to stick them on. Fortunately I had a few envelopes with me and mailed one to you.

    Your letter stating you had secured a sheet of the inverts reached me soon after six last evening just as I was starting for a dinner party. On my return I telephoned you unsuccessfully at 10.30 and with better luck after 11.

    As a result of this conversation and of the fact that I was the first to answer your inquiry, and for other considerations of value, it is understood between us that you are not to dispose of the sheet, or of any part of it, without first affording me an opportunity to purchase, and that if I will pay an amount equal to the highest bona fide offer which you receive or obtain up to 11.30 P.M. Wednesday, May 22, 1918, you are to sell me the sheet.

    The connection was perfect and I heard you clearly so do not think there could be any misunderstanding. I am enclosing a dollar in order that there may be no question that I accept your proposition as above stated.

    Possibly it will be convenient for me to be in Washington to-morrow (Friday) evening or Saturday as I am planning to go to Philadelphia and Baltimore within a few days and could run over from Baltimore and see you.

    Yours very truly,

Perry replied to Robey's telegram and letter with his response dated May 16, 1918. Perry had received Robey's letter at 6 PM the same day it was mailed and offered to buy the sheet and enclosed a $1 silver certificate as a deposit.

"As a result of this conversation and of the fact that I was the first to answer your inquiry, and for other considerations of value, it is understood between us that you are not to dispose of the sheet, or of any part of it, without first affording me an opportunity to purchase, and that if I will pay an amount equal to the highest bonafide offer which you receive or obtain up to 11:30 P.M. Wednesday, May 23, 1918, you are to sell me the sheet."

    Robey went to New York City on Friday, May 17th in an effort to sell his sheet. He did not receive an acceptable offer and stopped off in Philadelphia to show the sheet to Philadelphia dealer Eugene Klein on May 19th. He sold the sheet for $15,000 to Klein two days later, who immediately resold it to the famous millionaire stamp collector Colonel Edward H.R. Green for $20,000. Green was the son of the famous miser, Hetty Green, the richest woman in the world. She was known as the "Witch of Wall Street."

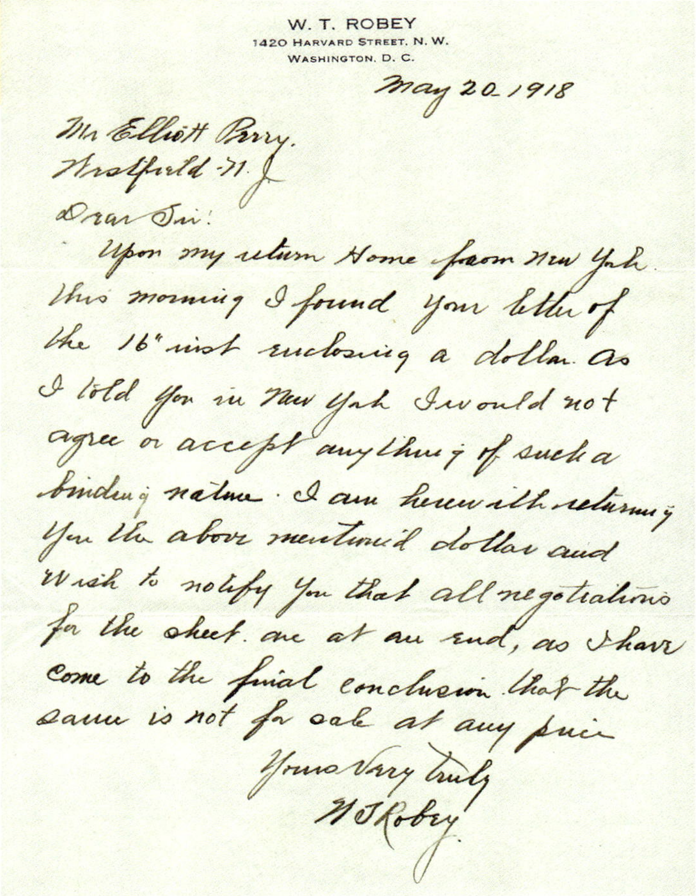

W. T. ROBEY
1420 HARVARD STREET, N.W.
WASHINGTON, D.C.

May 20 1918

Mr Elliott Perry.
Westfield N.J.

Dear Sir:

    Upon my return Home from New York this morning I found your letter of the 16" inst enclosing a dollar. As I told you in New York I would not agree or accept anything of such a binding nature. I am herewith returning you the above mentioned dollar and wish to notify you that all negotiations for the sheet are at an end, as I have come to the final conclusion that the same is not for sale at any price

Yours very truly
W T Robey

Robey wrote this letter to Perry returning his one dollar deposit

WHAT HAPPENED TO THE SHEET?

Eugene Klein
Photo from American Philatelic Research Library

When Eugene Klein delivered the sheet to Colonel Green, he suggested that it be broken up to allow other stamp collectors to own an example of the invert. He suggested selling the singles on the bottom row and far right row (the straight edge copies) for $175 each and $250 each for the fully perforated copies. This would allow Green to recover the cost of his investment and pay Klein a commission. He could then keep the remaining twenty stamps and own them at a very nominal cost (plate block of eight, center line block, left arrow block, and the lower left corner block).

Before Klein broke up the sheet, he numbered them very lightly in pencil on the back in the lower right quadrant from 1 to 100. This has allowed the stamps to be traced and followed over the years since the sheet was broken up. After the first ten stamps were sold quickly for $250 each, the price was increased to $350. Only two straight edge copies were sold initially, the balance remaining in Green's collection. In 1920, a copy sold at auction for $675 and in 1924, one was privately sold for $750. The $1,000 level was finally achieved in 1928 and gradually increased, even staying immune from the effects of the Great Depression.

Hetty Green - The Witch of Wall Street

From her early days as a child, Hetty Green's desire was to become the richest and most powerful woman in America. She achieved her goal by losing her dignity, love, and respect. She was very skilled in making money from her shrewd real estate and stock market investments, her initial fortune inherited from her New England whaling and ship owner ancestors. Most of her life she lived in a dilapidated apartment in Jersey City and rode to New York City in community coaches because she "couldn't afford" cabs. She did not want to spend money on soap, wore old dark rags for clothes, and haggled over prices. She loved to make money but did not want to spend it. She once spent hours in a coach looking for a two cent stamp she had misplaced.

When her daughter wanted to get married, she insisted her future son-in-law sign a legal document waiving any rights to her fortune. This was before the widespread use of the pre-nuptial agreement.

A picture of Mrs. Hetty Green made by a newspaper photographer at Morristown, N.J., in 1909
Photo from the book "The Witch of Wall Street" by Boyden Sparkes and Samuel Taylor Moore

"I have never achieved my ambition, which is to spend one day's income in one day."

Hetty died in 1916 at the age of 82. Her estate was worth over $100,000,000, an amount equivalent to billions after adjusting for inflation. Over $9,000,000 of her estate was in cash. Not a single cent was left to charity!

Edward (Ned) H. R. Green was never in the military but given the title Colonel by a friend in 1910. When he was a young boy, he would resell the morning paper in New York City after his mother read it to earn spending money. Even though Hetty loved her son dearly, there was one thing she could not do—spend money.

When he was fourteen, he was coasting on a sled down a steep hill, fell off, and dislocated his knee cap. He suffered excruciating pain but she could not bear to spend money to get him medical treatment. She had tried various means of treating the dislocation, the last one being the use of hot sand. This caused the flesh to slough off. Hetty, two or three years after the injury, dressed up as a beggar and finally took her son to a physician. Ned was taken to Bellvue hospital as a charity patient and treated until the physician found out his mother was Hetty Green. She left his care when he wanted to be paid in advance and five years after the accident, the leg was amputated due to gangrene.

Col. Edward Howland Robinson Green, Mrs. Green's son, who inherited half of her possessions

Photo from the book "The Witch of Wall Street" by Boyden Sparkes and Samuel Taylor Moore

After his mother's death, Ned started spending his inheritance and shortly thereafter began collecting stamps, currency, and many other collectibles. Money was no object. He was once quoted as saying "I have never achieved my ambition, which is to spend one day's income in one day." Colonel Green died in 1936 at the age of 67. There were 41 copies of the Jenny invert left in his estate. His holdings were sold in a series of auctions in the 1940's. Some of the rare currency notes in this book were also undoubtedly once part of his collections.

Here is Mrs. Green in the black & forbidding costume in which she was accustomed to appear on her daily rounds of the financial district of New York

Photo from the book "The Witch of Wall Street" by Boyden Sparkes and Samuel Taylor Moore

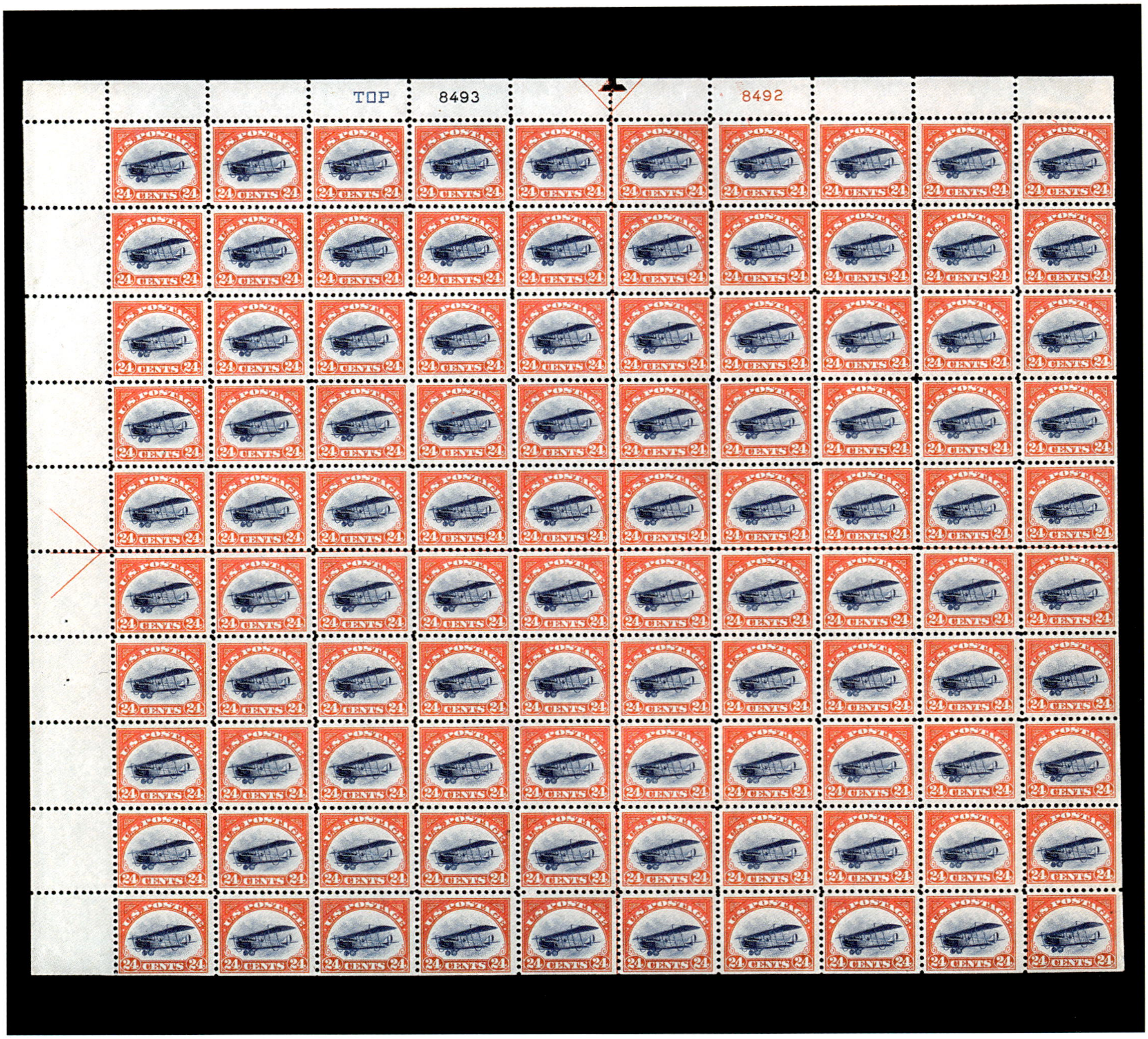

Full sheet of 100 stamps from the second printing

The word "TOP" in blue ink was used in the second printing of the stamp to avoid a repeat of the error. However, in an abundance of caution, a second "TOP" in red ink was shortly added to a third printing to help inspectors spot any further errors. The single blue "TOP" is extremely rare today due to the brief press run.

There is no text on the stamp saying "Air Mail." Nevertheless, the purpose of the stamp is clear from the design itself which incorporates an engraving of the Curtis Jenny Biplane.

What did Robey do with the Money?
He Sold the Jenny Invert Sheet of One Hundred for $15,000.

What did Robey do with the $14,976 profit? He bought a car for himself and a furnished house for his wife without a mortgage. Those two purchases used up all of his money.

His daughter Louise developed polio in 1923 at the age of six, and lost the use of her lower extremities. Robey and his wife mortgaged the house and used that money to pay for extensive medical care including physical and occupational therapy. This dedication to their daughter allowed her to fully recover from the effects of polio.

There are very few photographs of William T. Robey. Here, in one of the rare ones, he is photographed with his daughter Louise at her wedding.

Robey never wanted any publicity but would continue to speak about his discovery at stamp shows and would appear on a few radio programs to talk about the inverts. He did not want to be photographed and this picture with his daughter is the only photo known to exist other than his U.S. Government ID photo. *Photos - Louise Robey Birch*

Louise Robey Birch and her husband reviewing her mother's collection of newspaper articles, letters, and memorabelia regarding the Jenny inverts

WHERE ARE THE INVERTS TODAY?

Col. Edward H.R. Green would frequently have his driver park his limousine on Nassau street. This was the center of philately in New York City. Stamp dealers would come to his car offering stamps & collections for sale.

The sheet of Jenny inverts bought by William Robey for $24 on May 14, 1918 became the world's most famous stamps. Six blocks of four, including the plate block, and 71 singles are known to exist. Over the years, there have been some interesting stories regarding the individual stamps.

Colonel Green put one invert back to back with a normal stamp in a transparent glass case for his wife, the so called "locket" copy. Mabel Green, who died in 1950, was never known to have worn it around her neck. One copy was accidentally dropped out of an album and ended up, damaged, in a vacuum cleaner. One block of four was stolen in 1955 at a stamp convention and exhibition in Norfolk, Virginia. The thief was never apprehended, but two of the stamps broken from the block were later recovered. Two have never been accounted for and are missing to this date.

In May, 2002, four of the known six blocks, were sold by Harry (Sonny) Hagendorf, president of Columbian Stamp Company, for approximately three million dollars. The four blocks are illustrated below and will always rank as one of the most desirable items of philately.

Harry (Sonny) Hagendorf

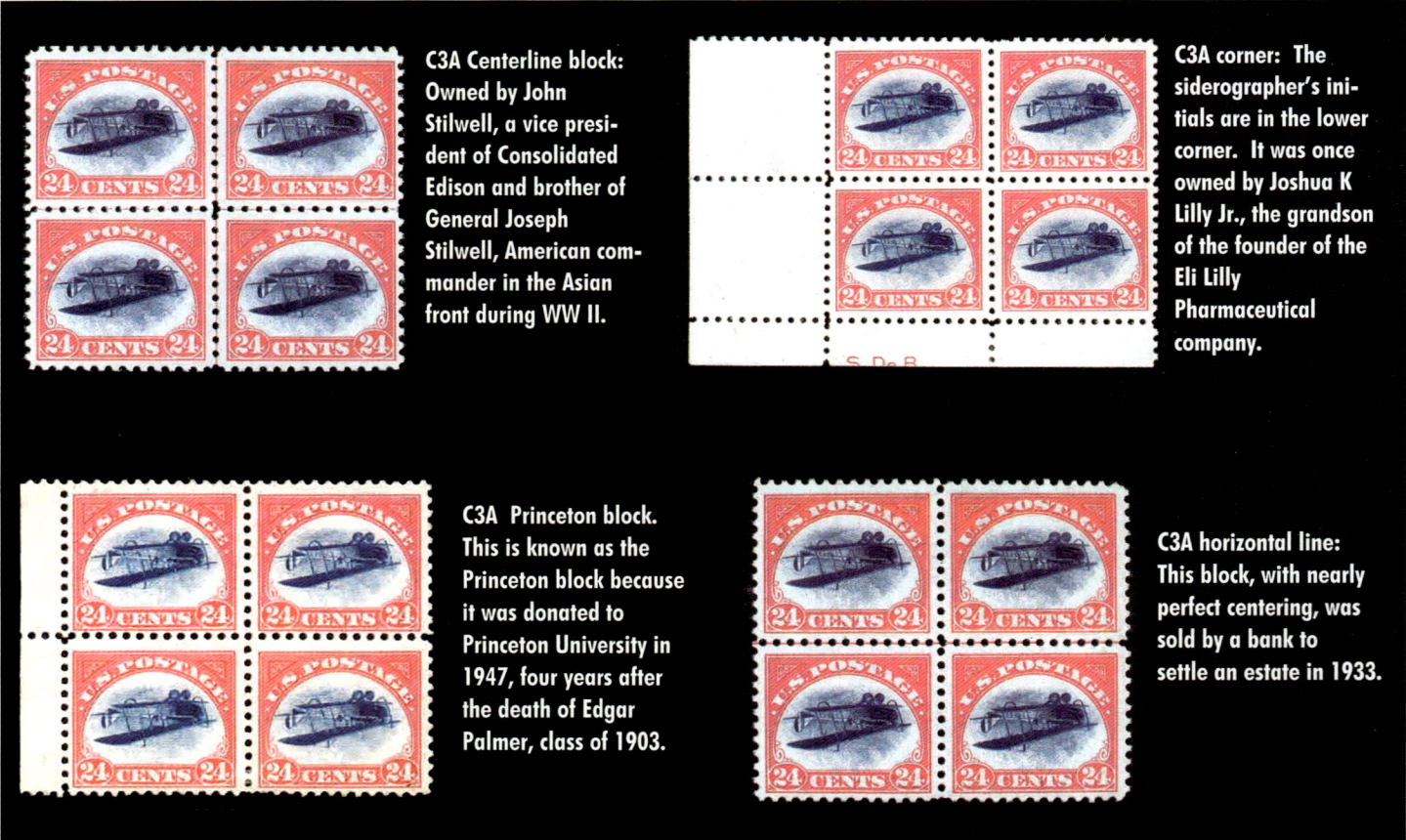

C3A Centerline block: Owned by John Stilwell, a vice president of Consolidated Edison and brother of General Joseph Stilwell, American commander in the Asian front during WW II.

C3A corner: The siderographer's initials are in the lower corner. It was once owned by Joshua K Lilly Jr., the grandson of the founder of the Eli Lilly Pharmaceutical company.

C3A Princeton block. This is known as the Princeton block because it was donated to Princeton University in 1947, four years after the death of Edgar Palmer, class of 1903.

C3A horizontal line: This block, with nearly perfect centering, was sold by a bank to settle an estate in 1933.

Chapter VIII

GOLD CERTIFICATES

Gold certificates are among the most beautiful and popular issues of United States currency. Not only were they redeemable in gold coin, but the backs are printed in a bright golden orange color. There were a total of nine different issues of gold certificates, but only notes issued 1882 and later were widely circulated. The first three issues were not even intended for circulation among the public and were used mainly between banks and for settling gold balances between clearing houses. Gold certificates were first made legal tender on July 12, 1882, and were payable for all public dues and debts including tariffs and taxes.

The last issue of the large size gold certificates were printed in 1913 (fifty dollar notes only) and 1922. They were widely used in circulation until President Roosevelt issued several executive orders requiring all persons "...to deliver on or before May 1, 1933, all gold coins, gold bullion, and gold certificates to a Federal Reserve Bank or member of the Federal Reserve System." Congress also passed in five days the Gold Reserve Act on January 30, 1934. It became illegal to even own gold certificates and most surviving examples were held in private collections, forgotten, left in safe deposit boxes, or stored overseas, primarily in Europe.

In 1964, the possession of the notes were finally legalized although, unfortunately, several rare specimens prior to that date were confiscated and either cancelled or destroyed by the Secret Service. Many collectors consider gold certificates the most desireable and colorful type of currency ever produced by the United States.

This $20 gold certificate is from the first issue of notes authorized by an Act of Congress, March 3, 1863. The first certificates were not issued until Nov 13, 1865, and no examples were ever sold at auction until 1990, when this particular example was purchased. It is the finest known $20 gold note of four known of the first $20 issue in private hands. There are two printed signatures and two hand signed signatures. A similar example was sold publicly in auction in June, 2000 for $528,000.

Oscar Fink

H. H. Van Dyck
The above signatures appear on the $20 and $100 gold certificates of 1863

This $100 gold certificate from the first series of 1863 is the only example that exists in private hands. Two other notes of this design are in the Smithsonian Institution-one autographed countersignature that was confiscated and cancelled and the other one with an engraved countersignature. Thus, this design is unique in private collections and is one of three unique notes featured on the cover of this book.

Although a black and white photograph of this note appears in a reference book, most dealers have never seen it, and its very existence was questioned in a 1990 Auction catalog when the $20 note on the prior page was offered for sale. Not only is this the only $100 gold note of this design, but it is a key to a complete type collection of gold notes or $100 type notes.

It is machine signed by Colby and Spinner and hand signed by two other signatures. It is a beautiful, unrestored high grade original note in almost uncirculated condition.

The only $10 large size gold certificate was issued in 1907 and 1922. Pictured is Michael Hillegas, who served as the first Treasurer of the United States from 1775 to 1789. He was originally a merchant from Philadelphia who became wealthy dealing in sugar refining and iron manufacturing.

Hillegas was a good friend of Ben Franklin and spent his entire fortune supporting the revolution, spending part of the war as quartermaster. He is buried next to Franklin in Philadelphia, near the Liberty Bell and Independence Hall.

An original document signed by King George III of England dated 1776, the same year as the signing of the Declaration of Independence

CHARLES R. DARWIN, 1809-1882

Charles Darwin - British Naturalist - 1809 -1882

Charles Darwin was born in Shrewsbury, England. He was the grandson of the famous physician and naturalist Erasmus Darwin, who had proposed a theory of evolution in the 1790's. His maternal grandfather was the successful china and pottery businessman Josiah Wedgwood. Charles' father was a physician. His mother Susannah Wedgwood Darwin, died when he was eight years old.

Darwin went to the University of Edinburgh to study medicine at the age of sixteen, but dropped out a year later and went to the University of Cambridge to become a clergyman of the Church of England. Darwin was independently wealthy and never had to earn an income. His most significant contribution to science was his theory of evolution through natural selection or the survival of the fittest. His famous book, On the Origin of Species by Means of Natural Selection was published in 1859.

Darwin married his first cousin Emma Wedgwood at the age of thirty. He and his wife had ten children, three of whom died in infancy. They lived in Downe, Kent from 1842 until Darwin's death in 1882 at the age of seventy-three. Darwin suffered from panic disorders and constant fatigue throughout his life. He is buried in Westminster Abbey.

Charles Darwin in the Galapagos. In 1831, Charles Darwin sailed to the Galapagos Islands on the HMS Beagle.

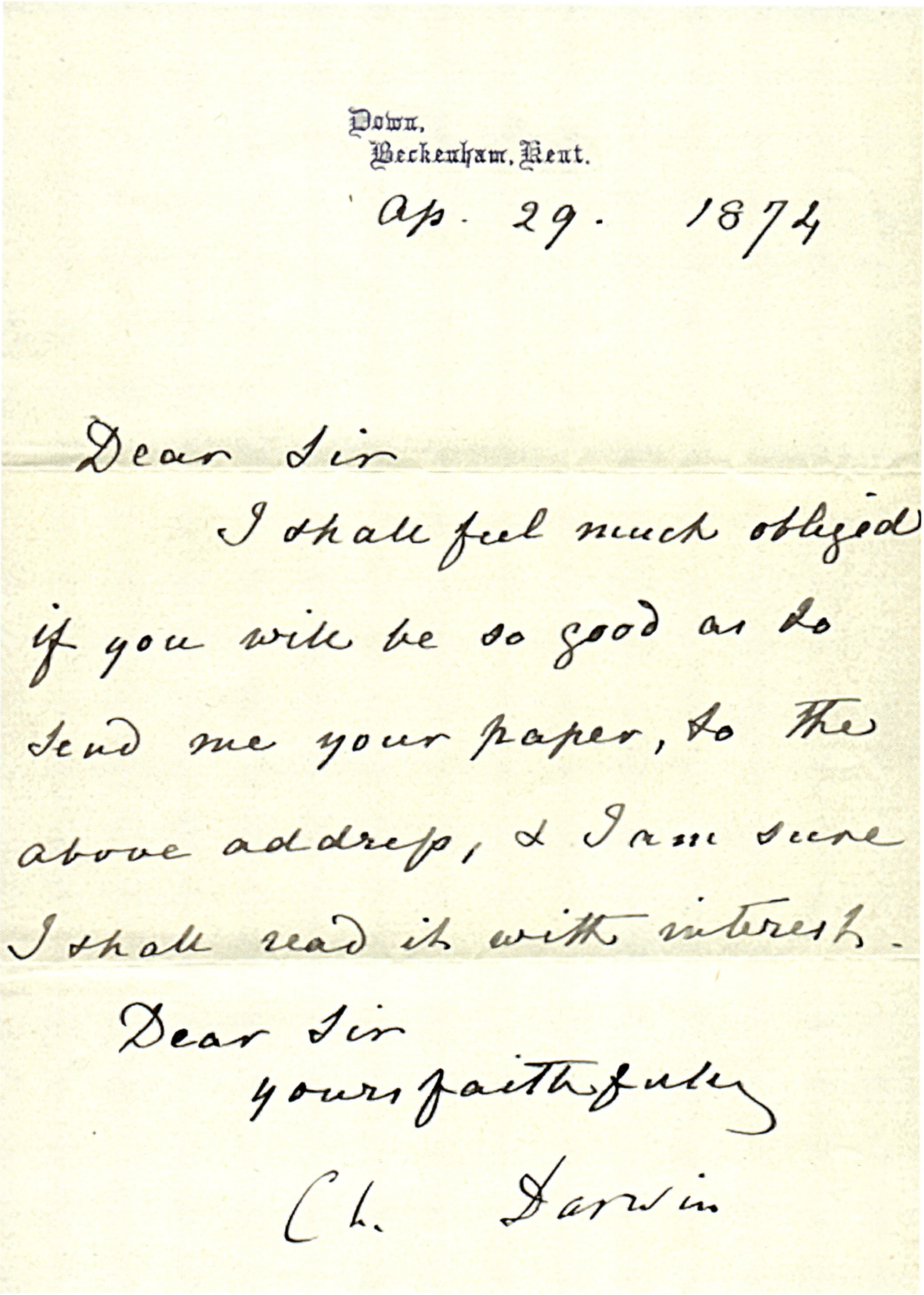

Down,
Beckenham, Kent.

Ap. 29. 1874

Dear Sir

I shall feel much obliged if you will be so good as to send me your paper, to the above address, & I am sure I shall read it with interest.

Dear Sir
Yours faithfully
Ch. Darwin

Letter written by Charles Darwin in his own hand, dated April 29, 1874

This triple signature $20 is crisp uncirculated and is the finest example known.

Portrait of President James Garfield, shot on July 2, 1881, by an embittered attorney who had failed to get appointed for a consular post. The multiple attempts to remove the bullet, which was not endangering any major internal organs or vessels, led ultimately to a systemic infection and his death on September 19, 1881.

Chester A. Arthur
21st President of the United States

The following letter was hand written by Chester Arthur on Christmas Eve, 1882, while he was the President on White House stationery. The White House at that time was known as the Executive Mansion. Letters written by Presidents in their own handwriting on White House stationery are rare and desired by collectors. Most letters were written by secretaries and only signed by the President. This letter came from the Forbes Magazine collection.

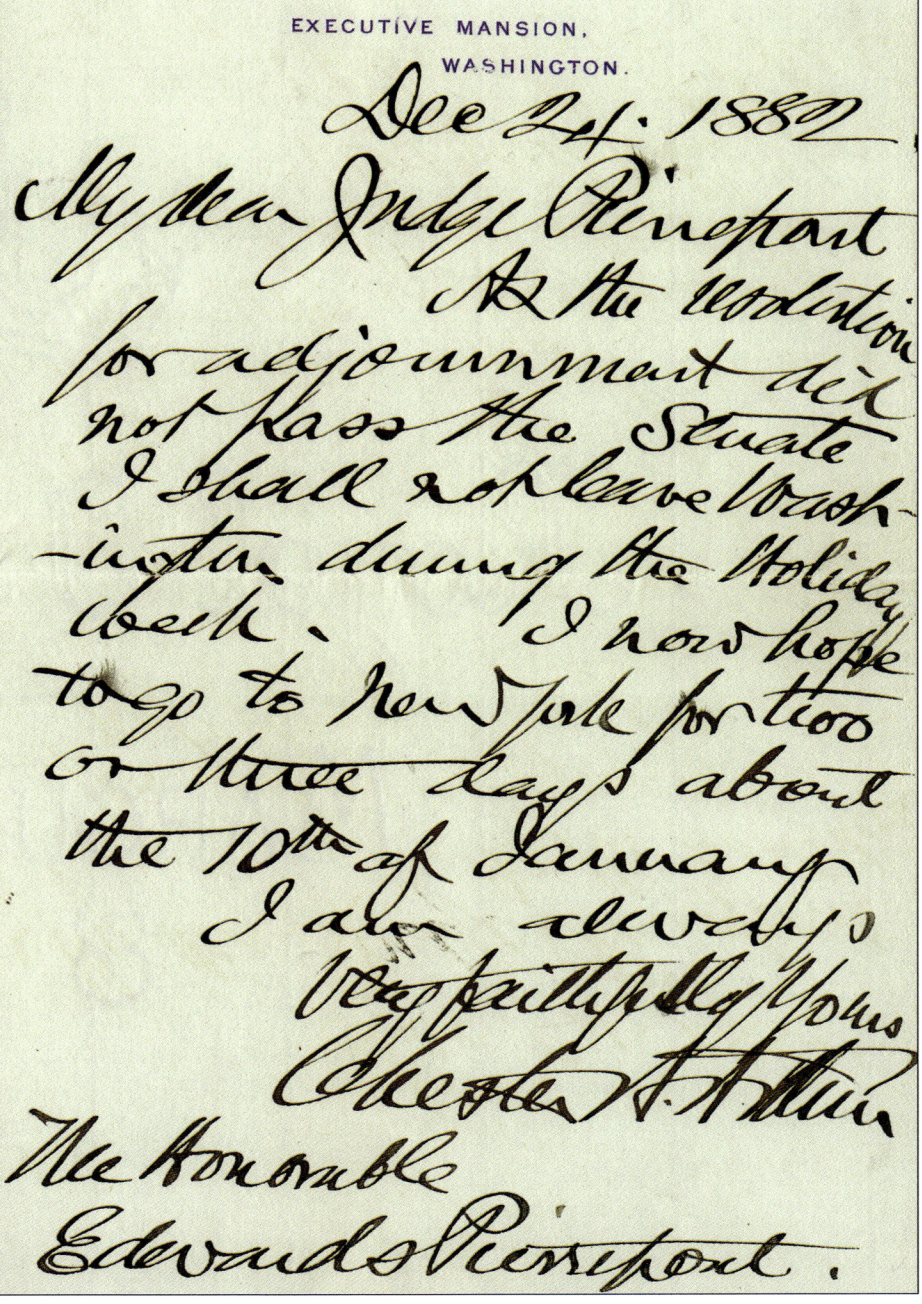

Text of the letter:

December 24, 1882

My dear Judge Pierrepont
    As the resolution
For adjournment did
Not pass the senate
I shall not leave Wash-
-ington during the Holiday
Week. I now hope
To go to New York for two
Or three days about
The 10th of January.

    I am always
        Very faithfully yours
        Chester A. Arthur

The Honorable
Edwards Pierrepont.

James A. Garfield
20th President of the United States

Although Garfield is remembered by most people as the 20th President of the United States who was assassinated after only four months in office, he was an officer in the Civil War, rising in rank rapidly from Lt. Colonel to Major General. He exhibited superb military leadership, had a sound understanding of battlefield tactics, and understood the important relationship between war and politics. Garfield is also known for stimulating the public's interest in civil service reform. He was replaced by his Vice President, Chester A. Arthur.

James A. Garfield, 20th president was assassinated after only 4 months in office

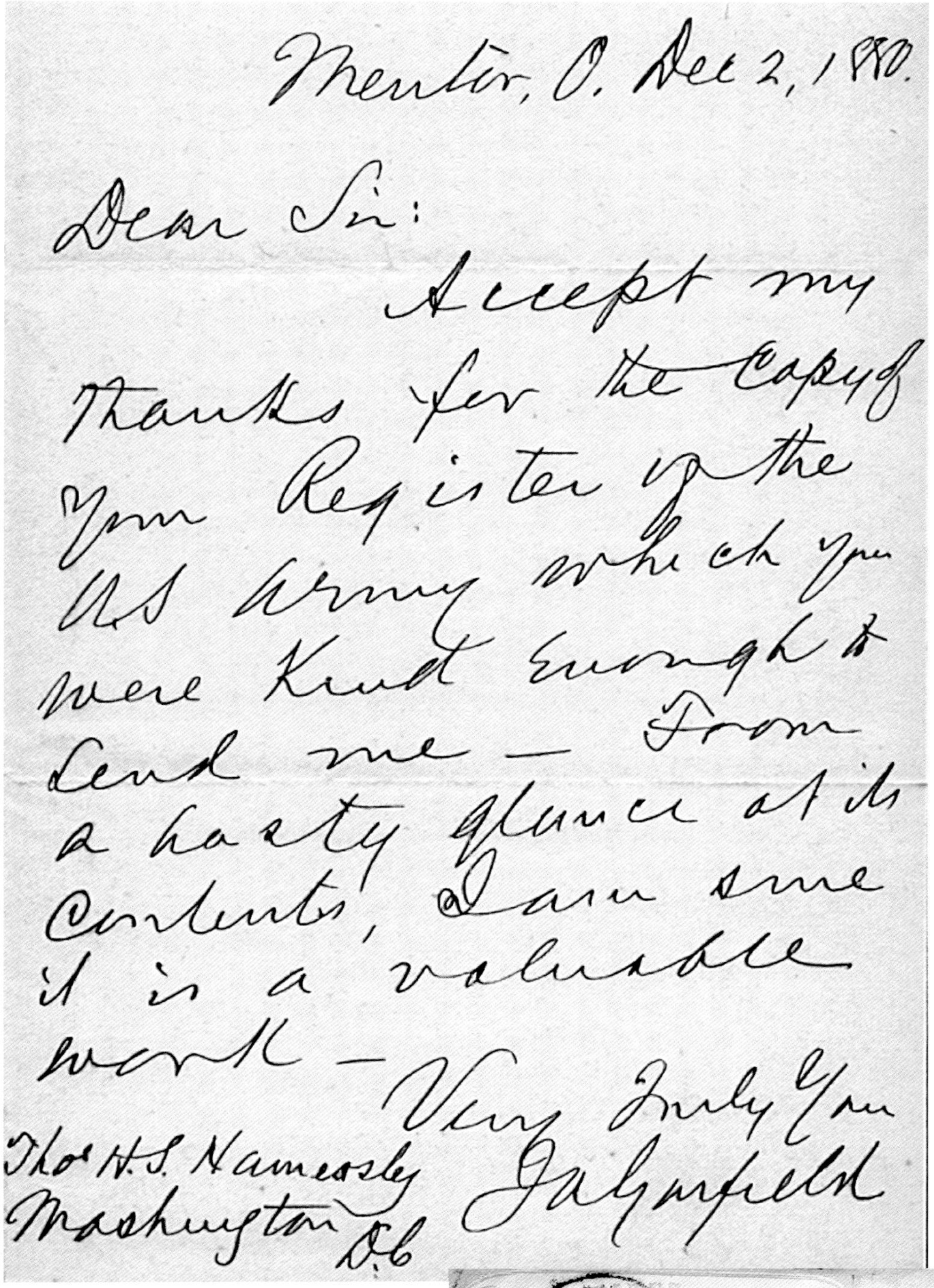

Mentor, O. Dec 2, 1880.

Dear Sir:

Accept my thanks for the copy of your Register of the US Army which you were kind enough to send me — From a hasty glance at its contents, I am sure it is a valuable work —

Very Truly Yours

J A Garfield

Thos H.S. Hamersly
Washington D.C.

Letter handwritten by James Garfield on December 2, 1880. The letter reads as follows:

Mentor, O. Dec 2, 1880

Dear Sir:
Accept my thanks for the copy of your register of the US army which you were kind enough to send me - From a hasty glance of it's contents, I am sure it is a valuable work -
Very Truly yours
J A Garfield

Thoe H.S. Namensley
Washington D.C.

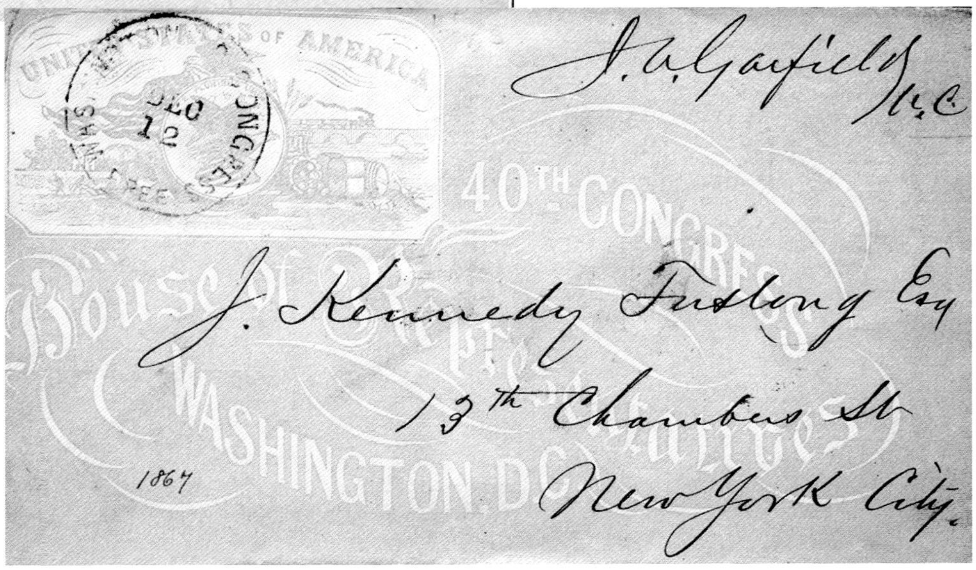

Shown right is a free frank addressed by James Garfield to a J. Kennedy Fuslong of New York City

This envelope bears the watermark of the 40th Congress

The above 1905 note is called the "Technicolor Note," due to its wide array of colors and red serial numbers. This colorful and popular note was only printed for one year during the Theodore Roosevelt administration.

"Keep it for your children and your children's children, and for all who come after you, as one of the great sights which every American, if he can travel at all, must see."
Teddy Roosevelt on the Grand Canyon

The $20 gold note was slightly redesigned for the 1906 issue and was not as colorful as the prior years note. Minor differences were also incorporated in the design of 1922. In 1928, currency was redesigned and reduced in size to current standards in an effort to reduce the amount of ink and paper used in currency production, thus lowering production costs.

Pictured above is a 1928 series gold certificate that was withdrawn from circulation in 1933

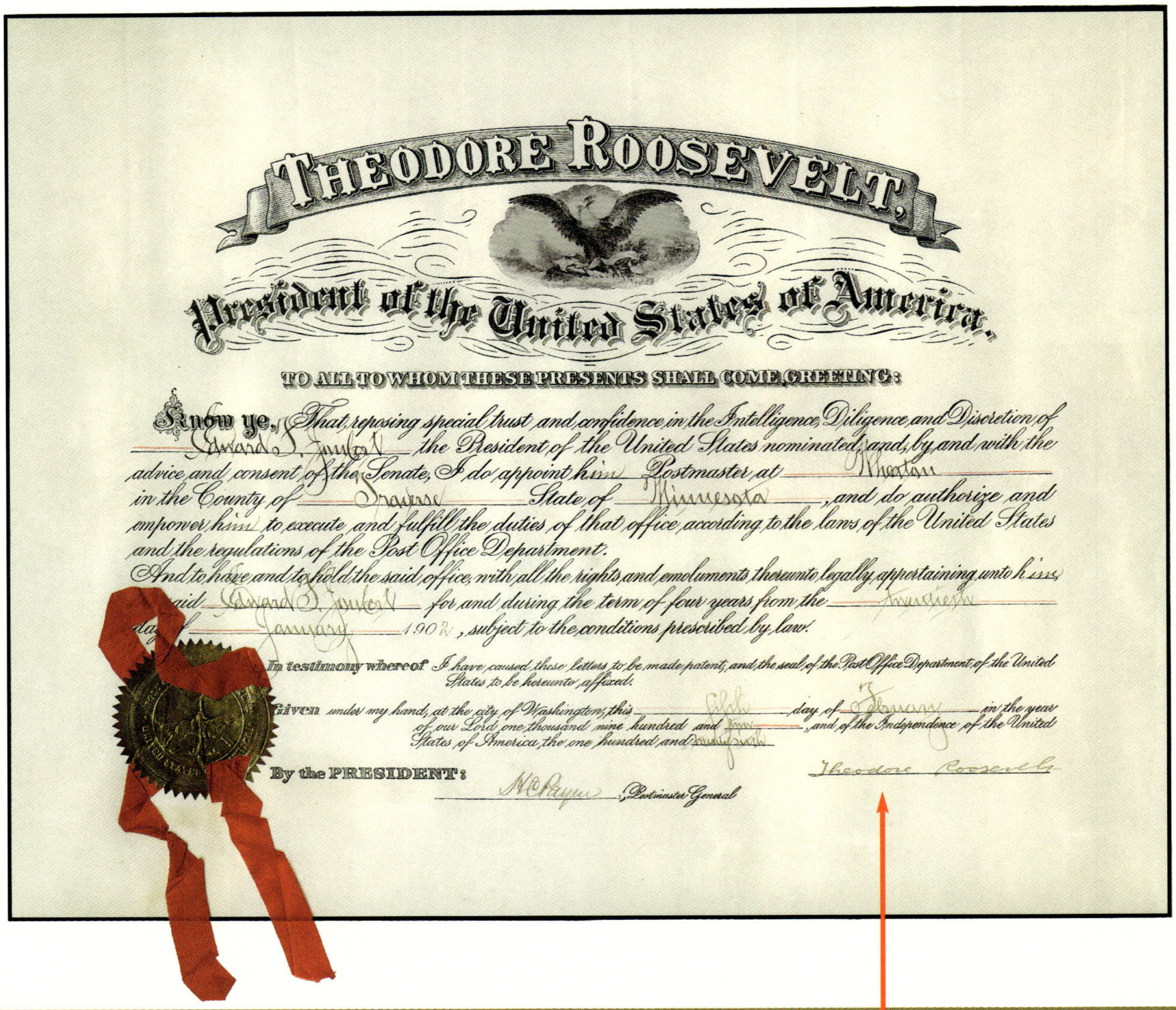

THEODORE ROOSEVELT,

President of the United States of America,

TO ALL TO WHOM THESE PRESENTS SHALL COME, GREETING:

Know ye, That, reposing special trust and confidence in the Intelligence, Diligence, and Discretion of [illegible] the President of the United States nominated, and, by and with the advice and consent of the Senate, I do appoint him Postmaster at Wheaton in the County of Traverse State of Minnesota, and do authorize and empower him to execute and fulfill the duties of that office according to the laws of the United States and the regulations of the Post Office Department.

And to have and to hold the said office, with all the rights and emoluments thereunto legally appertaining unto him the said [illegible] for and during the term of four years from the twentieth day of January 1902, subject to the conditions prescribed by law.

In testimony whereof I have caused these letters to be made patent, and the seal of the Post Office Department of the United States to be hereunto affixed.

Given under my hand, at the city of Washington, this fifth day of February in the year of our Lord one thousand nine hundred and two, and of the Independence of the United States of America, the one hundred and twenty-sixth

By the PRESIDENT:

H.C. Payne, Postmaster General

Theodore Roosevelt

Signature of Theodore Roosevelt is illustrated on an original certificate appointing the Postmaster in Minnesota, February, 1902

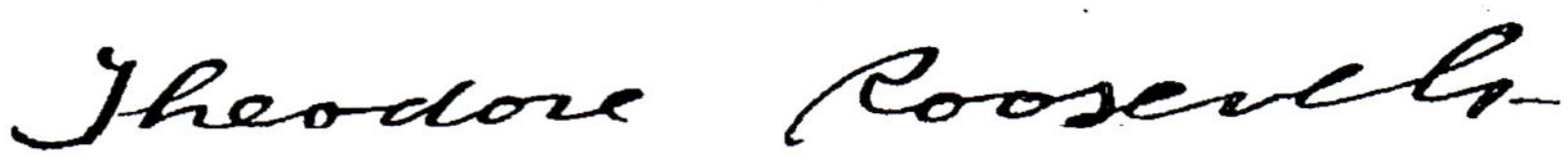

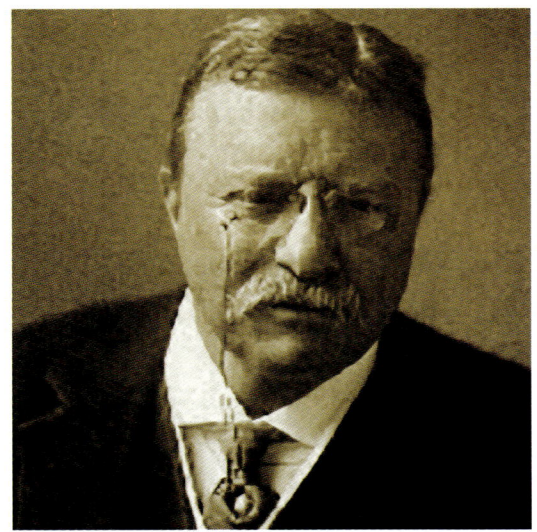

Russia and Japan had been at war since February, 1904. On June 8, 1905, Theodore Roosevelt, sensing a need for world peace, met with the two powers in Portsmouth, New Hampshire, to mediate the end to the war. The final peace accord was signed September 5th and Roosevelt received the Nobel Peace Prize that year.

Theodore "Teddy" Roosevelt was the colorful and dynamic personality who dominated the American political landscape from 1900 until World War I. He became the 26th president of the United States following the assassination of William McKinley in 1901.

WILLIAM McKINLEY (1843-1901)
Twenty–fifth President of the United States (1897-1901)

President William McKinley

This letter was written July 25, 1896, one month after his nomination as the Republican candidate for President

WILLIAM McKINLEY,
CANTON, OHIO.

July 25th, 1896.

Mr. John A. Bower,
    Care Dilworth Bros.
        # 957 Penn Ave.
            Pittsburgh, Pa.

My dear Sir :

For your suggestions of the 22nd. inst., please accept my thanks.

Yours very truly,

W M Kinley

Ida McKinley retained the free frank privilege after the assassination of her husband, President William McKinley. This letter was postmarked February 12, 1902, and written to Mrs. Myron T. Herrik.

PAN–AMERICAN EXPOSITION OF 1901

The Pan-American Exposition of 1901 was held in Buffalo, New York from May 1 to November 2, 1901. It covered a site of 342 acres. It attracted eight million people from all over the world. The African, Eskimo and Mexican villages were among the most popular attractions. The Exposition celebrated the harmony among the nations of North, South and Central America, after the end of the Spanish-American War of 1898.

Shown right, the official logo for the Pan-American Exposition of 1901 at Buffalo, New York

Original admission ticket to the 1901 Pan-American Exposition.
Adult admission to the Exposition was fifty cents for adults and twenty-five cents for children. If you came on Sundays after 7 p.m., admission fee was discounted by fifty per cent. The daily program cost five cents. There were 36 restaurants, 15 kitchens in concessions and villages, and 57 soft drink stands on the grounds. The average rate for a hotel room was one dollar per person a night.

This Exposition was a great opportunity for the United States to showcase new inventions and technology. It featured the first electric typewriter, the Blickensderfer. The Brownie Camera No. 2, with detachable winding key was a highlight of the Exposition. The amazing Electric Tower showed the world America's technical superiority. It was illuminated nightly by thousands of brightly colored light bulbs. Buffalo was also "showing off" its new electric streetlights and trolley car.

One of the modern advances in medical technology on display at the Exposition of 1901 was the infant incubator. For a dime, the public could enter a building called, "Infant Incubators" and view premature babies being cared for in a new incubator.

One of the most popular exhibits at the Exposition was the "Infant Incubators." Hundreds lined up to visit the exhibit.

Inside, visitors viewed premature babies being cared for in this amazing new invention

305

Series 1928 Five Hundred Dollar Gold Certificate

President McKinley and his wife Ida stepping from the train as they arrived at the 1901 Pan-American Exposition. The next day as Mrs. McKinley was at the home of the president of the Exposition, the president was asinated by a Polish anarchist.

Photo: McKinley Memorial Library

1901 stamps issued by the United States to commemorate the Pan-American Exposition

An historical event happened in the fall of the Exposition. On September 6, 1901, President William McKinley was shot by Leon Czolgosz, a Polish citizen affiliated with the Anarchist movement. It was an extremely hot day and many people had handkerchiefs in their hands to wipe the excess sweat from their foreheads. No one noticed that Czolgosz had a handkerchief wrapped around his right hand. He shot the President as he extended his hand to him. He was wounded in the upper abdomen. President McKinley died eight days later of peritonitis. His Vice President, Theodore Roosevelt, became President on September 14, 1901.

Crowds around the hospital while McKinley was undergoing surgery Photo: University of Buffalo archives

ADVERTISING COVERS

It was not unusual for business letters mailed in the 19th and early part of the 20th centuries to have advertising on part of the envelope promoting their products. These cachets are interesting and colorful reminders of our past and are in great demand from collectors.

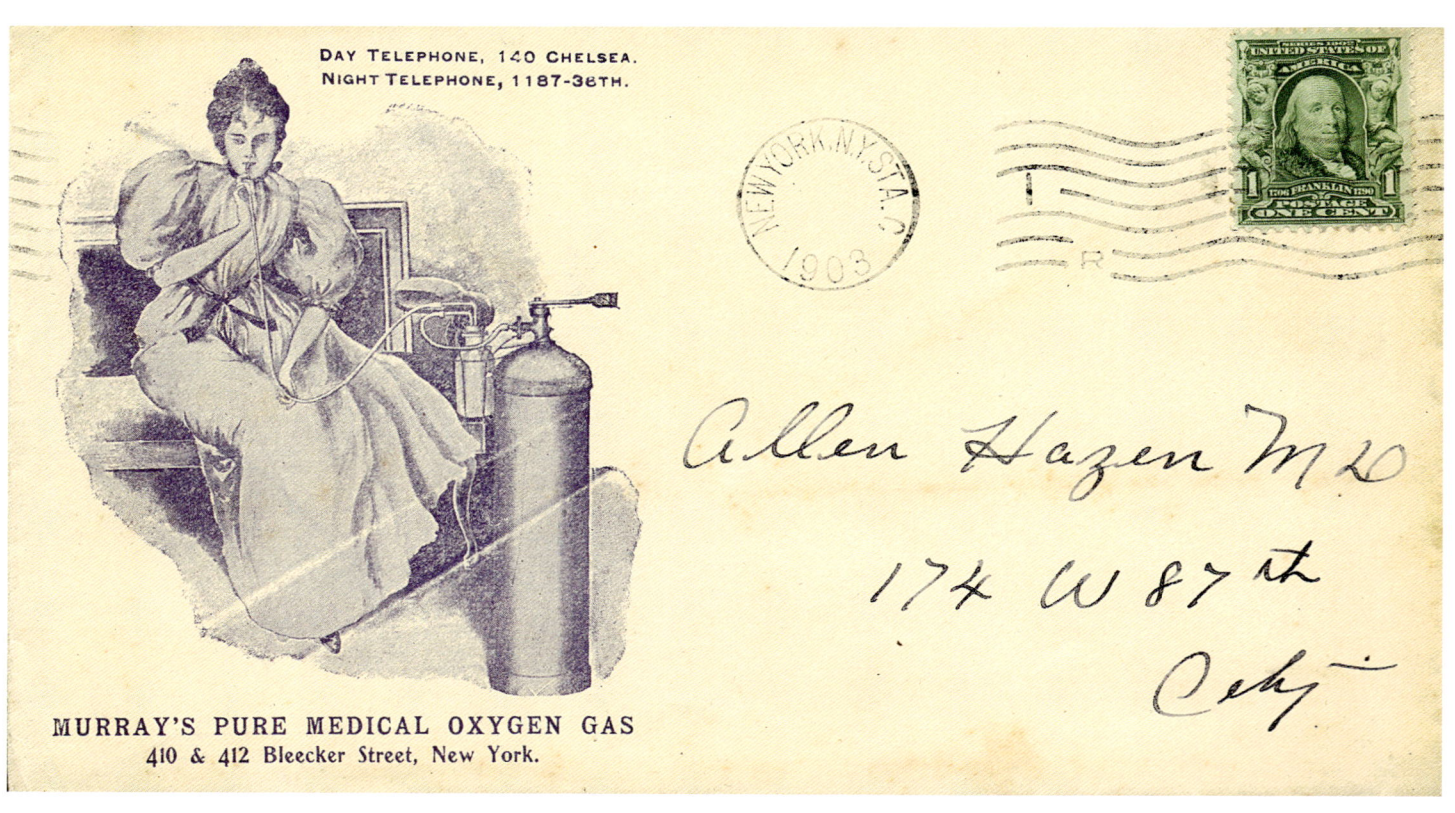

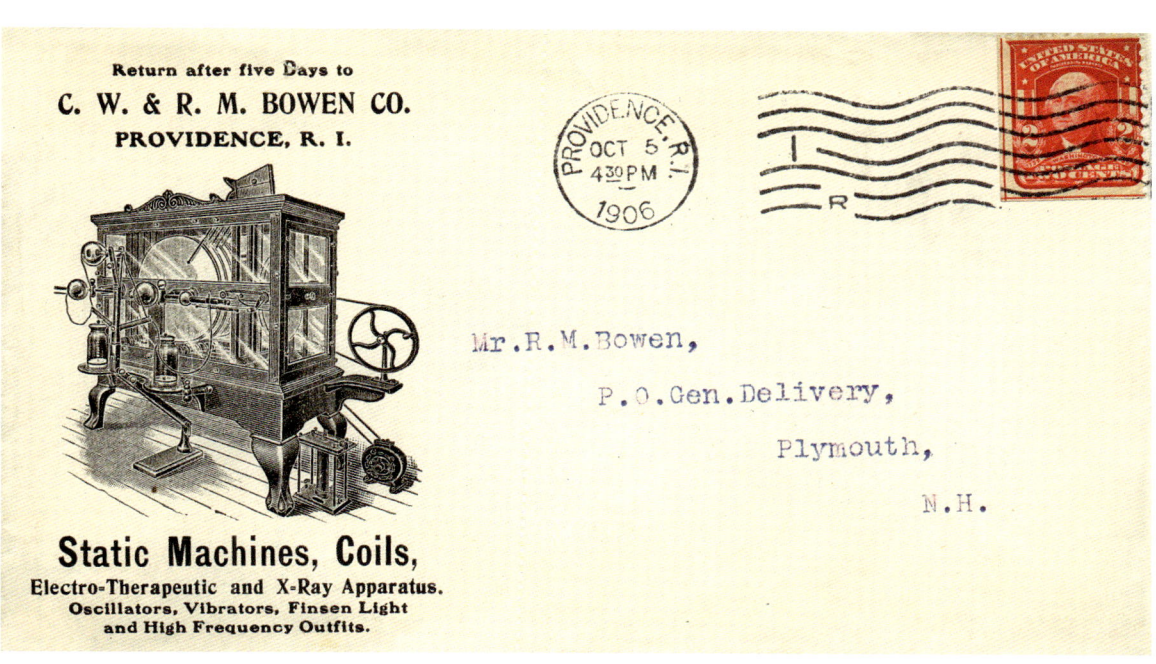

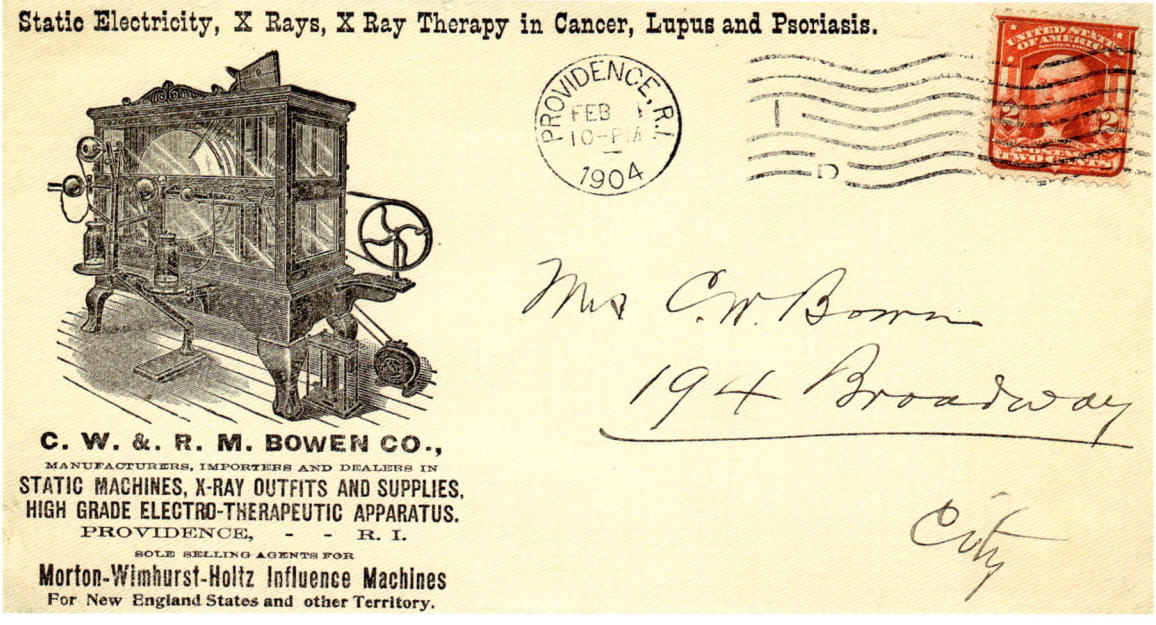

CALVIN COOLIDGE (1872-1933)

Calvin Coolidge - Thirtieth President
1923-1929

Calvin Coolidge was born in Plymouth, Vermont on July 4, 1872. He was given the birth name John Calvin Coolidge, but in early adulthood dropped the John, and was called Calvin Coolidge. Coolidge's father was a jack-of-all-trades, teacher, storekeeper, farmer, politician, and a mechanic. His mother Victoria Moor Coolidge died when Calvin was twelve.

He graduated from Amherst College cum laude, and entered law and politics in Massachusetts. He advanced politically from councilman, to mayor of Northhampton, to the house in Massachusetts, to state senator, to lieutenant governor, and governor of Massachusetts. He served as Vice President under President Harding and became the 30th President of the United States when Harding died in office.

He was a very popular President. His first message to Congress in 1923 called for isolation in foreign policy, tax cuts, a strong economy and limited aid to farmers. He was known as a man of few words. But as President, he was so kind and patient as to be photographed in Indian war bonnets or cowboy dress. He greeted a variety of delegates to the White House daily.

Coolidge married Grace Ann Goodhue at the age of thirty-three. She was the daughter of a Vermont mechanical engineer. She was a teacher at the Clarke Institute for the Deaf in Northhampton. Grace Coolidge was a woman of natural charm and good humor.

President Coolidge demanded and received efficient and economical performance in all government operations. He was most successful as President. He died in 1933 of coronary thrombosis at the age of sixty-one. He was buried in his family plot in Plymouth Notch, Vermont.

The Coolidge Homestead

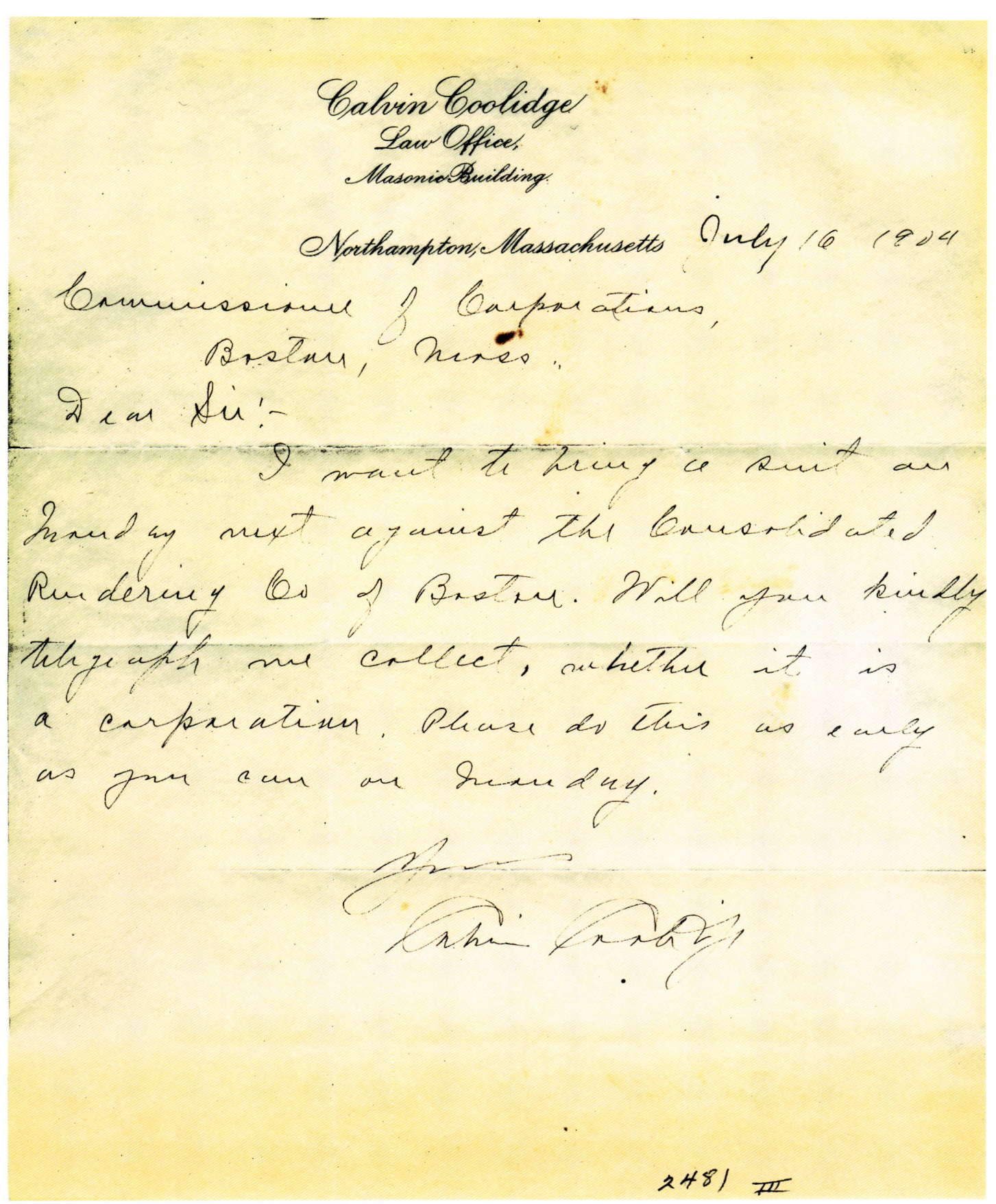

Letter written by Calvin Coolidge when he was 32 years old and a young lawyer in 1904

Admiral Richard Byrd Naval Aviator and Polar Explorer

Admiral Richard Byrd

Richard Byrd was born in Virginia in 1888 and attended the U.S. Naval Academy in Annapolis, graduating in 1912. He retired in 1916 due to an ankle injury but was recalled to duty during World War I and learned to fly as a naval aviator. Byrd was an accomplished seaplane pilot, navigator (flying over water out of sight of land), and developed techniques for nighttime landings.

His interest in exploring the South Pole began after his pioneering flights over Greenland and the North Pole from 1925-1926. Byrd's initial exploration was supposed to be on a dirigible but President Coolidge canceled that plan in 1924. He flew over the arctic in 1925 as part of a Navy expedition and in 1926 on a privately financed flight.

The first Antarctic expedition was planned in 1928 and was supported by public financial assistance. This was the first use of an airplane, aerial photography, snowmobiles and other scientific technology to explore Antarctica. He returned to active duty during World War II and was appointed commanding officer of the United States Antarctic Service.

In 1926 Richard Byrd put his expertise in aviational navigation to work and challenged the public's imagination by being the first to fly over the North Pole. This photograph was taken moments before the first polar flights on May 9, 1926. Byrd himself was the navigator while Floyd Bennett was the pilot.

Photos:
Ohio State University Archivist Raimund Goerler and Richard Cullather of the Byrd Polar Research Center.

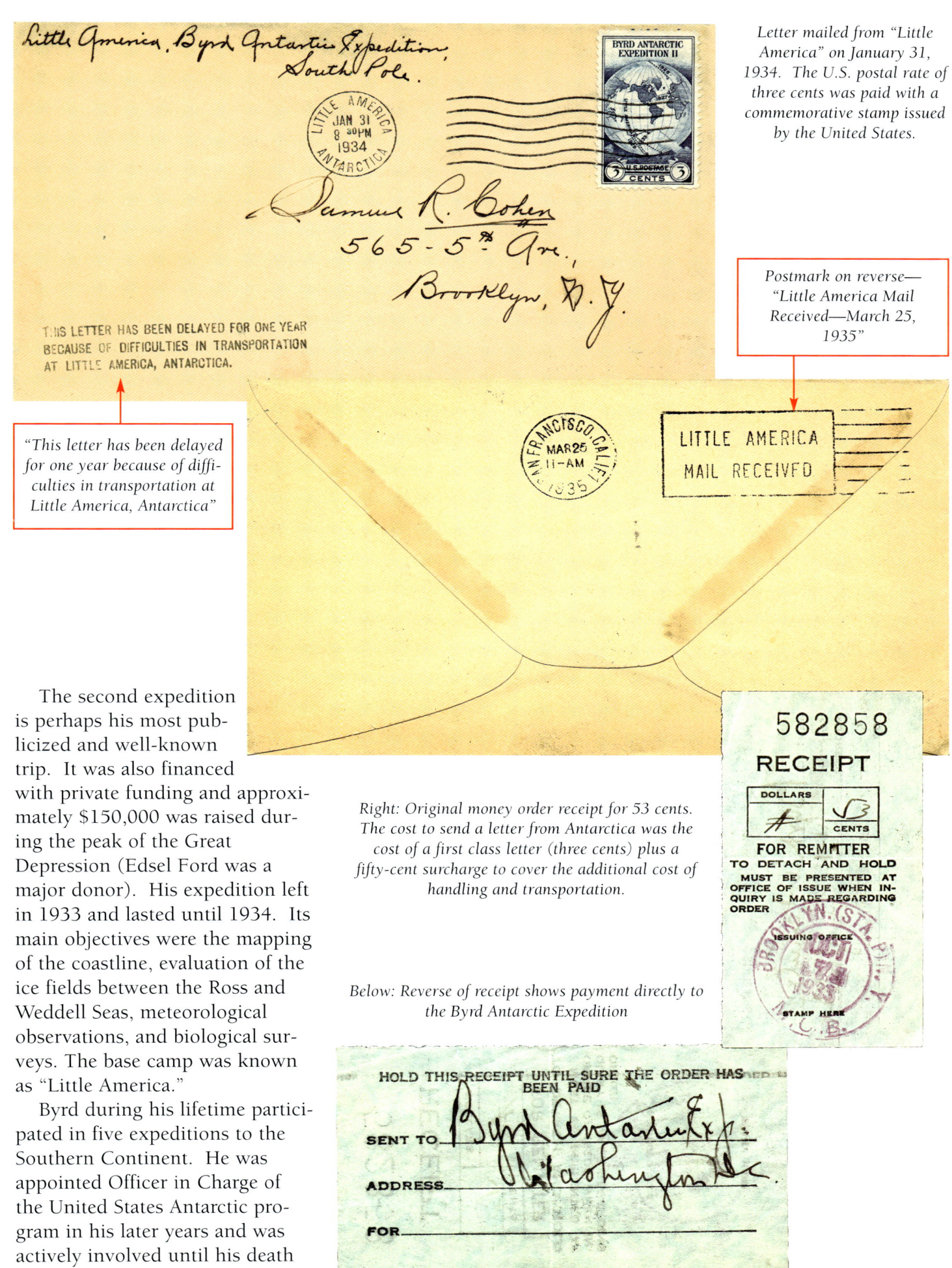

Letter mailed from "Little America" on January 31, 1934. The U.S. postal rate of three cents was paid with a commemorative stamp issued by the United States.

Postmark on reverse— "Little America Mail Received—March 25, 1935"

"This letter has been delayed for one year because of difficulties in transportation at Little America, Antarctica"

Right: Original money order receipt for 53 cents. The cost to send a letter from Antarctica was the cost of a first class letter (three cents) plus a fifty-cent surcharge to cover the additional cost of handling and transportation.

Below: Reverse of receipt shows payment directly to the Byrd Antarctic Expedition

The second expedition is perhaps his most publicized and well-known trip. It was also financed with private funding and approximately $150,000 was raised during the peak of the Great Depression (Edsel Ford was a major donor). His expedition left in 1933 and lasted until 1934. Its main objectives were the mapping of the coastline, evaluation of the ice fields between the Ross and Weddell Seas, meteorological observations, and biological surveys. The base camp was known as "Little America."

Byrd during his lifetime participated in five expeditions to the Southern Continent. He was appointed Officer in Charge of the United States Antarctic program in his later years and was actively involved until his death in 1957.

Above: Ten Mile River Scout Museum
William A. Stumpp, Gov. Al Smith, Admiral Byrd at Camp Ranachqua (Kanawaukee Lakes)

Photo: TMR Scout Museum

Admiral Richard E. Byrd, Paul Siple, Major Murray Wiener USAF, and IGY representative Edward Goodall, stand in front of the Little America I/II radio antenna towers. The top of this tower was originally 70' above the surface of the Ross Ice Shelf on which the station was first constructed in 1928-29. For some reason the abandoned buried station (30 miles west of LA5) was a frequent VX-6 tour stop for the media and DV's.

Photo from 90° South

Dauer Antarctica Expedition-December, 1987

The authors in Antarctica in December, 1987 on a scientific expedition. In front of them are old whale vertebral bodies. Radiological analysis can be useful in identifying diseases and nutritional states from skeletal remains.

Who was Really the First to Fly?

Samuel Langley, in 1896, was the first to build heavier than air machines capable of sustained, although uncontrolled flight.

Langley's aerodrome on its unsuccessful launch over the Potomac River
From the collection of the Smithsonian Air and Space Museum

They were unmanned and powered by steam engines. Langley's first manned aircraft was powered by a five-cylinder engine and was flown by Charles Manley. It was launched from a catapult on a houseboat in the Potomac River and both times the "aerodrome" snagged on the catapult and crashed into the river. Langley also had a design fault in that he did not account for the fact that drag would be increased exponentially when he enlarged his scale developmental model up to full size.

His last flight was December 8, 1903, just nine days before the Wright Brothers flight at Kitty Hawk, North Carolina. It is widely believed that if he did not suffer the catapult failures, Langley would rightfully have been known as the inventor of the first manned heavier than air-controlled flight.

Langley was also appointed the assistant secretary of the Smithsonian in 1887. He died in 1906 after suffering his second stroke, shattered by his failure to be the first to fly.

It was believed by the Wright Brothers that because of Langley's affiliation with the Smithsonian, they were denied the recognition they deserved of being the first to fly. Many historians felt that Langley was really the first to fly in spite of his failure to successfully launch his aerodrome from the catapult. In their own form of protest, the Wright Brothers sent their flying machine to the British Museum, where it resided on public display for nearly a quarter of a century.

In 1928, correspondence was started between Orville Wright (Wilbur had died in 1912 of typhoid) and Senator Hiram Bingham. Bingham was a Senator from Connecticut from 1924 to 1933 and was trying to negotiate the return of the Wright flyer to the Smithsonian where it belonged. Illustrated on the next page are the actual letters between Orville Wright and Senator Bingham to return the flying machine to the Smithsonian. The controversy was resolved by a joint resolution of Congress that had the National Academy of Science independently make the determination. The flying machine finally came to its rightful home.

Senator Hiram Bingham, 1875-1956

Supreme Court of the United States
Washington, D.C.

March 3, 1928.

My dear Senator:

I have yours of March 1st. I don't know anything whatever about the controversy between Orville Wright and others. The Secretary, Mr. Walcott, was very familiar with it, but I don't think the matter was ever brought before the Regents to take any formal action. I presume, without knowing, that the letter which Mr. Wright wrote me was handed to Secretary Walcott. I think perhaps if you desire information about it, the best person to consult is the present Secretary of the Smithsonian Institution, Dr. Abbot.

Sincerely yours,

Wm H Taft

Hon. Hiram Bingham,
United States Senate,
Washington, D. C.

Letter dated March 3, 1928 between William Taft, Supreme Court Chief Justice and previously President of the United States from 1909-1913, to Senator Bingham. The Chief Justice of the Supreme Court serves as an ex officio member of the Smithsonian Board of Regents.

"I don't know anything whatever about the controversy between Orville Wright and others."

The Wright Brother's first airplane flew at a speed of about 6.8 miles per hour at its first flight in December 1903

ORVILLE WRIGHT
DAYTON, OHIO

February 20, 1928.

My dear Senator Bingham:

I have your telegram of this date asking whether I would be willing to place our first aeroplane at Kill Devil Hill, if an adequate memorial building were erected there; and urging my approval of the suggestion. I also had a telegram several days ago from Congressman Lindsay C. Warren on the same subject.

I answered Mr. Warren that I did not think Kitty Hawk would be a suitable place for permanently exhibiting the machine since it is too inaccessible and the plane would be seen there by comparatively few people. Under ordinary circumstances the number of people actually seeing the machine would not have been so important, but under present circumstances it is important as a means to help overcome the adverse propaganda put out by the Smithsonian. Some years ago the Smithsonian started a campaign to take from Wilbur and me credit for work which we, and we alone, had done. While the Smithsonian has repeatedly given us credit for being the pioneer aviators, it has tried to take from us the credit for the scientific work of which our first aeroplane was the outgrowth.

I have sent the machine to the British Museum because that is about the only place where it will be seen by as many people and will have the prestige it would have had in our own National Museum.

As I can not in this letter enter into a full explanation of these matters, I am sending you a statement I wrote a short time ago for one of the aeronautical magazines, but which I believe has not as yet appeared in print. I am also sending a copy of a letter which I wrote to the Chancellor of the Smithsonian a few years ago. These may give you some idea of my objections to the attitude of the Smithsonian.

I appreciate most sincerely the kindly interest you have taken in securing recognition for us.

Sincerely yours,
Orville Wright

Senator Hiram Bingham,
Washington, D. C.

Letter dated February 20, 1928

"I have sent the machine to the British Museum because that is about the only place where it will be seen by as many people and will have the prestige it would have had in our own National Museum."

Orville Wright

ORVILLE WRIGHT
DAYTON, OHIO

March 8, 1928.

Dear Senator Bingham:

Thank you for your letter enclosing a copy of Congressman McSwain's joint resolution to determine which was the first heavier-than-air flying machine. This resolution came as a surprise to me. I had suggested, several years ago, an investigation by some impartial scientific body. I would have hesitated to suggest a congressional investigation for fear of its becoming involved in politics. After considering Mr. McSwain's resolution I am inclined to think that this is probably the best course.

I am not well enough acquainted with the organization of the National Academy of Science to know whether an impartial committee would be appointed by it, since practically all of the officers of it are connected with different government institutions at Washington, which have more or less relations with the Smithsonian. The assistant secretary is a Smithsonian man. Of course, I know that if this bill passes, immediately the Smithsonian will begin making recommendations for appointments to the commission, probably through the secretary to the President. But if the men appointed are really big men, and are not dependent on, or expecting in the future, financial or other assistance from the Smithsonian, I believe the appointments will be as good as could be expected from a national body.

Sincerely yours,
Orville Wright

Honorable Hiram Bingham,
United States Senate,
Washington, D. C.

Letter dated March 8, 1928

"Thank you for your letter enclosing a copy of Congressman McSwain's joint resolution to determine which was the first heavier-than-air flying machine. This resolution came as a surprise to me."

Orville Wright

Orville Wright, 1871-1948

Wilbur Wright, 1867-1912

Samuel Langley, 1834-1906

The first manned flight in history: December 17, 1903. At 10:35 a.m. Orville Wright takes off into a 27 mph wind. The distance covered was 120 feet; time aloft was 12 seconds. Wilbur is seen at right. Picture was taken with Orville's camera by John T. Daniels.

Charles A. Lindbergh
1902 - 1974

The last year that large size U.S. currency notes were printed was in 1928. The reduction in size of the notes began in July of 1929. Two years earlier, in 1927, Lindbergh flew non-stop from Roosevelt Field on Long Island to Le Bourget Field near Paris.

Charles Lindbergh left New York on May 20, 1927 on his historic flight to Paris. He landed 33 hours and 29 minutes later after a flight of 3,625 miles. His interest in becoming the first person to fly solo across the Atlantic was motivated more by the $25,000 prize than the fame that would await him.

Charles Augustus Lindbergh

Top photo: Charles Lindbergh with The Spirit of St. Louis which he flew non-stop from Roosevelt Field on Long Island to Bourget Field near Paris

Right: Lindbergh and his wife Anne often flew with him when he pioneered new air-mail routes

Photos - Library of Congress

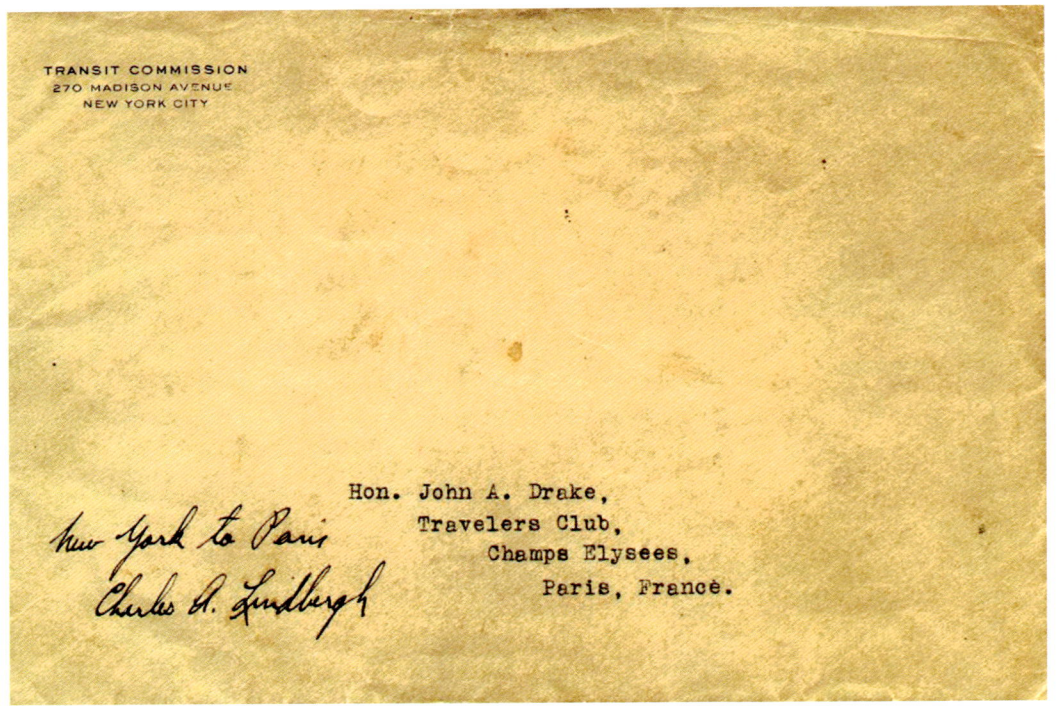

Above: The original oil and gas stains shown on the front of the envelope were left by Lindbergh's hands and can still be seen today

He was assisted in getting passport clearance prior to his flight by Charles Lockwood, the New York Transit Commissioner. Lockwood also gave Lindbergh a letter of introduction to John Drake at the Travelers Club in Paris to carry with him on his historic flight. Drake was a leader of American expatriates in Paris and a friend of the U.S. ambassador, Myron T. Herrick. Lindbergh did not carry any mail with him in order to preserve fuel, and this famous letter is one of only three or four that were personally carried on board the " Spirit of St. Louis."

TRANSIT COMMISSION
270 MADISON AVENUE
NEW YORK

CHARLES C. LOCKWOOD
COMMISSIONER

May 16th, 1927

Hon. John A. Drake,
Travelers Club,
Champs Elysees,
Paris, France.

Dear Mr. Drake:

This letter will introduce to you Captain Charles A. Lindbergh, who made the non-stop flight, alone, from San Diego, California to St. Louis, - from St. Louis to New York, and now from New York to Paris.

He is a very fine, clean-cut young man and I have told him he could look to you for advice in Paris, and that you would be glad to meet him.

Best personal wishes, I am

Sincerely
Charles Lockwood.

This cover and enclosed letter were first auctioned in 1964. At that time, the largest group of bidders ever connected by telephone for a stamp auction were aggressively attempting to acquire this historical item.

Cover and enclosed letter carried on Lindbergh's flight, autographed in his own handwriting "New York to Paris Charles A. Lindbergh"

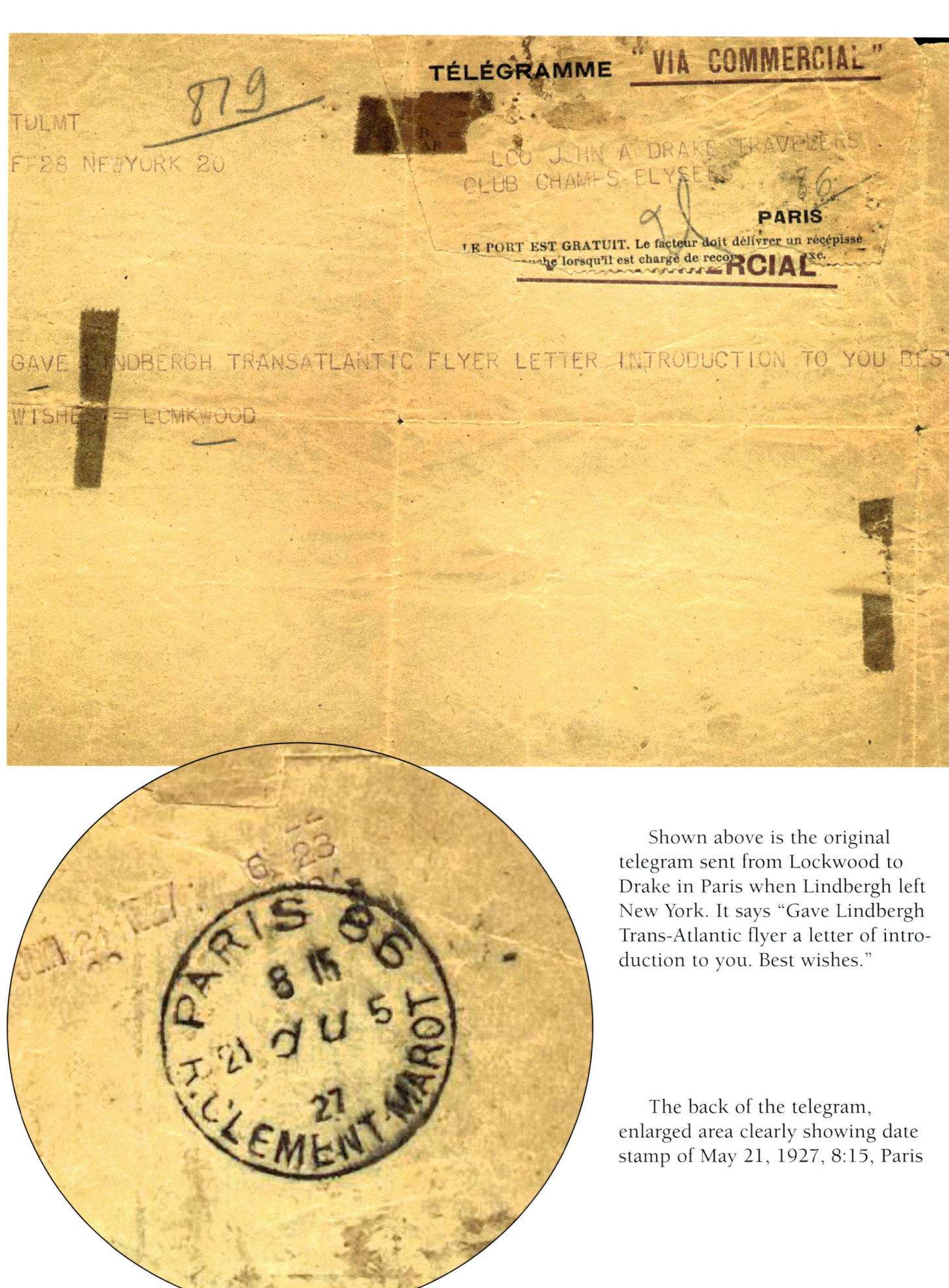

Shown above is the original telegram sent from Lockwood to Drake in Paris when Lindbergh left New York. It says "Gave Lindbergh Trans-Atlantic flyer a letter of introduction to you. Best wishes."

The back of the telegram, enlarged area clearly showing date stamp of May 21, 1927, 8:15, Paris

Charles Lindbergh was a contract air mail pilot before his transatlantic flight. Pictured below is a letter carried on an airmail test flight from Springfield to Chicago on April 10, 1926. Flown covers on planes piloted by Lindbergh that bear his autograph are eagerly sought after by collectors. Lindbergh personally signed the cover on the lower left – "C.A. Lindbergh Pilot."

The daily report for contract mail from Springfield to Chicago, dated November 26, 1926. Lindbergh was the pilot and personally signed his name at the lower right.

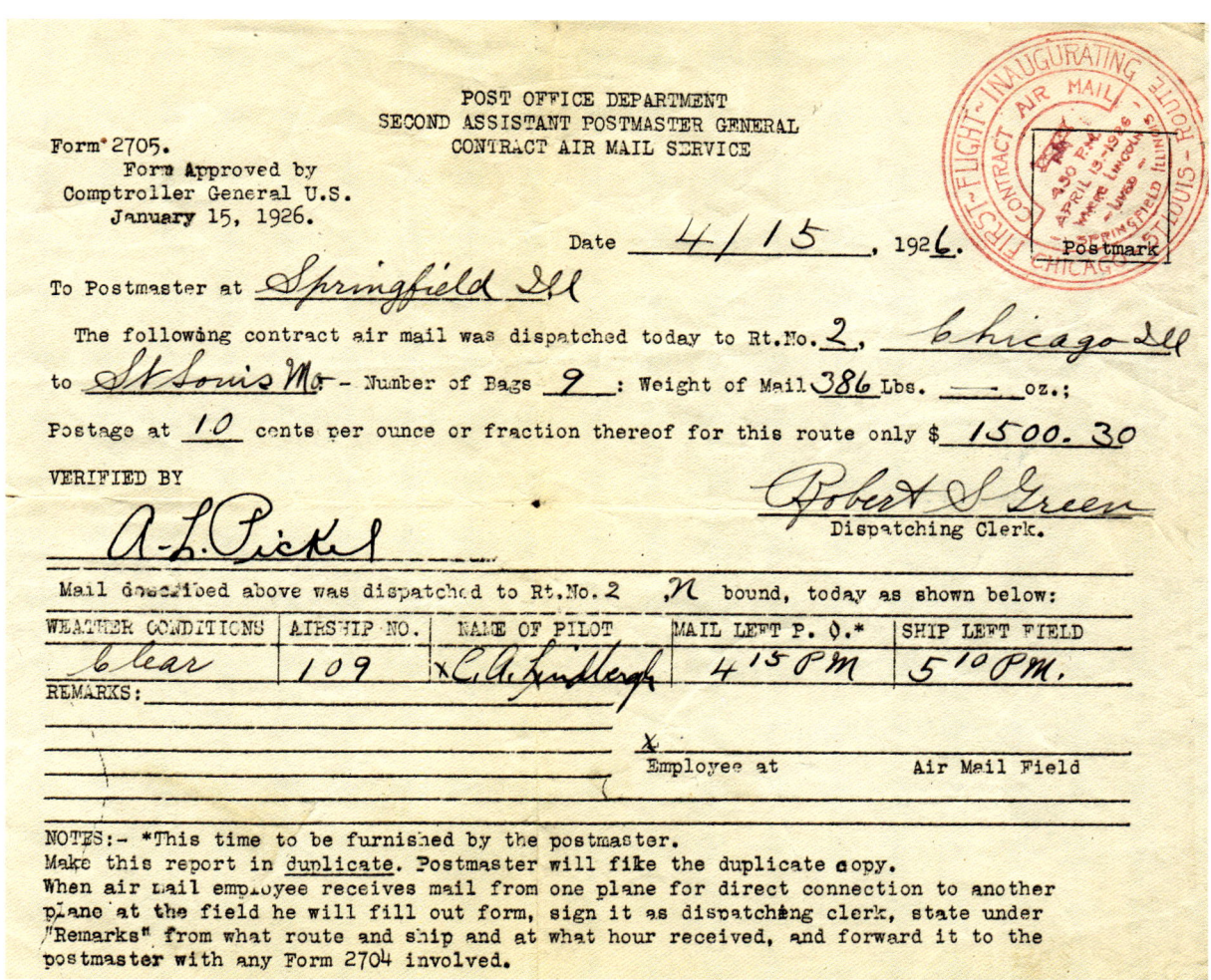

Contract with the Post Office Department dated 4/15/26 for delivery of mail from Chicago to St. Louis. This flight carried nine bags of mail weighing 386 pounds. C.A. Lindbergh signed as pilot.

At Lindbergh's request, the post office department granted him permission to once more carry the mail on his old assignment, which he did on February 20, 1928.

This registered mail cover is signed "C.A. Lindbergh Pilot" and features the 10 cent airmail stamp showing the "Spirit of St. Louis." These covers were overstamped with a horseshoe shaped cancel (Lucky Lindy) with the wording "Lindbergh again flies the airmail."

Lindbergh, upon his return from Paris, presented this autographed photo to Charles C. Lockwood

AMELIA EARHART, 1897-1937
Pioneer Aviator

Amelia Earhart

Amelia Earhart was born in Atchison, Kansas, at the home of her grandparents. Her grandfather, Alfred Otis, was one of Atchison's leading citizens. Amelia's father was a lawyer, but was not well-liked by her grandfather, for not providing the family with a larger income and a higher social status.

When Amelia was a teenager her father began drinking heavily. He was fired from his position at The Rock Island Railroad Company. Amelia's mother Amy, disturbed with her husband's drinking, left with Amelia and her younger sister Muriel, to live with friends in Chicago.

After high school Amelia trained as a nurse's aide in Toronto. A year later she enrolled as a pre-med student at Columbia University. She was an excellent student. With only a year completed at college, her parents who were now re-united, and convinced her and her sister to move to California with them.

Shortly after arriving in California, Amelia's father went with her to an "aerial meet" in Long Beach. She took her first flight the next morning in an open cockpit biplane for ten minutes over Los Angeles. She fell in love with flying from that moment on. She immediately began taking flying lessons from a woman pilot, Anita "Neta" Snook in Long Beach.

By the age of twenty-five, Amelia set a woman's altitude record of 14,000 feet. Her life changed forever in 1928 at the age of twenty-nine. Amelia Earhart was asked by George Putnam, a New York publisher, to be a passenger on a trans-Atlantic flight. She would be the first woman to fly across the Atlantic. Her official title was "commander" of the flight but she was only a passenger. When she landed back in New York, everyone was interested in interviewing her, and not the two pilots. President Calvin Coolidge sent her a personal congratulatory note.

Amelia became a well-known spokesperson for the airline industry. She was appointed assistant to the general traffic manager at Transcontinental Air Transport (later known as TWA) to find women interested in flying as passengers.

Following the divorce of George Putnam, Amelia married him at the age of thirty-four. They had much in common. They both loved flying, the outdoors, books and sports.

On May 20, 1932, precisely five years after the Charles Lindbergh flight, Amelia Earhart became the first woman to fly the Atlantic solo. Her flight took her from Harbor Grace, Newfoundland to Londonderry in Northern Ireland.

Amelia Earhart at age 29-setting the altitude record of 14,000 feet

"After midnight the moon set and I was alone with the stars. I have often said that the lure of flying is the lure of beauty..."

Upon Amelia's return to New York she was presented with keys to various cities and a tickertape parade. President Herbert Hoover presented her with a special Gold Medal from the National Geographic Society. She was voted Woman of the Year in 1932.

After touring the country on lecture tours, she began plans for an around the world flight. Amelia selected Fredrick Noonan, a former navigator on the Pan American Pacific Clipper, to accompany her. Noonan was very familiar with the Pacific Area.

Their flight departed from Los Angeles, California for Florida on May 21,1937. They continued from Miami, Florida, June 1 bound for San Juan, Puerto Rico, proceeding on to Africa and the Red Sea. They flew on to Bangkok and Singapore. Amelia took ill with the flu and delayed their trip to Australia until the end of June.

By July 2, 1937, Amelia and Noonan left with approximately enough fuel for twenty-one hours of flying. The head wind speed had increased by 10-20 mph. She made a radio contact, being on course for Howland Island, south of Honolulu at 8:00 A.M. At 8:14 P.M. that evening, the last voice contact was made with Amelia Earhart. She was never heard from again.

President Roosevelt authorized an extensive search of the area, but to no avail. By July 18th the search was abandoned. Amelia Earhart and Frederick Noonan's plane were never found.

Several archaeological visits to a remote Pacific Island have recovered physical evidence that Amelia's flight may have landed there, after failing to find Howland Island.

On May 20, 1932, Amelia Earhart became the first woman to fly the Atlantic solo

Solo Trans-Atlantic Flight of Amelia Earhart

Cover #16 of 50—Personally signed by Amelia Earhart

On May 13, 1932, Amelia Earhart flew alone non-stop from Newfoundland to Ireland. This duplicated Lindbergh's feat five years earlier.

To commemorate this event, she carried fifty specially cancelled and numbered flight covers with her. They are canceled with a 1-1/2 penny stamp from Great Britain and a 5-cent United States airmail stamp.

WALT DISNEY, 1901-1966

Walt Disney was born in Chicago, Illinois. His father, Elias Disney was Irish-Canadian and his mother, Flora Disney was German-American. Walt had four brothers, Roy, and one sister. He moved with his family to Marceline, Missouri and spent much of his early childhood on a farm. At the age of sixteen, Walt moved back to Chicago and studied Art at night at the Academy of Fine Arts.

Disney joined the American Red Cross at the age of eighteen, where he spent a year in Europe driving an ambulance decorated with his drawings and cartoons. He returned to the United States and was hired by the Kansas City Film Ad Company. He primarily made cartoon ads for the current movies.

At the age of twenty-two Walt decided to move to Los Angeles to join his brother Roy. They constructed a camera stand in their uncle's garage to begin animated and live-action film. They moved from there to the rear of a Hollywood real estate office. Shortly after, they received a contract from a New York firm for their first feature, "The Alice Comedies." This featured a real girl and her adventures in an animated world.

Walt Disney-one of America's most successful entrepreneurs

Walt Disney married one of his first employees, Lillian Bounds. They had two daughters, Diane and Sharon. His daughters described him as affectionate and understanding. He did have a temper but was always there for them. Walt's daughter, Diane Disney Miller, once said:

"Daddy never missed a father's function no matter how I discounted it. I'd say,"Oh, Daddy, you don't need to come. It's just some stupid thing." But he'd always be there, on time."

Mickey Mouse was created when Disney was twenty-seven years old and Mickey made his screen debut in "Steamboat Willie." The first sound cartoon premiered at the Colony Theatre in New York City on November 18, 1928.

"To all who come to this happy place, WELCOME! Disneyland is your land. Here age relives fond memories of the past...and here youth may savor the challenge and promise of the future. Disneyland is dedicated to the ideals, the dreams, and the hard facts that have created America...with the hope that it will be a source of joy and inspiration to all the world." -Walter Elias Disney, 17 July 1955

Photos-The Walt Disney Family Museum

Practically everyone loved Mickey..."the children who thought he was funny, the philosophers who thought he represented America's raucous individualism, the esthetes who saw in him the first successful adjustment of linear design to the fluttering motion of the films"
Quote from Life Magazine-circa 1930

In 1932 at the age of thirty-one Walt Disney won the first of his thirty-two Academy Awards for the film, "Flowers and Trees." He went on to produce the first full-length animated feature movie, "Snow White and the Seven Dwarfs." It premiered at the Carthay Circle Theater in Los Angeles. The production cost was a little over $1,499,000 during the Depression. This cost was unheard of at this time. During the next five years Disney completed many full-length classics as, "Pinocchio," "Fantasia," "Dumbo," and "Bambi."

Perhaps the most painful time in Walt's life was in 1938. He bought a new home for his parents in Burbank, California to be close to his studios. Less than a month later his mother died of asphyxiation caused by a faulty furnace. Disney felt guilty about her death the rest of his life.

By the 1940's Disney was employing more than one thousand artists, animators, story men and technicians in his Burbank, California studio. During World War II be helped the war effort by producing propaganda films for the armed forces and providing comedy films to boost civilian and military morale. A total of eighty-one feature movies were released in Disney's lifetime.

Walt Disney achieved his goal of developing the world's most famous entertainment centers in California and Florida. Disneyland Park opened in 1955 in Anaheim, California.

Disney helped to purchase forty-three acres of land in Central, Florida. He planned to have an amusement theme park, a hotel vacation center and his E.P.C.O.T. Center. (Experimental Prototype Community of Tomorrow) Walt Disney World opened in 1971 and EPCOT opened in 1982 after Walt had died. Walt Disney died December 15, 1966 at the age of sixty-five. He has been named among the most successful American entrepreneurs.

Letter Signed by Walt Disney on Walt Disney Productions Stationery
"The Hall of Presidents"

This letter, dated June 16, 1961, discusses a show designed for the New York World's Fair in 1964, "combining the techniques of a motion picture production and stereophonic sound, along with a 3-dimensional "Hall of Presidents." Disney was attempting to raise money from the corporate sector to sponsor the development of what would become one of the most popular and memorable attractions in the Disney theme parks.

WALT DISNEY PRODUCTIONS
500 SO. BUENA VISTA ST. • BURBANK, CALIFORNIA • CABLE ADDRESS: DISNEY

June 16, 1961

I am writing you about a matter which I believe may be of interest to you.

On Wednesday, June 28, at 2 p.m., we are having a presentation at the Johnny Victor Theatre, located in the R.C.A. Exhibition Hall on 49th Street between 5th and 6th Avenue, of a show designed for the New York World's Fair - 1964-65 combining the techniques of a motion picture production and stereophonic sound, along with a 3-dimensional "Hall of Presidents."

It is a dramatic presentation of our Constitutional form of government and the role our Presidents play in preserving the Constitution. I believe it is vital at this time that it be brought before the people of the United States as well as our many foreign visitors because it is entirely applicable to the problems of today.

The purpose of this presentation is to interest some American enterprise to sponsor it.

Although I will be unable to be present since we now have several pictures in production abroad, I have arranged for these special presentations by my staff because the time element is so important. Personally, I will be most anxious to hear from you on your reactions to the show.

Mr. Jack Sayers, of our Staff, will be in New York in advance of the show and I would appreciate it if you would advise him whether or not you can attend. He can be reached anytime after Tuesday, June 20th, at the Walt Disney Office, 477 Madison Avenue, New York, Plaza 9-3880.

Sincerely,

Walt Disney

WALT DISNEY

NO AGREEMENT WILL BE BINDING ON THIS CORPORATION UNLESS IN WRITING AND SIGNED BY AN OFFICER

HARRY HOUDINI, 1874-1926
World Famous Escape Artist

Harry Houdini was born in Budapest, Hungary with the given name of Ehrich Weiss. He took his stage name from the great French magician Jean Eugene Robert – Houdini. He later changed his name legally to Harry Houdini.

He won world fame as an escape artist from an airtight tank that was filled with water. Houdini's other shows featured magic tricks, escapes from chains and handcuffs and demonstrations of what he referred to as "spiritualist fraud."

In his most famous escape in January 1906, Houdini escaped from the Washington, D.C. jail cell of Charles Guitean, the assassin of President Garfield. He assured his place in history as both a famous jail breaker and handcuff king.

Houdini began to star in Hollywood silent films. Two of his films were the "The Master Mystery" and "The Grim Game." In 1921, the magician founded the Houdini Picture Corporation. Its first film was "The Man from Beyond." Houdini was the first magician ever to be honored with a star on the Hollywood Walk of Fame.

Harry Houdini

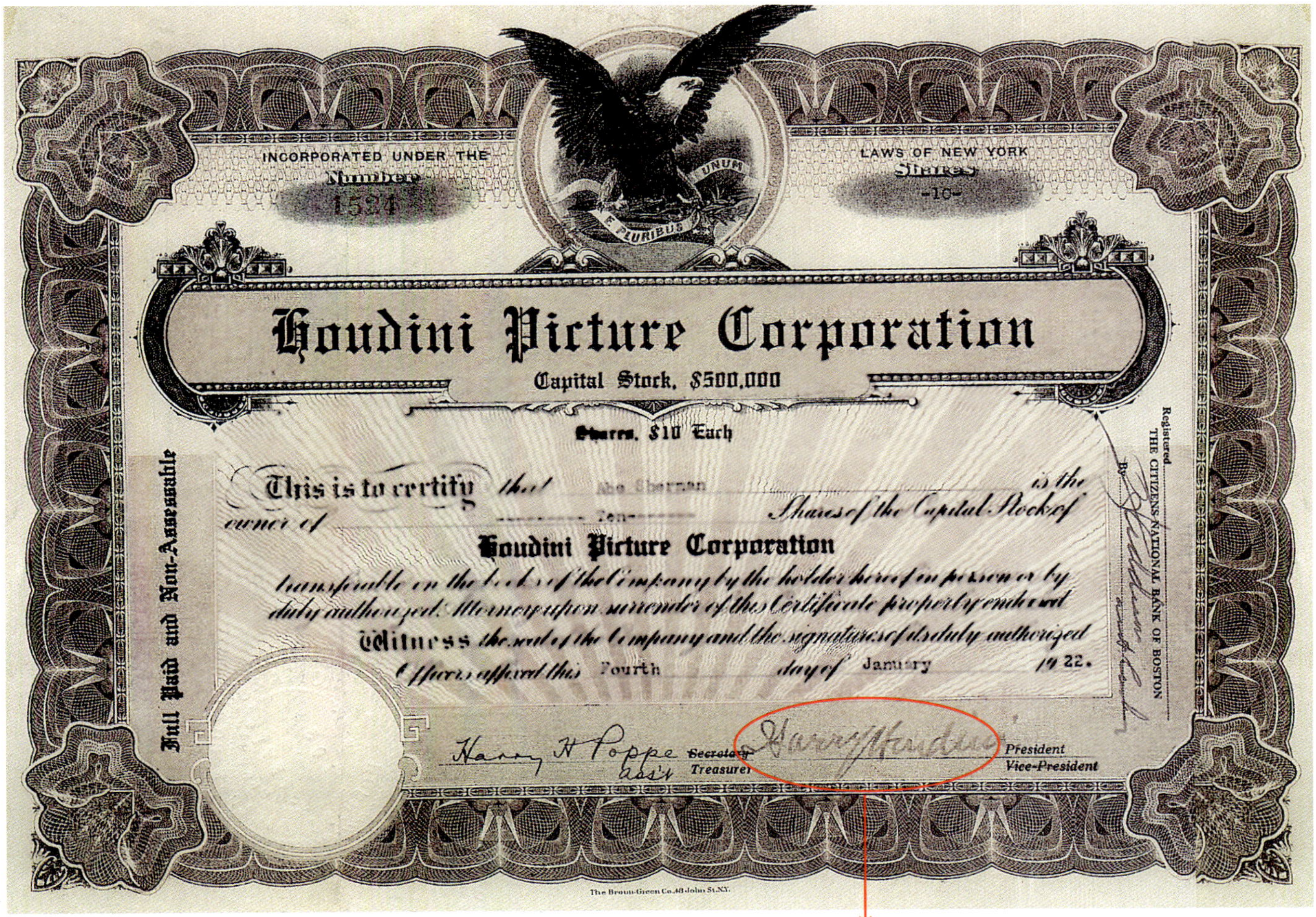

Stock certificate of the Houdini Picture Corporation-circa 1922 - Harry Houdini signed it as President

Harry Houdini wrapped in chains making one of his famous escapes at a performance in Washington, D.C.

In 1913 he introduced his legendary Chinese Water Torture Cell. This was the same year his mother died which was a great shock, as he was in Europe and not told of his mother's illness. He was also the first to perform the largest stage illusion to that day, making the largest object known at the time, an elephant, disappear. This was done in 1918 at the Hippodrome in New York City. According to Houdini the elephant Jenny, weighed 10,000 pounds. Houdini was very creative and introduced and invented many magic tricks that are depicted at the Houdini Museum in the Scranton, Pennsylvania Pocono region. After escaping underwater Houdini would often hide under a dock forcing people to think Houdini might have drowned. At the opportune moment Houdini would make his reappearance. Houdini had great strength and agility that he used in accomplishing his stunts. Houdini also spent many hours studying, practicing, and conditioning. For Houdini's underwater stunts, Houdini would practice holding his breath in the bathtub for up to four minutes. He also stayed in an underwater "coffin" for over an hour.

On October 22, 1926 while performing in Montreal, a young athlete from McGill University asked Houdini if he could actually withstand punches to his stomach, as was rumored. Before Houdini could prepare himself by tightening his stomach muscles, the student began punching Houdini repeatedly in the stomach. Houdini did not know it at the time, but his appendix was ruptured. He continued on to Detroit where he collapsed on stage and died on Halloween 1926, of peritonitis from the ruptured appendix.

Poster advertising Houdini's "Water Torture" stunt

334

ALBERT EINSTEIN - 1879-1955
Genius among Geniuses

Albert Einstein was born in Ulm, Wurttemberg, Germany. He began his early education in Munich. At the age of sixteen he failed an examination that would have allowed him to study for a degree as an electrical engineer. At seventeen he renounced his German citizenship and was not granted a Swiss citizenship until five years later.

At the age of twenty-one Einstein did succeed in graduating as a teacher of mathematics and physics. He had a difficult time finding a job, until he was hired as a mathematics teacher in a Swiss High School.

His next position was for seven years with the Swiss Patent Office. It was at this time he completed numerous theoretical physics publications and his theory of relativity.

At the age of twenty-six Einstein earned a doctorate from the University of Zurich. He went on to become professor of theoretical physics at the University of Zurich and he occupied the same position at the German University in Prague.

Albert Einstein - 1905

In 1921 at the age of forty-two Einstein made his first visit to the United States and was impressed with the American interest in his work. He lectured and toured throughout the United States. He accepted an offer for life at the Institute for Advanced Study in Princeton, New Jersey.

At the age of sixty-one he was granted permanent United States residency. Einstein's health began to deteriorate the last five years of his life and he died, at the age of seventy-six, of a ruptured aortic aneurysm.

Einstein when he was professor at Princeton University

Einstein at 76 years old, shortly before his death

CALIFORNIA INSTITUTE OF TECHNOLOGY
PASADENA

March 7th 1933.

Mr. Roland W. Ziege,
2547 Aubert Ave.,
Chicago, Ill.

Dear Sir:

      You could do the most important preparatory studies very well out of books at home, and lateron when conditions are better attend a university. The most important thing is the right kind of books. I am not familiar with the instruction books in the English language. It will be best for you to go to a Professor of Physics at the University of Chicago and ask him for the books best suited for your purpose and also for the requirements to go to college lateron.

      Yours very truly,

      A. Einstein

Typed letter signed by A. Einstein on California Institute of Technology stationery, dated March 7, 1933

Harry S. Truman

*Thirty-Third President
1945-1953*

Truman was born in Lamar, Missouri, in 1884. He grew up in Independence, and for 12 years prospered as a Missouri farmer. He was married to Elizabeth Virginia Wallace Truman. As President, Truman made some of the most crucial decisions in history including the use of the atomic bomb on Japan.

THE WHITE HOUSE
WASHINGTON

April 7, 1952

Dear Erma and Fred:

Many thanks for your kind sentiments and understanding thoughts concerning my decision not to be a candidate for re-election. Mrs. Truman and I both appreciate your good wishes a great deal and we will show your letter to Margaret when she returns from her concert tour. It will indeed be fine to enjoy life leisurely once more and, naturally, we are looking forward to the time when this privilege will be ours.

The confidence the people reposed in my leadership will always be a source of gratification to me and I am glad to have your words of commendation. It has been a wonderful privilege to serve my country in the Presidency and, of course, I shall not cease in my efforts for peace.

Very sincerely yours,

Harry Truman

Mr. and Mrs. Fred Bowman,
3940 Frontier Avenue,
Chicago 13,
Illinois.

Letter signed by Harry Truman while President on White House stationery

Fifty Dollar Gold Certificates-Series 1882

Silas Wright was born in Massachusetts on May 24, 1795; his family was involved in politics and farming. He was elected State Senator of New York, United States Senator, and Comptroller of New York State. He was nominated as the Vice Presidential candidate in 1844 but turned it down so that he could run for Governor of New York. In that race, he defeated Millard Fillmore. In that same year, on May 24th, Samuel F.B. Morse sent the first words by telegraph "What hath God wrought?"

Silas Wright - U.S. Senator from New York

This $50 note has the large red seal. It is the only specimen existing outside of government holdings. It originated in the Grinnell collection and is in extremely fine condition.

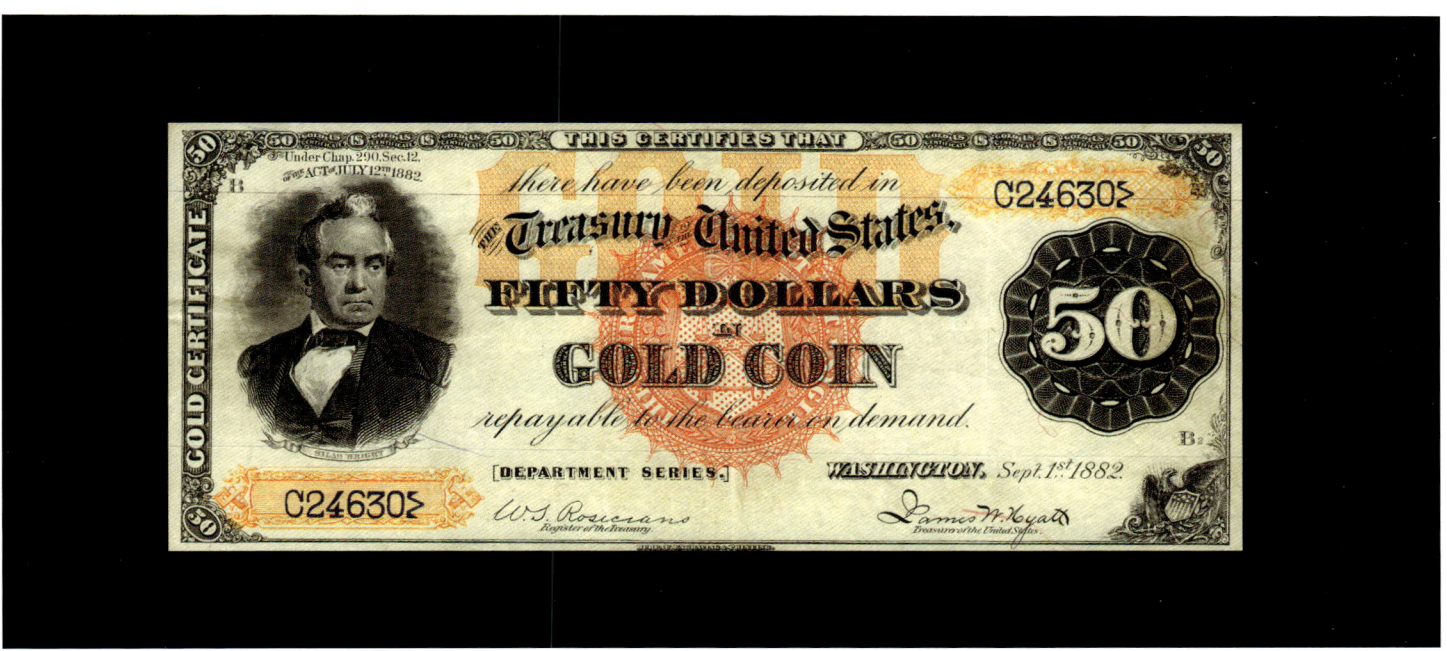

Samuel F.B. Morse
Inventor of the Morse Code for Telegraphy Communications

Samuel F.B. Morse

Samuel F.B. Morse was well known as an American inventor and painter. He was best known for inventing the Morse code, used for many years to send telegraphic messages over wires.

Morse was born in Charlestown, Massachusetts in a devoutly Calvinist family. He graduated from Yale University in 1810. The following year he left to study in London at the Royal Academy of Arts. Morse was a successful portrait painter but was unable to support himself financially. He spent the next years working on his inventions. He had little training in electricity but realized that pulses of electric current could convey information over wires.

In 1842, he was given $30,000 from Congress to construct a telegraphic line between Baltimore and Washington. On May 24, 1844 he was successful and tapped out the famous message, "What hath God wrought!"

To support himself later in life Morse was dependent on dividends from different telegraphic companies. Several European countries paid him a gratuity for use of his system. The two coasts of the United States were linked by telegraph in 1861.

For years a version of the Morse code has been an integral part of ham radio exams. Below is the QSL card (used to acknowledge communication by short wave radio) of the author's call sign WB4HNM.

This is used to provide written confirmation of communications with other ham radio operators around the world

Historic Message, 24 May 1844
This paper tape recording of the historic message transmitted by Samuel F. B. Morse reads when decoded, "What hath God wrought?" It was sent by him from the Supreme Court room in the Capitol to his assistant, Alfred Vail, in Baltimore. Morse's early system produced a paper copy with raised dots and dashes, which were translated later by an operator. Across the top of this historic achievement, Morse has given credit to Annie Ellsworth, the young daughter of a good friend, for suggesting to him what message to send. She obtained it from the Bible, Numbers 23:23. The Papers of Samuel Finley Breese Morse Manuscript Division.

Samuel F. B. Morse, was once a portrait artist but turned to inventing to make his fortune. He dreamed up the idea of an electromagnetic telegraph in 1832. An experimental version was made in 1835 and a practical system was not constructed until 1844. It was that year he built a line from Baltimore to Washington, D.C. The model illustrated on the right incorporates basic features of the 1844 receiver. He then applied for an application for a patent, which was granted in 1849. The patent describes a method for marking dots and dashes on paper. The telegraph became so popular than in ten years after the first telegraph line opened, 23,000 miles of wire crisscrossed the country. The development of the West was profoundly affected by Morse's telegraph. It made railroad travel safer, and allowed businessmen to conduct their operations more profitably.

Courtesy of the National Museum of American History, from the U.S. Patent Office

The first telegraph line was constructed between Baltimore and Washington on May 24, 1844

This photo was taken circa 1930 and shows telephone and telegraph poles of the day

This is the last issue of large size $50 gold notes. The 1913 and 1922 series are very similar but have minor differences on the obverse over the "50" printed in gold ink to the left of Grant's portrait.

Series - 1913

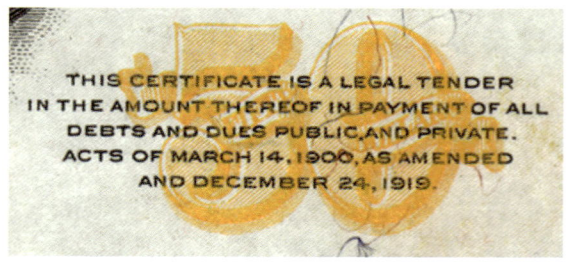

Series - 1922

The $100 note above with an engraved third signature is the only note available to collectors (there are two in the collection of the Federal Reserve System). The condition is choice, almost uncirculated, but it is as bright and fresh as the day it was printed. It originally came from the Grinnell collection and was first publicly auctioned on March 10, 1945.

This small brown seal $100 is unique in private hands

Thomas Benton was elected as a Senator from Missouri in 1821. He believed in the importance of using gold and silver to purchase public land in order to discourage speculation. This idea was legalized by President Jackson in 1836 after Congress defeated his resolution. This resulted in discouragement of land speculation and helped settlers develop the West.

Thomas Benton

Andrew Jackson

Portrait of Thomas Benton

The large red seal $100 pictured above is the match to the unique $50 large red seal. It is extremely rare and is the finest of two known to exist, not including the two lower grade examples in the Government collection. It also originated from the Grinnell collection.

Large brown seal from 1882

Series 1922, the last issue of large size gold certificates

$500 gold certificate, series 1882, from the Grinnell collection

$500, series 1922. The last of the large size notes and in almost uncirculated condition; it is the finest example of this design known to exist.

One thousand dollar gold certificate, series 1882, Portrait of Alexander Hamilton

Letter signed by Alexander Hamilton to Brigadier General George Clinton

> Head Quarters Camp at
> Middle Brook June 10, 1777
>
> Sir,
>
> By his Excellency's command, I am to desire you will give orders upon the Deputy clothier General at Picks-Kill, for the necessary supply of the clothing for the four companies raising under your direction. It is not however intended, that more shall be drawn, than a sufficiency for the number of men actually enlisted.
> I am Sir
>
> Your most obedt Servant
> A Hamilton ADC

The 1907 gold certificates were redesigned and are one of only three $1000 bills that utilize the dollar sign. Although usually only one note of each seal type or design has been utilized in this book, all five different signature varieties of the 1907 issue are illustrated.

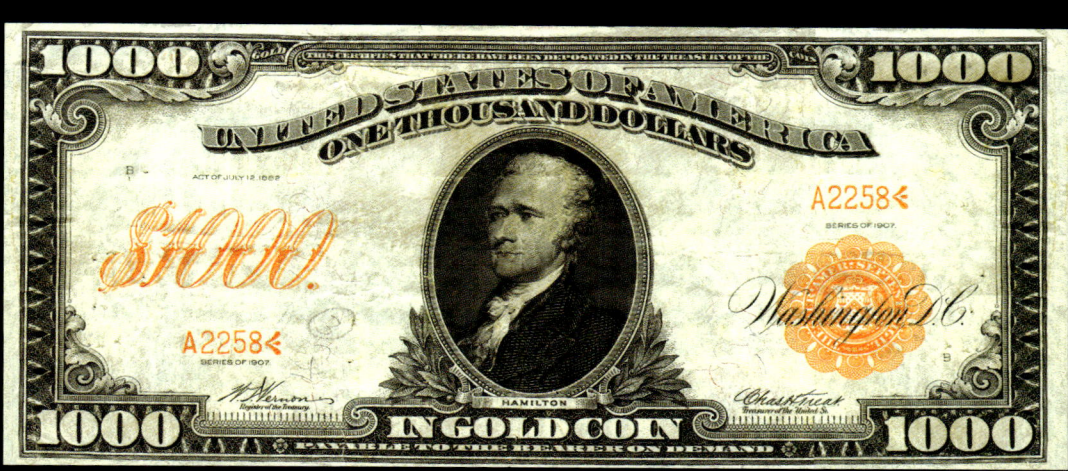

This note signed by Napier and McClung is the only example known to exist. It is even missing from the collections of the Federal Reserve System and the Smithsonian Institution.

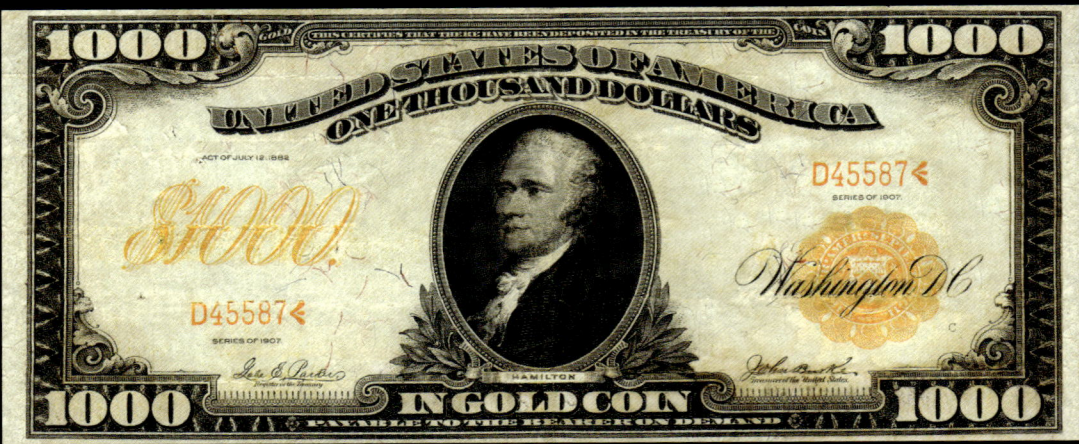
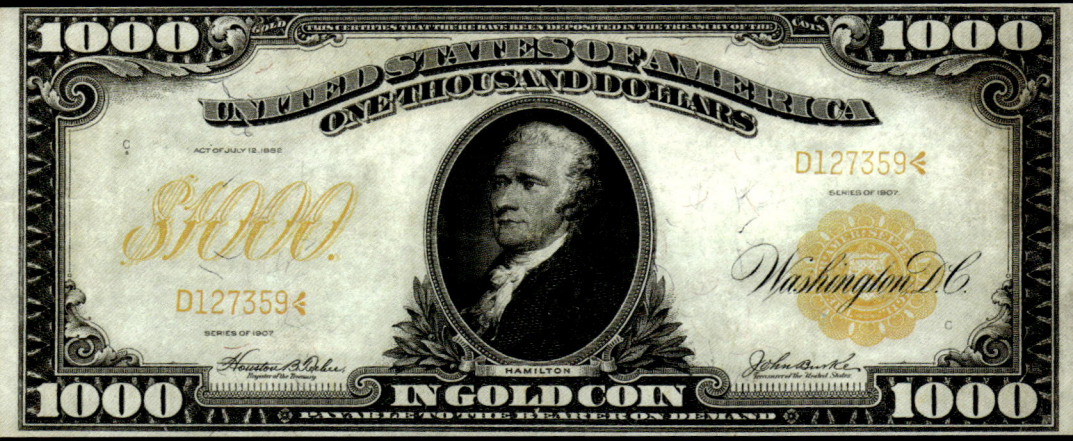
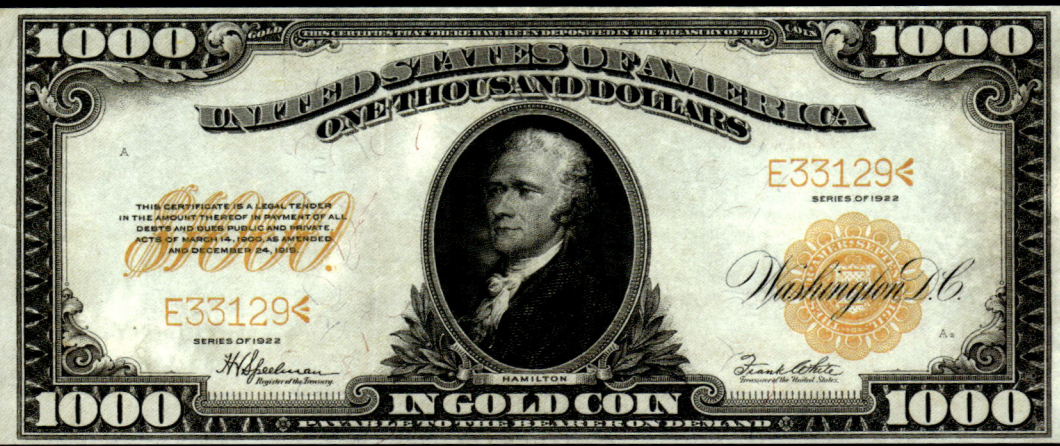

Series 1922

Chapter IX

National Gold Bank Notes of California

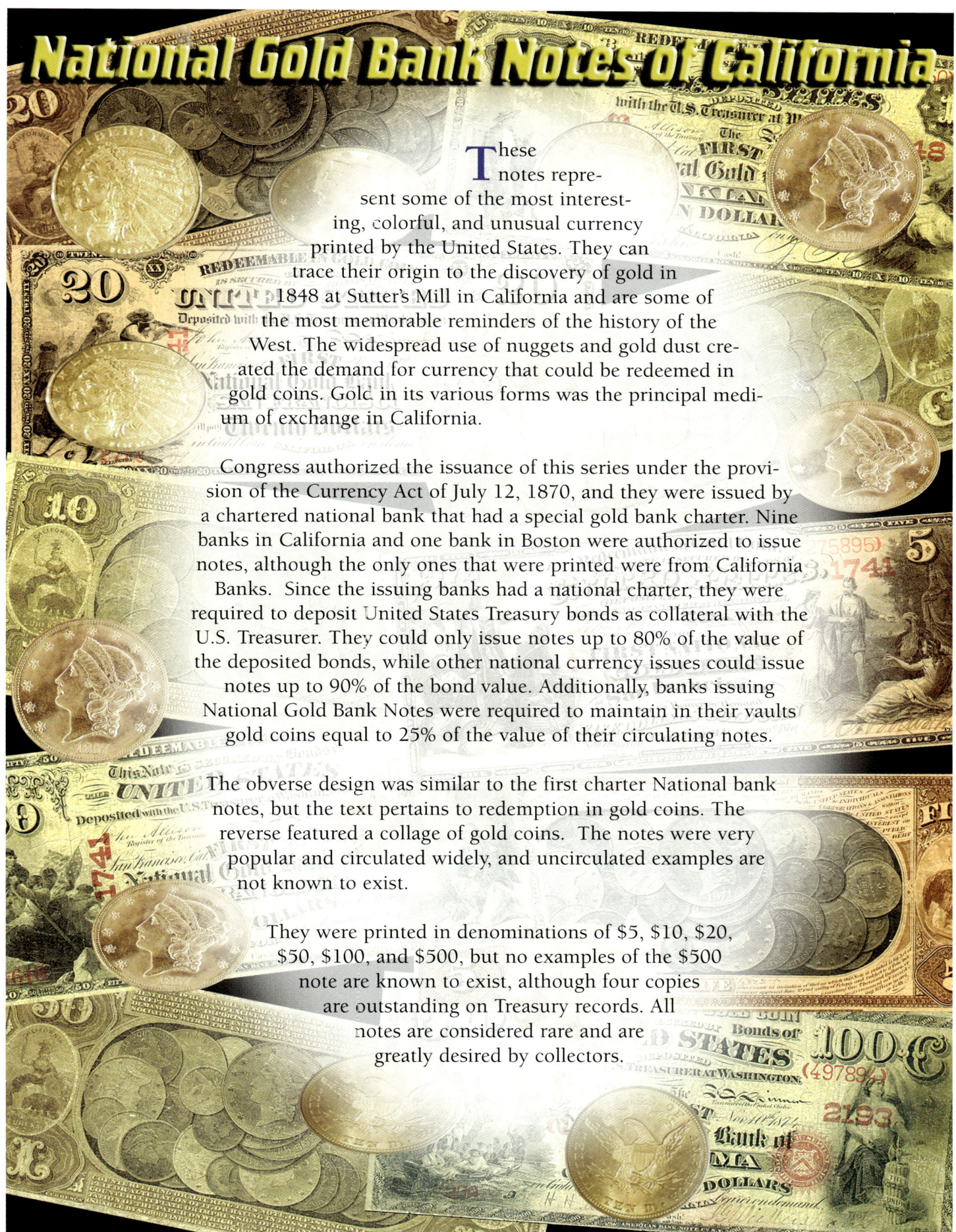

These notes represent some of the most interesting, colorful, and unusual currency printed by the United States. They can trace their origin to the discovery of gold in 1848 at Sutter's Mill in California and are some of the most memorable reminders of the history of the West. The widespread use of nuggets and gold dust created the demand for currency that could be redeemed in gold coins. Gold in its various forms was the principal medium of exchange in California.

Congress authorized the issuance of this series under the provision of the Currency Act of July 12, 1870, and they were issued by a chartered national bank that had a special gold bank charter. Nine banks in California and one bank in Boston were authorized to issue notes, although the only ones that were printed were from California Banks. Since the issuing banks had a national charter, they were required to deposit United States Treasury bonds as collateral with the U.S. Treasurer. They could only issue notes up to 80% of the value of the deposited bonds, while other national currency issues could issue notes up to 90% of the bond value. Additionally, banks issuing National Gold Bank Notes were required to maintain in their vaults gold coins equal to 25% of the value of their circulating notes.

The obverse design was similar to the first charter National bank notes, but the text pertains to redemption in gold coins. The reverse featured a collage of gold coins. The notes were very popular and circulated widely, and uncirculated examples are not known to exist.

They were printed in denominations of $5, $10, $20, $50, $100, and $500, but no examples of the $500 note are known to exist, although four copies are outstanding on Treasury records. All notes are considered rare and are greatly desired by collectors.

Issued by the First National Gold Bank of San Francisco in 1870

The reverse shows an engraving of gold coins similar in appearance to a photograph. Coins are illustrated from $1 to $20 and have a total face value of $211.50. The reverse is the same on all denominations of National Gold Bank Notes.

For many years before the Golden Gate Bridge was built, the only way to get across San Francisco Bay was by ferry; and by the early twentieth century the Bay was clogged with ferries

A view of Lombard Street in San Francisco

Issued by The First National Gold Bank of Oakland in 1875

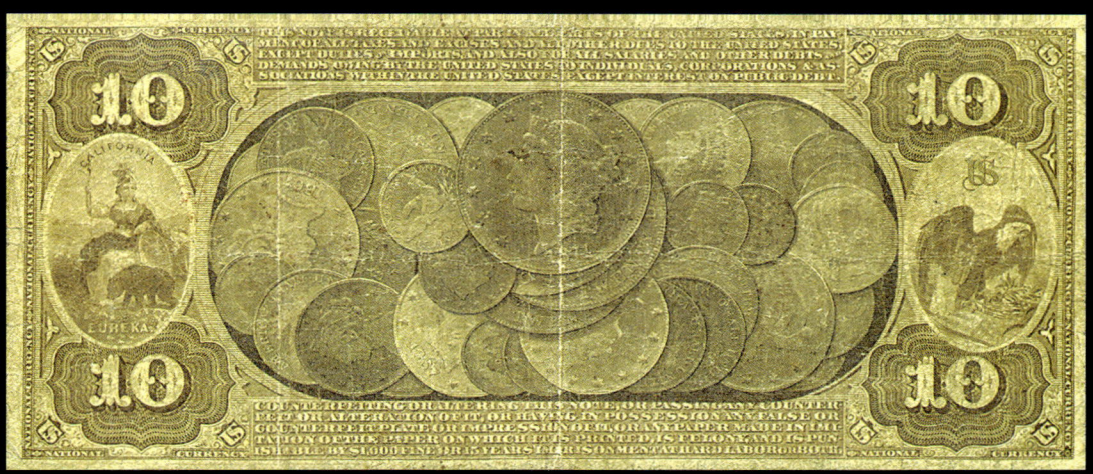

The paper used to print these notes has a yellowish coloration, which was an attempt to imitate the color of gold. All specimens of National Gold Bank Notes were printed with a red Treasury seal.

View of the Oakland California skyline from Lake Merritt. You can shop for fresh produce at the Saturday Farmers Market or take your kids to the Rotary Science Center.

Issued by the First National Gold Bank of San Francisco in 1870

The obligation states "This note is secured by bonds of the United States deposited with the U.S. Treasurer at Washington…..The (bank name and city) will pay ….. Dollars to bearer in gold coin on demand…This note is receivable at par in all parts of the United States in payment of all taxes and excises, and all other dues to the United States, except duties on imports, and also for all salaries and other debts and demands owing by the United States to individuals, corporations, and associations within the United States, except interest on public debt."

Left: Walking up Market Street towards the Call Building, San Francisco, just before the great earthquake of 1906

Right: Destruction of the buildings from the 1906 San Francisco earthquake

Issued by the First National Gold Bank of San Francisco in 1870

All denominations of this series of notes were widely distributed and used in California, circulating also with gold and silver coins. Western Americans generally preferred the use of coins with an intrinsic metallic value or currency notes backed by coins.

Only seven examples (one permanently in a museum) of the $50 denomination are known to exist

Immigrants crossing the plains
Engraving by H.B. Hall Jr-1860

View of San Francisco from Stockton Street
Photographer unknown. Published in "The Fantastic City," 1932

Issued by the First National Gold Bank of Petaluma in 1874

Eight notes of this denomination are known to exist from all banks. A total of 4,400 notes were printed, 400 from Petaluma.

Above: Downtown Petaluma at Center Park, circa 1918. Few cities of its size in America have earned the reputation that Petaluma can claim. Petaluma has gone from being one of California's largest cities (1860's), to the World's Egg Basket (early 1900's), to the World's Wristwrestling Capital, and home of the Largest Outdoor Quilt Show in California (current).

Left: Andrew Carnegie (1835-1910), the steel magnate who was establishing free libraries throughout the country, took his philanthropy to Petaluma just after the turn of the century. The cost of the proposed building was $16,000, of which Carnegie, paid $12,000.

Chapter X
Colonial Currency

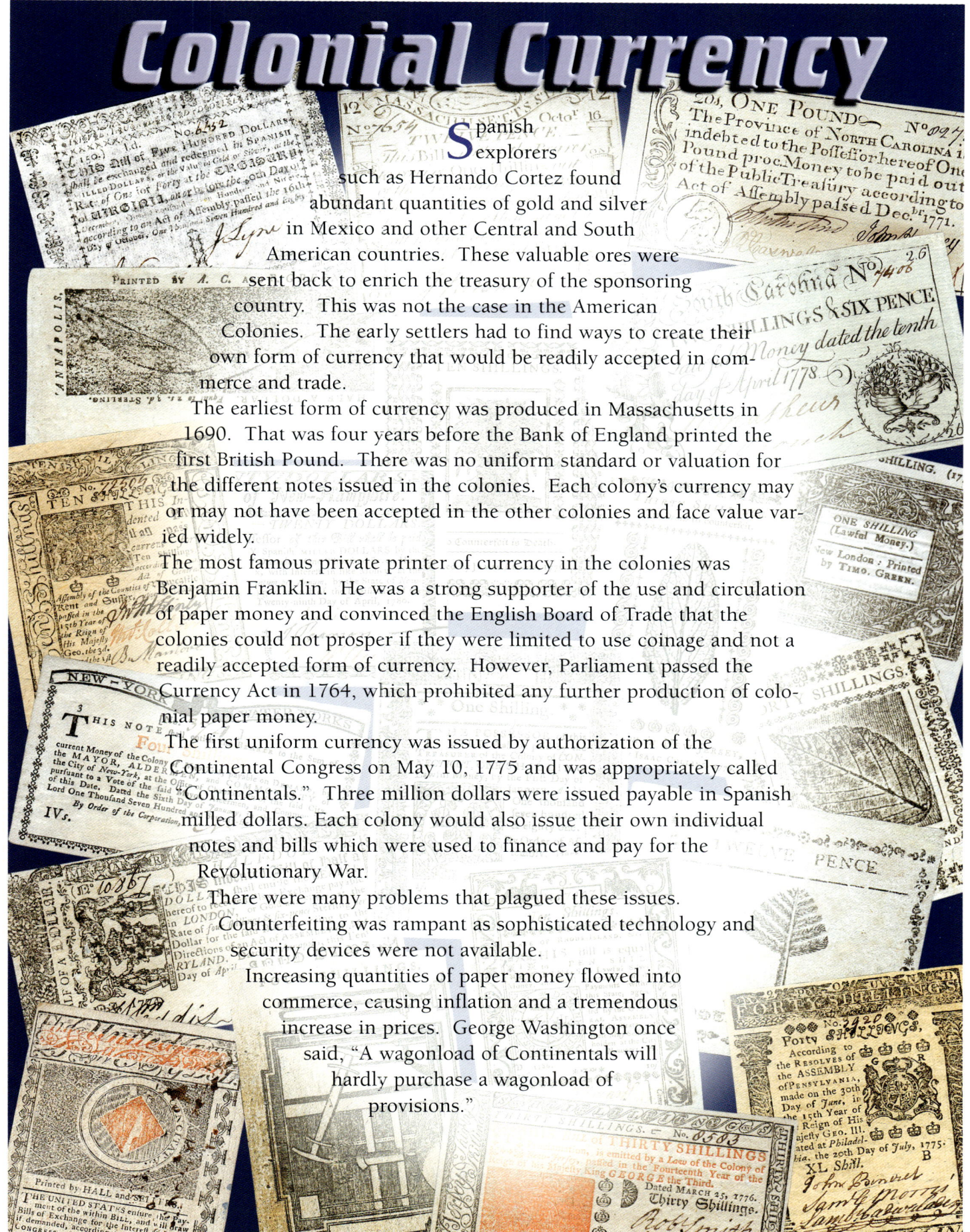

Spanish explorers such as Hernando Cortez found abundant quantities of gold and silver in Mexico and other Central and South American countries. These valuable ores were sent back to enrich the treasury of the sponsoring country. This was not the case in the American Colonies. The early settlers had to find ways to create their own form of currency that would be readily accepted in commerce and trade.

The earliest form of currency was produced in Massachusetts in 1690. That was four years before the Bank of England printed the first British Pound. There was no uniform standard or valuation for the different notes issued in the colonies. Each colony's currency may or may not have been accepted in the other colonies and face value varied widely.

The most famous private printer of currency in the colonies was Benjamin Franklin. He was a strong supporter of the use and circulation of paper money and convinced the English Board of Trade that the colonies could not prosper if they were limited to use coinage and not a readily accepted form of currency. However, Parliament passed the Currency Act in 1764, which prohibited any further production of colonial paper money.

The first uniform currency was issued by authorization of the Continental Congress on May 10, 1775 and was appropriately called "Continentals." Three million dollars were issued payable in Spanish milled dollars. Each colony would also issue their own individual notes and bills which were used to finance and pay for the Revolutionary War.

There were many problems that plagued these issues. Counterfeiting was rampant as sophisticated technology and security devices were not available.

Increasing quantities of paper money flowed into commerce, causing inflation and a tremendous increase in prices. George Washington once said, "A wagonload of Continentals will hardly purchase a wagonload of provisions."

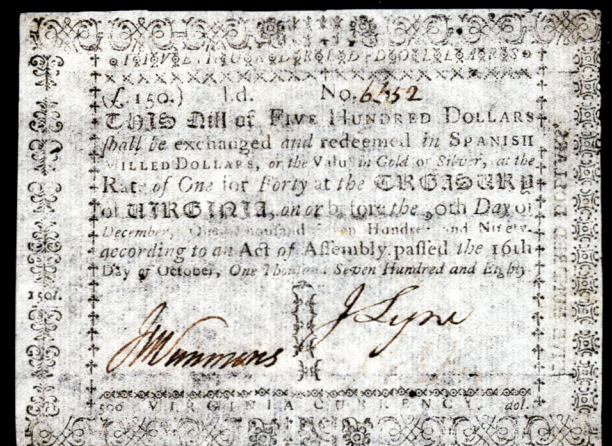

Virginia—Founded in 1607 by the London Company

$500 note exchangeable for Spanish milled dollars October, 1780

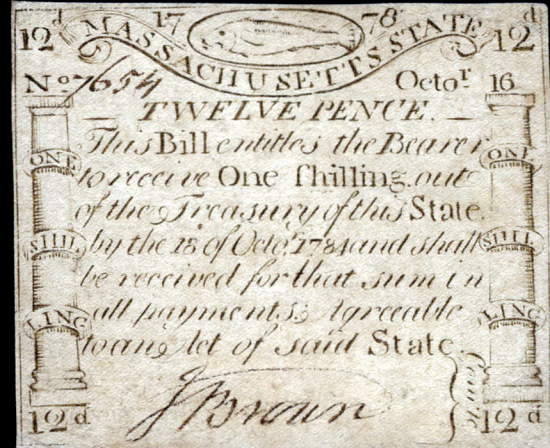

Massachusetts—Founded in 1620 by the Puritans

One shilling note which is equivalent to twelve pence
This note was printed by Paul Revere

Engraving of a Pine tree—October, 1778

A colonial family portrait of Dean Berkeley and his entourage - Painted about 1730 by John Smibert
Yale University Art Gallery

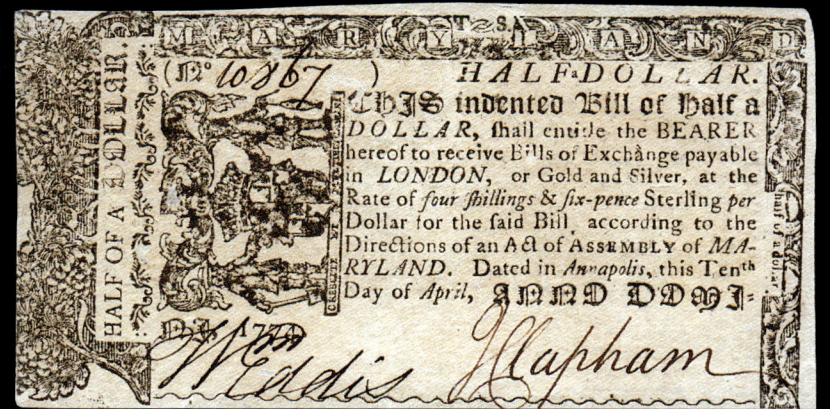

Maryland—Founded in 1634 by Lord Baltimore

Half dollar dated April, 1774
Signers were John Clapham and William Eddis

Printed in Annapolis by A.C. and F. Green
Equal to two shillings and three pence

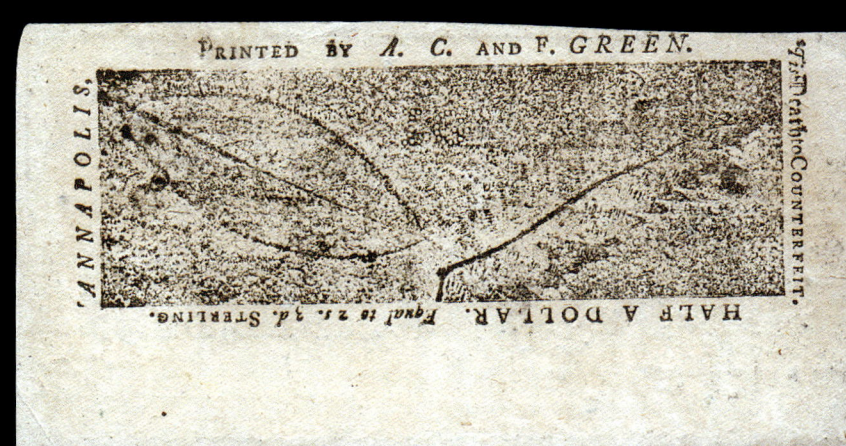

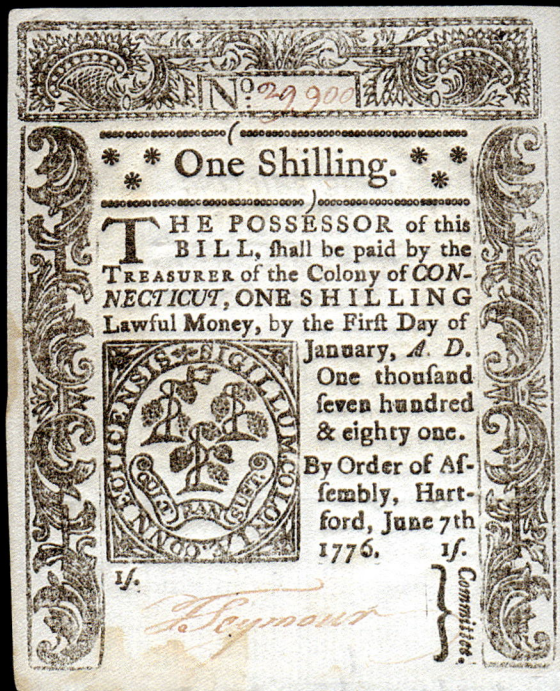

Connecticut—Founded in 1635 by Thomas Hooker
Signed by Thomas Seymour, June, 1776

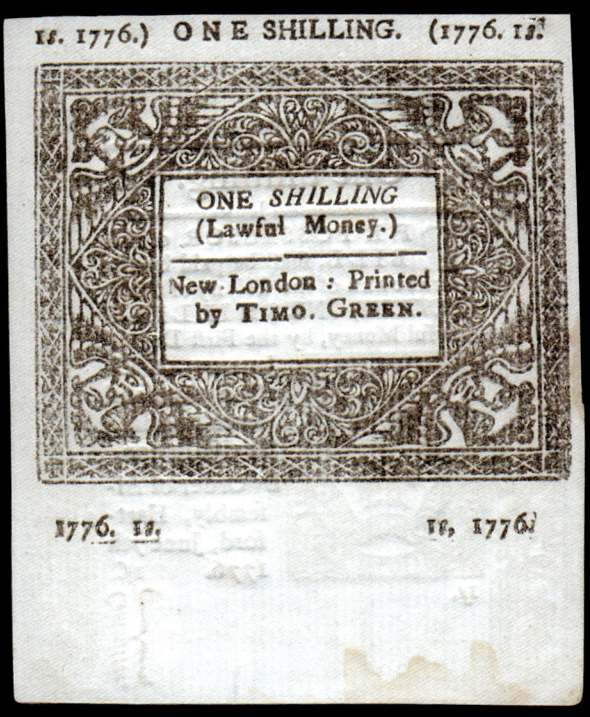

One shilling (lawful money)

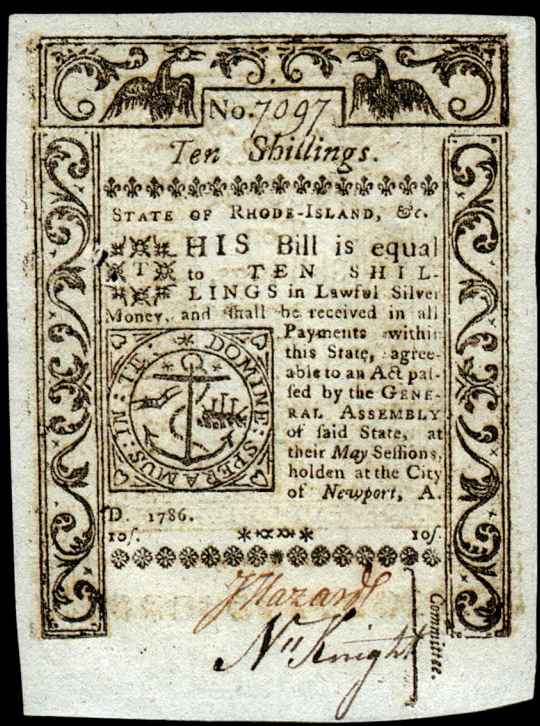

Rhode Island—Founded in 1636 by Roger Williams

Equal to ten shillings in lawful silver money
Dated May, 1786, signed by Jonathan Hazard and N. Knight

Printed by Southwick and Barber
96% of the issue was burned by the State between 1793-1803

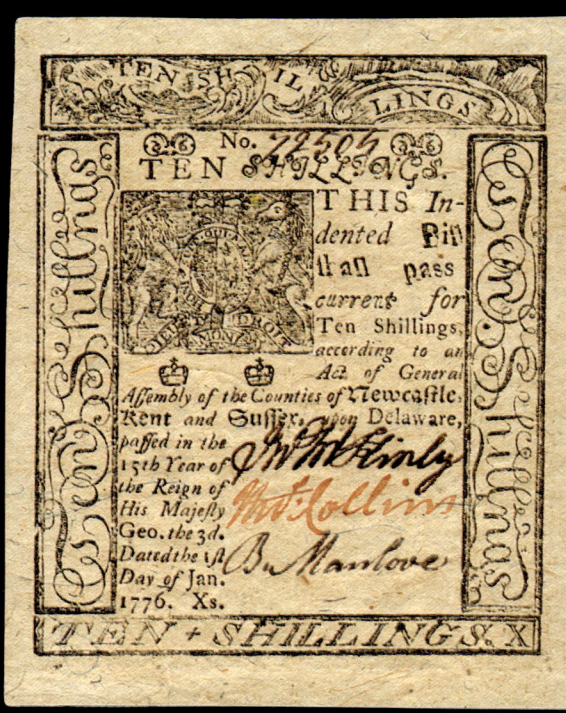

Delaware—Founded in 1638 by Peter Minuit and New Sweden Company

Ten shillings issued January, 1776
Signed by John McKinly, Thomas Collins, and Boaz Manlove

Printed by James Adams - "To Counterfeit is death" warning

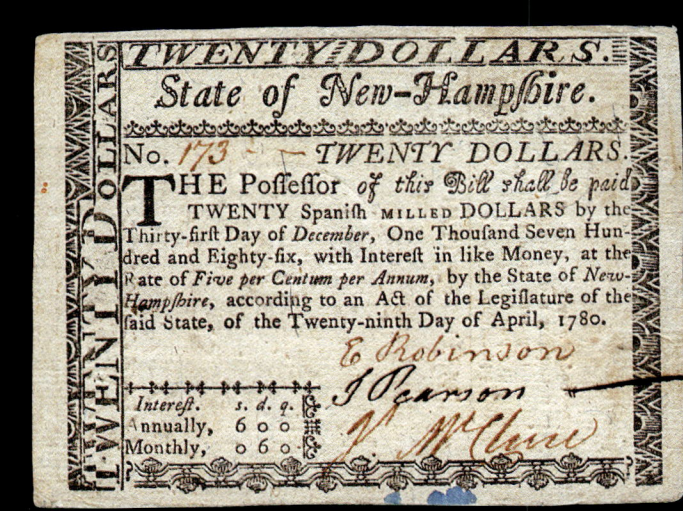

New Hampshire—Founded in 1638 by John Wheelwright

Twenty dollars issued April, 1780
Signed by E. Robinson, Joseph Pearson, and James McClure

Printed by Hall and Sellers in Philadelphia on watermarked paper
This was a Guarantee Note (redemption guaranteed by the U.S. Government). This note is very rare in this condition (almost uncirculated) as 95% of the notes of this type are hole canceled

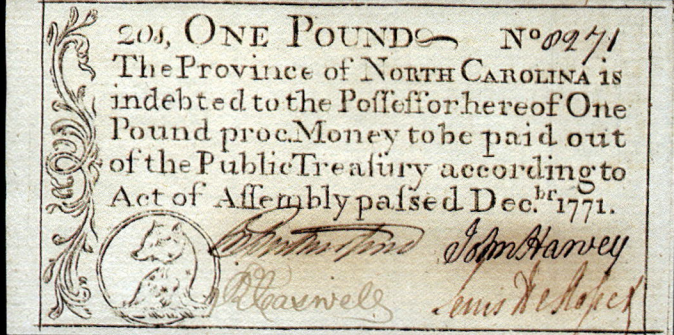

North Carolina—Founded in 1653 by the Virginians

One pound dated December, 1771
Design features a bear representing the constellation Ursa Minor

Allison Dauer is a student at the University of North Carolina at Chapel Hill. It is the oldest public university in the United States; the cornerstone was laid October 12, 1793.

North Carolina state flag

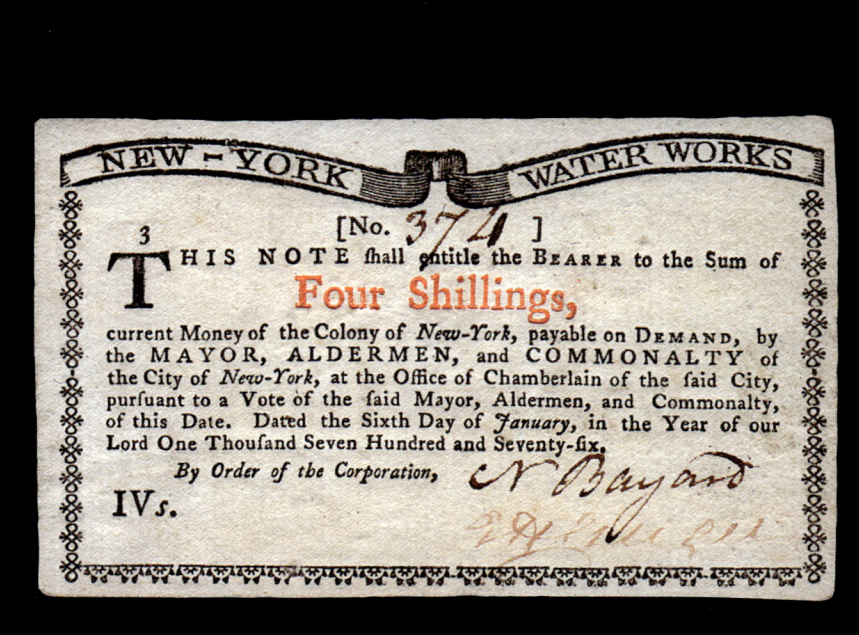

New York—Founded in 1664 by the Duke of York

Four shillings dated March, 1776
This unusual series was used to fund the New York water works

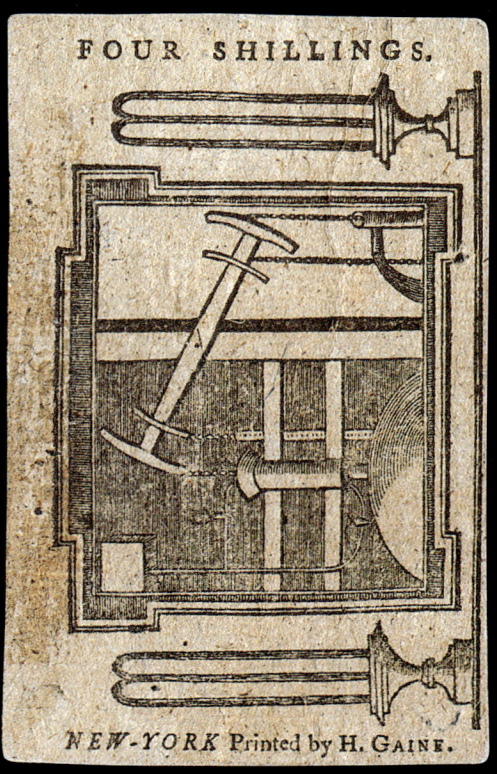

Interesting engraving of a portion of the water pump system

Penn's Treaty with the Indians, Painted in 1771 by Benjamin West
Pennsylvania Academy of the Fine Arts, Philadelphia

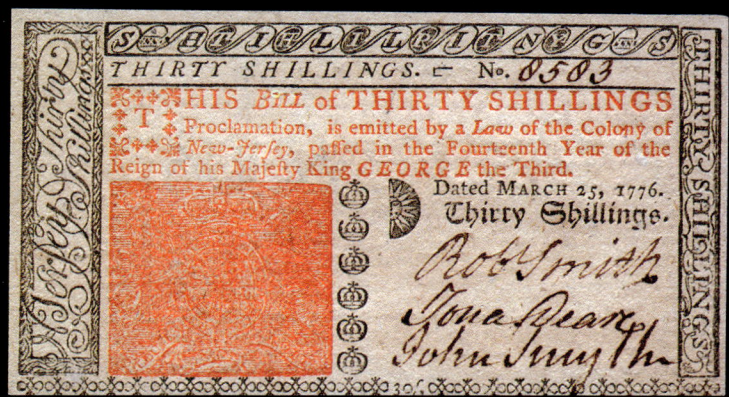

New Jersey—Founded in 1664 by Lord Berkeley and Sir George Carteret

Thirty shillings dated March, 1776

Printed by Isaac Collins on paper watermarked "New Jersey"

South Carolina—Founded in 1663 by eight nobles with a charter from Charles II

Two shillings and six pence, dated April, 1778
Printed on thin paper on one side only from engraved copper plates

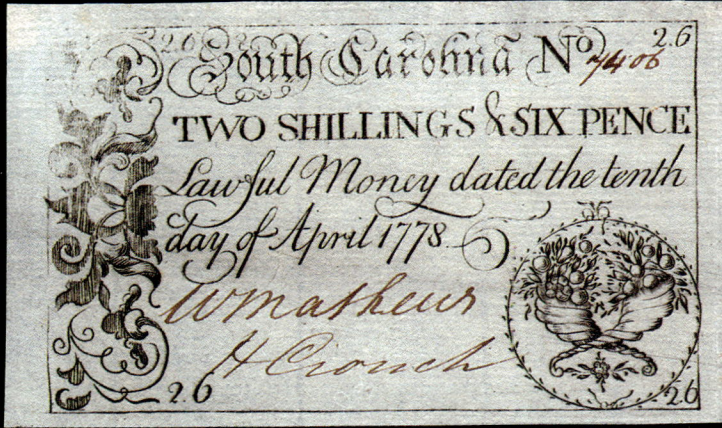

The Boston Massacre, the beginning of the Revolutionary War
Illustration from a Broadside 1770

Francis Scott Key reaches out towards the flag in "The Star Spangled Banner" by Percy Moran
Prints and Photographs Division, Library of Congress.

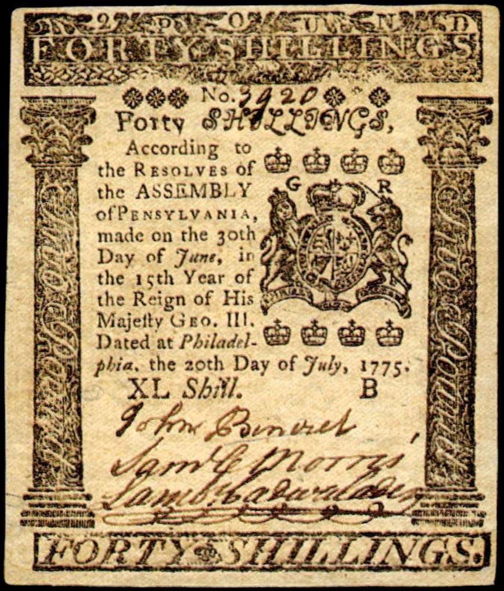

Pennsylvania—Founded in 1682 by William Penn

Forty shillings dated July, 1775
This issue was known as resolve money because the approval of the Royal Governor was not received

Georgia—Founded in 1732 by James Oglethorpe

Two dollars in Continental Currency Dated September, 1777
Five signatures, blank reverse

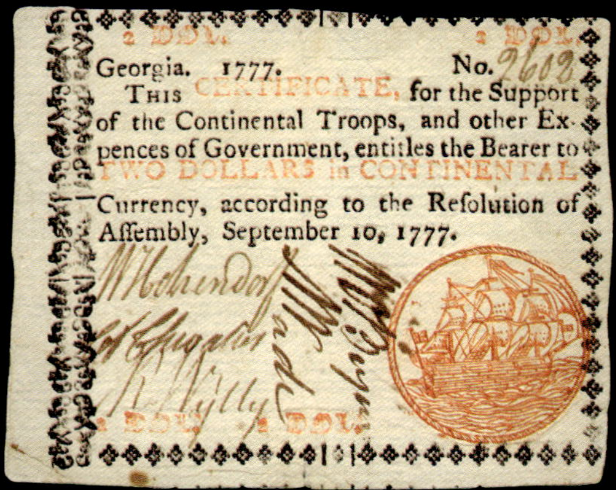

Printed by Hall and Sellers on paper containing mica flakes and blue silk thread

Congress ultimately redeemed Continental Currency at the rate of forty dollars per bill to one dollar in coin in 1780. In 1790 and 1791, currency could be exchanged at a 100/1 ratio for U. S. Treasury bonds bearing 6% interest. The bonds were finally paid off in 1813 but any currency, not exchanged for bonds became totally worthless. Thus, the term "Not worth a Continental" has forever been a part of our history.

A network of railroads grew up to unite the country. Train arrivals and departures were exciting events in the quiet towns of the 1800's.
Photo: American Heritage

Chapter XI
National Currency

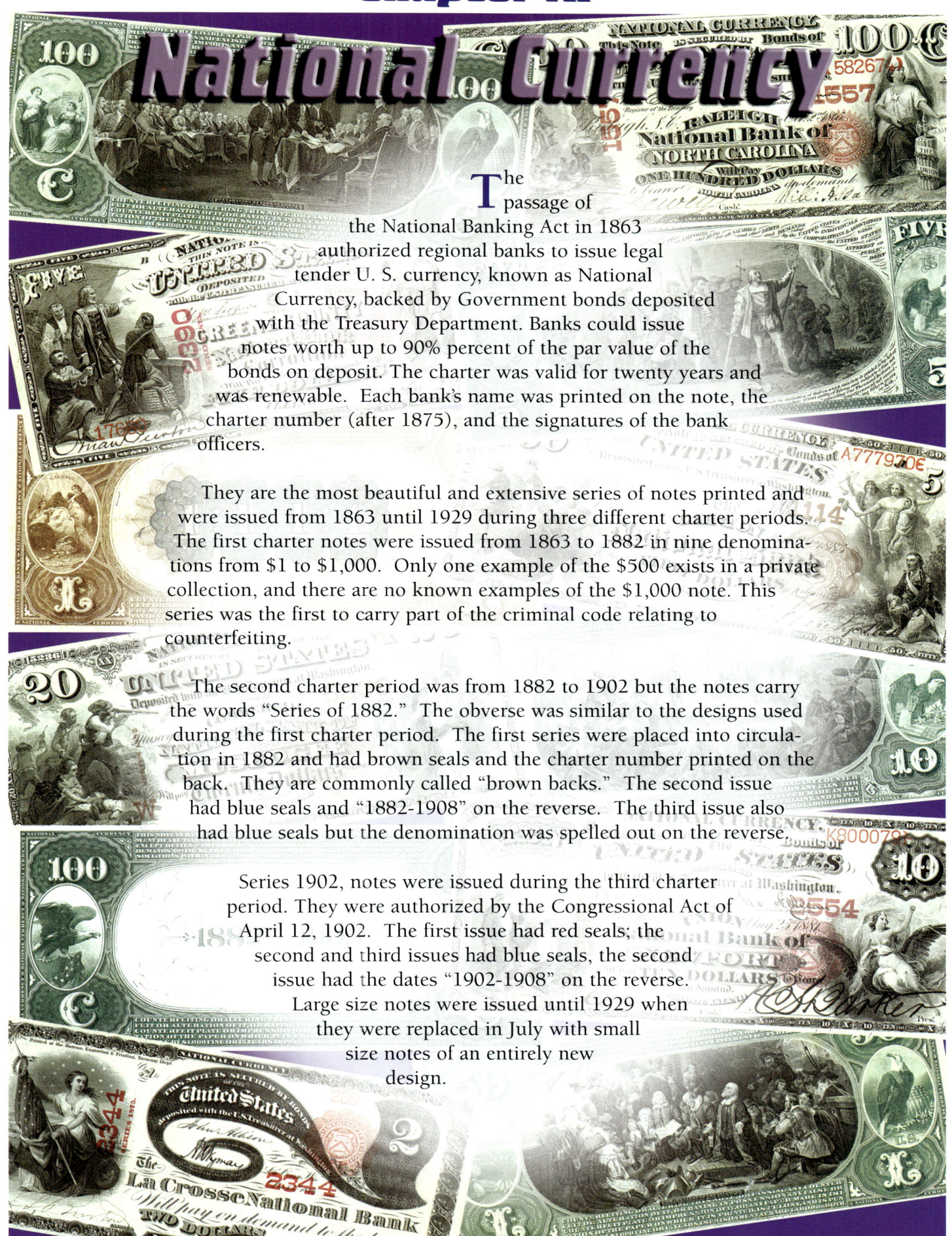

The passage of the National Banking Act in 1863 authorized regional banks to issue legal tender U. S. currency, known as National Currency, backed by Government bonds deposited with the Treasury Department. Banks could issue notes worth up to 90% percent of the par value of the bonds on deposit. The charter was valid for twenty years and was renewable. Each bank's name was printed on the note, the charter number (after 1875), and the signatures of the bank officers.

They are the most beautiful and extensive series of notes printed and were issued from 1863 until 1929 during three different charter periods. The first charter notes were issued from 1863 to 1882 in nine denominations from $1 to $1,000. Only one example of the $500 exists in a private collection, and there are no known examples of the $1,000 note. This series was the first to carry part of the criminal code relating to counterfeiting.

The second charter period was from 1882 to 1902 but the notes carry the words "Series of 1882." The obverse was similar to the designs used during the first charter period. The first series were placed into circulation in 1882 and had brown seals and the charter number printed on the back. They are commonly called "brown backs." The second issue had blue seals and "1882-1908" on the reverse. The third issue also had blue seals but the denomination was spelled out on the reverse.

Series 1902, notes were issued during the third charter period. They were authorized by the Congressional Act of April 12, 1902. The first issue had red seals; the second and third issues had blue seals, the second issue had the dates "1902-1908" on the reverse. Large size notes were issued until 1929 when they were replaced in July with small size notes of an entirely new design.

First Charter Period
Issued from February 25, 1863 to July 11, 1882

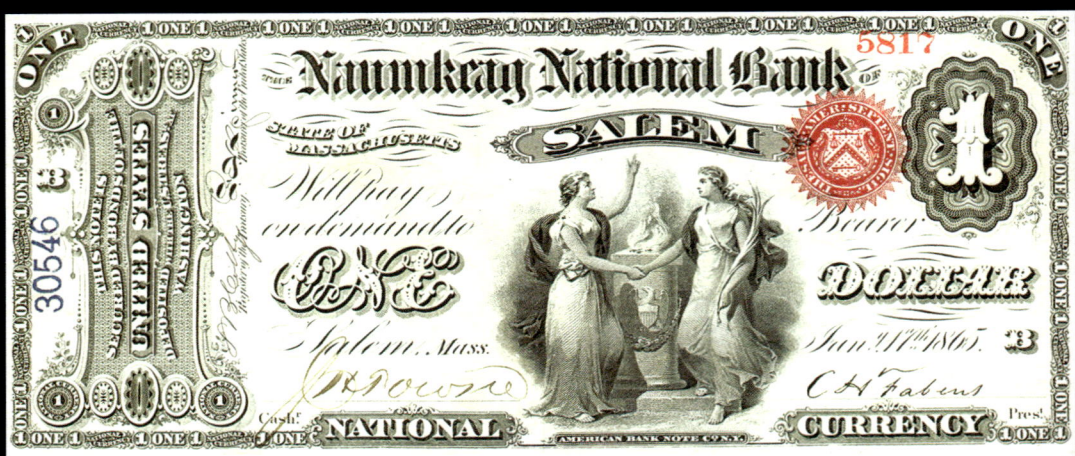

State of Massachusetts - Small Red Seal with Rays
Two allegorical maidens before an altar

Landing of the Pilgrims
This is the same design used on the reverse of the $5 Federal Reserve Notes of 1914 and 1918

Territory of New Mexico - New Mexico became a state in 1912 - Small Red Seal with Rays

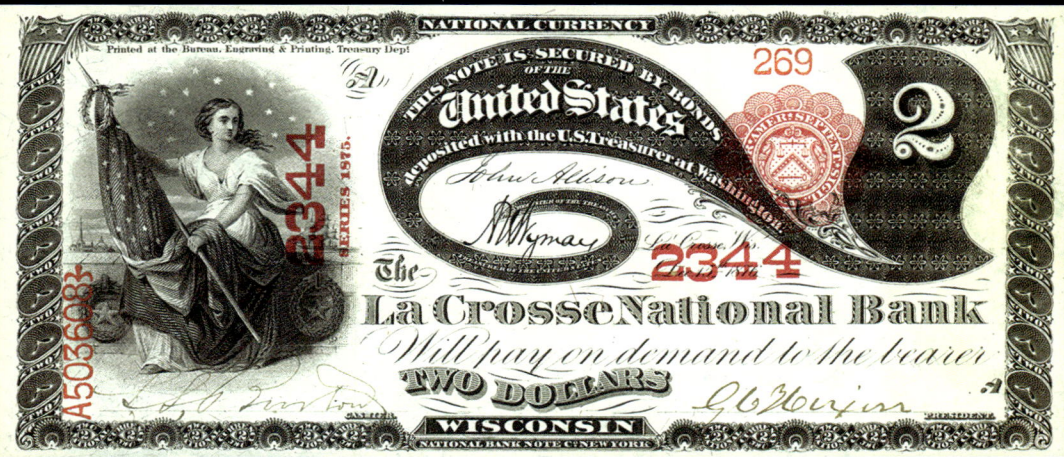

Allegorical figure of a woman holding the American flag
State of Wisconsin - Small Red Seal with Scallop

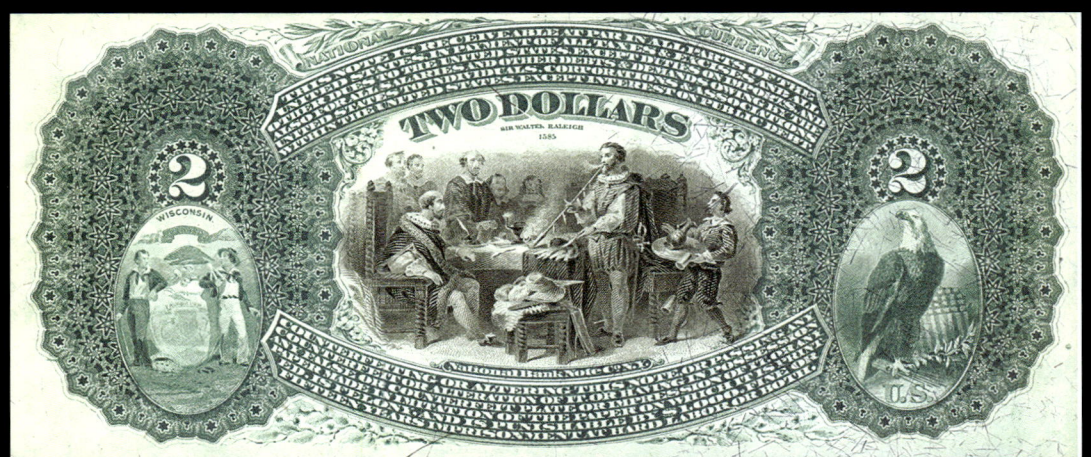

Portrait of Sir Walter Raleigh
He is shown in England in 1585 exhibiting tobacco and corn
that he brought back from America

State of California - Small Red Seal with Rays

This note is commonly referred to as "The Lazy 2" because of the side orientation of the "2".

The design on the left is Columbus in sight of land. The painting on the right is the presentation of an Indian princess representing America
State of Ohio-Small Red Seal with Rays.

"The Landing of Columbus" a painting in the U.S. Capitol

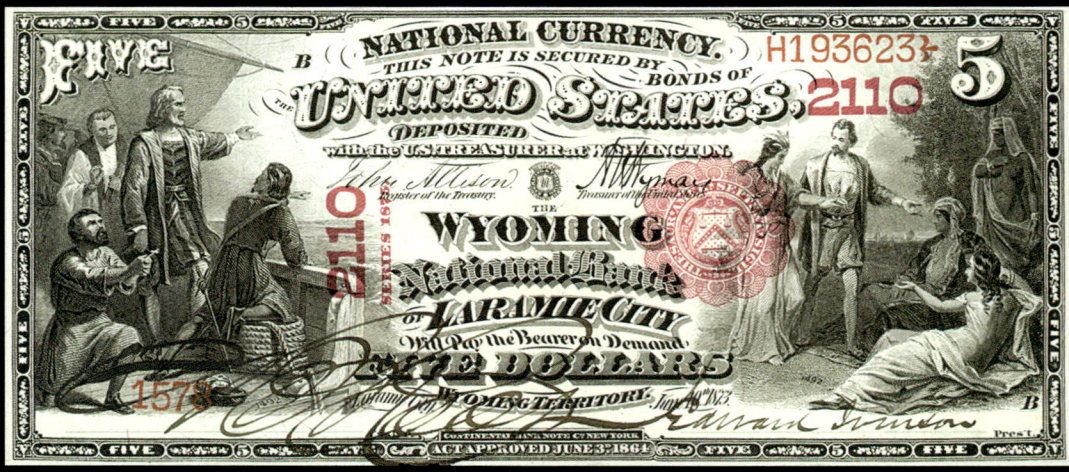

Territory of Wyoming
Wyoming became a state in 1890 - Small Red Seal with Scallops

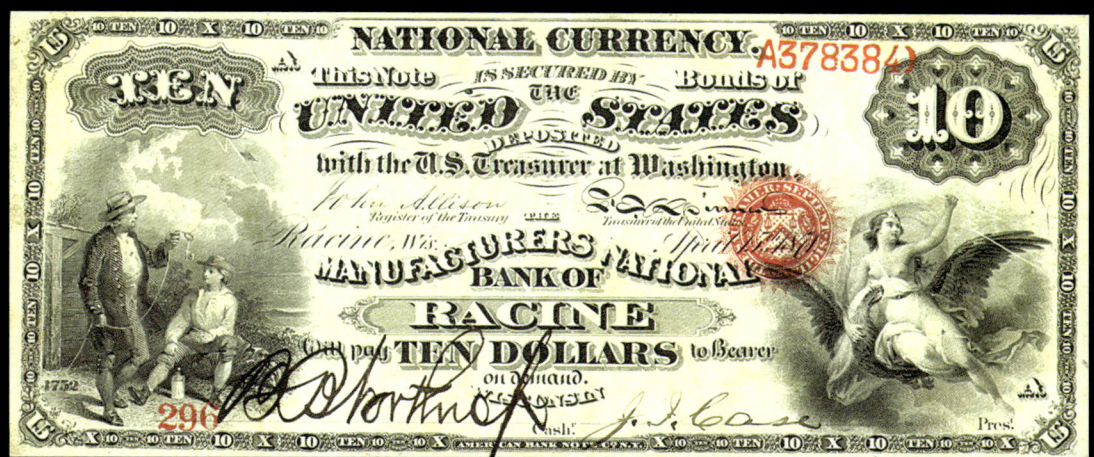

State of Wisconsin - Small Red Seal with Rays

This is the same painting of DeSoto discovering the Mississippi that appears on the 1918 $500 Federal Reserve Note

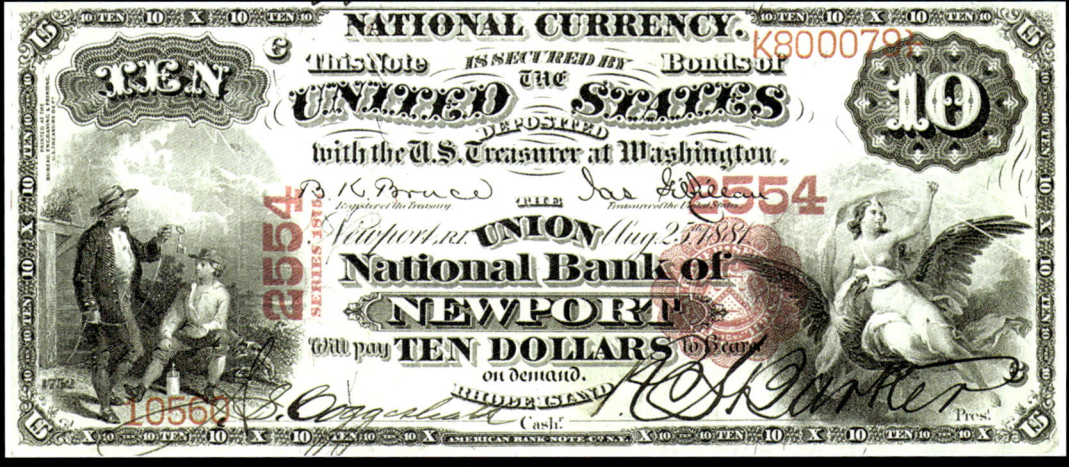

State of Rhode Island - Small Red Seal with Scallops
On the left is Ben Franklin attracting electricity with a kite attached to a key. At the right is a painting of "Liberty" holding a bolt of lightning and flying on an eagle.

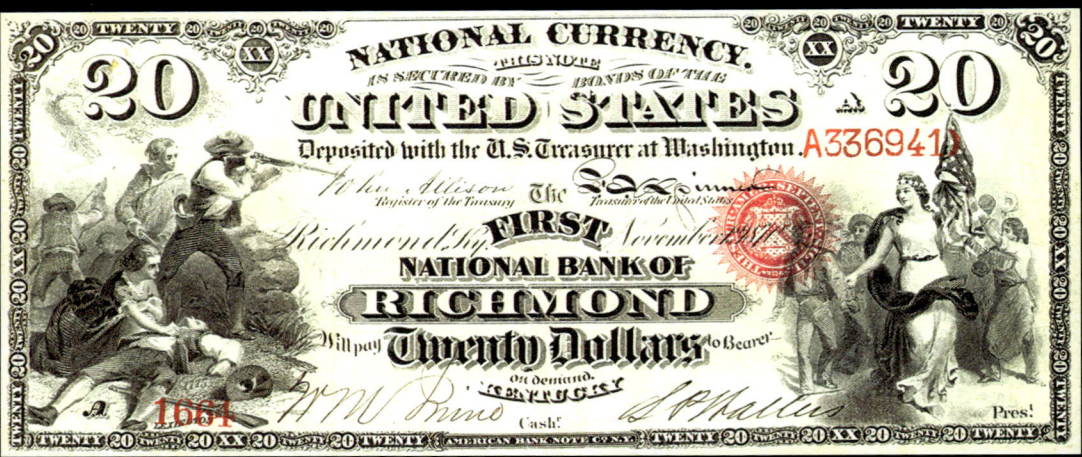

State of Kentucky, Small Red Seal with Scallops
The scene on the left depicts the Battle of Lexington, April 19, 1775

The Baptism of Pocahontas, painted by John Chapman

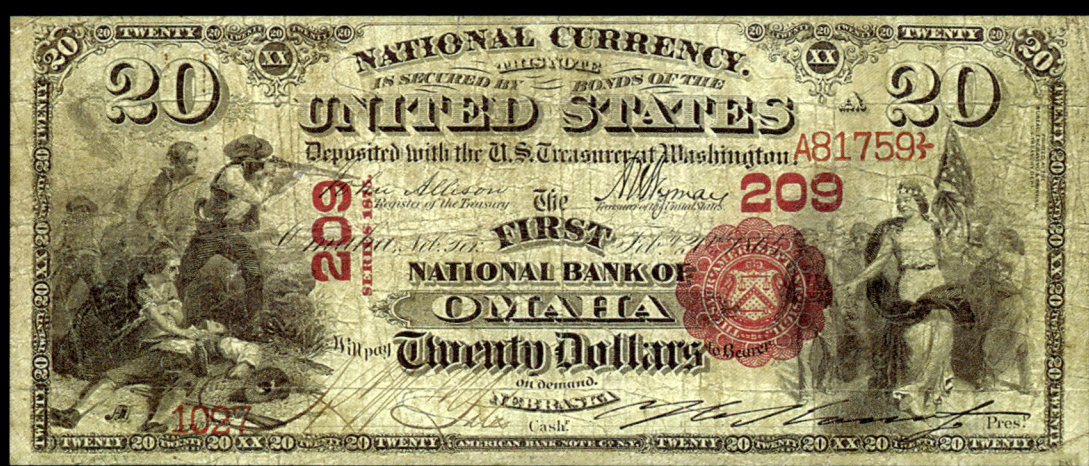

State of Nebraska, Small Red Seal with Scallops

State of Ohio, Small Red Seal with Scallops
Washington Crossing the Delaware and Washington Kneeling at Prayer

The Embarkation of the Pilgrims, painted by Robert Weir

State of Illinois, Small Red Seal with Scallops

State of North Carolina, Small Red Seal with Spikes
On the left is the Battle of Lake Erie, painted by W. H. Powell

The Signing of the Declaration of Independence, a painting by John Trumbull.
This is the same design on the reverse of the current two dollar bill.

State of Ohio, Small Red Seal with Scallops

Five Hundred Dollar National Bank Note - First Charter

An allegorical figure representing the Spirit of the Navy is on the left and the steamship Sirius arriving in New York in 1838 is engraved on the right

The reverse is engraved from a painting by John Trumbull and illustrates the surrender of General Burgoyne to General Gates at Saratoga on October 17, 1777

This note is unique in private hands; two other copies of the original series are permanently impounded in the U.S. Government collection.

Second Charter Period Issued from July 12, 1882 to April 11, 1902
First Issue—Series of 1882 with Brown Seal and Brown Back

Territory of Dakota—Became the States of North and South Dakota in 1889
Portrait of James Garfield

The numbers 2823 seen on the reverse and obverse represents the charter number of Sioux Falls National Bank

State of New York

Each bank issuing National Currency had its own unique charter number.

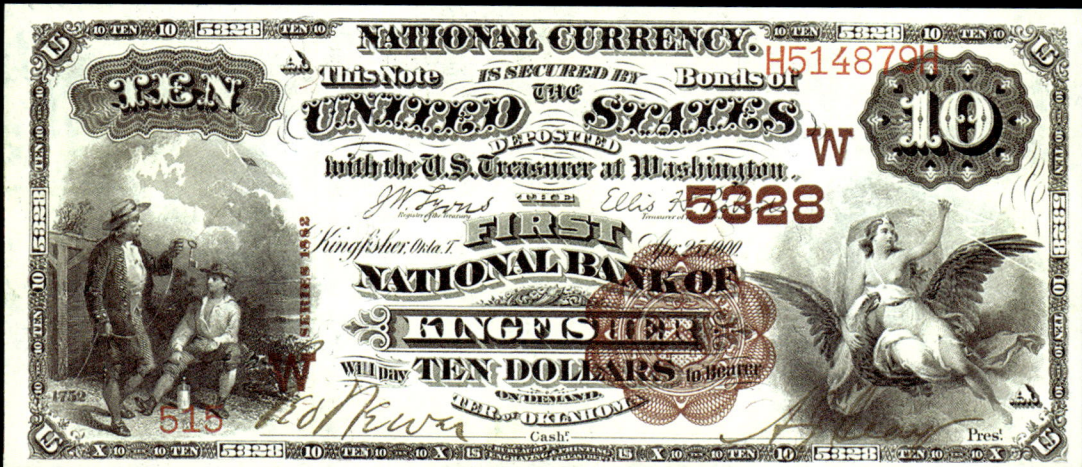
Territory of Oklahoma—Oklahoma became a state in 1907

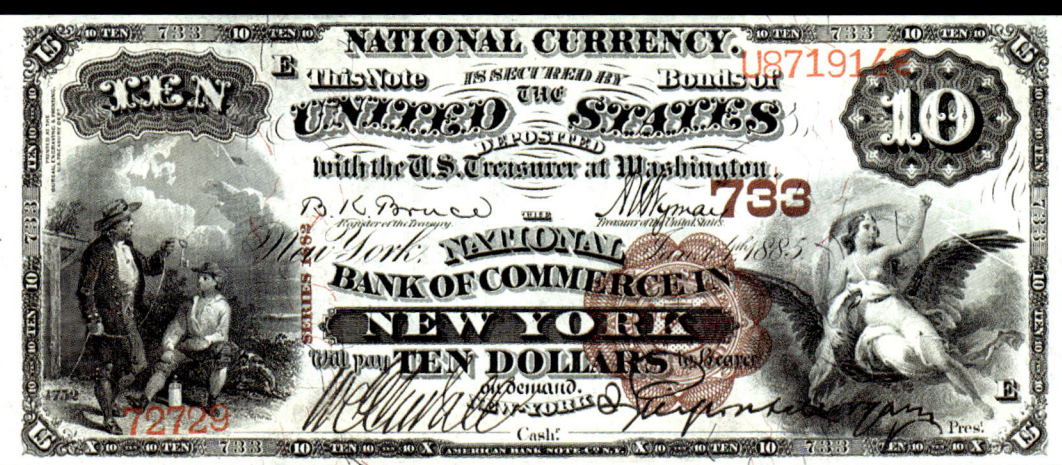
State of New York

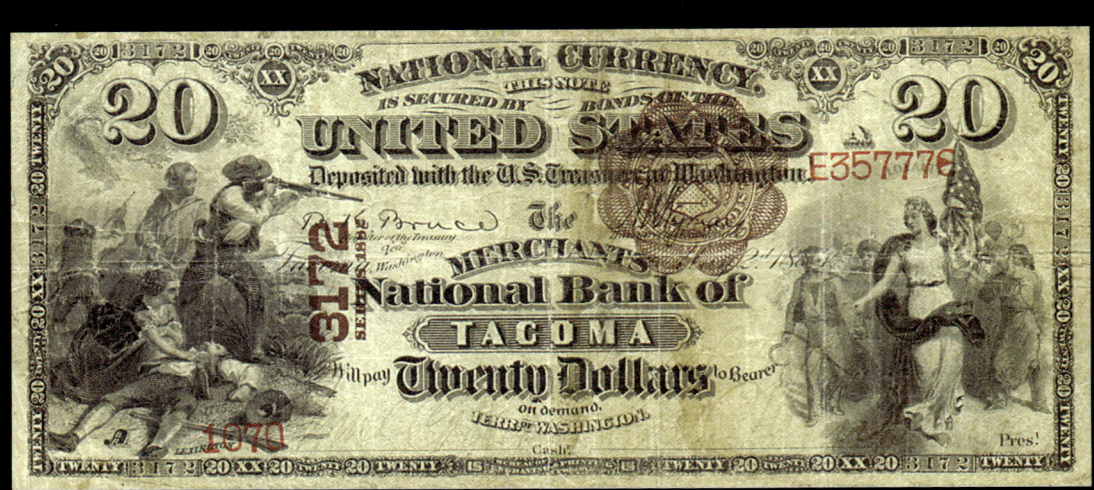

Territory of Washington—Washington became a state in 1889

Muscogee—Indian Territory

The Indian Territory existed from 1834 to 1907. The State of Oklahoma was formed in 1907 from the Indian Territory and the Oklahoma territory.

State of New Jersey

Clinton, the quintessential American small town, is nestled in the hills of Hunterdon County, New Jersey. A charming historic shopping area, cherry tree-lined streets and a river meandering through it makes Clinton a picture perfect hamlet.

Several lovely restaurants enhance the downtown shopping experience. From warm cozy eateries to outdoor dining on the river, Clinton offers a variety of restaurants from which to choose.

State of Washington

Territory of Utah - Utah became a state in 1896

Second Charter Period, Second Issue–Series 1882
Blue seal and "1882-1908" on Green Back

State of Kentucky

State of Pennsylvania

State of Pennsylvania

State of New York

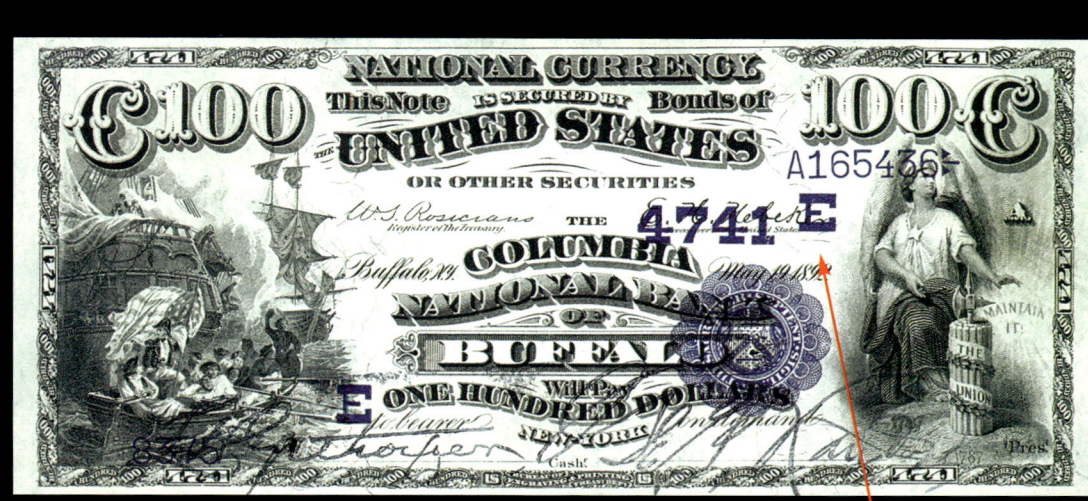

State of New York

When National Currency notes were worn out and sent to the Treasury Department for destruction, an inventory by hand had to be made of each note and the issuing bank and serial number. As the number of notes in circulation rapidly increased, letters were printed on the notes next to the charter number beginning with the second issue of the Second Charter. These letters corresponded to the geographic part of the country they originated from in order to make sorting easier. Thus, the following letters were used:

N—New England
E—East
S—South
M—Mid-West
W—West
P—Pacific

"E" represents a bank in the East

Second Charter Period, Third Issue - Series 1882
Blue Seal with denomination spelled out across Green Back

State of Pennsylvania

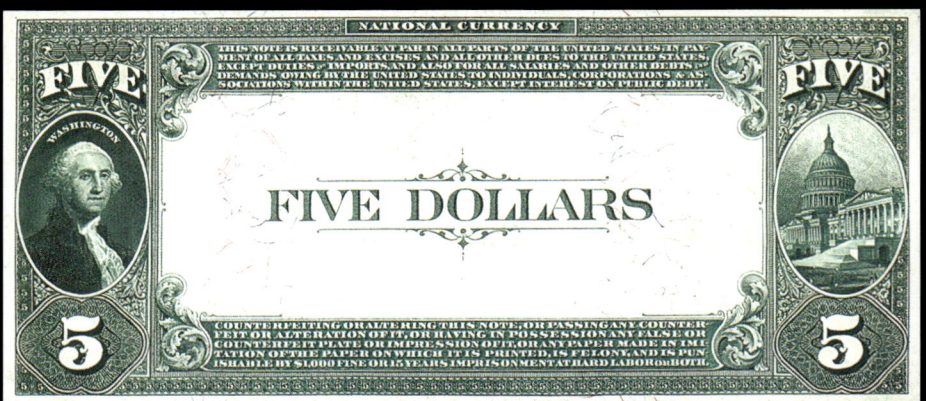

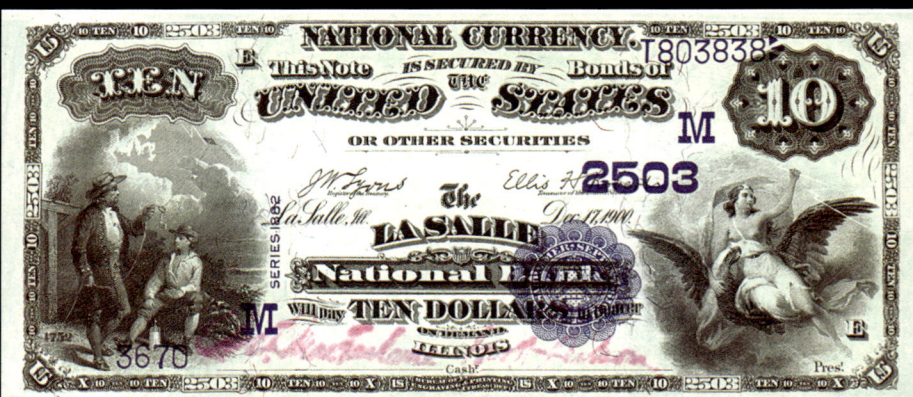
State of Illinois

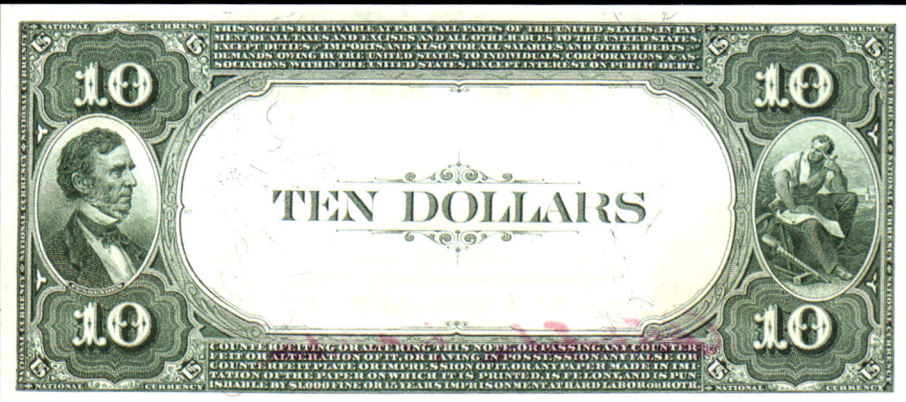

State of Illinois

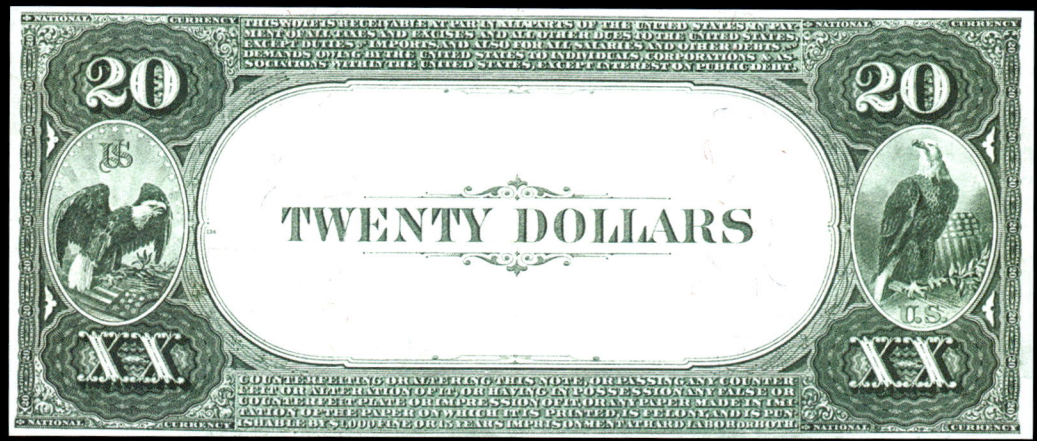

State of Louisiana

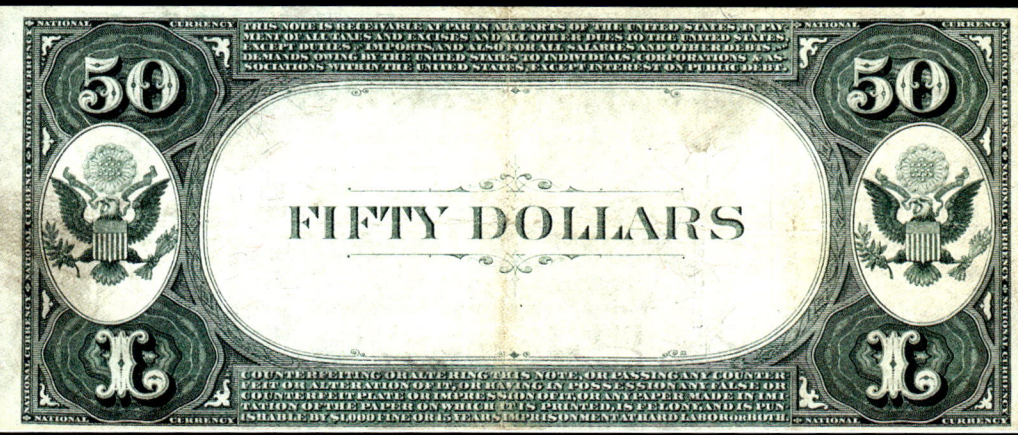

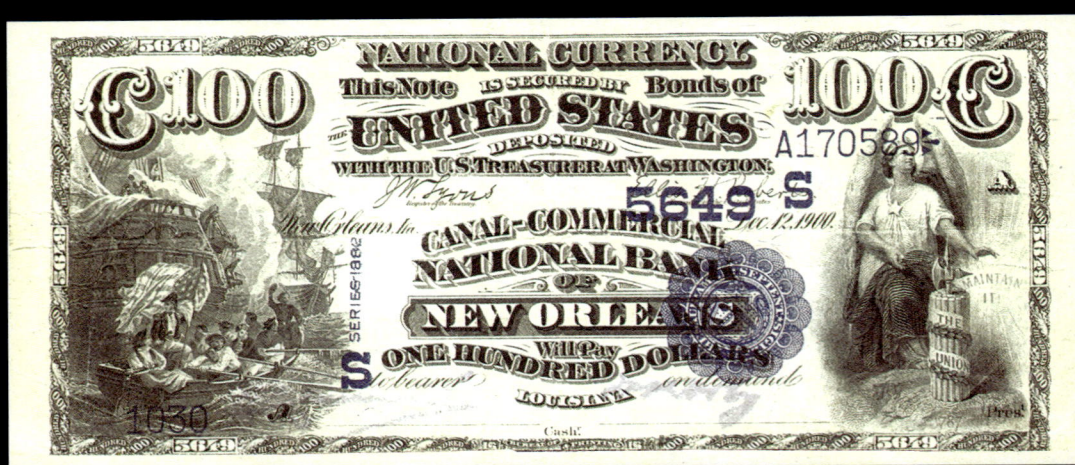

State of Louisiana

Although they are Series 1882, these notes were issued from 1919 to 1921. Other denominations of this series were printed over various years from 1916 to 1922.

The $100 notes were only issued at two banks: The Winters National Bank of Dayton and the Canal-Commercial National Bank of New Orleans. A total of 3,100 were printed and 2,857 were issued. Only four examples are known to exist, making this one of the rarest and most desirable of National Currency notes.

Mardi-Gras in New Orleans, Louisiana

THIRD CHARTER

Dated April 12, 1902 to April 11, 1922

Series 1902 – Issued from 1902 to 1929

Third Charter Period, Dated April 12, 1902 to April 11, 1922
Series 1902 - Issued from 1902 to 1929

First Issue - Red Seal
Second Issue - Blue Seal with "1902-1908" on back
Third Issue - Blue Seal without "1902-1908" on back

Third Charter Period, Dated April 12, 1902 to April 11, 1922
Series 1902 - Issued from 1902 to 1929

Reverse features "The Landing of the Pilgrims"

Territory of Arizona—Arizona became a state in 1912

State of Massachusetts

State of Pennsylvania

Portrait of William McKinley-Twenty-fifth President of the United States 1897-1901
(Assassinated at the 1901 Pan American Exposition)

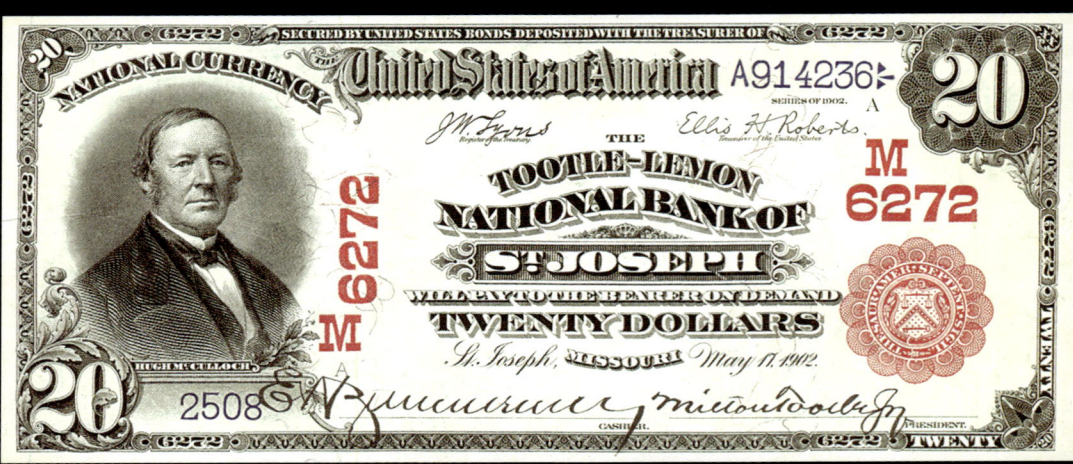
State of Missouri

State of Texas

State of Wisconsin

Portrait of Hugh McCulloch, Comptroller of the Currency from 1863-1865 and Secretary of the Treasury from 1865-1869 and 1884-1885

State of Missouri

State of Illinois

State of Illinois

Portrait of John Sherman - Secretary of the Treasury from 1877-1881 and Secretary of State from 1897-1898

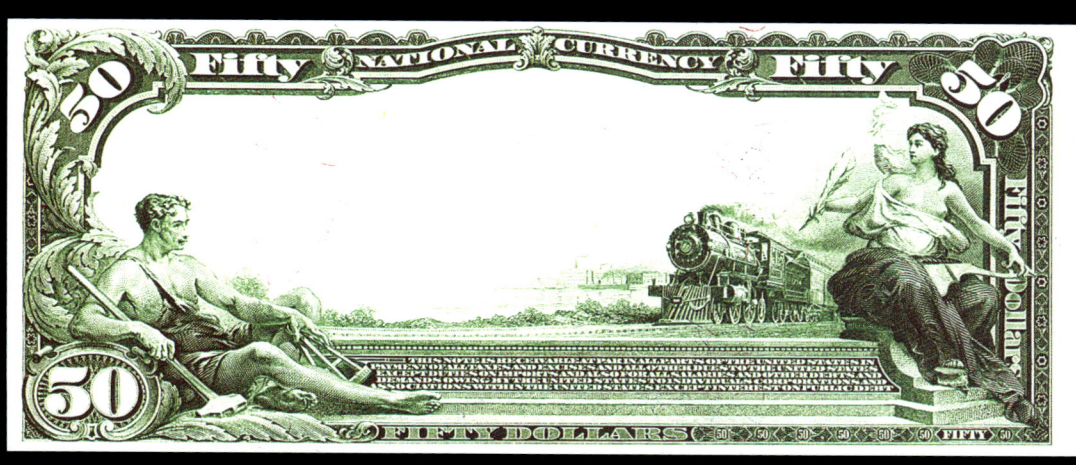
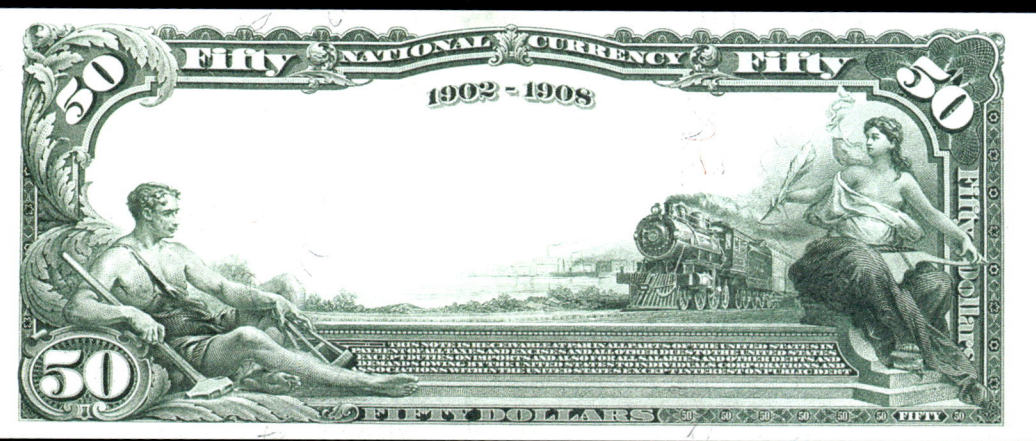
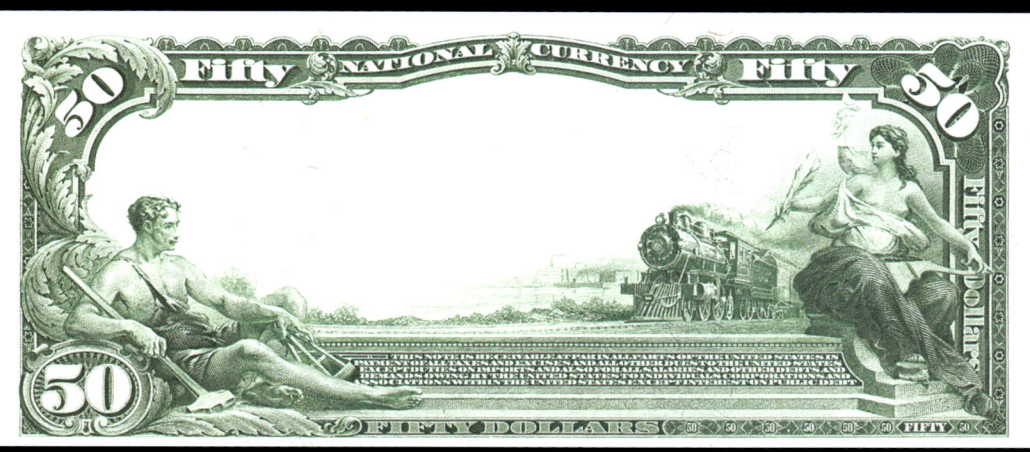

State of Pennsylvania

State of South Dakota

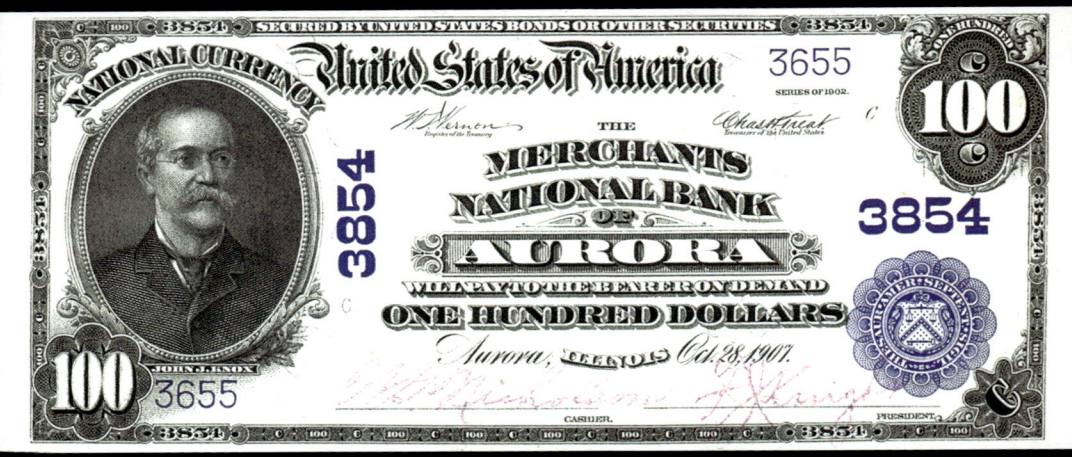

State of Illinois

Portrait of John Knox-Comptroller of the Currency from 1872-1884

National Currency with Unusual Names

Brokenbow, Nebraska

Intercourse, Pennsylvania

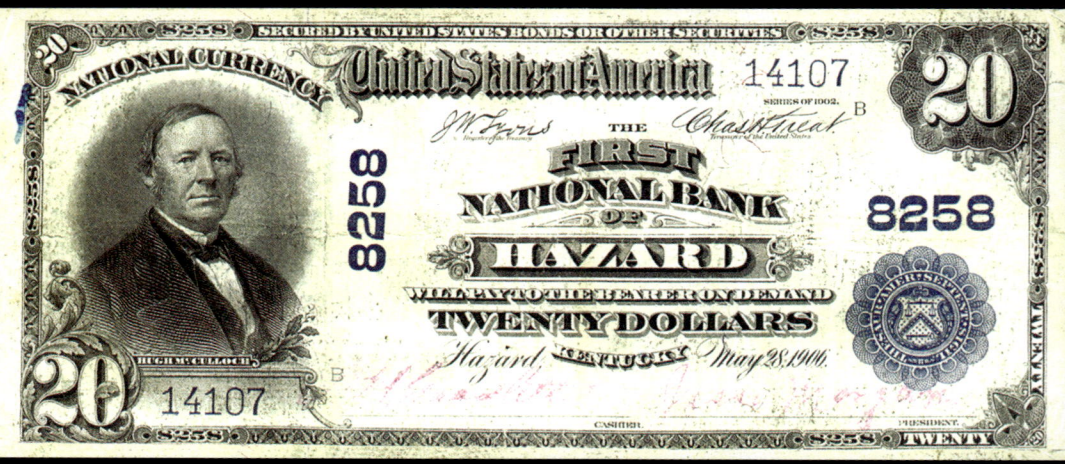

Hazard, Kentucky

National Currency

Good Thunder, Minnesota

Sleepy Eye, Minnesota

Serial number 1 issued by Florida National Bank of Miami.
This bank was later acquired by First Union and subsequently by Wachovia.

National Currency from Brockway, Pennsylvania
Brockway is the hometown of Joanne (Schlemmer) Dauer

Series 1929

Issued June 23, 1920 - The town was originally called Brockwayville

The original home on Main Street in Brockway where Joanne Dauer lived with her parents and nine brothers and sisters. Her brother's dental office (Dr. Ed Schlemmer) is on the first floor at the site of the original Schlemmer's Market grocery store.

Reproduction of Schlemmer's Market from the Dauer Museum of Classic Cars

ACKNOWLEDGEMENTS

This book could not have been written without the dedicated and enduring efforts of my wife Joanne. The past eighteen months have seen long hours scanning images, researching stories, and typing manuscripts with her help and assistance. Joanne was also nice enough to sometimes leave the light on for me in the bedroom, the many nights I would continue working until 4 or 5 a.m..

Dr. Donna Shalala has written a gracious and memorable forward. It has been indeed a pleasure to be working with her at the University of Miami.

Dean Oakes, respected currency dealer and author, will not only be known as the expert on the "oat bin hoard" but he stimulated my early interest in collecting, and helped establish important items in our collection.

We thank Sonny Hagendorf, a friend and professional philatelist, for his assistance in acquiring the historical documents and stamps. He is the person that motivated us to write this book.

Dr. Jeff Prince, Associate Professor of Biology at the University of Miami, spent many hours over our house proof reading the book after a game (attempted) of racquetball. Janet O'Connell, teacher and guidance counselor at Taravella High School in Broward County, provided all of those necessary commas, semicolons, and other punctuation, we haven't used in years.

Steve Sawitz, owner of Joe's Stone Crab Restaurant was gracious enough to share his family history with us and enabled us to include one of the most famous and well-known South Florida landmarks. Thanks to Millinda Sinnreich for introducing us to Susan Nowling, who helped edit and write that part of the manuscript.

We want to especially thank Fred Wolfe, graphic artist, who spent hundreds of hours with us designing and laying out the pages and his wife Sandra for helping us check the final proofs.

It was my anonymous collector friend(s), loaning me what notes I was missing, that enabled the complete type collection of United States currency to be seen for the first time in full color. It is hoped that this will be a valuable and important reference book that for years will stimulate and interest people to appreciate the early days of our great country.

Our children were very patient during the preparation of this book. Thank you for all of the hours away from you, that we spent on its preparation. We hope it will be a permanent reminder of our love and dedication to you.

J.C.D. and E.A.D.

The rare currency pages illustrated in this book are available as beautiful 17"x22" glossy posters

The six beautiful posters illustrated below are featured in American History as Seen Through Currency. They are reproduced from high resolution digital files using the latest technology. Printed on 100 pound glossy cover stock, they are suitable for framing. They are available in a limited edition of 250 author signed and numbered prints. Each poster is 17"x22" with the image size being 15-1/2"x 20".

For an additional $10.00 charge, any page in the publication can be reproduced as a poster with the same specifications. There is a $4.95 shipping and handling charge on poster orders. Outside the U.S.A. shipping charged at cost. Sales tax is extra where applicable.

Item POS-1

Item POS-2

Item POS-3

Item POS-4

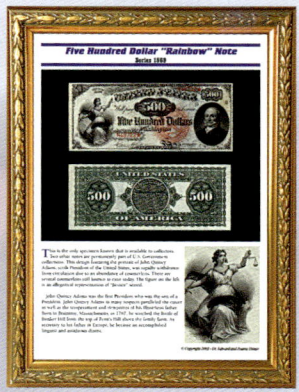
Item POS-5

Item POS-6

TO ORDER POSTERS

Special Limited Edition Poster.....................................$39.95
Signed by the authors

Shipping and handling-add...$4.95

- 17" x 22" Format • Glossy stock • Full color
- Beautifully printed • Suitable for framing

YES! Please send me
These beautiful posters from American History as Seen Through Currency

__Copies of POS-1 __Copies of POS-2 __Copies of POS-3
__Copies of POS-4 __Copies of POS-5 __Copies of POS-6 $_____
Custom posters are available from any page in the book
__Posters of page(s)_____ from the book at $49.95 $_____
Shipping and handling-add $4.95 per poster $_____
Florida residents add 6% sales tax $_____
Total enclosed $_____

Sorry, no credit cards accepted. Money order, personal or business check OK. Make check payable to: Edward A. Dauer, M.D. Please allow 4 to 6 weeks for delivery.

Name_____

Address_____

City_____ State_____ Zip_____

Mail to: Posters from American History as Seen Through Currency
4850 W. Oakland Park Blvd., Suite 145, Ft. Lauderdale FL 33313
Telephone: 954-739-0978 • Fax: 954-739-2587 • www.amhistoryuscurrency.com

Note: Frames are shown for illustrative purposes only and are not included.

It's exciting to be taken back in time as we learn about events and people, many which are depicted on our paper money

LIMITED EDITION AVAILABLE

Never before has a book been published illustrating in full color rare U.S. currency plus historical documents written by some of America's most famous people

- Limited to 100 books
- Real Leather-bound
- Gold Embossed Cover
- Full Color Slip Cover
- Author signed and numbered

Just one of the many stories in the book. Read about the history of the Bureau of Engraving and Printing. It was in a single room of the Treasury building on August 29, 1862, that the Bureau was born. See vintage photos of the bureau's printing pressroom.

A Beautiful History Book that you will Keep for Many Years

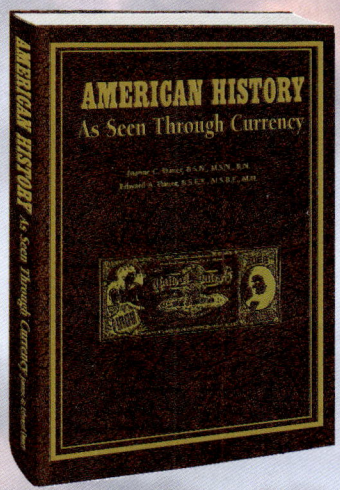

When you remove the glossy full color dust jacket, what is revealed is an elegant case bound cover in imitation dark brown leather for the regular edition and real leather for the special edition. Gold embossed artwork decorates the front of the book which is repeated on the spine. The cover has the look and feel of a fine historical publication that is usually only found in museums and ancient libraries.

TO ORDER BOOKS

Regular Hard Cover Book with Dust Jacket...$79.95	Leather-bound Limited Edition with Slip Cover...........$250.00
Shipping and handling-add................$3.95	Signed by the authors Shipping and handling-add..................$3.95

- 9"x12" Format • 400 pages • Full color
- Beautifully hard bound • Dust jacket

YES! Please send me
American History as Seen Through Currency

__Copies of the regular hard cover edition at $79.95 ea. $_____
__Copies of the leather-bound limited edition at $250.00 ea. $_____
Shipping and handling-add $3.95 per book $_____
Florida residents add 6% sales tax $_____
Total enclosed $_____

Sorry, no credit cards accepted. Money order, personal or business check OK. Make check payable to: Edward A. Dauer, M.D.
Please allow 4 to 6 weeks for delivery.

Name_____
Address_____
City_____ State_____ Zip_____

American History as Seen Through Currency
4850 W. Oakland Park Blvd., Suite 145, Ft. Lauderdale FL 33313
Telephone: 954-739-0978 • Fax: 954-739-2587 • www.amhistoryuscurrency.com

We Hope you Enjoyed Reading
AMERICAN HISTORY
As Seen Through Currency
A Pictorial History of United States Currency
Featuring Some of the Rarest Notes and Documents Ever Published

This edition is distributed to the coin and currency community by Heritage Numismatic Auctions and Currency Auctions of America

To join the free online community of almost 100,000 numismatists, review the over 400,000 past auction prices realized archive (with full descriptions and images), and learn how to collect or sell currency and other collectibles more knowledgeably.
Please visit *www.CurrencyAuction.com or call 1-800-872-6467*